"*Michael Dean gets it.*"

—ian

$30
WRITING
SCHOOL

"Michael Dean gets it."

—LYDIA LUNCH, novelist/musician

$30

WRITING SCHOOL

Michael W. Dean

ISBN: 1-59200-486-5

Library of Congress Catalog Card Number: 2004103486

Printed in the United States of America

04 05 06 07 08 BH 10 9 8 7 6 5 4 3 2 1

Thomson Course Technology PTR,
a division of Thomson Course Technology
25 Thomson Place
Boston, MA 02210
http://www.courseptr.com

SVP, Thomson Course Technology PTR:
Andy Shafran

Publisher:
Stacy L. Hiquet

Senior Marketing Manager:
Sarah O'Donnell

Marketing Manager:
Heather Hurley

Manager of Editorial Services:
Heather Talbot

Senior Acquisitions Editor:
Kevin Harreld

Senior Editor:
Mark Garvey

Associate Marketing Managers:
Kristin Eisenzopf and Sarah Dubois

Project Editor:
Brian Proffitt

Course Technology PTR Market Coordinator:
Elizabeth Furbish

Copy Editor:
Gene Redding

Interior Layout Tech:
M H Associates

Cover Designer:
Mike Tanamachi

CD-ROM Producer:
Brandon Penticuff

Indexer:
Kelly Talbot

Proofreader:
Sean Medlock

Tracy Hatfield,
Michael Kelley, and
Michael Joseph Woody

Acknowledgments

Thanks: Lydia Llam. Kevin Harreld. Kimberly Valentini. Jack Dean. Amelia Worth. Greg Dale. Tiffany Couser. Mike Di Luna. Skip Lunch. Carla Segurola. Saby Reyes-Kulkarni.

About the Author

MICHAEL W. DEAN is an author, filmmaker, and musician who lives in Los Angeles. Dean is the author of *$30 Film School*, *$30 Music School*, *The Simple Pleasures of a Complex Girl*, and *Starving in the Company of Beautiful Women*. He has been reviewed in *Spin Magazine*, *Maelstrom Rock 'n' Roll*, *The Face*, *New Music Express*, and *Film Threat Magazine*. Dean has also directed and produced the critically acclaimed music and art documentary *D.I.Y or DIE: How to Survive as an Independent Artist*. He sang and played bass in the San Francisco band *Bomb* and has released 12 records with five bands on labels ranging from independent to Warner Brothers.

Contents at a Glance

Contents

Introduction

I Work in a Coffee Shop

I work in a coffee shop. But I don't wait on people and bring them coffee. I sit in a coffee shop and write. A lot of people here do the same; I see a lot of laptops with the bagels. But the difference is, I actually make a living at it.

I can tell you how to do this.

Who This Book Is for and Why Another Book on Writing?

When you pitch a book to a publisher, one of the things you have to do is explain why the book is different from other books on the same subject. This book is different for the same reason that the other books in this series, *$30 Film School* and *$30 Music School*, are different:

♦ My books are not for wannabes. They don't promise overnight fame. They offer realistic goals and a map to reach them. This book is for people who are willing to *work*, who genuinely love the written word, and who want to write *important* things that affect the world deeply. They are not for people who buy the hottest laptop and the latest software and tons of books on writing and then never write. This book is for people who want to *write*.

♦ Like the other books in this series, this book covers *everything*. My film book talked about everything from how to buy a camera to how to make DVDs and get a distribution deal. And I've done this. My music book told you how to buy a guitar, how to play it, and on up through how to book a world tour. I've done this. And for this book, I'm covering everything from the difference between a noun and a verb through getting a book deal or even self-publishing (and booking a world tour). I've done this.

I write books because I love books. I can't really see any other reason to write. It's hard to get rich writing, and I can guarantee that most people who get rich at it love books and love writing anyway. You have to love the written word to put in the years of hours needed to get recognition.

As a kid, I spent a lot of time in the library. (Lest you think, "nerd!," know that I also spent a lot of time in *back* of the library, but that's another book. . . .) The library seemed magical to me. I loved the look, the feel, and even the smell of books.

I loved to be *among* books. I usually had five or six checked out at once and would multitask, two decades before I ever touched a computer. I would read several books at once on several different subjects and fill my head with as much knowl-edge—both practical and arcane—as possible. (It's funny how much some of that "useless" knowledge has allowed me to thrive later in four or five seemingly unre-lated fields at once. Everything I know influences everything I do). I drank up words with an addictive thirst.

I envisioned that the people who created these books were magical beings who lived enchanted lives in castles in England. They sat in ornate gardens typing while hot and cold running servants brought them tea and opium. After a morn-ing of plucking lightning out of the sky and bringing it to mortal humankind via his manual typewriter, the saintly writer would nap and later be carried by a horse-drawn carriage to have lunch with the king.

I *really* wanted to be a writer when I grew up.

Now I am less interested in chasing the rock-star aspects of being an artist and more interested in just making quality art. The funny thing is that, when you give up wanting that recognition and money stuff, sometimes it finds you anyway. It has with me.

But I'm not sitting in an extraordinary castle in England. I'm sitting in my favorite unspectacular coffee shop in my lower-middle-class neighborhood in Los Angeles. Someone is waiting on me, but he's my peer, and I have to tip him. And after a morning of writing, I will take a nap, and then drive my 1981 Toyota Supra to have lunch with my really cool lover (who I met though my writing).

All things considered, I have a pretty good life.

You can, too.

> — Michael Dean
> Echo Park
> August 2004

Chapter 1

I'm Living the Dream

$30
WRITING
SCHOOL

I write and I'm living the dream. I'm doing something I love on my own terms *and* getting paid for it.

I'm writing this while traveling. I live in Los Angeles, but at this moment I'm sitting at the kitchen table of a really cool, really pretty woman I just met in Dublin, Ireland.

I enjoy writing. I would write this book even if I made no money. (I did that with my first novel. I worked 10 years on it and barely broke even.) But I'm getting paid well. Per hour it works out to more than I made when I worked 9-to-5 in an office, and more than what I made digging ditches.

And that's just the advance. I'll get more down the line from book sales.

I set my own hours. And I wake up really excited *every day*. I feel *useful*. If I were to die today, at age 39, I would have done more in my life than most people have. And I'm planning on living a long time.

I usually get up and write a bit in the morning and then hit it some more in the evening. Throughout the day I get ideas and jot them down, or bark them into a portable tape recorder and use them later.

I get to do things that I could never do when I had a steady job. Like travel the world. And take a nap whenever I feel like it. And work when I feel like it. I work under very cool conditions that are better than the best job I've ever had (and exponentially better than some of the *worst* jobs I've had).

I have a strong sense of purpose. I love getting up in the morning because I know every day that I am doing something that *matters* with my life. I get to reach people. I write this sentence knowing that it will end up in a book, and knowing that at least 20,000 people will read it—maybe a lot more.

I move people. I get fan e-mails every day and at least one "You changed my life" e-mail a week. That never happened when I was temping as an administrative assistant or digging ditches or working as an elevator operator in a ballet school.

At least once a month, someone tells me I inspired him to quit his job and pursue art full time.

People give me their art and other gifts (someone gave me a new TV recently). They offer their thanks, praise, and "a place to stay if you ever find yourself in _____."

And occasionally, they offer me their love.

I am writing this, my fourth book, on a laptop while traveling all over Europe. I'm on a working vacation to promote my film and play some music. I also have a few stops to promote my second book, which is in stores now. I am also working with my editor via e-mail (downloaded at Internet cafés along the way into the laptop) on the final revisions for my third book, which is finished and will be out soon.

I can write anything and write it well. I've written really good novels, screenplays, songs, advertising copy, cover letters, poems, legal pleadings, manifestos, mission statements, and about a billion damn fine e-mails.

The ability to write is not confined to one area. If you learn to write, you can write. Period. I've written cease-and-desist letters that made people cease and desist. I've written press releases that got press. And I've written words that got young ladies I didn't know knocking on my door wanting to meet me.

NOTE

I write my own legal documents sometimes. It would be illegal for me to recommend that you do the same, and I would never recommend that you do anything illegal.

I love the freedom that being a writer gives me. I wrote most of my last book while in cafés on a film tour around America and Canada. I did much of the editing for that book on my back porch in Los Angeles, listing to birds chirp with my feet up on the railing, sitting in the sun, sipping iced coffee.

But this lifestyle has its downsides. My shoulders hurt at this moment from being hunched over a keyboard. I get big paychecks infrequently, rather than small ones every week. So I have to have discipline to make it work.

I don't have a boss, so on any given day, I don't have to work at all. Sounds great, right? The reality is that if I skip too many days in a row, I'll end up homeless, so I need to make myself work every day even without a boss yelling at me. I have to come up with good ideas to write about continually. I have to be able to organize and edit those pithy sentences into persuasive paragraphs, intriguing chapters, compelling books, and an original series. And I have to do it consistently well, on a deadline.

It can be a lonely life. I spend a lot more time alone and in my home than most people, probably more than is healthy. When someone with a regular job is done for the day, she's done. When she finishes her workweek, the weekend belongs to her. With few exceptions, I work some *every* day and *every* night.

Four out of the five people alive in my immediate family are published writers. One of my sisters wrote a book for Cornell University. My brother and dad both have written newspaper articles. Ink runs in the Dean family blood. But that's not the whole story. The rest of my success is because of *work*.

A lot of people glamorize the life of the professional writer, but these folks aren't always being honest about what it requires. You won't buy a house on your first try: I'm a fairly successful writer, in every sense of the word, and I still rent an apartment.

Many people who fancy themselves writers are putting the mansion before the work. They really have no idea about what it takes to be unfailingly great, to get published, and to make a living.

But I am honest, and I do know what it takes. And that's what I'm going to tell you in this book.

Chapter 2

Myths & FAQ

$30 Writing School

There are a lot of untruths about writing. I'm here to dispel them.

Here are a few of the myths:

- You need a college education to write.
- You need fancy hardware and software to write.
- You need to quit your day job to write.
- You need to move to New York, Los Angeles, Paris, or out in the country to write.
- Writing will make you rich and famous.
- "The first million words you write are junk."
- Real writers have insomnia.
- You need to drink a lot of coffee to write.
- You need to ruin your life to write.
- Writers don't have time to read.

Okay. Let's debunk these one at a time:

You need a college education to write.

Not true. At least not for me.

I started writing only a couple of years after I could read. (I was a gluttonous, ravenous reader by age five.) I got kicked out of high school and went to college at 17. Flunked out of college. When I was 30, I went back to college (the John Adams campus of San Francisco City College). I completed the curriculum called Microcomputer Business Application Certificate program, and picked up some of the basics of English I'd missed or forgotten from the first time around.

It doesn't hurt to take some English classes. Most writers do. There are exceptions—Hubert "Cubby" Selby, Jr. (check out the interview on the CD-ROM that comes with this book) is an amazing and celebrated writer who ignores standard rules of grammar and punctuation. He went to sea with the Navy rather than going to college. Now he teaches English at college. (USC in Los Angeles).

NOTE

Cubby died two months after I wrote that sentence the first time. He was quite a trooper, teaching class right up to three weeks before he left us. He went to class every day, breathing oxygen from a tank while he taught. We adored him and will miss him a lot.

I think the reason so many famous writers went to college is less that college fosters or teaches good writing, and more that people who can afford to go to college can afford to sit around and write. Great working-class writer Jim Goad says, "The reason there aren't many working-class writers is that the working class are too damn busy *working* to write."

The king of the working-class writers, Charles Bukowski, *did* go to college. But he wasn't an Ivy Leaguer. He went to Los Angeles City College, which had free tuition back then.

You need fancy hardware and software to write.

False. I'm writing this on a cheap off-the-shelf laptop. It's not the top-of-the-line model. It cost me $650 new, after rebate. (This is in early 2004, when the top-of-the-line ones are still selling for nearly $2,000. You could probably find an old desktop computer that would work fine for a hundred bucks, or for free if you have a friend who's upgrading and generous.) I'm writing in Microsoft Word, which is the program most technical writers, novelists, magazine writers, and other serious writers use (except screenwriters, who usually use an inexpensive program called Final Draft). I'm even using a seven-year-old version of Word, Word 97. I am always in favor of *not* updating software just because new versions are available, unless there's something you can't live without in the newer version.

John Grisham writes by hand on yellow legal pads, as he was trained to do in law school. (My dirty little secret is that I love his work and devoured his first 10 or so books. I stopped when he quit writing about lawyers and judges. I tried reading his tome on Dust Bowl Oakies, but I fell asleep after about 40 pages. Conventional wisdom would dictate that if you can write about one subject well, you can write anything. It isn't always true. Sometimes you gotta just write what you know.)

Many great novels were written on manual typewriters. Hemingway wrote on one. Cubby wrote *Last Exit to Brooklyn* on one. Iggy Pop's compelling autobiography *I Need More* was dictated to tape and put together by someone else. I wrote much of the first draft of my first novel by mumbling into a Dictaphone. Shakespeare wrote with a feather quill by candlelight.

I think that writing on a computer makes it easier to correct and edit. But it also makes more people think they can write. And most of them suck. (You don't, because you're reading this book.) People who suck don't buy the *$30 School* series of books. They buy the ones next to my books on the same shelves, the ones that promise you'll get rich and famous. I promise only to help you be *good*.

I would recommend you use some sort of computer that's running some version of MS Word. You don't need fancy stuff to write. You just need to write.

You need to quit your day job to write.

This is a lie, and it ties in with the Jim Goad quote. Jim wrote his *Redneck Manifesto* every night after coming home exhausted from a long shift doing manual labor. I wrote much of my first novel *at* work, temping as a receptionist or administrative assistant in San Francisco's financial district. I was using the skills I'd learned in that damn Microcomputer Business Application Certificate Program, both to perform the job and to get away with working on my stuff on their resources. I would sit there in a tie and mismatched suit, shuttled away in the corner of some multinational conglomerate, and enter numbers into an Excel spreadsheet, or answer their phones with repetitive redundancy. "Hello. The Very Large Corporation of America. How may I direct your call? Hello. The Very Large Corporation of America. How may I direct your call . . . ?" But at the same time, I'd be regaling myself with tales of low-budget rockstardom in a Microsoft Word document opened up on The Very Large Corporation's computer. The trick is to hit Alt and the Tab key when you hear your boss coming. It will switch from one program to the other. Make sure you e-mail it to yourself at home often or keep it on a floppy disc, because this type of at-will employment can end at any time. And it often does, especially if you're writing some sex-and-drugs-and-rock-and-roll crap at your desk on their dollar.

You need to move to New York, Los Angeles, Paris, or out in the country to write.

Not in the least. I can write anywhere, any time. I've written stuff that's been published, writing all over the world while traveling. I've written at sidewalk cafés in Paris (see Figure 2.1).

Figure 2.1 *Me working on this book at a sidewalk café in Paris.* Photo by John Rosania.

TIP

Coffee shops in Paris charge you four times as much for your cup of coffee if you have it at the sidewalk tables than if you have it inside at the bar.

I've written in New York. I've written on planes over the English Channel. I've written in a backyard in Belgium. I've written in crowded airports, in squats, in high-rise offices, on Greyhound busses, in libraries, coffee shops, bars, business centers in hotels, beautiful gardens, ugly parking lots, many people's houses and apartments, and in radio stations prior to being interviewed. I'm writing this paragraph in my friend's living room in Houston, Texas. (At 11:47 a.m. on December 25, 2003 — don't get me started on Christmas. . . . Let's just say I would *much* rather be sitting alone writing this than opening presents with some family.) Most of what I've written I wrote in a very boring studio apartment in a very boring residential neighborhood of Los Angeles, but it could have been anywhere. I didn't move to LA to "make it." I moved to LA after 16 years in San Francisco because LA has cheaper rent and better weather.

So, I can do my work from anywhere in the world, but at the moment I live in the best of all possible worlds.

January 13, 2004. Weather.com sez:

- Los Angeles: 76 degrees
- Jamestown, NY (where I grew up): 20
- Boston: 37
- Tempe, AZ (where my best friend lives): 75
- Detroit: 25 (But feels like 16 with wind. This is where my best friend just moved to Tempe from.)
- San Francisco (where I lived for the 16 years prior to moving to LA): 51
- Houston: 64
- London: 45
- Berlin: 41
- Paris: 45

I will say this: Living in Los Angeles may not have made me a better writer, but I do think it makes people take me more seriously. I didn't get a book deal until I moved there, and it may have a small bit to do with the return address on the queries I sent out.

NOTE

I'm thinking of moving to a smaller town where I could have good weather but more room for the same cheap rent. (Send suggestions to kittyfeet70@yahoo.com. Extra points if you'll be my girlfriend for the first three months I'm in your town.) The thing about LA is, it has cheap rent (for a big city—I live in a studio apartment and pay $564 a month—and have a yard and live in a safe 'hood) and good weather. My dad said, "If you want the same weather and want to live in America, look at your map and draw a line from Los Angeles to Atlanta. Then live within 100 miles either way of that line." I did this exercise, but noticed that anywhere on that line outside of Los Angeles would pretty much put me in the Bible Belt.

Writing will make you rich and famous.

Probably not. I make a wage (not much — a dollar a book on these, believe it or not), and I've met a few girls that like me from my books. (Not from *$30 Film School*, though. Every fan letter I've gotten for it is from a guy. A girl I'm dating says it's because girls buy the book but don't wanna bother me. It's okay, girls. Bother me.)

But I don't get recognized on the street, usually. Writing probably will not whisk you sky-high out of the ghetto into a vortex of love and sex and money. If that's your plan, buy lottery tickets. You'll have a better chance. Or sell munitions. Seriously. Write only if you *love* to write.

The first million words you write are junk.

Writing teachers are fond of this, especially writing teachers who have never sold anything. It's a nice rule of thumb. But I published my first novel, and people really liked it. It was rough around the edges and didn't have much of a story, but it was compellingly constructed and a good read.

If you are a natural born writer, "The first million words you write are junk" may be true, but only if you count every word you ever write from the minute you start writing as a child. Include every paper you write in school, every note you write to a girl or boy you like, every job application you fill out, and every e-mail you write, and this old warhorse *might* be true. But probably not.

Basically, I think the inference here is that you need your first million words to develop your style. Your style is a combination of your voice and your mannerisms. Mannerisms are part of style. One of mine is using a lot of parenthetical constructs and asides (such as this). But a bigger part of your style, the part that people will attempt to imitate if you are hugely successful on an economic level, is basically what you write like. It's your voice, literally. It's your choice of words and subjects, your rhythm, and your bounce. It's your soul. And that is one thing people cannot successfully steal or copy.

I developed my voice literally from my voice — from telling stories out loud. I've always liked to tell stories, and people have always asked me to tell them. That's where I worked out my voice. Putting that on paper was just a matter of practice.

There definitely is truth to the idea that the more you write, the better you get, so write whenever and wherever you can. You can write good stuff before your first million words, but you probably won't astound people consistently until you've written a lot. People liked my first novel, but between that and writing *$30 Film School* I wrote a lot. Most of it never even got published, but it was writing and practice. A lot of people who read *$30 Film School* say it's the best book they've ever read. Only a few people (mostly drug addicts and other criminals) said that about my first novel.

Real writers have insomnia.

Nope. Some do. Chuck Palahniuk, who wrote *Fight Club*, does, and he even worked it into the plot. I do, but mine is sort of reverse insomnia. I go to sleep fine but wake up too early a lot. This is because I'm very excited to be alive. I get up and work for a few hours and then go back to sleep. I slept 5½ hours last night and got up and wrote this half of this chapter this morning. I'm gonna finish up and go back to sleep. I've written about 2,000 words (the curious number of words being exactly 2,345 words to be exact) this morning. That's 2 percent of the final book (judging from a word count of approximately 100,000 words in the first two books of this series). Two percent of a book written in one sitting. About two hours. I just earned the right to go back to bed. And it *is* Christmas day. Writing is my present to myself.

Technically, reverse insomnia does count as insomnia. There is a writer's coffee shop in Los Angeles called Insomnia that's open late and full of laptop-toting wannabe screenwriters. But you don't *have* to have sleep issues to write.

You need to drink a lot of coffee to write.

Okay. This one is true. At least for me. But I don't drink it after 6:00 p.m. or I'm up all night. Not up all night and productive, just up all night and lying in bed, staring at the ceiling, wishing I were asleep.

You need to ruin your life to write.

Not true.

I once heard a Hollywood screenwriter speak at a book signing in Los Angeles. Like most events featuring charismatic writers, most of the questions in the Q&A were from writers wanting to know how to write.

This just goes to show how easy it is to call yourself a writer. A writer asking how to *write?* Would a swimmer ask how to swim? Wow. . . . Anyway, this also leads into the "You don't need to move to a big city to write" category, because a lot of people move to Los Angeles thinking that life there will inspire them to start writing. If they really were writers, they'd already be writing in Kansas City or Bakersfield or Podunk—yes, there is such a place, in Connecticut.

Anyway, this screenwriter probably gets asked that "How do I become a writer?" question every day. Not surprising. He is one of the unofficial muses of plucky writers who move to LA and demand that the City of Angels sparkle for them, *now*, because it worked for him. He came here (from New York, mind you, the city writers are supposed to move *to*, not *from)* with nothing and became a household word in several industries.

So I'm at Skylight Books bookstore on Vermont Avenue in the trendy Los Feliz 'hood of LA, sitting in the back of about a hundred people gathered at the screenwriter's feet. This kid, probably 19 or 20, raises his hand after the reading and cuts right to the cat, "Hi. How can I become a writer?" Without skipping a thump, the writer 'torts out, "Ruin your life, hurt people, and apologize in print."

I thought this was pretty funny, and it actually worked for him. It sort of worked for me, but it can be exceedingly bad advice. It's what Stephen King called "The Hemingway Lie." It's the lie that to be a good writer, you have to ruin your life with drink or drugs. Stephen King was a drunk and a cocaine addict at the beginning of his career, too. Hmmmmm. . . . It probably sounds like I'm not making the best case against this sort of behavior. But the point is that these people were great *despite* the drugs, not because of them. It's like they were so great that they were able to write with a lead noose around their wrists.

I recently saw Hunter S. Thompson on TV. He was bloated and seemed paranoid and not very bright. I would venture that the drugs and booze have taken their toll. It didn't seem cute.

Figure 2.2 *"Die Trying."* Cartoon by Cassidy Coon.

I think I nailed this well in my novel *Starving in the Company of Beautiful Women*:

> "It takes more than a six-pack and a typewriter to be great. For every great original like Burroughs or Bukowski, there are two million junkie/drunk hacks clutching their pens while they die in the gutter, claiming to be artists."

So, you *don't* need to ruin your life to write.

If you're not writing *without* a bottle in your hand, you're not gonna write *with* one.

Writers don't have time to read.

Not true at all. I think you have to *love* reading to be a writer.

I read all the time. I'm reading three books at the moment, as well as doing author review on this book and living a full social life.

But don't read books you feel you should, if you don't like them. Especially fiction. (Occasionally I'll read a how-to on something I'm into, if it's something I want to learn about and there aren't better-written books with the same info.) It's like Cassidy Coon says, "Fiction shouldn't be like eating your vegetables."

I finally realized this and took it to heart. I think we are trained otherwise in high school, where we are forced to read dusty old "classics" against our will. These days, if a book doesn't *compel* me in the first five pages, I put it back on the shelf.

(See the color photo Cassidy took of me captioned "I like to read" in the goodies folder on the CD. I sit there and read some almost every day I'm home.)

Interview

FAQ

Frequently asked questions about writing and getting published.

This is a much shorter version adapted from a long interview with Michael W. Dean done in Nuremberg, Germany, in the middle of Michael's self-booked film/music/book tour.

The interview is by Marika (see Figure 2.3), founder of *Provokator Magazine* (www.provokator.org) from Prague in the Chezc Republic.

The complete interview is on the CD-ROM that comes with this book. Note that I added a few questions for this FAQ that were not in the original interview. Lesson one of *$30 Writing School*: Feel free to repurpose your art and sample yourself.

These questions are stuff people ask me a lot.

I'll give the short-form answers here and then expand on them in the rest of the book.

Figure 2.3 *Marika.* (Photo by Michael W. Dean. All photos in this book by Michael W. Dean unless otherwise indicated.)

How did you come to write your last book, $30 Film School?

A stranger wrote me an e-mail and asked, "How do I make a movie?" and I spent an hour answering her e-mail.

Then six months later this other guy sent me another e-mail that asked, "How do you promote a movie?" and I spent an hour answering him. I saved those two e-mails and expanded on them until it was like 15 pages and became the outline of the book.

I don't like to waste words and actions. I will often use things twice like that.

Describe to me the fine art of the interview.

I think it was Connie Chung who said, "All good interviews boil down to one question: 'What's it like to be you?'"

I heard that and it made sense. That's what I go for.

A good interview is not a situation of a lower person sitting wide-eyed before a star. A good interview is a collaboration between peers.

What is your philosophy on life?

It changes. My life has a definite character arc.

I read this book called *Zen Guitar*, which blew my mind. It made me reconsider and examine everything in my life. I started corresponding with the author, Phil Sudo, but then he got cancer. I ended up interviewing him three weeks before he died. (The video of this interview is on the Extras part of the *D.I.Y. or DIE* DVD.) It's an amazing interview. His book *Zen Guitar*—anybody should read it, even if they don't play guitar—is kind of like Zen *life*. It's about music, but there are no chord charts. It's just about doing art for the right reasons instead of for feeble-witted reasons. I met him, and it was one of those situations where you meet somebody and they just go (*Michael gently taps Marika in the center of her forehead*) like that, and it just goes into you. Like the Universe, God, whatever is going through somebody *into* you. That really changed me.

To me, a good story about football can reach me even though I don't like football. It's not the subject. It's about people's motivation and heart. Passion is universal.

A good novel, a good interview, a good documentary, a good drama, or even comedy, they all touch something—a common human thread. That's bigger than "What kind of guitar picks do you use?", which is meaningless to me.

What helped you get published?

One thing that I've realized as a writer is that you need editing. Part of editing is having a beginning, a middle, and an end.

Like with film, an outline helps. I had a definite idea of where I wanted it to go, but once you start laying stuff into the timeline, the film kind of tells you where it wants to go. Same with a book.

I don't think everything I do is golden, and I spend a lot of time proofreading and rewriting, which I think is important for any writer, musician, or artist to do.

How do you get cool interviewees? How did you finish a film or book and follow through all the way to the end?

If you do stuff right, people are interested in working with you. A big compliment I've gotten was from Ian MacKaye, who told me that he was amazed that I actually got my film done. He said that a lot of people have interviewed him on video, and almost none of it has seen the light of day. He said that I pursued this in an almost aggressive manner and got it done.

My aggressive manner pisses people off sometimes, but it gets the job done.

Ian helped me get to interview Henry Rollins for the *$30 Music School* book, and it took about 90 seconds to set up. Just sent an e-mail, made a call, and got in my car that minute. As an artist, you have to be ready to answer any marching orders. But it was easy and cool. And Rollins told me he liked the interview so much he's planning to use it in one of his upcoming books. I like that. Again, it's a collaboration.

Ten years earlier I probably would have moved across the country to get to word-jam with Rollins and have it end up in one of his books. Today it's just a car trip across town.

Things get easier the more I do this stuff. And it just kinda comes to me because I do the incessant footwork. I have structured my life in a way that I do what I like to do for work, therefore I am a workaholic and totally dig it. I am not afraid of work. I like *doing*.

This girl at a reading I did in Paris told me that "dreaming is better than doing." I was really attracted to this girl until she said that. It just killed it. That's the lamest attitude I could imagine.

I have always been a big fan of Thomas Edison. He said "genius is one percent inspiration and ninety-nine percent perspiration."

I've said it before and I'll say it again—any junkie lying in the gutter has a tattered notebook full of great ideas, but he didn't follow through with them. When I was a junkie, I had five or six notebooks filled, with about 10 or 20 ideas per page. Hundreds of ideas.

Since getting clean, I've spent years working on only two of those ideas (this book series and the *D.I.Y. or DIE* documentary). And I'm making a living, traveling the world, and *changing* the world for the better every day. Ideas and dreams alone are useless.

So you're process oriented instead of goal oriented?

I used to be very goal oriented and I've become more process oriented over the last few years. This is ironic because it actually helps me meet my goals better.

You learned the structure of writing by trial and error?

Basically I've always had the punk-rock attitude, "You can't tell me anything, man." As I get older I am learning that I *can* learn new tricks. It's smart to listen to people who can already do the stuff you want to do.

I don't think you have to go to school for four years to learn anything. But I think it doesn't hurt to pick up a book, and it doesn't hurt to ask someone who is already doing it.

Everybody has an opinion, but opinions are useless. Experience is better. If you want to learn how to work out in the gym and get in shape, you don't go to the guy who reads books about working out and isn't in shape—you go to the guy who's in shape and ask how he did it.

Getting back to editors.

The way I write books is to make each chapter a separate document. That's really important. And do some kind of outline. That's absolutely necessary for a non-fiction "how-to" book, and I think it wouldn't hurt to have a one- or two-page outline for a novel.

The outline can change as it goes on. It's not set in stone. It's a living guideline to help you. It's not like work or homework or something.

Leonardo da Vinci said, "This block of stone has an angel in it, I just have to let her out." You have to envision your result at least a little bit before you start.

The main editor on the *$30 School* series is the Acquisitions Editor, Kevin Harreld. He's the guy who signed me to Muska & Lipman/Course/Thomson (though I'm free to work with other publishers). He's the guy who guides me in the overall direction of the project. He's very smart and has done a lot of success-ful books in every capacity—from editor to author to sales.

The other editors I worked with were the Project Editor, Sandy Doell, who catches mistakes and examines the overall structure and direction of the book, and two tech editors, Michael Prager on *Film School* and Michael Woody on *Music School.* Sandy doesn't just catch misspellings and bad grammar, she also has a very good feel for my stuff and sees what I'm trying to do and makes suggestions to strengthen it for the reader.

NOTE

After I wrote this, Sandy got busy on another project. So the Project Editor on this book is the very capable Brian Proffitt. This sort of mutability of involvement is one thing I love about the writing (and film) world . . . you aren't committed to the same people. Ever.

The tech editors worked only on the chapters that were technical. A tech editor is basically a guy who does a lot of proofreading of technical manuals. He's really computer intuitive. He can look at anything (even if he hasn't used the program) and catch what you've said that doesn't make sense or isn't clear. He will even download a demo and go through everything you describe (and try it). I have had good ones: Michael Prager is an author of technical manuals and books himself, and Michael Woody is a really smart guy and long-time friend and collaborator of mine who totally "gets" me.

There is also a Copy Editor who just mainly catches typos and grammatical errors.

*How did you go about publishing your first novel (*Starving in the Company of Beautiful Women*)?*

Non-fiction is generally sold on a query, a proposal, and two sample chapters. There's an almost rigid formatting and convention for writing the proposal. The query is almost like a cover letter, asking, "Do you want to see this?" You always send that as a body of an e-mail, not as an attachment, unless you are asked to send an attachment.

Fiction usually has to be completed to be sold. It's not sold on just a proposal and sample chapters. And you are more likely to sell non-fiction (and are more likely to get an advance). Fiction's really hard to sell, and it has to be completely done—

proofread and everything, and they'll still ask you to make changes, but it has to be complete to sell.

I formatted the proposal to industry-standard format. It got me an agent, but the agent was unable to sell *Starving*. After a year we split amicably. He was probably sick of dealing with me anyway. I was pretty high maintenance at that point in my life.

So I just self-published it. I got a "borrowed" copy of Quark, learned page layout. Did it myself and took it to a printer.

Contacts—that's what agents are all about. The way books are sold, publishers and agents are almost all in New York, all in like a five-square-block area. The agents and editors all know each other, and once a week they go out to lunch with an editor from each publisher and pitch books to them. The idea of an agent is as a go-between, which I kind of resent on principle—the idea of a go-between. I can see why they exist; so that the publisher doesn't have to sift through the piles of crap. The agent does it for him.

A reputable agent has a track record. The publisher knows that if he takes something, it's going to be good. Chances are they can sell it.

A lot of things that are agented get sold really quickly. My book *$30 Film School* got sold within a month of me signing with my agent (Kimberley Valentini at Waterside).

How do you live?

Simply and smart. Writing has very little in the way of guarantees. It's freelance work, it's not a secure vocation. You get a big check, and then you won't get any money for many months. It's a lot different than having a 9-to-5. You need to make your money stretch.

Have you learned over time to deal with criticism differently?

Yes. I just heard a guy tonight who walked out of my movie and said, "I don't like this movie." But there are 65 people in there watching it who are very interested in it. Five years ago, I would have been totally bummed. I would have heard only that one negative comment.

And anybody who puts me down, I'm like, "Okay, let's hear *your* band. Let's read *your* novel."

Somebody once said to me, "if something has wings it will fly." That doesn't necessarily mean you'll become a billionaire, but it means it will get out into the universe because the universe loves art.

Stuff that's cool has a way of getting made and a way of finding distribution and an audience.

Conclusion

So. This concludes our debunking and our enlightening—all the stuff you didn't learn, for one reason or another, in school (or learned and forgot). Now it's time to move on and grapple with the basics of English. Time for English 101.

Chapter 3

English 101

$30 WRITING SCHOOL

Some of this stuff you may already know. This chapter is sort of like the section in *$30 Music School* where I showed the basic chords on the guitar, but a few chapters later, I was telling you how to book a world tour. People who could already play guitar told me that they learned something from the chord chapter. So you can skip this English basics part if you think you already know it all, but you might not want to!

I'm a high school dropout. Sort of. Well, I say that for lack of a better term, because there isn't an easy term like that for what I am. More accurate might be "community college dropout." But there's more.

I went to an all-boys religious school for kids who weren't really bad kids yet. It was a school for kids who were on their way to being bad. I hadn't stolen cars yet, but I probably would have if I hadn't gotten sent to the school.

I got kicked out in the summer between eleventh and twelfth grades. I'd written a letter to Mick Jagger asking him to buy the school and turn it into the Jagger School for Boys. In the letter I'd called our headmaster a "fat, bald, overtly Christian old fart." I sent the letter to the wrong address, and I'd forgotten to put my name on the envelope, but the school address was printed on it. The letter was returned and got opened by the headmaster to see to whom to return it, and I got kicked out.

I called the guidance counselor from my old school (Westfield Academy and Central School in Westfield, NY) at his home. He came in on his summer break and met with me. He recommended that I go to college! (Maybe he'd remembered what a pest I'd been in elementary school and wanted to cut his losses.) He said, "You can go to college in Jamestown and get concurrent credit for it for both high school and college. Natalie Merchant did it last year." (Singer Natalie Merchant went to the same small high school and college as I did, a year ahead of me. The counselor perhaps felt that she'd been a bit of a pill, too.)

So I did. I went off to college at 17, had my own apartment, and partied a lot. I barely passed. But at the end of the year I got to go back to my old high school where I hadn't been in five years, put on a cap and gown, and get a diploma with people I barely remembered.

I went back to the college the following year (so I wouldn't have to go get a job) and flunked out. (I got four Fs and an A the last semester. The A was in an independent project for my radio broadcast class, where I just spent all my time recording my music.)

So that's what I am. I'm not a high school dropout, but I am something.

Many years later, I went to San Francisco City College and took some English classes for kicks and actually *learned* something. But other than that, I would say I'm mostly self-taught.

Now I am a professional writer. I think that would surprise my teachers. I am a horrible speller. In high school, that would indicate that you probably were not destined to make your living as a writer. But then along came affordable computers, word processors, and spell check, and I was off and writing for pay.

I used spell check extensively. Of course, you still have to look at what you're doing, because it won't know the difference between "their" and "there." But spell check rocks.

There was a time, hundreds of years ago, when writing was not standardized. The old belief was that if you could understand what word it was, it was fine. This is no longer the case with most people, but there are some schools of thought that believe grammar doesn't matter. Usually beatnik schools.

There is writing that does work while defying conventional rules. e. e. cummings used unconventional capitalization. Hubert Selby, Jr., has his own entire system of grammar and punctuation (for starters, he replaces the apostrophe with a slash mark. See his interview movie on the CD-ROM for more on this). But you can read Selby's writing. His stuff is really easy to follow, easier than some stuff that follows all the rules precisely.

Basically, I would say, try to make it as good as you can and follow the rules. But don't use the grammar check in Word. I think it sucks. It is too damn literal. It takes forever to get through a page.

To disable grammar check, go to Tools/Options.

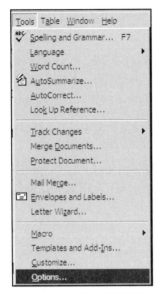

Figure 3.1 *Go to Tools/Options.*

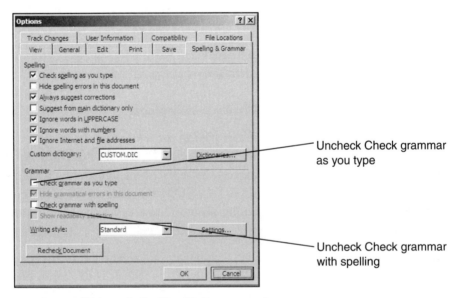

Figure 3.2 *Click on the Spelling & Grammar tab*

Uncheck Check grammar as you type and Check grammar with spelling at the bottom of the pane, and click OK to save.

Grammar Time

Good writing is *way* more important than perfect grammar. But if people have to wade through the mistakes, they're not going to find your writing easy to read.

If you *must* invent your own system, do it for a reason and *be consistent.* Then it doesn't seem like a mistake. It becomes a *style.*

Here's a thing that's been going around the Net for so long that no one can really say who came up with it:

> "Aoccdrnig to a rscheearch at Cmabrigde Uinervtisy, it deosn't
>
> mttaer in waht oredr the ltteers in a wrod are, the olny iprmoetnt
>
> tihng is taht the frist and lsat ltteer be at the rghit pclae. The
>
> rset can be a total mses and you can sitll raed it wouthit
>
> porbelm. Tihs is bcuseae the huamn mnid deos not raed ervey lteter
>
> by istlef, but the wrod as a wlohe."

A lot of my writing breaks the rules, but I usually know when I'm doing it, and I'm doing it for a reason. I like to have the basic rules of grammar in place and the spelling as good as it can be.

A lot of my writing is creative writing that can discard the rules when it wants to. Sort of like ad copy. In advertising, you'll have a sentence that is not even a sentence, such as "20% off!" or "the best thing you'll ever buy." Some ad copy, such as "Buy now!," actually *is* a complete sentence, even though it doesn't seem like it. You say there's no noun in "Buy now!"? Actually, there is. It is tacitly assumed that this sentence actually reads "*You* buy now!", so the "You" is the noun. Knowing this makes your breaking the rule a conscious decision, not sloppy idiocy. You'll look better if you learn the rules before you break them. It's like an abstract painter is going to be a lot better if he learns how to draw realistically first, because then he can paint his impossible nightmares a lot more clearly.

(The pros always make it look easy!)

I try to make my work airtight. I don't like typos, but a few still slip through into the final copy of my book. (Of course, then I go through *that with a red pen and make changes for the second printing, as demonstrated in Figure 3.3).*

(Look on the CD in the Goodies folder for Book Being Proofed for Second Pressing—LowRez. You can see my marks more easily on that.)

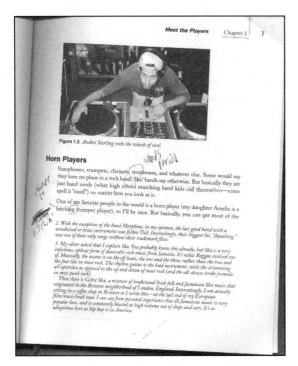

Figure 3.3 *A book being proofed for second printing.*

Keep in mind that because of the way page layout is done, the designer can't easily repaginate. So I don't bother with suggestions of "we should add more here" or whatever, because they really can't. I make marks only if something is dead wrong or really hard to understand. Basically, they have to make all the corrections in the same space as what they're changing.

With proofreading, I try not to do too much in a day. I only have a few hours' worth in me in a given day, if I want to stay accurate. When I start glossing over the text quickly, it's time to put it down and go on to some other task. Or take a nap.

English is the fourth most common language in the world, after Mandarin, Hindustani, and Spanish. However, it is by far the most common *second* language. Much of the world can speak some English, and it's the international language of commerce, industry, and science.

English is pretty difficult as a language. Even native speakers tend to make mistakes. The most common mistakes are *so* common that if you get rid of them, you'll be doing pretty darned well.

Parts of Speech

In case you slept through third-grade English like me, let's examine the very basic parts of English.

Let's look at this sentence: The red kitty swiftly ate the bat in my room.

"The" is an article.

"red" is an adjective.

"kitty" is a noun.

"swiftly" is an adverb.

"ate" is a verb.

"the" is an article.

"bat" is a noun.

"in" is a preposition.

"my" is an adjective.

"room" is a noun.

Nouns are things, people, and places.

Verbs are actions.

Adjectives modify nouns.

Adverbs modify verbs, adjectives, and other adverbs.

Articles substitute for nouns.

Prepositions are describers for where: in, on, over, under, etc.

If you're still confused, borrow the DVD of *Schoolhouse Rock* from your local library; a place, by the way, where books are still kept.

—Michael Woody

"Punks Not Dead"—Grammar Errors

I'm gonna go through a few of my pet peeves with grammar.

This chapter does not cover all the rules for the English language. There are other rules and exceptions, but here are some basics and some of the stuff most commonly done wrong.

Apostrophes

Misplaced and Missing Apostrophes

Many people don't know when and where to use the apostrophe character ('). There was a famous pin that people used to wear that said "Punks Not Dead" on it. I have also seen that phrase painted on the back of people's leather jackets. It should, of course, be "Punk's Not Dead" because in this case, it is a *contraction* for "Punk Is Not Dead." The apostrophe, in this case, is substituting for a missing letter.

Unnecessary Apostrophes Used

There are a lot of them. People generally seem to think that the only rule for the use of apostrophes is, "If you don't know if there should be one or not, by all means, put one in."

Figure 3.4 *Errors in a sign in Los Angeles. "TUNE UP'S" should be "TUNE-UPS." (Maybe the tagging is the graffiti form of proofreader's marks. Who knows?)* Photo by Michael Dean.

People often use them incorrectly to make stuff plural. The plural of "pet peeve" is not "pet peeve's," it's "pet peeves." The plural of "CD" is not "CD's," it's "CDs." The decade is '70s or 1970s, not 70's or 1970's.

Someone posted on my Web board about a film she was making: "…a documentary about the presence and influence of Puerto Rican's in Hollywood."

"Puerto Rican's" should be "Puerto Ricans." Astonishingly, the person who wrote this works as a technical writer for a living!

Figure 3.5 *At 608 Folsom Street in San Francisco, there is a plaque on the wall with a typo in it. It's especially ironic, because the plaque says that it was the original site of the Typographer's Union.* Photo by Dattner.

NOTE

"Irony" is one of the most improperly used words. As they say in the movie *Reality Bites*, irony is when the implied meaning is the opposite of the actual meaning.

Most people don't know irony when they see it. When most people say "that's ironic," the situation is not actually ironic. It's merely interesting. Interesting does not equal ironic. You can easily have one without the other.

A fat guy named Slim is ironic. So is a tiny, sweet dog named Cujo or Killer. Some would say the name "Patriot Act" is ironic, also.

This is ironic:

The judge sentenced Jay to 40 hours of community service working at the community music center where he used to pay to hang out.

This is merely interesting:

I like cats and ended up working at a cat shelter that sells rare cats for the Russian Mafia (see Figure 3.6).

Figure 3.6 *Russian Mafia kitty.* Cartoon by Cassidy Coon.

Necessary Apostrophes Not Used

This one is pretty common, even in signs and names of companies. Janes Flowers. Toms Carburetor Repair. Amelias Cat Detailing. These would indicate plural, not possessive. They would be remotely accurate only if these companies were owned by two Janes, two Toms, and two people named Amelia, respectively. Even then, they would be Janes' Flowers, Toms' Carburetor Repair, and Amelias' Cat Detailing.

When an apostrophe is used to indicate possession, it is harkening back to some archaic construct from Olde English. *Michael's hard drive* really means *Michael his hard drive*, meaning "the hard drive belonging to him, Michael." *Skip's lunch* really means *Skip his lunch*. Same with girls, too: *Tiffany's cheese* means *Tiffany his cheese*, meaning the cheese belonging to Tiffany.

The one exception to this is "its," meaning "that which belongs to it." "Its" is written "its" to avoid confusing it with "it's," the contraction for "it is." Get it? (See Figure 3.7.)

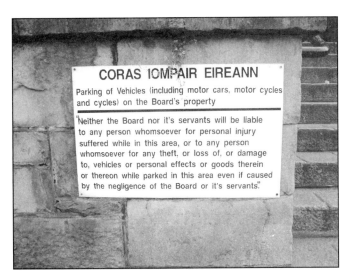

Figure 3.7 *Errors in a sign in Ireland. ("It's servants" should be "Its servants.")* Photo by Michael Dean.

This rule also works with things like "the day's receipts," meaning the receipts of the day. A day, not just people, can own something.

It gets a little complicated when you are making a plural possessive. A cat that's owned by two nuns would be "the nuns' cat." (Technically it should be "the nuns's cat," but the **s's** thing is too awkward, so it is usually changed to just **s'**.)

"My friend's band's lyrics" would mean lyrics belonging to the band of one of my friends.

"My friends' band's lyrics" would mean lyrics belonging to the band with several of my friends.

The Sandra Bullock/Hugh Grant movie *Two Weeks Notice* should have been called *Two Weeks' Notice*. The notice belongs to the two weeks.

(How can a company spend millions making a piece of "promo art" and then not pay someone 10 bucks an hour to come in and proof it? And of all the people who work on a big Hollywood movie, how come no one spoke up? Fear of losing his job? Another example of all that is wrong with Hollywood.)

Hyphenation

There are a lot of rules about hyphens (-), but the most common mistake is not knowing where to put the hyphen when you want to use two words to describe a third word. (This is basically a noun and an adjective, or two nouns, forming a compound adjective to modify a noun, if you must know.) Examples are "dog-eared book," "cat-tongued kiss," or "twenty-minute rant." The first two are forming one unit to describe the third word. You use the hyphen to show which two words out of the three are being combined. This makes it less confusing. You know which word goes with which.

For example, a blue-green god is different from a blue green-god. The first one, blue-green god, would be a god that is colored a mixture of blue and green. Blue green-god could be a green god that is feeling sad.

Seven-nation army

is different from

Seven nation-army

A "seven-nation army" would be an army made up of soldiers from seven different nations. "Seven nation-army" wouldn't really make much sense.

Hyphenation can be used with three words, not just two:

> I will nibble Lydia's nape sometime in the not-too-distant future.

> The naked (hairless) cat cost a lot: a dozen one-hundred-dollar bills.

The exception to hyphenation rule is as follows: Use it if it adds clarification, and omit it if doing so doesn't add confusion:

> Senior citizen dance

> Social Security cuts

> New Age crap

The hyphen is used only when the first word is a noun or an adjective. It is not usually used if the first word is an adverb or ends in "ly":

> Aptly named kitten

> Organically grown kitten

Also, *any* phrase that contains the word "self" is hyphenated, regardless of how it's used:

> self-published

> self-esteem

> self-hatred

> self-abuse

> self-love

A and An

A kitty. A movie. An atrocity. An amusement.

If the noun you are describing begins with a vowel sound (a, e, i, o, u), use "an" before it. If it begins with a consonant (all the other letter sounds), use "a" before it.

Note that you're working off the *sound* of the word, not the actual letter that starts the word. For example:

> a URL

not

> an URL

(URL is pronounced "you are ell." Y sounds get "a," not "an" before them.)

Another example:

> I would rather squat in *a* Unabomber-style shack with DSL than own a swanky townhouse with all the trimmings if I couldn't create art.

Of course, you would break rule this if you were doing dialogue for a character who talks street. Like on *The Simpsons*, when a stoned guy from Cyprus Hill says, "I can't remember. Did we order a orchestra?"

Commas

Commas are tricky. Basically, they are used to break up a sentence to make it easier to understand.

I used to have an English teacher who would say, "Just put a comma where you'd take a breath reading it out loud." This sort of works, but not really.

There are scores, if not hundreds, of rules for comma use. Listing all of them is beyond the scope of this book (If you want to know all of them, or are having trouble sleeping, read a few hundred pages of *The Chicago Manual of Style.)*

A few of the most common and important (and also most commonly broken) rules of commas are these:

> Put in a comma when joining two sentences:
>
> > I bit your sister, but she liked it.
>
> Put a comma before an introductory clause:
>
> > Because he relapsed, his girlfriend left him.
>
> Put in a comma with dates:
>
> > April 4, 1983, is my lover's birthday.
>
> Put in a comma with addresses:
>
> > P.O. Box 29704, Los Angeles, CA 90029-0704 is my address.
>
> Put commas in a list:
>
> > I enjoy sleeping, listening, biting, moaning, slapping, and kissing.

In this book, we always use the serial comma.

Put a comma before a quote (as in the *Simpsons* example used previously).

Put in a comma for a parenthetical clause (part of a sentence that makes something else more clear, but that the sentence can function without):

> I wanted to take my cat, Charlie, on the road to Europe, but Lydia said it was a bad idea.

This could function without the parenthetical clause just fine:

> I wanted to take my cat on the road to Europe, but Lydia said it was a bad idea.

It's called a parenthetical clause because the part separated by commas could just as easily be separated with parentheses:

> I wanted to take my cat (Charlie) on the road to Europe, but Lydia said it was a bad idea.

(Note that the term "parenthetical" can describe either the parenthetical clause itself or a sentence containing a parenthetical clause.)

Exception to all comma rules: *A comma can be used where it is not indicated, if using it makes the sentence easier to understand.*

Footnotes and Endnotes

Footnotes are sort of separated parentheticals at the bottom of the page, such as this[1] (see bottom of the page). I like them because they are almost like hypertext Weblinks, but on a printed page. Actually, it's probably the other way around. Hypertext Weblinks were probably invented to imitate footnotes.

I've always liked footnotes. You used to see them more often than you do now. They are usually used only in scientific journals and other academic text, and even then, often only for bibliographic references and attributes for quotes and statistics.

I used them in my novel because I like them. Even though I did them as footnotes (Insert/Footnote in Microsoft Word), they ended up as endnotes (all at the end of the document rather than at the bottom of each page). This happened because Quark 4.0, the page layout program I used, would not add them as footnotes. Footnotes would have had to be cut and pasted in carefully by the page layout person. Quark 6.0 does footnotes automatically, which saves a lot of work.

---

[1] This is a footnote.

I always liked the idea of David Foster Wallace's book, *Infinite Jest*. It's a 1,088-page novel with endnotes that alone are longer than some novels. In fact, some of the endnotes have footnotes!

I read the endnotes of his book, but I haven't read the book. But the endnotes are a good read all by themselves.

Ellipses . . .

Ellipses are those dots after a sentence or phrase to indicate missing words or that something keeps going . . .

You use three dots in the middle of a sentence to show that something was removed or to indicate a pause:

Something was removed:

The review of *$30 Film School* said, in part, "This is the best filmmaking book I've read. Michael Dean really knows his stuff, but . . . I think he is a criminally minded little brat who has a thing or two to learn about life."

Indicating a pause:

She said that in the end I'd change my ways and . . . ahh, never mind. It's not important.

You use four dots at the end of a sentence, because it's the period that would normally come at the end of that sentence plus three dots as above:

Jessica told Charlie cat to stop eating grass. . . .

Semicolons (;)

Semicolons are like super commas. They're used to put order to confusion when you have too many commas:

My goal is to promote this film and get it shown on TV, PBS, and cable, and at theaters, youth centers, high schools, universities, and film festivals; and to travel to, and personally present it, at the same.

Semicolons can also join two sentences where a cause and effect is indicated:

I bit Cassidy's nape; therefore, she made little squeaking noises.

Colons (:)

A colon is used to add a list or a resulting example after a full sentence:

> I have only six needs to be a happy man: loose shoes, a cat, some tongs, a pretty girl, a laptop, and a coffee machine.

You also can use a colon to separate a clause from a complete sentence, if that clause is the example or result of the action in the complete sentence. If the clause is a complete sentence, you begin it with a capital letter:

> Okay, there is one reason that I could see favoring a typewriter over a computer: You have a complete lack of distraction.

If the clause is a *not* a complete sentence, you do not begin it with a capital letter:

> Okay, there is one reason that I could see favoring a typewriter over a computer: lack of distractions.

Who/Whom

These are very misused. People often misuse "whom" when they're trying to sound smart. They end up sounding stupider than if they hadn't tried. "Who" is a subject; "whom" is an object:

> Who is going to bite my nape?

> To whom were you directing your nape biting?

When in doubt, just skip it. This usage is dying and being taken out of the English language slowly. "Who" will work most of the time.

Ending a Sentence with a Preposition

Ending a sentence with a preposition is a no-no to most English teachers. I do it whenever I feel like it. *Not* doing it is often difficult and involves creating awkward sentence structure as a workaround:

> "I want to know who you've been talking to."

and

> "She wants to know whose nape you've been biting on."

Both sound good, and much better than:

"I want to know to whom you've been talking."

and

"She wants to know on whose nape have you been biting."

(I would use this type of sentence only out of the mouth of a snooty character, to demonstrate her snootiness.)

Beginning a Sentence with a Conjunction

Conjunctions (and, but, or, nor, if), according to some English teachers, are not to be used to start a sentence. This is archaic. Do it if it works:

She has been biting a nape. But she didn't bite *my* nape.

Stress

I use *italics* a lot to stress certain words. It *does* make a difference. It is one of the things that makes my writing seem more conversational, because people stress words a *lot* when they're talking to you. Don't *over*do it, but it *can* help. It makes a *big* difference in how stuff is perceived. Read each of these out loud, stressing the italicized word:

I like to pet mean cats.

(I, as opposed to you or someone else, like to pet them.)

I *like* to pet mean cats.

(I enjoy it. Might be a reply to someone saying, "I hate petting mean cats.")

I like to *pet* mean cats.

(Might be a reply to someone saying, "I like to bite mean cats.")

I like to pet *mean* cats.

(Maybe I don't like the nice ones.)

I like to pet mean *cats*.

(As opposed to dogs.)

Figure 3.8 *I like to pet mean cats.* Cartoon by Cassidy Coo.

Italics are the best for showing stress. Don't use <u>underlining</u> to stress stuff. It looks crappy in books, as it cuts off the bottom of the letters j, y, g, and so on.

And don't use ALL CAPS, because it looks like YELLING! I usually don't use **bold**, either. I just think *italics* look the best.

Italics are used for the titles of full-length books, movies, and albums:

> *$30 Film School*
> *Chasing Amy*
> *Blood Sugar Sex Magic*

"Quotes" are used for the titles of articles, short stories, poems, short films, and individual songs:

> "Michael Dean's Findings on the Squats of Europe"
> "The Raven"
> "I Left My Band in San Diego"
> "Ode to a Cat"

Capitalization

There are a few ways to capitalize a sentence or phrase to indicate how it is being used, and to make it clearer exactly what it is referring to. They are: Title Case, Sentence case, and ALL CAPS.

Note that in Title Case, the first letter of most words is capitalized, but very short words such as "a", "the", "of", and "on" are not.

In Sentence case, only the first word of the sentence is capitalized. (Of course, other words that are always capitalized, like proper names, are also capitalized.)

In ALL CAPS, every letter is capitalized.

Title Case:

Starving in the Company of Beautiful Women

Sentence case:

She loves the works of Dean and other critters of his ilk.

NOTE

You can toggle between these three cases in Word by highlighting a sentence or phrase, pressing the Shift key, and repeatedly pressing the F3 key at the same time.

Don't be random with capitalization (or any other conventions of English). It will look like a mistake. If people have to hunt and peck through your inconsistencies to find your brilliance, they probably ain't gonna bother.

If you decide to break a rule, do it universally. In my first novel, I capitalized the words Beauty and Beautiful every time they came up. I did this for two reasons. One is that there is an old chestnut my first creative writing teacher in high school laid on me. He said that the words Beauty and Beautiful were overused by inexperienced writers (especially poets) to the point of laughability. When people are making their first attempts to express something deep, those are often the only words they can come up with. Secondly, I wanted to stress that the protagonist was in love, even obsessed, with Beauty. In women. In life. In love, dreams, drugs, music, and God. He wanted to bathe in the embryonic blanket of beauty with every cell of every pore.

Only one person ever figured this out, that I know. As I'll explain later, one reviewer said, "I guess it's his religion." Yup.

ALL CAPS:

> IF YOU MAKE SOMETHING ALL CAPS, IT USUALLY LOOKS LIKE YOU ARE YELLING!!!!!!! USE IT SPARINGLY!!!!

Days of the week, months of the year, planets, people's names, and places are always capitalized:

> I left for Cleveland to visit Mars the first Tuesday in June, and took Cassidy, and her dog Fluffy, with me.

Was/Were

"Were" is usually the plural past tense of "was":

> She was. We were.
>
> I was. We were.

It is also used when describing something that isn't or never will be:

> "If I were her father," not "If I was her father."
>
> "If I were a rock star," not "If I was a rock star."

("We're" is a contraction of "we are.")

Anyway/Anyways

It's always *anyway* (or *any way*, but that means "any way." *Anyway* is a placeholder word, like "ummmmmm." *Anyways* isn't a word.

Then/Than

Often confused. "Then" implies time:

> Then I left. Things were better then.

"Than" implies comparison:

> Charlie is fatter than the other cat, Tiger Woods.

There/Their/They're

Often confused.

"There" implies place:

Charlie is sleeping over there today.

"Their" implies ownership:

I don't know what the cats told you, but it's their problem that the mice and bats are missing.

"They're" is a contraction of "they are":

They're coming for dinner.

Again, to review:

They're going over there and bringing their mice.

Quotes and Parentheses

Double quote marks ("") go around something someone said:

Debbie said, "I wanna nibble your nape."

NOTE

If you end up with quote marks that face the wrong way, such as " instead of ", you can do a search and replace in Word that will take care of it (Edit/Replace). Just search " and replace with " (both going the same way), and it will know which to put where. Then do the same with single quotes, replacing the ' character with the ' character. It's a good idea to save a backup copy before doing any global replaces like this.

Make sure there is no space before or after any of the marks in the search field, or it will search and replace that, too.

If it's a quote within a quote, you use single quotes inside:

"Jim said he ran into Debbie, and she told him, 'I wanna nibble Michael's nape.'"

(Note both single and double quotes at the end of a quote within a quote.)

If you want to extend a quote over several paragraphs, you put the quotation marks at the beginning of the quote in each paragraph, and at the beginning and end of the last paragraph:

> I ran into Debbie. She told me a lot of stuff. She said, "If you see Michael, tell him I wanna bite his nape.
>
> "Also tell him that he left his cat-handling tongs over at my apartment. The tongs are taking up space, and I am no longer handling cats, so he should come get them.
>
> "And the stuff he told my turtle was not good. Now the turtle wants to go off and join a rock band."

The same rule works for parentheses over several paragraphs:

> (I know that living in Prague seems like a bad idea. But it's working out for several of my friends, so I'll consider it.
>
> (Marika lives in Prague, and she says that it's cheap to live there, and she likes it. She thinks I'd like it, too, because there are lots of pretty, bored, artistic women who would really like me.
>
> (It sounds fun, but I don't wanna go halfway around the world. Besides, who would feed and love Charlie in my stead?)

Paragraphs

Sentences are the basic building blocks of writing, but knowing how to structure paragraphs is where the art and the voice really come together. There are a few guidelines for this, but mainly you start to do it by feel the more you write (and read).

When to Use

A paragraph is a collection of sentences that represents one complete line of thinking. Paragraphs can be as short as one sentence and as long as several dozen sentences. Most paragraphs are between three and twelve sentences.

There is a rule that a paragraph should never be one sentence in formal writing. I break this rule a lot in my writing. I will very occasionally use a one-sentence paragraph to make something stand out more.

A page in a book usually has between two and five paragraphs. Keep in mind that a page in your word processing program is about a page and a half in a book. One single-spaced page in Microsoft Word, 12-point type, Times New Roman font, with the default top, bottom, and side margins, averages around 500 words. A page in an average book is about 325 words. In tech-type writing like this, it's less, because there are a lot of pictures and a lot of white space. I think the space is to allow the text to breathe, which probably aids the retention of knowledge.

It's sometimes rather hard to know where to end one paragraph and begin the next begin. I give careful consideration to this when I'm proofing a chapter or article the first time through. I tend to write in a sort of trance, a stream of consciousness. I'm a right-brained out-of-body writer or something. So then, when I switch over into left-brained proofreading mode, I try to read it out loud (at least in my mind, but sometimes with my lips) and try to let the page tell me where it wants to be. Then I draw a paragraph mark (¶) next to where I want to make a paragraph break. Then I usually draw a circle around it so that I won't miss it later. I do this with most of my proofreading marks. And I always use a blue or red pen. It's easier to see on a white page printed with black ink.

There will be more on proofreading later, but basically, I make all my marks, then I go through and enter all the marks on the paper into the computer file.

Line Breaks Rather Than Tabs

Most people do paragraphing like this, with each paragraph beginning by hitting the Tab key, and no vertical space between paragraphs:

> The writer was a swell cat. He certainly liked the ladies, and they certainly liked him. It was almost a burden at times. He would be on a deadline, attempting to create another brilliant "textbook that doesn't suck," and he would be accosted by women clamoring for his attention.
>
> There was usually one in his bed, one on the way out, and another on the way in. Often, there'd be one making plans to fly in from somewhere a few weeks from now.
>
> And as if that wasn't enough distraction, there was his cat. This darned cat, which he loved beyond comprehension, was a mewling, scritching little flucker. The kitty loved to jump on his face and wake him up at 10:00 a.m., which is at least an hour before the writer fancied to rise.

Kitty would also cry outside his door for half a day or until he let her in. The writer was fond of saying, "If that cat were a human woman, I'd put a restraining order on her."

I paragraph it like this, with no tab character, and one line of vertical space between each paragraph:

The writer was a swell cat. He certainly liked the ladies, and they certainly liked him. It was almost a burden at times. He would be on a deadline, attempting to create another brilliant "textbook that doesn't suck," and he would be accosted by women clamoring for his attention.

There was usually one in his bed, one on the way out, and another on the way in. Often, there'd be one making plans to fly in from somewhere a few weeks from now.

And as if that wasn't enough distraction, there was his cat. This darned cat, which he loved beyond comprehension, was a mewling, scritching little flucker. The kitty loved to jump on his face and wake him up at 10:00 a.m., which is at least an hour before the writer fancied to rise.

Kitty would also cry outside his door for half a day or until he let her in. The writer was fond of saying, "If that cat were a human woman, I'd put a restraining order on her."

I just like the way it looks. I do it both in fiction and non-fiction. It makes things easier to read, too, and it actually puts fewer words on each page, which makes it easier to meet by-the-page deadlines! (Though that isn't a problem with me. I tend to overwrite, not underwrite. In a 500-page book, the editor usually has me cut about 90 pages. This is fine and makes for a stronger book, because we usually cut the weakest 90 pages.)

Paragraphing One Line

Sometimes, to stress the importance of one line, I will just hit Enter and give it its own line, without quite making it a separate paragraph. It's sort of a half-paragraph. I will often do this when the second paragraph is a single sentence that actually belongs in the first paragraph, but I make it a separate sentence to stress it. As far as I know, I made it up, and it works. :) It's often good for a sentence that sums up the last paragraph of a story, or one that gets the last word. (I do this a lot in e-mails, too.) Here's an example of where it do it with the line about cats:

> The writer had, as they say in Europe, "a complicated life." That's their phrase over there for dating more than one person. I think that the way he had set things up in his life was to foster that, although to ask him, you'd believe him to be a victim of circumstance beyond his authority.

> And then there was the thing about the damned cat. . . .

Double Spaces

Conventional typing dictates that you hit a double space at the end of a sentence. This is an old practice and has become sort of archaic for some reason with the advent of computers. It is acceptable, and even more proper, to single space everywhere in a document. I will even massage the text when I am done with a chapter by doing a search and replace to eliminate all the double spaces (I tend to accidentally hit a few here and there). To do this, go to Edit/Replace. In the Search field of the dialogue box that comes up, hit the spacebar twice. Then in the Replace field, hit the spacebar once. Then hit Replace All. (For some reason, this won't work when the Track Changes feature is in use. More on this feature in Chapter 8, "Working with an Editor.")

Numbers

Numbers less than nine are usually written out:

> One. Three. Seven. Nine.

After nine, numerals are usually used:

> 11. 22. 3,878.

The main exception is that if a number from each category is used in the same sentence, you usually pick one or the other and stick with it:

> The cost of the seven cats was over three thousand dollars total.

There are a billion other rules in English, but, in my experience, these are some of the most commonly broken. Follow these rules and you'll look better than about 90 percent of everything that lands on most editors' desks.

Chapter 4

Outlines Rule

$30 WRITING SCHOOL

You probably wouldn't take a trip to a place you've never been without having a map, or at least some sort of plan. An outline is your map for getting stuff done when you're creating a new book. It's a game plan, a playbook, a mission statement.

Almost all people who write professionally, or even just write well, use some form of an outline.

Why an Outline?

I hated the idea of outlines when I was in school. I felt that an outline was tainting my flow, impeding my purity, and just generally pretty square.

Well, I got away with not using them a lot when I wrote poems, songs, and even a few essays. (I was probably writing some sort of outline in my head without realizing it.) But when I tried to write a book without an outline, I was lost and had to learn the value of (and the process for) outlines pretty quickly.

Separate Documents

I highly, highly, highly, highly recommend that you start each chapter of a book as a separate document (see Figure 4.1 and Figure 4.2).

I wrote *$30 Film School* as one long document, and later I had to cut it up to make it easier to edit. (Another reason to do it in separate documents is that, if someone somehow intercepts one chapter and puts it on the Internet without your permission, one chapter is better than the whole book.) Also, making it one long document made it more scattered and less focused, which required a nearly complete rewrite.

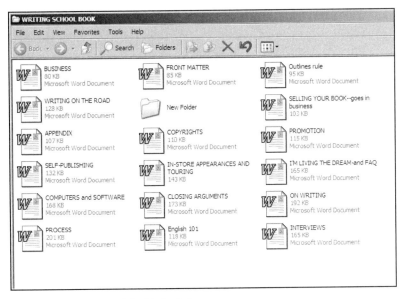

Figure 4.1 *Folder with this book in progress.*

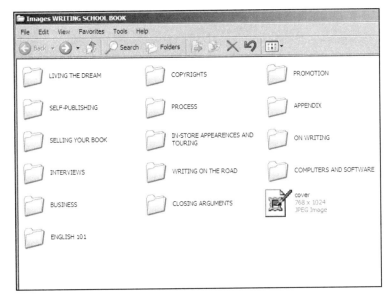

Figure 4.2 *Folder with this book's images in progress.*

When I turned in *$30 Film School*, the editor decided that it was too scattered and made me rewrite it. (I was mad, but he was right. Telling you what you need to do is part of an editor's job. And rewriting it made for a much stronger, more focused book.) It was much harder to do, because it was one long document. I think that, all in all, I would have shaved four months off the writing of the book if I'd simply done two things differently. (Four months is a long time. It's the *total* time it took to write *$30 Music School*.) One is to start with a folder of separate documents— one for each chapter. The other is to write an outline.

Don't worry about numbering your chapters until AR (author review—the final stage of going back and forth via e-mail with the editors before going to press). You will probably end up consolidating some chapters that run short, and creating two chapters out of one of the longer ones. Also, don't number your figures until author review, for the same reason. I just give them names such as "The folder of this book in progress.jpg" or "The folder of this book's image folders in progress.jpg" and add the figure numbers later as we're doing the final AR.

> **NOTE**
>
> Having separate documents will make it easier to write, organize, navigate, and edit your book. Also, a short document will open, close, and save more quickly, and a long one will crash more frequently than a shorter one.

Writing an Outline

I highly, highly, highly, highly recommend that you start each book with an outline.

After I come up with a book's title (we'll cover titles in Chapter 6, "How to Write"), I write the table of contents. That's the list of chapter titles, arranged in a logical order. I usually start with about five or six chapter titles, type them up, and print it out. Then I look at it and see where there could be more subjects and add them, and rearrange things into a more logical order. Sometimes I do this all in one sitting, and sometimes I find it best to do one part and then go work on other projects and come back to it another day.

There is much to be said for the power of the subconscious mind to work stuff out in the background while you're not thinking about it. You'll get better at this the more you do it.

NOTE

I hate to waste paper, but it's easier for me and a lot of folks to edit on paper than on a screen, so I print out stuff frequently. If you feel bad about killing trees, you can recycle, go out and plant some trees, or use recycled paper (available at most office supply stores). It costs a few pennies more than regular paper.

I make my edits on paper with a pen and then enter the edits into the computer file, print it out, and go through it again. I require fewer passes the more I write, because I get better at envisioning stuff in my head.

Basically, the key to writing outlines is learning to picture a logical flow of information. A lot of writers start out thinking they are good because they can craft a stunning flow of words. But a sentence does not a book make. You have to be able to construct your brilliant sentences into paragraphs and chapters that work as a whole on all levels.

One reason that an outline makes this work is because it's an example of things on the micro level controlling the macro level. Picture each chapter as a state and the book as a country. If the infrastructure of a bunch of states is out of order, the country is in disarray. The smaller makes up the larger, and the smaller not only influences the larger, but also actually drives and controls it.

It is much easier to make changes in an outline and then guide the overall book than to just start writing and figure it out later. The latter attitude drives the creation of a lot of crappy books.

We will cover this more in Chapter 6, "How To Write," but while you're writing an outline, you should think about the beginning, middle, and end. You should think about supporting your claims. And you should think about logical progressions.

Beginning, Middle, and End

Most good writing follows this pattern, even some of the more experimental fiction writing. Basically, at the level of sentence, paragraph, chapter, and book, you have all three. You state an idea, you expand it, and then you restate it. Sort of like that old Army cliché: "They tell ya what they're gonna tell ya, then they tell ya, then they tell ya what they told ya."

Beginnings and endings are usually shorter than middles, but in a way are more important. Beginnings pull you in. If a paragraph, chapter, or book has a lame beginning, there is a chance that some people won't even finish it. The end of a chapter is the part that has to segue smoothly into the next chapter, and the ending of a book is the part people remember the most. On the other hand, with a lot of books, the first line is the one people remember. "Call me Ishmael" is remembered as the beginning of *Moby Dick*. More people can name that line than can name the author. The first line of a book can immediately set the mood for the whole thing. Who can forget the first line of Hubert Selby, Jr.'s, book *Requiem for a Dream*: "Harry locked his mother in the closet."

You will use information on beginnings, middles, and endings later when you're actually writing the book, but keep it in mind when you are writing the outline. It will help you flow your micro thoughts in a direction that will flow your macro ones in the same direction later.

Supporting Your Claims

Good writing is logical, and even fiction supports its claims. If you make up a universe where water flows upstream and people can trade brains, you have to create some logical new science for that universe to explain why. People are willing to suspend disbelief, but it's easier if you give them a good reason to do so.

Again, you will use this later when you're actually writing the book, but keep it in mind when you are writing the outline.

Logical Progressions

This is probably the most important idea in writing. Good writing sets up things to flow from one thing to another thing in a way that makes sense to the reader. It is generally accomplished by having the end of one idea remotely related to the next idea. If they are not related, it is good to relate them with some sort of "glue," such as a sentence or two that explains why the reader should be willing to make the jump from one to another. For example, I often type a letter to someone, proof it, and then realize that paragraph five and paragraph eight should be switched to make a more logical flow.

The same is true on a larger level with book writing. Sometimes I'll even cut part of one chapter into part of another chapter later. Creating any linear art (for instance, I use this same idea when editing video or when rearranging the song order during the final stages of making a CD of my music) means knowing that there are two aspects to editing. One is good planning that makes things work. The other is knowing when to give in to it and let the art tell *you* where to change stuff when you are in the later stages.

You will use this later when you're actually writing the book, but it is used when you are writing the outline. You want to have things flow logically in the table of contents and the outline.

Writing a TOC

I start with my title, and then I create the table of contents (TOC). This starts with just a list of chapter ideas. You expand that to the outline, you expand that to the long outline, and then you use that to write the book.

Here's the first draft TOC for this book:

Chapter 1: I'm Living the Dream
Chapter 2: On Writing
Chapter 3: Process
Chapter 4: Computers and Software
Chapter 5: Selling Your Book

Chapter 6: Business

Chapter 7: Writing on the Road

Chapter 8: Self-Publishing

Chapter 9: In-Store Appearances and Touring

Chapter 10: Copyrights, etc.

Chapter 11: Promotion: Telling the World

Chapter 12: Closing Arguments

I run this by my project editor — the person at the publisher who oversees the bigger picture of it all. He probably makes a few suggestions to tweak the overall project. We go back and forth and do some fine-tuning to fix the whole thing.

If you don't have a publisher and editor yet, you do this yourself, as preparation for the book proposal (more on that in Chapter 11, "Selling Your Book").

Then I make a folder of blank documents, based on the TOC, and name them. I make these documents using an MS Word template from my publisher (on the CD-ROM that comes with this book as goodies/ tech book template—Course Technology) that contains certain extra styles in the Style drop-down menu. For instance, they have their own presets for the way they like to set up things such as Tips and figure captions. This is used to do the final page layout in Quark.

I *always* insert page numbers using the Insert Page Number function in Word. This automatically renumbers as you type more. You need page number because otherwise, when you print out a chapter and proof it, the pages will not be numbered, and you'll be lost.

I use the Word default of Times New Roman as the font, but I change the default font size from 10 point to 12 point from the Font drop-down.

I make one blank document from my publisher's template, add page numbers, copy it 10 to 20 times, and rename each one with a chapter name. Then I cut and paste my outline into each page.

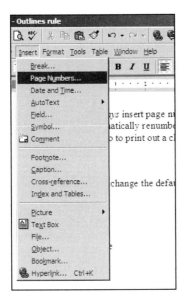

Figure 4.3 *Insert/Page Numbers.*

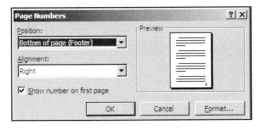

Figure 4.4 *Hit OK.*

Figure 4.5 *Font size picker.*

Changing the Default Template in Word

You also can make a template with your preferences (font size, font, page numbers, and so on) and save it to overwrite the default Word template.

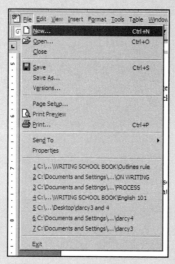

Figure 4.6 *Go to File/New.*

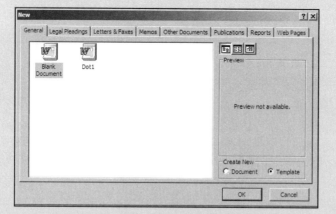

Figure 4.7 *Pick Template rather than Document in the bottom right corner. Hit OK. Make the changes you want to appear in your default template. Change the default font, font size, tab, and indenting, add page numbers, and so on.*

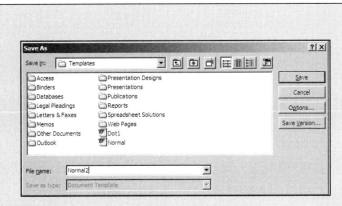

Figure 4.8 *Save as Normal2.*

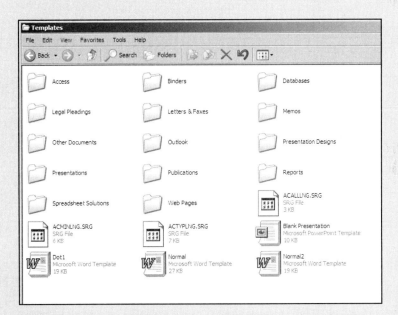

Figure 4.9 *Open the folder called C:/Program files/Microsoft Office/Templates.*

continued

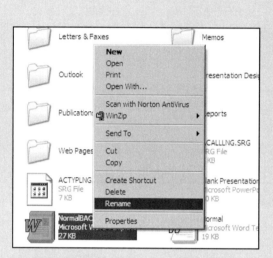

Figure 4.10 *Right-click on the Normal template.*

Figure 4.11 *Rename it NormalBackup. Then rename Normal2 as Normal.*

The next time you open Word, your new preferences will appear as the default template.

Then I start writing one of the chapters, filling in the blanks and rounding out ideas, sentences, paragraphs, and chapters. I generally write about 1,200–2,000 words at a time and then put it down. Sometimes I'll just write a paragraph, and sometimes I'll write nearly a whole chapter. But it's mostly about 2,000 words and then I stop. I'll go do something else—answer e-mail, set up promotional appearances, pet my cat, or grab a nap with one of the girls I'm dating. I feel that once I've done a bunch of work, I can go do something else. But it's usually something creative.

My goal is 1,000 words a day. On a good day I can knock this out in an hour. If I do 3,000 words in a day, I still try to write at least 1000 words the next day.

The middle of the process of writing a book is the hardest for me. The outline, the first two chapters I write (not always the first two chapters of the book), the last few chapters I write, and author review are easy in comparison. I have heard the same thing said of writing the second act of a three-act screenplay.

Average length for a novel is about 75,000 words. The *$30 School* series are all around 100,000 words each. This means that, theoretically, I should be able to write a novel in two months and a *$30 School* book in three months. In reality, it takes a little longer than that because there is also the editing, image production, and CD-ROM production, with its associated video editing and so on. But it's all good.

On the rare occasion that I get writer's block, I still have stuff to do. I can always edit. Or do promotion.

NOTE

I would never recommend that you ignore your friends, but it's okay to set good boundaries. If I'm feeling distracted, it helps my chances of working uninterrupted if I unplug my phone and turn off my Internet connection while working. I often do this all day when on a deadline. Sometimes I'll go to the Down Beat café because my wireless connection does not work there.

Occasionally I'll go out to the country with one of my lovers to her lake house and get away from it all to work. More likely I go there to recharge my batteries. I find that I usually write better in the city with not too much distraction and background noise than in the idyllic countryside. If I need quiet, I just become partially nocturnal for a while and work while the loud-ass city humans sleep.

One advantage of using an outline is that it pretty much eliminates writer's block. You have a battle plan of what to write about, and you write it. You don't have to work in order; you can jump around. I do. But you need a list of what to write about.

How to Write an Outline

This is imperative for non-fiction, and it is even indicated for fiction, such as a novel (and *especially* for a screenplay). Writing an outline will not cramp your creativity. In fact, it will release your creativity. It will enable you to worry less about the structure later and just get lost a little bit in the fun of creating. It's your road map to an untraveled terrain.

Basically, an outline is a blueprint. It's a recipe for a meal you are making out of words. It's not absolute, in the same way a good cook will use a written recipe but then improvise on the fly as she's working, adding her own flourishes to make it art. You will do this, too, but please—I can overstate it with reiterating repetitive redundancy and still not say it enough—*write an outline*.

An outline needn't be any more complicated than a slightly elaborated TOC. Just think of 10 or 20 chapter ideas you want to write about, and then refine from there. You can do it the official way with Roman numerals and letters, or you can do it my way. Here's the official way:

1. Chapter Title
    A. subheading
        I. sub-subheading
        II. another sub-subheading
        III. yet another sub-subheading
    B. subheading
        I. sub-subheading
        II. another sub-subheading
    C. Subheading
        I. sub-subheading
        II. another sub-subheading

III. yet another sub-subheading

IV. the fourth sub-subheading

2. Another Chapter Title

etc. . . .

etc. . . .

etc. . . .

For a full-length book, this outline would probably be three to five pages long.

I opt for a longer, less structured format, which is basically my own shorthand for everything I plan to write about. Below is the short final draft outline of this book. (Note that it is basically an expanded TOC.) I later expanded this into a much more detailed 10-page outline. It's called "Writing School Outline" and is on the CD-ROM in the Book Proposals folder.

CHAPTER 1: I'M LIVING THE DREAM

Opening motivational speech for aspiring professional writers.

Interview with me that briefly answers the most commonly asked questions.

CHAPTER 2: ON WRITING

Pros.

Cons.

Do you need an English degree?

Who does what? Writer, agent, publisher, editor, tech editor, copy editor, publicist.

Good writing versus bad writing (with examples).

CHAPTER 3: PROCESS

Myths

"Hemingway lie" (booze).

You have to go somewhere else to write.

"First million words you write are junk."

English basics.

    Spelling.

    Grammar.

    First-person, second-person, third-person.

    Overall story structure.

    Linear versus nonlinear.

The rules and how to break them.

Research and fact checking.

CHAPTER 4: COMPUTERS AND SOFTWARE

    Typewriter versus computer.

    Laptop versus desktop.

    Mac versus PC.

    How much computer do you need?

    Keyboard shortcuts.

    Other hardware:

        Palm and Handspring.

        Alphasmart.

        Dictaphone.

    Software:

        Word processing.

        Zip.

        FTP.

        Voice recognition.

        Page layout.

CHAPTER 5: SELLING YOUR BOOK

    Fiction versus non-fiction.

    Writing a query—format.

    Writing a proposal and sample chapter.

    Agent: pros and cons.

Negotiation.

    Types of contracts.

    What advances are for.

CHAPTER 6: BUSINESS

Can I make a living?

    Taxes.

    Insurance.

    Inconsistency of checks.

Alternate writing jobs.

Keep everything win/win (in life, too).

CHAPTER 7: WRITING ON THE ROAD

Equipment needed:

    Cables, adapters.

    Voltage converters.

    Backup drivers.

    NIC cards and cables.

Using college networks for free without permission and getting away with it.

Finding and using business centers (Dublin airport example).

CHAPTER 8: SELF-PUBLISHING

No shame in being self-published if you're great.

    Mark Twain.

    Henry Rollins.

Make sure it's good. Again, proof. A lot. Get help.

Problems I encountered with printer.

Chapbooks.

Internet publishing.

Alternate models: CD+, DVD, etc.

CHAPTER 9: IN-STORE APPEARANCES AND TOURING

Booking a tour even if your publisher won't.

Keeping a good balance.

How.

Where.

Booking.

Advancing the show.

Accommodations.

Crossing borders. Passports.

Staying healthy on the road.

Doing a Q&A—dealing with hecklers, making it work for you.

How to be interviewed.

Archiving all your press.

CHAPTER 10: COPYRIGHTS ETC.

Copyrights, patents, and trademarks.

Slander and libel.

Fair use.

CHAPTER 11: PROMOTION . . . TELLING THE WORLD

The Web, e-mail.

E-mail lists.

Fax.

Flyers.

Stickers.

Writing a press release.

Word of mouth.

Creating a buzz.

Getting people to help.

Getting on TV.

CHAPTER 12: CLOSING ARGUMENTS

> Integrity and drive.
>
>> Art Karma.
>
> Workflow:
>
>> Be on a mission.
>>
>> Make art that inspires other people to fight for you.
>>
>> Work ethic.
>>
>> Self-definition.
>>
>> Dealing with critics.
>>
>> Art is all.

INTERVIEWS WITH WRITERS

APPENDIXES

Compare this short outline and the longer one on the CD. You'll see that there is a logic to all this. Basically, the way I work is this:

- Come up with an idea. And maybe a title.
- Write down the main points I want to cover.
- Expand this into a TOC.
- Expand the TOC into an outline.
- Expand the outline into a long outline.
- Create separate documents for each chapter.
- Cut and paste each chapter content of the long outline into each chapter document.
- Flesh out each chapter's points within the chapter document into more. And more and more. And more.
- Rewrite several times.
- Have someone proofread it, make changes. Have someone else proof it, and then work with an editor until it's nearly perfect.

I went through about five versions of this outline before I got to this final version. Basically, I started with the chapter titles and wrote a little bit about each one. Then I printed it out and made marks with a pen. I did a lot of cutting and pasting based on these marks, moving subheadings to different chapters and moving different chapters to different places in the order so it made more sense. I also split a few long chapters into two chapters each. Then I printed it out and did the same thing four more times. A few of those times I e-mailed it to a few smart friends and had them make a few comments. I took part, but not all, of their advice.

Also compare this to the actual table of contents in the book you're holding. Note that the order of things has probably changed a good bit as I was writing and as we were editing.

Sometimes I make a new TOC in the middle of a project to reflect this. Check out the document "Updated TOC music school book—done after book was started" in the Book Proposals folder on the CD-ROM.

Conclusion

That's it for outlines. This chapter was sort of a pause after our English 101 refresher. This chapter is to see how you would take that English 101 and put it to good use.

Now that you know all that, let's get it *on*. This chapter was high school in *$30 Writing School*. The next few are college.

Chapter 5

English 102

$30 WRITING SCHOOL

We covered about six semesters' worth of basic English in about an hour in the two previous chapters. Now that you've mastered that, pick up your books and go next door to the moderately advanced class, English 102. Here you'll learn about writing outlines for fiction. And you'll also take the basics and expand on them to put things together and *write*.

How I Write Fiction

Fiction is, to me, the essence of writing. Creating non-fiction, like the book currently clutched in your grubby little hands, is nifty, for sure. It gives back to the world, helps people avoid making the same mistakes I made (It allows them to just make different mistakes), and is more likely to cover your fiscal needs on planet Earth than fiction is. However, gentle reader, it is *fiction* that really seems like *writing* to me.

Non-fiction helps explain the existing world, whereas fiction invents *new* worlds.

NOTE

I am writing this chapter in the front row of a showing of my film to a group of punk rock kids in Lyon, France. I turned the brightness down on the laptop screen, but I'm being totally rude. If it were someone else's movie, I'd be asked to leave. But I am here to speak, so whatever. Call it performance art.

Outlines for Fiction

Some good fiction has been written without an outline, but I still recommend using one. Not so much a chapter-by-chapter breakdown like you'd have with non-fiction, but some preproduction notes will certainly help you to extract something grand out of the universe.

With fiction, I start with a one-page breakdown of what the story is.

I remember I had a wonderful girlfriend (and best friend) from Switzerland named Marie. Marie had a very European outlook on a lot of things. When I'd tell her about a movie I liked and recommended, she'd say, "What's the story?"

I loved that. Most Americans would ask, "Who's the star?" or "Who directed it?" or even just how many car crashes it has. But when you are asking about a book or movie, basically what you really want to know is, "What's the story?"

So the one-page breakdown is just that. It's what happens. It's a quick look at who does what, and the result.

Then I do a character sketch. (This and the breakdown are worth doing for a novel, as well as a screenplay.) I list the two or three or five main characters and write a bit about them—age, race, sex, height, weight, childhood, and something about their likes and dislikes. My preferred method is demonstrated in the following Note.

NOTE

Cash Newmann.

Male, 31 years old. Short. Skinny and muscular. Blond hair. Blue eyes. A few tattoos. Loves life, rock music, and cats, and has a weakness for women and narcotics. Spiritual but not religious. Wants to be in love monogamously with every woman he meets.

Molested by neighbor at age eight. Parents divorced when he was nine. Rather intelligent, but dropped out of high school to tour with a band.

Melody Annabella.

Cash's main girl, she's 26. Doctoral candidate at UC Berkeley. English major. Minor in pharmacology. A little taller than Cash. Shapely, not thin, not fat. Long brown hair, brown eyes.

Alcoholic dad committed suicide with a shotgun in front of her when she was 14. She's always attracted to messed-up men.

Raised by aunt, who was a chemist for the U.S. Army.

Thinks like a scientist, loves like a whore.

You could also do this with bullet points, like this:

- Cash's main girl
- 26 years old
- Doctoral candidate at UC Berkeley
- English major, minor in pharmacology
- A little taller, and smarter, than Cash
- Shapely, not thin, not fat
- Long brown hair, brown eyes

You might not even reveal all these details in the book. You might describe some of these attributes, but these little sketches, or *backstories*, are mainly for you, the writer. They help me get to know my new babies a little better and conjure up a mental picture of them more easily. Once I can see a blurry picture of a character in my mind's eye, the character will become sharper with the passing weeks. *She* will tell *me* what kinds of things she'd do and say.

Your outline needn't go into extreme detail about locations, situations, and so on. Include maybe the main points, such as, "Begins in the Australian Outback, progresses to the city of London once the primary objective has been presented. Ends up back in Australia."

What's In a Name

Character names are a tough call. You want them to be interesting and appropriate, but not to the point of drawing attention away from the character arc. (The character arc is the journey of growth that a character experiences throughout the story.) Not distracting from the arc is one reason I nixed the idea of naming a girl April May June in my new novel. It's a cool name, but not that believable. People would concentrate on the name and have trouble "suspending disbelief" to forget they're reading a book.

A great book, like a great movie, will make a person forget they're consuming fiction. They will *believe*. (This is one reason people stalk movie stars, and to a lesser degree, novelists. They imagine themselves to have real relationships with imaginary characters.)

> **NOTE**
>
> Final Draft is a great script writing and formatting program. It's available from www.FinalDraft.com and there is a demo on the CD of this book: (We will cover it more in Chapter 10, "Software.") It has a great built-in database of character names (look under Tools/Names). Also, check maps. The London tube (subway) map is a reliable source of stunningly cool names. I'm pretty sure that's where they got the last name for the guitarist Nigel Tufnel for the movie *This Is Spinal Tap.* (Tufnel is a tube stop in London.) A lot of maps are available for free online.

Other Story Elements

As I said, a well-written book seems like it just "happens." We rarely think about the fact that someone sweated blood for a year or so creating and perfecting it. But they did. And you will. But you would be smart to think ahead a little about the person, tense, tone, and other stuff before you start writing. It will help make your words soar off the page and worm deeper into the cortex of the reader.

Person

A narrative is said to be first person, second person, or third person. First and third person are the most common.

First person means the story is being told from the viewpoint of the protagonist. The protagonist is the main character in any story, typically the person the story is happening *to*.

Example:

> She stumbled into my office. I looked her up and down. She was a tall drink of Uzo, with legs from here to Wednesday. She said, "I need you to find this man," and threw a tattered photo on my cluttered desk. I lit a drink, poured a smoke, and said, "How much dough you got, dollface?"

Third person means the story is being told from the viewpoint of an omniscient observer, an entity like God (or Santa Claus) that can see everything that happens to all the characters in a story all the time. This can work, and a lot of novels are written like this, but it tends to be less personal than first-person writing.

Example:

> She stumbled into his office. He looked her up and down. She was a tall drink of Uzo, with legs from here to Wednesday. She said, "I need you to find this man," and threw a tattered photo on his cluttered desk. He lit a drink, poured a smoke, and said, "How much dough you got, dollface?"

Stories often switch from third to first person, in that the narrator is telling the story in first person, and the dialogue is in third person.

Other than this, you probably don't want a narrative to switch person, but if you do, be damn well aware of it, do it for a reason, and make sure it works.

Second person means the story is happening to *you*, the reader. Here's an example:

> She stumbled into your office. You looked her up and down. She was a tall drink of Uzo, with legs from here to Wednesday. She said, "I need you to find this man," and threw a tattered photo on your cluttered desk. You lit a drink, poured a smoke, and said, "How much dough you got, dollface?"

It is very rare for a whole book to be in the second person. It's pretty bizarre, but it can work. Examples include *Bright Lights, Big City* by Jay McInerney, the *Choose Your Own Adventure* series, and *Half Asleep in Frog Pajamas* by Tom Robbins.

NOTE

2/19/2004

Diary Entry:

I just bought a copy of *Bright Lights, Big City* used on Amazon for 20 cents. It was three bucks with shipping.

I wanna read it because I've decided my next book is gonna be a novel written in the second person, and people tell me that's one of the only books written like that.

My friend Tracy said that if anyone can pull it off, it's me.

My writer friend Deb DeSalvo joked, "You could make it a codependent's diary and start each paragraph with 'You SHOULD.....'" LOL.

A note on the "omniscient observer" idea. Many novels (and most movies) use it a lot, even when told in first person. Like the character will be saying, "I knew she was right . . . I am sort of a weasel." And then the next paragraph will be, "Meanwhile, across town, the super villain, the Prober, sharpened his probes and his wit," or whatever.

I consciously avoided this in my latest novel, *The Simple Pleasures of a Complex Girl.* And I had my editor look for it, and catch the one or two places I slipped into it. I considered it a fun challenge to avoid it consciously. You don't need to do the same, but be aware of it so you know when and why you use it.

(The editor of which I speak was my smart (and foxy!) friend Carla Segurola, who I paid to help proof the chapters for me before submitting the book to publishers. It was fun. I was on tour, I'd e-mail the day's work to her in Hollywood, and she'd proof it and send it back. We used the Track Changes feature in Word. More on that in Chapter 8, "Working with an Editor." Also, Carla said I could print her e-mail address and let it be known that she offers this service for others. It is julycarla@yahoo.com.)

Tense

There is past, present, and future tense.

> Past tense: Marie and I rescued many cats.
>
> Present tense: Marie and I rescue many cats.
>
> Future tense: Marie and I will rescue many cats.

Again, be aware of them, don't switch betweem them in mid-paragraph, and if you do switch between them in mid-paragraph (or even mid-story), be damn well aware of it, do it for a reason, and make sure it works.

Active and Passive Verbs

Active voice tends to work better. Again, be aware of the differences and switch only if there's a reason.

> Passive present tense: The book about insanity in cats is being taken home.
>
> Active present tense: I'm taking home the book about insanity in cats.
>
> Passive past tense: The book about insanity in cats was taken home.
>
> Active past tense: I took home the book about insanity in cats.

Linear versus Nonlinear Structure

A linear plot goes forward in time. It begins at the beginning and goes through to the end. It's a chronological progression.

A nonlinear plot jumps around a lot. It can employ flashbacks, concurrent plots, parenthetical concentric stories, or something even weirder, like going forward and backward at the same time such as in the movie *Momento*. This can make a story a lot more interesting, but it also can risk confusing the reader or viewer. A lot of stories, especially movies, intentionally attempt to confuse the viewer. It's that hoary old "surprise ending" where everything is *not* what it seems.

If you do this, again, be aware of it, do it intentionally, and make sure it works. That's pretty much the rule of breaking rules.

NOTE

Learn the rules first. Then break them with confidence to achieve a desired result that cannot be reached within the boundaries of those rules.

Tone

A conversational tone is okay in most novels. It also works in some non-fiction books (like this one). It is usually not appropriate in most technical or academic writing. Reporting in newspapers is usually written in a non-conversational, "just the facts ma'am" tone, to give the illusion of impartiality to the biased editorial policies of some papers. (The exception is that weekly columns in newspapers often are in a very conversational tone.) Magazines can be conversational or not. The more successful ones usually have a well-done mixture of both tones.

You want to consider two basic things when choosing your tone. One is the readership. A fanzine put out by and for punk rockers is going to have a much more lax approach than a technical paper written by and for scientists at a major university.

I've challenged this convention with the books in the *$30 School* series. While "how-to" books are sometimes written in a down-to-earth, friendly manner, I pushed it to the extreme. I've yet to read a book in the *Dummies* series where the author has a footnote referring to his former heroin use or a sidebar about how a car crash made him reevaluate his life, or gives tips on dealing with non-monogamous relationships a few chapters after giving tutorials of using various computer programs.

This turned out to be a major selling point. Go on Amazon.com and read the reader reviews of *$30 Film School* or *$30 Music School*. Many people talk about how they love the tone of the book, and a good number of them say it was the best book they've ever read.

The other consideration with tone is "your tone versus your character's tone." They can be the same thing or two different things. An example of the writer's tone being the same as the character's is Hubert Selby, Jr.'s *Last Exit to Brooklyn*. (I use him a lot for examples, but why not? He rocks.) In that book, both the narrator and the characters have a very *street* way of speaking. An example of the writer's tone being different than the character's is when John Grisham does dialogue for uneducated hicks (which he does a lot). The tone of the writing is educated, but when he does the dialogue, it's pure bumpkin in tone.

If you use slang, keep in mind that it changes with time. It can make your book seem really dated really fast. I tend to avoid it, to give my novels a fighting chance at longevity.

Clarity of Subject

This is a tricky one. Basically, you wanna make sure that the *it*, *he*, *she*, or whatever you are talking about is clear as the sentences and paragraphs get more complex:

> I was talking to Tom about the cat party for Michael and wanted to make sure he knew about it.

It's hard to tell if "he" refers to Tom or Michael (or maybe even the cat).

You might have to restructure it as:

> I was talking to Tom about the cat party for Michael and wanted to make sure Michael knew about it.

Or consider these sentences:

> I want to make sure the project is going well. I have a TV interview coming up and will be keeping it going as planned.

Is the "it" the TV interview or the project? See what I mean? You might need to restructure it as:

> I want to make sure the project is going well. I have a TV interview coming up and will be keeping the project going as planned.

It is important to write clear sentences. Part of being clear is making it easy to tell what the subject is and what the object is. For instance, in this sentence, it's hard to tell who "him" and "he" refer to:

> Michael and Francois walked to the record store, and he told him he didn't know which record to get.

This is clearer, but stilted:

> Michael and Francois walked to the record store. Michael told Francois that Michael didn't know which record to get.

This rearranges things to be clearer without being stilted:

> Michael and Francois walked to the record store. Michael said, "I don't know which record to get."

I recently sent this to my agent in an e-mail:

> "I don't know if you n' your man like jazz, but my friend Bob Sax has an excellent jazz quartet in San Diego. If you want, I can find out when they play for you."

After I sent it, I realized that the second sentence sounds like Bob Sax is going to give a concert just for my agent and her man. This is not what I meant. I should have written it as:

> "If you want me to, I can find out when they're playing."

The way to check the readability of your work is to read it aloud, or have someone else read it out loud. This will make it obvious to you what works and what doesn't—what flows and what is stilted.

Foreshadowing

Foreshadowing is a hint early in a story at something that will come up later. A good example is in the movie *Demolition Man*, when Wesley Snipes' character says something like, "I'd lose my head if it wasn't attached." Of course, near the end of the film, he is decapitated.

Foreshadowing is a good device to give continuity to a story. Just don't overdo it.

Character Arc

As I said, a lot of fiction sucks. Some is great, but the basic Beatnik premise of "just write, don't plan, and don't ever edit, because editing will taint your purity" is a drug-fueled copout. On the other end of this spectrum is calculated fiction that is pretty much written by the numbers as far as being predictable in a cool and unpredictable way, such as John Grisham or Stephen King. Personally, I would rather read Grisham than most Beatniks. Part of that is the fact that Grisham and King are *really* good writers, but part of it is that their stories are exactly that. They're *stories*, as opposed to the "just a bunch of stuff that happens" angle of much writing. King and Grisham write taut thrillers based on a formula that also is present in a lot of movies. It is no surprise that every book they write eventually seems to become a major motion picture. Their books read like movies.

NOTE

I've even been guilty of it myself in the past. Like in a review in www.NightTimes.com, J. Gordon called my novel *Starving in the Company of Beautiful Women* "an On the Road for the 1980s punk rock set." She said, "Dean's book is full of overly long narrative, typos . . . (many intentional, such as his mysterious compulsion to capitalize the letter B in the word Beautiful), his religion (I guess), made-up words ("squimmery" is just great), and invented spellings like Gurl, Chix, etc." She probably has no idea that I also rewrote and edited the hell out of that book! But she does go on to say, "Now let's counter that with the fact that Dean's a hell of a storyteller with vivid imagery, and some 'Beautiful' prose occasionally sneaks out through the muck."

The little bit of Beatnik fiction that is excellent usually follows a character arc, even if the author is unaware of it. Check out the video interview with Hubert Selby, Jr., on the CD-ROM that comes with this book, where he talks about having no idea about three-act structure and character arc, even though his stories usually have both. Again, two of his books have been turned into major motion pictures. (And *excellent* ones at that: *Last Exit to Brooklyn* and *Requiem for a Dream* are far more creative than most flicks.)

The Hero's Journey

Movies are often written with a blueprint for the character arc It is commonly called "The Hero's Journey." This blueprint basically catalogues a lot of what people, deep in their souls, want to see. What they want their heroes to do. What viewers *wish* they could do themselves. They can't, so they pay Han Solo or some character played by Will Smith or Matt Damon to do it for them.

I hear you saying, "I thought this book was about *writing*, not movies." Well, my friend, the things that work in movies work in novels too. A lot of novels fail because they ignore the need for a *story*. The writer becomes so in love with the force of her words that she forgets to write a story. More than anything else, people want stories.

Also, books written with stories in mind are far more likely to become adapted into movies. Movies are *written*. They are produced from scripts that some writer wrote. When you hear some dumb moviegoer saying, "Wasn't that cool what Nicholas Cage said in that flick?", that moviegoer is cheating someone. Nicholas Cage didn't come up with it. Some guy with a bad back sitting in a coffee shop pecking away at a laptop said it first. (And got paid damn well to say it.)

This is another thing we forget—movies aren'tjust spontaneously generated from the mud. They are created by writers. (And this is the reason that many movies are *about* writers. Ever notice that? We write what we know.)

You can write movies. There are a million books on screenwriting, but the main thing you need to know is that you need a story. Other than that, you can learn to write dialogue by listening to people on the street and by watching movies. You can learn formatting simply by reading the short tutorial in Final Draft. You can learn that scripts are written differently than books—more sparse, leaving more to the visual aspect—by watching movies and studying scripts. (You can buy scripts in book stores, or download them free online. Search Google for the words "Scripts Free Download Movies" and you'll find some.) There is also one of my scripts on the CD.

Remember: great movies, *and great books*, start from great stories.

We want to live vicariously through the characters in our favorite books and movies. We want the heroes to take risks we could never take and, conversely, reap rewards we will never taste.

I fought this idea in my book *$30 Film School*. I held out that a good story could be "just a bunch of cool stuff that happens." But I am revising my statement, with an asterisk. My new statement is, "Movies and books needn't be as predictable as most Hollywood and bestseller fare, but you would still do well to study the stuff that works, historically speaking."

Figure 5.1 *The Hero's Journey.* Cartoon by Cassidy Coon.

The asterisk would be, "There are a million variations and a million cool, original things you can do within this framework. Once more, if you are gonna break the rules, you at least should *know* the rules first."

Writer's Books

I highly recommend *The Writer's Journey* by Christopher Vogler, and Stephen King's *On Writing*. And of course, the book in your hot little hands.

- Stephen King's *On Writing* (named after the Hemingway book by the same name) is just plain good. It's very informative, funny, sweet, and down to earth. My only complaint is that he denigrates big-selling fiction by other writers in his same class and calls 'em hacks. I think King thinks he's a hell of a lot more literary than he actually is. I would love it if he were just satisfied with his very cool place in the world: the foremost

Figure 5.2 The Writer's Journey.

producer of amazingly well-written pulp fiction that serves mainly as inspiration for good popcorn movies.

◆ *The Writer's Journey* is by Christopher Vogler. This is a pretty damn amazing book. It kinda slayed me as I read it. It made me want to get in touch with the dude and interview him. (I e-mailed him, he agreed, and then I guess, got sidetracked and never replied to my follow-up e-mails trying to set a place and time for the interview. So I've gone into more depth here to cover what I assume he might have talked about.)

The crux of the whole biscuit is that almost all stories, at least successful stories, share common bonds. (By "successful," I mean economically successful, like big Hollywood movies, and also stories that just succeed in the collective unconsciousness, like fairy tales and stuff like that.) These common bonds include the hero:

◆ Starting off in a safe, boring world.

◆ Being called to action by a defining event.

◆ At first refusing the call.

◆ Finally accepting the call.

◆ Trying to solve his problem, and failing.

◆ Meeting a mentor who helps him grow.

- ◆ Passing tests that make him stronger.
- ◆ Finally being pure of heart enough to solve the problem.
- ◆ Living happily ever after and bringing new and helpful knowledge back to his people when he returns to his safe, boring world.

NOTE

The Hero's Journey can have variations. Not all elements have to be in this order, the normal length, or even present. But if you study it a little, you'll be astounded at how universal it is. Especially with the "mentor" stuff and the "refusing the call" stuff. Almost all movies have the hero refusing what they're called to do at first, and later accepting it (usually after it becomes personal—like they have to do it to save grandma's farm or whatever.)

A rather funny and very literal refusal of the call is in the movie *Rock Star*. The young guy in the cover band gets a literal call—a phone call—from his all-time favorite band asking him to join. He thinks it's his buddies playing a prank and hangs up on them. Literally "refusing the call."

This is seen in everything from the Bible to Shakespeare to the film *Independence Day* to the *Harry Potter* to *South Park: Bigger, Longer & Uncut* series (both books and movies) to *Armageddon* to *Lord of the Rings* to "VH1: Behind the Music," and pretty much everything in-between. *Adaptation* makes fun of it. Heavily. But *still* relies on it.

The Writer's Journey really doesn't have any new information, but it has it all in one place and is pretty spot-on. A lot of it is based on the Joseph Campbell writings about "The Hero's Journey" (and Vogler admits this). Campbell called it the "Monomyth" rather than "The Hero's Journey," but it's the same thing.

(My mom was watching a lot of videotapes of Campbell speaking in her last few months alive after being diagnosed with cancer. Campbell had a pretty unique worldview, and my mother felt that watching the tapes helped prepare her for the next world. And she was a very smart lady . . .)

The Writer's Journey isn't a bestseller. The cover of my copy, which is the second printing, boasts "Over 60,000 sold." Sixty-thousand is a very respectable number, but you'd have to add a zero or two to that to keep pace with any single book by Stephen King. However, most successful Hollywood movie producers and directors are among those 60,000. *The Writer's Journey* is a cult classic among industry professionals. It is required reading for new executives at several major movie studios.

NOTE

Mine is an old printing. Vogler later told me that they're up to 120,000 sold now.

While it is aimed primarily at people writing for film, I think it would certainly be of interest to anyone writing anything, anywhere. If you are a good writer, and, read *The Writer's Journey* and then write a novel, I'm sure the novel will be infinitely more readable.

NOTE

To help you understand this all better, look on the CD in the "Hero's Journey worksheets" folder. In there you'll find a blank worksheet you can use to map the main points of the Hero's Journey in films and books you like. Also included are a few of these already mapped by me and some people on my mailing list. (That's another cool thing about being a writer—you can build a fan base and collaborate with them on projects easily and quickly when needed.)

I would recommend watching the movie or reading the book without mapping the first time through, just to enjoy it. Why kill the fun, right? Then go through a second time and map it. And after watching it once, it doesn't take as long to map. I mapped *Rocky* in fifteen minutes the day after I watched it. It's pretty easy, especially if you use the chapter access stuff on the DVD menu, and set up your DVD player to display the timecode on the screen.

Keep in mind that just because people making formulaic popcorn flix work from the Hero's Journey idea, it doesn't mean you'll be boring if you use it. The idea is about "format, not formula," and you can take what you like and leave the rest. There are infinite possibilities for working within this Hero's Journey concept and staying true.

NOTE

I also highly recommend *Zen Guitar* by the late Phil Sudo. This slim volume is not about writing at all. It's about music, but on a larger level, it's about life. I think this book would be more valuable to a writer than almost any book on writing.

Also check out the interview with Phil Sudo on the Extras section of the DVD of my film *D.I.Y. or DIE: How to Survive as an Independent Artist*. (The DVD is actually called *D.I.Y. or DIE: Burn This DVD.*) It's pretty damn cool. I shot the interview as Phil was dying of cancer, and he still has more lust for life than most folks do on a normal, healthy day. And it even sort of follows the Hero's Journey, all in six minutes, with very little editing. Many documentaries do follow some variation of the Hero's Journey. Sometimes you'll even find elements of it in a 60-second commercial or one-page memo. People like it. A lot. And they respond to it. Especially the part near the end when the hero dies in some way and is then reborn. Our hearts *soar*. I even get misty-eyed at that point while watching dumb movies that I feel are below me. I feel tricked, but the trick *works*.

One could get into endless "chicken and the egg" arguments about the Hero's Journey, whether people want to see it because it's innate, or if it's innate through societal conditioning because it's used in so many movies and books. I'd say it's one from column A and one from column B. And then I'd say, just check it out and learn it, and then do whatever the hell you want. It's helpful just to know that it exists.

Conclusion

I know we've covered a lot quickly. But this isn't grad school, and I don't get more money for keeping you here longer, as they do in college. I wanna give you some tools and some wisdom and then cut you loose on the world. Ready?

We've fine-tuned your basics of English in a crash course that hopefully didn't hurt much. Did it? Go take a break, get a drink or take a nap, and we'll start writing for real now.

Chapter 6

How to Write

$30 WRITING SCHOOL

"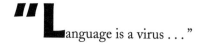anguage is a virus . . ."

—William S. Burroughs

"Writing consists of the ability to make human emotions out of dry symbols that have been pounded into thin layers of dead trees."

—Michael W. Dean

> **NOTE**
>
> Some might say it's pretty damn presumptuous to quote oneself. And even more so to do it in the same breath as William S. Burroughs. But hey, if you don't believe your own hype, no one else will. That's rule number one of *this* school.

A lot of people say they're writers. And a lot of people sit around in coffee shops with expensive laptops pounding out words. But a lot of them will never get published because, to get published, you have to have three things: talent, drive, and perseverance. We'll talk about all that here. This is the chapter where we move beyond just *writing* and work on *being a writer*.

What to Write About?

They say, "Write what you know." I agree. But I also say, "Write it well, and *rock*." You need to write a lot to be good. Get no-pay or low-pay jobs writing for local magazines and newspapers to practice. Just write.

Some of my best writing is just for one person. A love note or a letter to a friend. I always try to write everything well.

Also, you can never tell what subject, and what way of writing it, will take off and be a hit. Maybe no one can know, although some seem to be able to.

I "know" a lot. About a lot of things. But for my commercial writing (like this), I try to focus on the angles that people might find useful, and I tell it in my own unique way. And maybe, with luck, some of it will become a meme (rhymes with "scream"). A meme is an idea that spreads like a virus, where the "idea is bigger than the person who comes up with it." See this article for a thorough explanation of the meme theory:

www.straightdope.com/columns/040213.html

Titles

It may seem like putting the cart before the cat, but often a good book comes out of a good title. A good title is important, not just to sell the book, but also because it helps *define* the work in the mind of the reader and the writer. It is *part* of the book, and part of the process of plucking the book out of thin air and making it happen.

I always try to come up with a catchy title, one that will drive me to write because I know I'm writing something great. And I want a title that will make people talk about the book once it's on the shelves.

A title can be kind of random, but the better ones aren't. *$30 Film School* is a killer title, and it sums up *exactly* what that book is about. Although you'd be amazed at how many people ask, "How much does it cost?" They usually think it's a book on how to make a film for $30, not a $30 book on how to make a film. It is, to the credit of those folks, sort of both.

Other killer titles:

- *War and Peace*
- *The Artist's Way*
- *Steal This Book*
- *Women*
- *Get in the Van*
- *How to Win Friends and Influence People*

A good title does not have to be short. It merely needs to be descriptive and catchy. My first book is a novel called *Starving in the Company of Beautiful Women*. No one forgets that title. I got the title idea when I was reading a story by Charles

Bukowski and noticed that he *was* starving in the company of beautiful women. (Or at least pretending to. I think that much of his earlier writing was not really him in cheap Los Angeles hotel rooms, drinking and hanging out with damaged beauties. I think it was him in cheap Los Angeles hotel rooms, drinking alone, and just *writing* about hanging out with damaged beauties. Which I think says even more about his fortitude as an artist.)

Your book cover is very important, too, and you will probably have an idea for the design, but just keep it as an idea for now. Worry more about the title, and especially about all those words that will go *between* the covers.

The publisher will probably come up with a cover design that is more commercial and catchier. You may hate it, but this might be one of those cases where you should just let them do their job because they are very good at it. (You need to learn to pick your battles. There will be more important things you'll want to fight for.)

On *$30 Film School,* I came up with a cover design, and Lydia Lunch took the photographs. My friend Jen Berkowitz was the model, and my friend Mike Kelley and I collaborated on the layout via e-mail. I thought it was excellent, and so did all my friends. Muska & Lipman came up with another cover and insisted on sticking with it. I was mad at first, but later I realized that their cover made people want to take my book off the shelf and look at it more than the one we designed. Lydia Lunch even liked Muska's final cover.

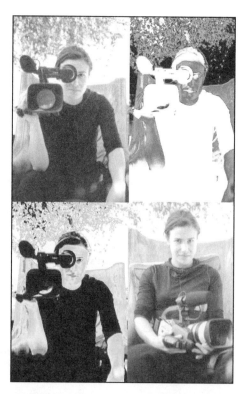

Figure 6.1 *Cover that we designed for* $30 Film School. *Model Jen Berk.* Photos by Lydia Lunch.

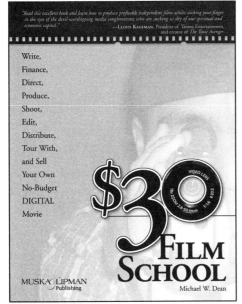
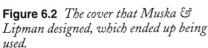

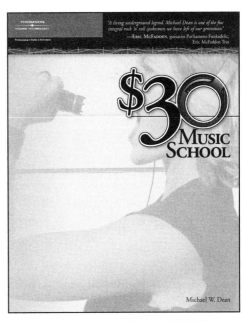

Figure 6.2 *The cover that Muska & Lipman designed, which ended up being used.*

Figure 6.3 *My cover photo for* $30 Music School.

For what it's worth, I took the photo on the cover of *$30 Music School*. When you play the publisher's game at first, sometimes you get more latitude later.

So. How about those other words, the ones *between* the covers?

Ideas

Keep in mind that before you come up with a good outline, you need a good *idea*. Or several of them. Good ideas often can be summed up in a few lines. (This is sometimes called the *pitch*.)

$30 Film School? How about, "A textbook that doesn't suck. A totally complete video-making tutorial, covering everything from picking a camera to booking a world tour for you and your movie, and everything in-between. No budget, no nonsense, no stars. Just kick-ass art and promotion, in simple terms, presented in a compelling way."

That's even a little wordy. (48 words, to be exact, and a concise pitch is usually considered to be 25 words or less. Sometimes in business this is called an "elevator pitch," a project summation so succinct that you can pitch it to someone in the elevator while he's on his way to work.) But it gets the point across. This could actually be used in a short cover letter to pitch an idea to a publisher or an agent, to see if they want to see more.

My pitch for *$30 Music School* is shorter: "Reach the world with your music, with no money. Learn everything from picking a guitar to booking a world tour."

But more to the point, the pitch is for *you*, to define what you're writing about and to guide you. If you make a good outline of a good idea, the book won't quite write itself, but it really will tell you where it wants to go. Let it. It will guide you as you guide it. Collaborate with the book like it has a consciousness, because effectively, it does.

Here's the tagline I came up with for my documentary movie *D.I.Y. or Die: How to Survive as an Independent Artist*: "A celebration of the Underdog. A profile of unique American artists working in many mediums, folks who consistently create great art regardless of a continuous paycheck." That pretty much sums it up, no?

NOTE

The pitch usually comes after you're done writing and you're trying to sell the project, but I'm encouraging you to come up with it first, because it will help drive the creation of the idea. And as we'll see in Chapter 11, "Selling Your Book," sometimes books are sold on little more than an idea.

Don't hold your ideas too dear. Don't keep all your cards in your pocket. If you talk your ideas around a little bit, you might get some useful feedback from unlikely places. And it is unlikely that anyone will steal your ideas. Ideas are a dime a dozen; it's the completion of them that's rare. Many homeless junkies have tattered notebooks full of great ideas they will never get around to executing.

I remember when a filmmaker friend of mine saw *D.I.Y. or DIE,* and he told me, "Damn, I wish I'd come up with that idea." I think he was missing the point. A good idea helps sell and promote and push a project, but you actually have to *finish* the project at some point. I have a dozen non-tattered notebooks full of ideas as good as

D.I.Y. or DIE and the *$30 School* series. Hundreds of ideas. These are simply the two that I've dedicated myself to for the last three years.

Dedication

I have two friends who joined a gym together in 1996. The idea was that they'd help each other stay devoted to it. Friend A went six days a week. Friend B went two or three days a week. Friend A teased friend B about not going as often and rode him hard about it. Friend B kept going and goes to this day. He looks great. Friend A got burnt out and stopped going after about six months. He's totally out of shape.

The same is true with writing. Find a schedule you like and keep to it. Writing is a lifelong occupation, and it doesn't come overnight. Even once it starts coming, it have to practice daily to get really good at it. Once you're good at it, people will want you to do it. You'll have an audience and maybe even some money for it, and you'll *have* to keep at it. (And at that point, having a serious ethic of daily work burned into your cellular memory will come in handy to keep you from falling behind or panicking.)

Don't force yourself to write too much per day, though. I can write for about two hours at a stretch, and edit for maybe two hours. Then I need to rest or do something else for a few hours and come back for a little more. Or not. After two hours, I become less effective. It is better for me to hold some off for tomorrow. And the next day. And the next. And the next . . .

I generally work on writing about four hours a day total. (Nice work if you can get it!) And that's my *job*! But I work Sundays, holidays, my birthday, every day.

I love the article about me in a German newspaper (reprinted on the CD-ROM in "Interviews with Michael Dean") where they said, "But you won't meet Dean a lot outside of his apartment, where the lights of computer and coffee machine turn on at 8 A.M. and thus commence the day. A cat purrs along to it."

I don't know where they got 8 a.m. (it's more like 9 A.M. or 10 A.M.—something must have been lost in translation when they interviewed me), but the rest pretty much sums it up. I get up and make coffee. My cat sits at my feet. I drink the coffee and sort of half meditate/half space out for about half an hour. I love that that is part of my workday. I would have gotten fired for doing that in an office.

Then I write.

Every day, I knock out my daily minimum, 1000 words, in an about an hour to an hour and a half. That sounds like a lot, but that's 16 words a minute. I type about 90 words per minute. (Install my program MouseCount in the Goodies folder on the CD-ROM. It measures your mousing and time on the computer and is useful in monitoring yourself so you don't get repetitive stress syndrome or "computer wrist.") Much of that time is spent staring into space, thinking what to do next.

I often do this in the morning. I sleep about six or six and one-half hours a night, get up, and hit it hard, rocking out words on my computer. I usually do this in quiet for the first hour, and then I put on music later in the morning. I work a few hours, and then I take a nap for a half-hour or an hour in the afternoon. The nap is important after all that intense thinking and writing. I get cranky without hitting the mat for a spell.

Then I get up, love myself real well (with or without a little help from my friends), drink coffee and start part two of a great day. Sometimes I write in the evening, sometimes I edit, and sometimes I just relax or work on a different project in a different medium, or answer e-mail and do interviews. Sometimes I work on writing more, usually with the TV on in the background. I get up and watch it when I want to take a break. I usually take a break to go watch the sunset, pretty much every day. Sometimes with more coffee, sometimes just petting a cat.

When I write in a coffee shop, I usually buy a daily paper and read it while I eat my breakfast, and then I write. Reading the paper relaxes me, and also gets the juices flowing. Sometimes I actually use an event from the day in my book.

NOTE

Coffee is a good tool to get the writerly juices a-coursin', but don't overdo it. A decade or two of way too much coffee can give you a heart attack.

I usually edit only in the afternoon or evening. It requires a clear head. In the morning, I'm lively enough to write, but not coherent enough to edit.

I'm writing more than usual currently. It's January 2004 as I type this. I'll be 40 years old in late May 2004, and I want to try to get this book out, or at least done and off to the printer by then so that I can say, "Well, I am 40, but I have four books, one movie, and twelve records out." That will make becoming old a little easier to swallow.

> **NOTE**
>
> Learn to type. Get good at it, using the standard touch method without looking at the keys. It's easy. Just get a chart, hang it up, and practice.
>
> You can't really write if you can't type.

I don't have a particularly regimented writing schedule, but I write a lot. Very occasionally, I'll write for four or five hours at a time. Other days, not at all. But keep in mind that I work in a lot of artforms—writing, filmmaking, music, painting, and photography—as well as a lot of public lecturing related to all of them. I also spend a lot of time doing promotion for all that stuff, so some days I may not be writing, but I am probably doing some sort of art. Even on days I don't work on writing a book, I'm probably writing a lot of e-mails. (Where I still try to write well. I strive to make my e-mails creative yet succinct. And I do spell check them.)

Not counting 100+ pieces of spam, I get about 80 e-mails a day that I have to read. And I send at least 60 e-mails most days.

I know writers who make themselves write every day. Some even set aside a time, such as every day from 10:00 a.m. to 3:00 p.m. Gosh. That sure sounds like a job to me. I'm a writer because I *don't* like having a job. I hate schedules imposed by others. (Although with schedules I impose on myself, such as a speaking engagement, or a musical performance, or showing a film, I am fastidious about being punctual.)

Here's what you should do: You should love writing enough that you will do some almost every day. If you don't want to do that, you shouldn't be a writer for a living. If you don't love writing enough on your own to do it a lot, go sell fried cheese in a mall. You'll be happier. Seriously.

And if you don't love writing, you *really* shouldn't do it as a hobby. Enjoying it is pretty much all you're gonna get from it if it's only your hobby.

Structure

Structure in art mirrors dedication in life. You need both, especially to hone your devotion into a career.

There are different forms of structure, but many kinds of art adhere to some variation of a three-act structure. This includes books, stories, pop songs, commercials, and especially movies. Like this:

- ACT ONE: You meet the characters and find out they have problems.
- ACT TWO: The characters run around trying to solve their problems. They fail but have a lot of adventures in the process. This is the bulk of the story.
- ACT THREE: The main character passes a trial by fire and something inside him changes. He is now able to master the problems he was unable to resolve before.

Keith Moon, drummer for the rock band The Who, said that people remember only your entrances and exits. While Keith had a pretty memorable exit, don't get fooled again into thinking that you can have a story without a good second act. In fact, a weak second act is where many screenplays and novels fail.

This three-act holy trinity is most obvious in films. Most Hollywood movies follow this formula to the iota, but you'll notice it almost everywhere you look, once you know about it. In short films and commercials, sometimes it's reduced to two acts: a set up and a knockdown, like in a joke. But it still usually has some aspect of "meet the characters, see their problem, see the problem solved." In the short two-act format, the middle act (not being able to solve the problem) is sometimes folded and fluffed into one of the other acts, or eliminated entirely.

Sometimes novels contain much less "story" than movies, and there is a literary heritage of allowing this. But the most effective and often commercially successful novels (and scripts) usually have a traditional linear narrative, no matter how hallucinatory and bizarre the details are that the author wraps around that framework. Arty Nelson said it's "poetry over math, and when it's done right, you don't see the math."

Non-fiction usually has some form of this three-act format as well. Most documentary films are structured and edited in a way that resembles the standard Hollywood comedy or dramatic blockbuster. (They'll sometimes even put some "redemption" near the end that feels tacked on.)

NOTE

"Documentaries are not scientific research to determine a truth. They are a defined bias maintained by a careful choosing of subjects who champion the presupposed thesis, and the deliberate consideration of the exclusion of clips that do not support the conclusion, achieved through creative editing."

—Michael Dean

This would be a good example of writing that is overtly erudite and pedantic and loquacious. But in this context (trying to sound somewhat pseudoscientific), it works.

We are so used to this formula that it is applied even in places that do not have a story, per se. Many textbooks even have some variation of this blueprint, in that they start with an introductory part, advance into a middle part, and wrap up at the end. Statement, example, and conclusion. This might work in a textbook chapter as Intro, Exploration, and Conclusion. I do it in this book. Each chapter has a short introductory graph (again, "graph" is writer speak for "paragraph"), then the bulk of the chapter, and then a conclusion. And that conclusion leads into and sets up the next chapter.

The three-act thing also works in the book as a whole. For instance, in the *$30 School* series, the first few chapters bring you into the world you are going to study, the middle chapters (the bulk of the book) explore and teach, and the "Closing Arguments" chapter wraps it up with a fine-tuning of the soul.

The first three books of this series, *$30 Film School*, *$30 Music School*, and *$30 Writing School*, function as a trilogy. I conceived the series that way. There may be more books after this. I may or may not write them. But these three were the three I intended to work together forever.

You will see this in Chapter 18, "Closing Arguments," sums up not only this book, but all three.

Speeches usually have three acts. So does a lot of well-thought-out public speaking, even if it's done on the fly.

Even a human life comes in three acts: youth, middle age, and old age. First is the learning stage, second is the doing stage, and third is the looking back stage. This was also summed up in the Riddle of the Sphinx from Egyptian myth "What walks on four legs in the morning, two in the afternoon, and three in the evening?" (The answer is man, who crawls on all fours as a baby, walks upright in his prime, and uses a cane as a third leg in the evening of his life.)

Chapters

There are usually between 10 and 30 chapters in a book. Each chapter is usually between 10 and 50 pages long. In non-fiction, they tend to be close to a uniform length throughout a book. This is because non-fiction is written from an outline and formulated in a way that helps make it easier to digest. Uniform chapter lengths help this—each chapter covers a separate subject and is about the length that the mind can easily comprehend before getting tired. It's basically one "unit" of a subject.

In fiction, there is usually more variation in chapter lengths. Fiction is more of a journey, and different stages of that journey can be of different lengths. I've even seen people make one chapter of a book very short—a single page or even a single sentence—to stress its importance.

NOTE

Keep a Dictaphone or a notebook by your bed. I do, and often I get up at night for a minute, scribble something down, and go back to bed. Do it. Trying to remember it won't work. You *won't* remember it in the morning.

When I started writing my first book (a novel), I basically had a list of great ideas and scenes. "This happened. Then this happened. And another thing happened. . . ." This is not a story. It's a scattered outline.

As I said, the three books I'm writing in this series follow the three-act formula. And they even work together as a set and reference each other in subtle and not-so-subtle ways. The series may end up having other books, but I doubt I'll write them. These three have more or less exhausted my expertise. The rest will probably get assigned to some other writer. *$30 Med School* and *$30 Law School*, anyone?

The three-act thing also works in a larger sense with most college courses. There are beginning, intermediate, and advanced classes. (These courses might use my books, so the course would contain three-part structure on the macro *and* micro levels.)

So you see, the three-act structure is seen in everything literary, from the tiniest part to the biggest part. It works in the smallest sense in a sentence. Many sentences have two sections, but sometimes three. They can work like little stories unto themselves.

Many paragraphs even have three-act structure: a short intro, the body, and the conclusion. It can be subtle, but it is often there.

Some people try to get around the formula, with varying degrees of success, and challenge the convention as stale by messing with it. But usually when this works, they are merely taking the three-act thing apart and putting it together in a new way. A good example is the movie *Memento* or the book *Alice in Wonderland*. (*Alice in Wonderland* is ripped off in every Hollywood movie where you find out at the end that the protagonist is dreaming or imagining or hallucinating some aspect of the events. This includes *Fight Club* and *Memento*, too.)

The grand poppy of the Beatniks, William S. Burroughs, invented a technique he called "cut-up." He actually took a blade and cut typed pages into sentences and phrases, and rearranged them at random. The result was more intriguing than readable, but it was a nice idea. He allegedly invented it when he came out of a drug blackout and had all the pages for his new novel all over his hotel room, and he had not numbered them. (As I said in Chapter 4, "Outlines Rule," I number the pages of a new document every time, before I begin writing.)

Burroughs' resulting book, *Naked Lunch*, is a far more interesting idea than an actuality, in my opinion. That man made amazing sentences but could never captivate me for even a full chapter, let alone a book. Burroughs also did cut-ups of taped audio recordings using a razor blade and several reel-to-reel tape recorders. This predated sampling, but that is essentially what he was doing. I *do* think *that's* pretty neat. ("It also resembles collage based on found art" adds Michael Woody, my good friend and the tech editor on *$30 Music School*.)

I never did buy the "Beatnik Lie" that the first draft of a book is the truest, and that any subsequent revision is befouling your innocence and integrity. Most Beatnik writing is brilliant for about 20 words, here and there, but cannot sustain my interest much longer than that. (I read those books only because I "should," because someone told me they were important. I would rather read a book I can't put down.) This is often the case with writing (or music, or film) produced under the influence of a lot of drugs. Bukowski was great because even though he was a drunk, he was a brilliant drunk, and he had some sober editors cleaning up the stuff. Bukowski also disliked most Beatniks.

What I am suggesting here is that you should be aware of this three-act structure, and maybe try to work within it a bit to give you a framework, before you try to change the world and come up with a new way of looking at things.

Building Blocks

Begin by learning to write a good sentence. Then work at combining these good sentences into compelling paragraphs.

Once you've mastered paragraphs, work on pages. Then chapters. Then sections. Then books. Then later you might be ready to master a series. It's all small steps, and it's a lifetime of work. I'm almost forty years old, I've been writing since I was five, and I feel that I'm just now starting to come onto my own as a writer with my own unique voice and the ability to make people feel and think.

Each paragraph and chapter should probably have a rise and fall: an arc, some sort of resolution. You will learn with experience and by studying the work of others. Then you need to plan, form, write, and edit your own work. Plan how to make words flow, not only within paragraphs, but also in how they relate to each other. A good book is not just a collection of paragraphs, but an intricate interweaving of interconnected words and sentences and paragraphs and chapters and sections and thoughts and nuance.

Someone once turned me on to the idea of "master sentences." It was presented to me as a study guide. He said to take a highlighter pen and go through a book and find the one sentence in each paragraph that sums up that paragraph. Then go back and read just the highlighted sentences. They will provide an instant summary of the chapter.

I don't really use this directly as an aid to writing, but it's a good thing to think about when considering the concord and harmony of the subtleties that tie things together and work to thread an arc throughout a book.

Amount

How much do I write? It varies. When I'm working on a book, I try to get in a thousand words a day. Sometimes I'll even check it with the Word Count feature, but I don't get too hung up on it.

I generally write between one and three hours a day. I seem to do stuff in-between, like answer mail or whatever. I can do it all.

A really good day is 2,500 words. But I have to do a lot more to make a book. It's not just writing. It's also editing, doing the images, fact checking, making the CD-ROM that goes in the back, and making the Web site. Also, there's promoting the book that just came out while I'm writing the next one. It's all a big fun ball of synergy.

I don't write 1,000 or 2,000 words of a new book every day, but I'm always occupied with something. My mind requires it. Sometimes I'm busy with other projects. For instance, I spent yesterday morning sending out press releases for *$30 Music School*, which came out this week (first week of January 2004), and spent the afternoon doing interviews concerning my film *D.I.Y. or Die: How to Survive as an Independent Artist*, which came out two years ago, but which seems to be increasing in popularity every day. It is also mentioned a lot in *$30 Film School* as an example, so sales of one thing drive sales of another. I try to make my life and my art work that way.

I often will take a bunch of notes that I made during a day or over a period of days and type them into a single document. Then I elaborate on those ideas, and cut and paste them into appropriate chapter documents to expand later. See the photograph of a couple of days' notes on the CD-ROM, called temp.jpg. Also note the file of the same notes typed and awaiting inclusion in the book (including this paragraph) as temp.doc.

I'm prolific but lazy in a way. I watch a lot of TV. I feel I could be doing more. All I do, and this is the key, is work consistently, a little bit at a time, all throughout the day, every day, over a very long time.

Content

A line in *The Player* (one of my favorite movies) has Tim Robbins' character listing the elements that a script needs in order for his studio to buy it and make a movie out of it. These elements include "heart, triumph, passion, fear, violence, sex, love, hope, action, redemption. . . ."

In the movie, this list seems intentionally a little trite, but it isn't that far off from what makes a good story. If you want your writing to move people, you might want to put some of these things in.

Different writers have different styles, and style is the main thing that makes them saleable. I am not pushing art over commerce. My entire MO is based on validating art that does not make money. But that is to encourage artists to not give up so they can develop their own style. Art that is great and powerful often *is* saleable. It's just sometimes hard to find someone to take a chance on it and sell it. Good writing is something people want to consume, and they are willing to pay for it.

You will not have a clear style of your own from the first paragraph you write. You will have to learn the basic technical aspects of English: It's very hard for someone to see your cool style if he has to dig through all your typos to find it. Don't kid yourself and think you're so great and magical and blessed that the audience (or the agent or publisher) will overlook it. They won't.

Gone are the days of daft and addled geniuses such as Bukowski and Hunter S. Thompson, turning in rambling, unnumbered pages and letting a good editor sort it out. Today's editors are willing to work with a good writer, but you gotta have your stuff *tight* before they'll even look at it.

This is probably because of the proliferation of computers. Time was when a writer had to lug around a manual typewriter. It was physically hard to use, and self-editing was difficult. You had to really think ahead a lot. Something as simple as moving a paragraph from the middle of a chapter to the end of the chapter involved retyping the entire thing.

NOTE

A long time ago, I owned one of the first "laptop" computers. It was made by Zenith, weighed 22 pounds, lasted a half-hour on a battery charge, and had no hard drive. It worked off of two 5-inch floppy discs, one with the operating system (DOS) and one with the word processor, Word Perfect 1.1, and the data files. When I'd pull it out in a coffee shop, people really thought I was insane. They thought it was science fiction, overkill, conspicuous consumption.

Today, in 2004, computers are everywhere. At this moment, I'm on a train in France, and probably every tenth person on the train has a laptop out. When it's easy to write, everyone writes. To be fair, no one on this train seems to be working on a novel, and none of them seem like young artist types. They are all businessmen and women, either working in Excel or answering e-mails offline. And they all have computers older than mine. Laptops cost much more in Europe than they cost in America.

Conclusion

You've gotta be great. You have to make your sentences, paragraphs, chapters, and books *breathe*. The words have to leap off the page and into the mind and life of the reader. A good book is a religious experience. It makes people go out of their way to tell others about it.

Write with conviction. Imagine that the little clacking keys on your computer have the force of a metric ton of dynamite, and they're pounding each letter into the eight million layers of papyrus and hemp that will comprise the totality of all the copies of your epic that will eventually be sold.

Write something that inspires that in others, and you're most of the way there. But you need to follow through to make a mark. Work at writing. Improve. Grow. Learn. Read. Listen.

> "Follow through and remember: 'It takes a while.' "
>
> —Li'l Mike Martzke in *D.I.Y. or Die*

Chapter 7

On Writing

$30 WRITING SCHOOL

So you wanna be a writer. Here we will go over the basics of what that involves. We'll talk honestly a little more about the dedication it requires. I'll try to scare you off, and if you don't run screaming, I'll show you more on how to write.

Why Write?

Writing is a very cool thing to do, and an even cooler thing to do for a living. It is incredibly freeing to set your own hours, be creative, and etch your thoughts into the world, reaching random people in far-off cities and countries.

Shortly before he died of cancer, my favorite author, Phil Sudo, told me, "I get e-mail from people all over the world, total strangers . . . really supportive. It's just amazing how you write this little book and it's like putting a message in a bottle and throwing it into the sea from an island. You don't really know who's going to get it. And to suddenly get all this feedback to see who's gotten it and how it's affected their life. It's amazing. I don't have to worry about my legacy if I'm to meet an early death. . . . I've said what I'm going to say. . . . If that's it, . . . I feel like I've got something out there in the world."

There are some very heavy pros and a few cons to being a writer. One of the pros is that you can do it anywhere. I'm writing this sentence on a train going from Rotterdam, Holland, to Paris, France. Pretty cool, no?

Figure 7.1 *Me in Paris, writing.* Photo by John Rosania.

Figure 7.2 *Me on a train between Manchester and London, England.*

Figure 7.3 *Me in Lyon, France, writing.*

Figure 7.4 *Me in Sheffield, England, writing.*

Figure 7.5 *My office, on my back porch in Los Angeles (cat: Charlie).* Photo by Michael Dean

Also, you can start *today*. You don't need years of training. It helps to have a good understanding of English (or whatever language you intend to write in), but you don't need a degree. I got kicked out of high school and flunked out of college.

Another pro is that writing is free. Other than the cost of getting a computer, which you probably already have, writing costs nothing. If you don't have a computer, you can write on paper. Remember paper? That's what writers wrote on for the first thousand or so years of publishing, until about 1970, when a few folks got things called "word processors." They weighed a lot, cost a lot, and were hard to use. Today you can buy a used desktop computer capable of running Microsoft Word for about $50, if you shop around. (Especially an older version of Word that will take less memory. And an newer version has more stuff to confuse you and won't make you a better writer. I'm sitting here in 2004 writing this on Word 97.) (Try eBay or the want ads in local papers, and on bulletin boards at colleges. You can get a comparable laptop for $125. It won't be screamingly fast (I just paid $650 for a two-GHz Toshiba that *is* fast), but it'll get the job done.

So yeah, writing is free. And if you're lucky and talented and driven enough to do it for a living, you may basically end up being your own boss to one degree or another.

Conversely, when you are your own boss, you have to have discipline. When you don't *have* to go to work any given day, you damn well better still go to work most days, even if your commute is only 10 feet.

Freedom does not come without responsibility.

Freedom also does not come without worry. Professional writing is not for the faint of heart. If you don't deal with rejection well, you should probably go work for someone else. If you wanna be your own master, you had better be brave.

NOTE

Get up and stretch. It's good for your back, hands, and spirit. This is hard sometimes when you're in the "zone," but if you notice you're dehydrated *and* have to pee, it might be time to step away from the computer.

Meditate. Be alone in the morning. I get up, make coffee, drink it, and sit on my back porch staring at the sky for 20 minutes. And I don't like to talk to anyone or even speak until I've been up an hour. This works for me.

If you are bad at budgeting, you should probably consider doing something else for your living and maybe just write for fun (and that's not a bad plan overall, ever). Paychecks in writing don't come every Friday (well, they might for some writers, but not for me). They come every three months and tend to be of ghetto-rich sizes and inspire me to go mad with spending if I'm not careful. And then I'm starving by the time the next one comes.

If you are a social creature, maybe you should go work in an office. As much as water-cooler gossip sucks, try living without it for a while. It's hard being me. I have to get up in the morning and gossip to myself about myself sometimes to stay sane. On really crazy days, I'll CC myself with little rumors via e-mail just to shake myself up.

Just kidding. But ya know, you *can* go a bit mad, not being around other folks much. Writing requires a sense of balance. You have to *have* a life in order to *write about life.*

In *D.I.Y or Die*, Stephen Elliot (author of the novel *A Life Without Consequences)* said writing "comes from that urge to be alone and to communicate at the same time . . . that need to get everything in my head out of my head. But instead of driving everyone crazy and telling them everything that's in my head, I just write it all down and then I just show 'em the good stuff."

Which leads to the fact that working as a writer is not just about writing. It's also about editing. You have to be able to edit yourself to a degree, be your own crap-o-meter, and know your gold from your mud. You have to do this before an editor will even want to take a look at you, and especially after you get a deal and have an acceptance letter. Self-editing's tough. And editing takes at least as much time as the actual writing. Maybe more time.

If you are not a self-starter, you should probably go work in a bank. Writing involves a lot of work, thought, and constant devotion. *Infinite Jest* author David Foster Wallace said that working on a book is like dragging a sick child around with you for several years. You have to care for it constantly and worry about it and think about and love it in hopes that it will turn out okay.

The main problem with trying to get attention as a writer is that *everyone is doing it.* I love the punk rock ethic of "anyone can make a record," but when anyone *can* make a record, anyone *does.* I will fight to the death for your right to make a record, but I don't necessarily want to listen to it.

The same is true of writing. Writing is *the* most inexpensive art form. It's *free*. People who can't really write can delude themselves into thinking that they can. Or more commonly, very new, unpolished writers believe that they are ready to be published. While I believe that everyone has *some* art in them, it takes years, decades, and a whole lifetime to really come into your own with writing. Too many people pick up a pen or computer and start pecking away and try to publish the next week (I know I did). And with the advent of the Internet, everyone *does* publish before they're ready.

But just because something looks nicely formatted on your screen doesn't mean it's good.

If this all sounds like naysaying to you, then you probably aren't ready to be a real writer. You probably want a book that will tell you how easy it is. If that's the case, simply put this book back on the bookstore shelf and grab one of the other books on either side of it. At least one of them will tell you what you want to hear (and probably will be a more popular book, so when you give up in a few months, you can resell it more easily than you could sell this book).

But if I haven't lost you yet, you *might* have what it takes.

You might be realistic and not afraid of work or rejection or whatever it takes to be a powerful, compelling, *literate* writer.

And you *might* make some money.

If you're still reading this, roll up your sleeves and let's *work*.

School or Not?

Let's go back to that school part for a minute. I've been writing forever. I was a published writer at the age of sixteen. It was a poem about autumn that was printed in the local paper.

I've written consistently longer and more thoroughly than I've approached any other of my pet endeavors and careers. (I also make music and films. And I'm good at them. I paint too, and enjoy it, but I'm not very good.)

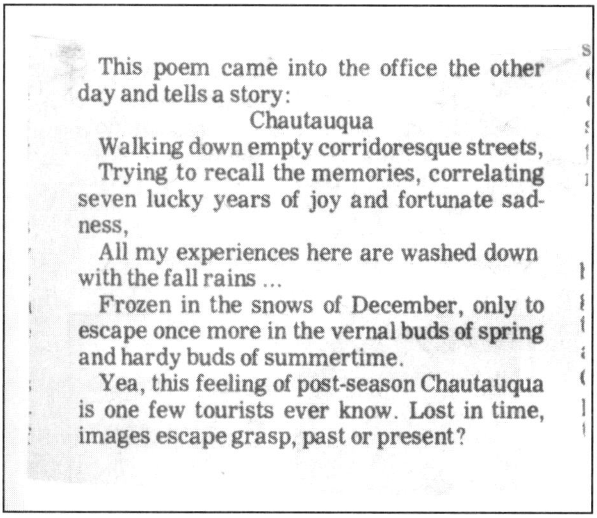

This poem came into the office the other day and tells a story:

Chautauqua

Walking down empty corridoresque streets,
Trying to recall the memories, correlating seven lucky years of joy and fortunate sadness,
All my experiences here are washed down with the fall rains ...
Frozen in the snows of December, only to escape once more in the vernal buds of spring and hardy buds of summertime.
Yea, this feeling of post-season Chautauqua is one few tourists ever know. Lost in time, images escape grasp, past or present?

Figure 7.6 *Scan of my first published work from* The Chautauquan Daily, *October 1980. (I learned to play guitar in the park in front of the office of this paper.)*

I was one, Alone, Down in The Dumps.
making up Scheduals For he and For me.
actully making Them up For No one.
Then, one night, There you where.
RANDOMNESS LED ME.
Through The Dark of mordor,
To The Light of galidrial,
I walked, looking For Love.
I'm NOT Alone any more.
When I walk with you to The Store.
Draw up some New routeins
Break our Barriers
Trying to Figure out The next chord
I'm still alone Inside.
Fighting my way to The outside.

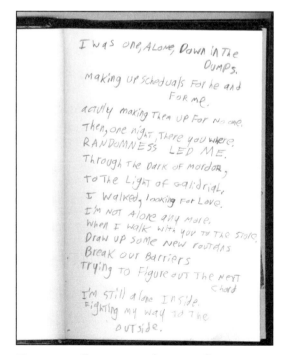

Figure 7.7 *Crappy poem from one of my notebooks when I was 14.*

I always intuitively understood the basics of sentence structure and was always a good storyteller. When I was 12, I got to hang out with 18-year-old kids because I could entertain them with words.

I can write. And more importantly, I can create and also *tell a story*. But I cannot, to this day, tell you what a "participle" or a "gerund" is. I do know a verb from a noun, but I rarely think about it. I am a horrible speller. (Not only did I have to look up "thoroughly" with spell check in a previous paragraph, but I had to type a few different attempts before I was even close enough for spell check to correct me correctly.)

I did go back to college and *not* flunk out when I was 31 years old. I took free part-time non-credit classes for 18 months at the John Adams annex of San Francisco City College. I took some English, some typing, some very basic computer classes (Intro to Microsoft Office) and job prep classes (basically just writing a resume and conducting, videotaping, and critiquing mock job interviews). Then I just went and put on a suit and temped in offices for a few years to make rent and to hone those skills. But mainly I just did a lot of work on my own. I wrote before work at my day job, I wrote at work at my day job, and I wrote after work at my day job. I became incredibly fascinated with computers and the endless well of knowledge that comes with them. I was just off a decade-long self-crippling run with hard drugs, lucky to be alive and pretty excited to not be sick every day anymore. I had planned to be dead and famous by age 30. When I turned 30 and turned out to be neither famous nor dead, I started putting a lot of energy into having a life and making art—for fun, the spark, and just the love of doing it. I learned to paint, learned filmmaking, kept playing music, and wrote every day.

NOTE

As a writer, I can work when I'm sick as a dog. And I'm sick pretty often for a healthy guy, probably the result of drug abuse and drinking before I sobered up and focused my energy like a laser.

It's nine years later and this is my fifth book. (I wrote another novel that I'm saving. It has not been published yet.) I'm working on the outline for my sixth book, a novel.

I would say that in order to write, you don't need a college education. You need the equivalent knowledge of a college graduate, but I got that without college. I would recommend that people instead consider the possibility of spending a couple of years living and traveling. Just make sure you are armed with the skills that it takes to get by in the world. If you do not have such skills, get them, whether it be through experience, non-credit classes, reading books, consulting willing experts, or all of the above. (Or even through college, if that's what you need to get this stuff.) Regardless, to survive in this world, you should be able to cook a little, balance a checkbook, compose an effective business letter, and communicate effectively in writing. Mainly, be able to talk to anyone about anything without fear (something that college usually does not teach).

Some jobs do require a diploma, but not because they require the skills that the diploma allegedly represents. No, basically what a diploma proves is only that you are capable of showing up at the same place at the same time for years and are comfortable sitting in little rows and being told what to do and liking it. And since most writing jobs are freelance, those are *not* the job requirements. The only job requirement for freelance writing work is basically the ability to create compelling copy under a deadline. And you also need a little bit of people skills, but only enough to be able to deal with an agent via e-mail and occasionally by phone. I had two book deals with my agent before I actually met her in person. And most of the time when I deal with her, I am sitting around in my underwear with a cat on my lap, something that would get you fired (and possibly jailed or institutionalized) in a conventional job.

NOTE

Concept in the beginning of the preceding paragraph borrowed from the book *The Sovereign Individual: Mastering the Transition to the Information Age* by James Dale Davidson and Lord William Rees-Mogg (Free Press, 1999).

Most writing jobs are handed out based on meritocracy (a situation based on merit). You can't bluff your way through most writing assignments. Well, maybe once, but there won't be a twice if you do. Conversely, I used to bluff my way though temp office jobs a lot. I would get a call and they'd ask if I knew a certain computer program. I'd lie and say, "Yes." They'd say, "Good. You start tomorrow."

That night, I'd go online and find a tutorial and learn some basic functions in that program and figure out the rest at the job, from the Help menu.

There are a few places where you will need an English degree. You will need one to teach at most places. Though I don't have one, and I get invited, and paid, to lecture at colleges. You will probably need a degree to be an editor at a big publishing house, though that isn't really a writing gig, per se. And those jobs are sometimes doled out without a college degree via nepotism (*who* ya know, rather than *what* you know—the opposite of meritocracy).

I always wondered why I couldn't get jobs that I could have gotten if I just had one more line on a resume, a line that said I had a degree. That conversation in my own head actually resulted in me coming up with the title *$30 Film School*. And led to this series. And this series is more commercially successful than anything I've ever done. I basically just started my own school.

And *many* people who spent 10 or 20 grand on "real" film school said they learned more from my film book (check the Amazon.com reviews). So my basic point is, *get the knowledge* and then do it yourself. Don't wait for permission or a piece of paper to prove your knowledge.

Where to Write

In high school English class, I had a really cool teacher, Ray Greenblatt. High school pretty much sucked, but he was one of the two teachers who were actually cool, actually cared about the students, actually inspired me, and actually made school almost bearable. (The other one was an art teacher, Mrs. Sanderson. I wonder: If it had been a business teacher, would I be doing something else with my life?)

Ray taught me two cool things, but they seemed unimportant to me at the time. One was the value of an outline. I rejected this outright for two reasons. One, I felt I was a free spirit and that using an outline was hobbling my creativity. Second, while I liked to write, I felt it was going to be of no use to me in later life. "I'm gonna be a rock star" was my general feeling.

I've already covered outlines.

The other thing he told us about was the importance of a clean, well-lighted, uncluttered space devoted entirely to writing. Ray Greenblatt was a published writer, but I felt that he couldn't tell me what to do and that I could be very selective about what he taught me. I actually didn't let myself learn much from him, but he did praise some of my writing, which is probably what I liked about him. (I always ignored the parentheticals after the praise, stuff like ". . . needs more focus . . . work on spelling . . . use an outline . . ." and so on.)

I've never had a clean, well-lighted, uncluttered *anything* in my life. I still don't. But I certainly do have a place devoted to writing. It's a very cluttered desk that is basically the center around which my entire apartment revolves. This desk is what draws the eye when you walk into my place, and everything radiates out from the desk—not by design, but by necessity. It's Feng Shui gone awry. Writing is my life. I'm married to the page.

But I can write anywhere and often do. I have several peripherals, from a laptop to an Alphasmart and a Handspring Visor with a keyboard (more on all this stuff in a few chapters). I also carry a tiny removable USB drive that weighs less than an ounce and is the size of my thumb. I carry it *everywhere* and often write on other people's computers, or public ones (Internet cafés or college computer labs), whenever I have a few moments free and feel like expressing myself. When all else

Figure 7.8 *My desk.*

fails, I always have a pen and a scrap of paper with me, or at least a pen. When there's no paper, I write on the back of my hand (I jokingly call this my "palm pilot") and work out the details later when I get to a suitable machine.

I'm actually at this moment sitting in a sidewalk café in Paris, sipping cappuccino while writing this. Isn't that the dream for all writers? The difference is, I don't care where I write. I did have a lot of fun today walking around

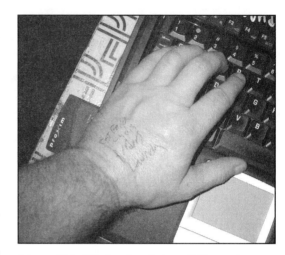

Figure 7.9 *My hand and the scribbles on it.*

this town, but I rarely look away from the screen to even know what city I'm in when I'm on this damn 'pooter (computer). But it's all good. All the work I do through my 'pooter enables me to travel anyway.

Figure 7.10 *Me in Paris, writing some more.* Photo by John Rosania

It's also pretty cold on the sidewalk in Paris at the moment. Which is probably not part of the typical writer's dream.

I had a friend who used to move about once a year from San Francisco to New York City and back to work on her novel. She kept thinking that she had to be somewhere else to write. She never finished that novel. In that time, I wrote my novel, and did much of it while at work doing reception at various law firms in San Francisco. In the past two years, I've written three 500+ page books, and I did most of it in my tiny little room in Los Angeles, usually with the shades drawn.

It's more about what's inside your head than outside your head.

Also, I think it is important to be able to write anywhere, even with distractions. If you constantly need the right atmosphere to write, you won't write much. It's kind of like London May's drumming advice on the CD-ROM of *$30 Music School*. He tells aspiring drummers to practice at home, without monitor speakers, with the air conditioning off, and to get good at using different drum kits so you won't be married to your own perfect setup. Because the reality is that as a working rock drummer (unless you are in a *huge* band with your own drum roadie), you will often have to use other people's drums or will have very little time to properly set up your own.

I can, and do, write anywhere, on anything. I like to write on my laptop, but sometimes I write on other people's computers. Maybe they have a sticky keyboard and don't have Microsoft Word and the battery on their laptop won't hold a charge and the power cable has a loose connection that keeps shutting off. But I can always make it work out.

I can write using the Graffiti pen commands on a Palm Pilot or Handspring. Today I wrote in a university computer lab that was very hot and was full of students talking in three different languages on cell phones all around me. I can type on my laptop standing up on a train, using my knee as a table. Right now I'm in a café (it was too cold outside, so I came in) that has two different dogs barking and a lot of people speaking French, which I don't understand.

When I can write, I feel free. In many social situations I'll leave to go write. (Or ruder yet, I'll *stay* and write.) But I also try to get out and socialize and travel and live a lot of life, so that I'll have things to write about.

Who Writes What, Where?

There is a joke that you can walk up to *anyone* in Los Angeles and say, "How's your screenplay coming?" and they'll start to tell you. I've actually done this. It is barely hyperbole to say that most people in this town are working on a script. People move here to "make it." Go to Insomnia Café on Beverly or the Coffee Table coffee shop on Rowena, or literally a hundred other places, and you will find, at *any* given time, between 15 and 30 people writing on laptops. I guarantee that between 14 and 29 of them are in Final Draft (a screenwriting program) writing a script. I think they actually think that they're gonna get discovered right there in the café or something. (There is another saying in LA that claims, "No script written on a laptop has ever sold," but I doubt that's true anymore.)

In New York City, cafés are full of people writing novels. In San Francisco, it's usually erotica, fierce political manifestos, or novels. Or fierce, novel, erotic political manifestos. Or these days, probably resumes.

Of all these people writing in all these places, very few of them will ever get their stuff published (less than one percent). And of those who do, not many (maybe two percent of that one percent) will be able to quit their day jobs.

Why do we do it? Because there is an amazing power to the written word. We are skywriting on eternity and making it available for all to see. Writers are *immortal* through the power of the published word. And that totally transcends any money we might make.

Good Writing versus Bad Writing

What constitutes good writing and bad writing?

- ◆ Good writing has a lot less to do with following grammatical rules than most English teachers would have you believe. In writing that mimics and even improves on conversational English (like this book), rules are broken constantly. I turn Grammar Check off in my word processing program. I never use it. It thinks almost everything I type is incorrect. For instance, a few pages back, I wrote this:

  "And editing takes at least as much time as the actual writing. Maybe more time."

Good Writing:

I ended up lost from my friends, alone in Paris. Walking along the Seine in the rain sure sounds romantic, but it sure ain't when it's bone-chilling cold out and you can't hail a taxi because there are exactly 1,034,085 Parisians attempting to negotiate the same act at the same moment.

It also would have helped me to know that it is illegal in Paris for a taxi to stop when hailed. You have to go to a designated taxi stand and wait. I finally realized that and went to one. There were over 100 people all trying to the get three available cabs.

I had missed the last train by seconds. My friends insisted on a long goodbye, which my gut told me would be pushing it logistically. I finally disengaged from their loving hugs and longing gazes and bolted down the subway steps, only to see the doors on the final train snap shut, and a posse of French drunks secure on the other side of the glass laughing at me and pointing.

How the hell can a world-class city like Paris organize the world's biggest all-night block party and then close the subway at midnight? Even stoner San Francisco runs the trains late for something as mundane as a ballgame.

I love Paris. But to me, this party scenario is indicative of why many hate France: The French know that they're so cool that they don't have to try to be convenient. At all.

Bad Writing:

We went to the party and I did not get back. Oh yeah, I was in Paris. I hate Paris. It was cold. They didn't plan. It's their fault. They Are Dum. The rain was wet and cold and came down in sheets. The sheets went into my clothes like a rainy hammer. I was as wet as a dog. I was as mad as a bull. In Paris they act like they are cool so why do I have to go?, I said. I lived in Frisko for long time and they run parties good and no one can't get go to stuff.

The first sentence begins with *and*. This is often considered incorrect. And the second sentence, *Maybe more time*, is not a real sentence at all. It has no subject, no object, no noun, and no verb. It is a clause. It is grammatically incorrect by itself. But it works for me, because I use a conversational tone, and conversational speech often uses clauses as sentences.

◆ Good writing usually *does* have correct spelling. Unless it's an intention-ally bad or odd spelling to make a point. Like when I write "girl" as "gurl" to imitate the whining cadence of an adolescent male who does not like girls.

◆ Good writing does not have to have big words, though some of my favorite good writing uses mostly simple English with an occasional and well-placed use of something a little tastier, without becoming overtly erudite or patently pedantic. (Like the last five words of that last sen-tence.)

◆ Good writing is frequently universal. Often (but there are notable and potent exceptions), good writing effortlessly strives to find the common thread in all human experience. It is less about the "how" than the "why." I can enjoy a well-written short story about a football player, even though I despise watching football.

There is an infinite number of examples of good and bad writing. But I'm gonna give you a dollop of each, and I think you'll see what I'm barkin' at.

By the way, good writing usually contains a natural mixture of short sentences and long sentences. Bad writing often features mostly one or the other.

Really bad writing is often stilted to the point of confusion: It often consists of run-on sentences. And it's hard to tell in these what the subject is and what the object is. It gets pretty damn confusing. Good writing, no matter how complex, is clear.

Research and Fact Checking

I use the Internet as I write. I keep an open Internet connection and often shift back and forth between Word and my browser. I will look up stuff like the spelling of a person's name (www.google.com), whether or not something's true or a rumor (www.snopes.com), what a word means (www.m-w.com—and be sure to sign up for their free word-of-the-day e-mail thing), and stuff like that. Sometimes if I don't know which of two spellings of a word is correct, I'll search both spellings in Google and go with whichever one returns more hits. This is right about 95 percent of the time.

www.snopes.com is a great resource for debunking myths, especially crap that people forward in e-mails (check the "Inboxer Rebellion" link).

When you want to put a URL (Web address) in a book, it's best to try it first in a browser to make sure it's correct (not mistyped) and working, and then cut and paste from the browser by highlighting it in the location bar and copying it to the Clipboard:

- Click once in the browser location bar (the place the Web address is displayed near the top).
- Hit Ctrl+A to select it.
- Hit Ctrl+C to copy it.
- Click once in your word processor where you want to paste it.
- Hit Ctrl+V to paste it.

In the first printing of *$30 Music School*, in Joan Jett's interview, I incorrectly put her Web address as www.joanjet.com (it's actually www.joanjett.com). It's one of those sites that someone registered to get traffic from idiots like me who mistype popular Web addresses. (My opinion is that this is pretty screwed up to do.)

Joan Jett loved my book, but she caught the mistake and told me. I had my publisher fix it for the second printing.

How to Interview People

I get interviewed a lot. I also interview people a lot. I often do both in my favorite coffee shop in LA, the Down Beat, a little café in my neighborhood (Echo Park). It's kinda fun, I have a table I like, and it's like my office. Some days I'm sticking a Dictaphone in someone's face, and sometimes someone is sticking one in mine. I like that. It seems fair somehow. Very egalitarian. Like how, back in the real punk rock days, the bands took turns at a show being the audience for each other.

NOTE

If you want to interview someone famous but you have no set contact, go through their publicist. It is that person's *job* to get them interviews. You can call their manager to find out who the publicist is. It will help if you are already published and can tell them about or show them your published work. It may also help if you write a cover letter, but have your agent send it to the publicist.

Permission

You should always get written permission to use an interview, or seomone's art, even if the person is your friend. I can't stress this enough. Of all the projects I've done, involving interviewing over 80 people, only two of them have turned into a nightmare. But those two would have totally sidetracked my career if I didn't have permission in writing. Basically, there were people who were unhappy in their lives and looking to take any glory away from other people. Percentage-wise, only two in eighty is actually pretty good.

I always get an e-mail from everyone I collaborate with, at the least. I send them an e-mail that says, "Is it okay to use the interview we're doing, for free, in my new book?"

They only have to reply, "yes," and I save the e-mail. (Complete with headers, to show when and where it was actually sent from. Don't worry, your mail program will do this automatically.)

If they delete the part where I asked them, I have them send a reply again without deleting my question.

Better than an e-mail permission is a written one with their signature.

NOTE

Nothing in this book constitutes legal advice. This is for information purposes only.

I use a release form tha you can find on the CD-ROM in the goodies folder called generic release.doc. It's protected me so far. Note that it not only grants you permission to use the interview or art, it also grants you permission not to use it. This is very important because sometimes in editing, it is necessary to cut something. It's the old "cut the song to strengthen the record" argument. You want to cover yourself. Some people don't have much of a life, and they think that you including them in a book is gonna make them rich and famous. How deluded is that? I write the damn books, and I ain't rich and famous! So if you have to cut them, they get upset.

Generally, the more that people have going on in their own careers, the less they care if you have to cut them out of your book. Truly happenin' people won't even notice. They're too busy with reality.

NOTE

If you have to cut someone from a project for space or time, send them a polite and short e-mail telling them this. And do it before the book comes out. That way they won't tell all their friends, "I'm going to be in a book," and look stupid when they aren't. And offer to help them with a job reference if they ever need it. That way they don't feel totally bad. If you cut them because they just plain sucked, don't tell them that. Be kind.

So anyway, cover yourself to use (or not to use) someone's words for free when they kick down a word jam and collaborate with you on some cool work.

Always be available to work for them like this for free, to return the favor. Always say, "Let me know if I can help you." But don't ask to be interviewed. People who are happenin' don't ask. It comes across as a little desperate. And desperate people don't usually make for good interviews. (Unless you're a news team, and you want sensational footage of a victim of some disaster or crime.)

Noting in a press release that you are "available for interviews" is not desperate, however. We will cover that in Chapter 16, "Promotion . . . Telling the World."

Tools of the Interviewer

Bring a tape recorder. Make sure you have fresh and backup batteries. Test the recorder when you get there. Record a little bit, hit rewind, and listen to it.

If you are doing an interview in a public place with background noise, consider going elsewhere, somewhere quiet. A car is usually good. If you must do it in a public place, have the person speak directly into the microphone on the tape recorder. Maybe pass it back and forth when you ask the question and when they reply. If they are close to the mic, it will make it a lot easier to understand when you have to transcribe it later.

If you do a lot of interviewing, get a Dictaphone. This is a small portable recorder that uses microcassettes and gets a good sound. Dictaphones are good things for writers to have anyway. They are good for jotting down ideas.

The Dictaphone company also makes a foot-controlled office model. They are often used by secretaries. (I want a secretary!) The foot pedal makes it easy to stop and start, which makes transcribing easy. I don't have one of those. I usually just import the audio from my Dictaphone into my computer and make an audio file of it. Then I can open it up in Windows Media Player (or better yet, Sony Pictures' SoundForge—it's easy to stop and start in an incremental, exact way in that program). Then I simply open Word and transcribe it. (This is a lot easier if you have two computers like me, but it can be done all on one with a bit of effort.) It's easy to stop and start in SoundForge, too—you just hit the Enter key to stop and the spacebar to start. Sometimes I also make it into an MP3 or several MP3s, and upload them for friends with lots of free time in different cities to transcribe for me. I give them credit in the book and a copy of the book.

Everyone wants to be mentioned in a book. Mentioning them is nice and can also get you a lot of favors. But don't ever abuse it. It's a privilege. Always use your powers for good. Never for evil.

TIP

A talented interviewer will make a fast temporary friend with an interviewee. But keep in mind that the person isn't your best friend now. When you are earnestly looking each other in the eyes and sharing your secrets in an interview, you are actually being candid more with the totality of the final readership, not with the interviewer himself. This can lead to resentment on both sides if people aren't honest with themselves (and each other).

How to Interview

Do your research. Check the person out on the Web. Don't ask obvious questions. Don't be stupid. When I went to interview Foetus for *D.I.Y. or DIE*, my first question was, "Where are you from?" He seemed annoyed and said, "I was born in Australia, lived in England, and I live in New York now." My second question was, "What was it like to work with David Bowie?" He seemed annoyed and said, "I don't know. I never have." (I thought he had for some reason.) I could have spent five minutes on the Web (even just on his Web site) and avoided both of those stupid questions.

Sometimes people make notes ahead of time with what they want to ask. I did this with Hubert Selby, Jr. Check out the Selby interview questions on the CD-ROM in the Goodies folder.

Sometimes it's a word jam. You just start talking and let it go where it can. Sometimes it's planned but has room to go off on tangents. I usually do that.

I heard somewhere that when asked how to interview people, Connie Chung said, "All interview questions basically boil down to 'What's it like to be you?'"

I agree and try to keep this in mind. Actually, I sometimes even finish up by asking them that directly.

Basically, interviewing takes practice, and you get better at it. You can practice on your friends if you've never interviewed anyone.

Accuracy

Ask people during the interview to spell out names and things you can't spell. They'll appreciate it.

After transcribing, I usually proof the interview and then ask the interviewee if he wants to check it for accuracy. If so, I put on Track Changes and explain this function to them. It is respectful to see if the person wants to check it, but it's a judgement call. You don't want to be waiting to get it back when you're on a deadline. Use your judgement.

Figure 7.11 *Me on tour in Germany. My auxiliary brain extender (a laptop) is in my shoulder bag. This pony was very sweet.*

Conclusion

$30 Film School took 18 months to write. *$30 Music School* took four months. *$30 Writing School* took about six months. (Keep in mind that a few of those months overlapped; I started writing *$30 Writing School* while I was on tour in Europe and later in Texas after teaching a film class. I was also doing author review for *$30 Music School* at the same time.) The first one took a long time because I was figuring out the process as I went along and didn't make an outline. The second one took the least amount of time because I was trying to prove something to myself. I think six months is about right, but it's still faster than most people could come up with a 520-page comprehensive textbook and CD-ROM. But then again, I drink a lot of coffee and don't go out much.

One reason it got easier to write each book is because I was being mentored by my great editors. Let's take a look now at what that entails.

Chapter 8

Working with an Editor

$30 WRITING SCHOOL

A lot of my work involves proofing and editing. This is the *big* difference in my being publishable or not. I always see people *writing* on their laptops in coffee shops, just tap tap tapping, clicking away their days. (Who pays their bills? Mommy?) But I never see people *editing* in coffee shops. (I sneak looks over their shoulders. I'm *always* curious as to what other writers are up to.) The fact that these people do not edit is probably the reason they are destined to never have their writing exist outside the coffee shop.

NOTE

I used to think that real writers didn't write in coffee shops, but recently I've actually started going out and enjoying it. I get up, check my e-mail, then pack the laptop up and go to the Down Beat and have coffee and a bagel, read the paper and then write for 60–90 minutes solid. It's good because I don't have mobile Internet access away from home, so I really *work*. It is also kinda cool to be around other people, as I've become rather antisocial with my ever-increasingly intense work ethic.

Stages of Editing

Don't make your editor do the grunt work. That's your job. Do the bulk of it before he even sees it, and then let him do what he does best: guide you as he hones the diamond in the rough.

It's not your editor's job to stroke your ego. That's your fans' job. If an editor doesn't complain, your writing is probably making her happy. If you need validation, write a book, get some fans, and hang your fan letters on the wall to read when you're feeling down. That's what I do.

Do a good job. Books are permanent. The editor ain't necessarily going to catch your minutia, and the less he has to work on the tiny crap, the more he can work on the bigger picture, and vice versa. The book certainly ain't gonna edit itself on the shelf. I've seen a lot of books, even from big publishing houses, with typos. Yuck.

You gotta be great. Do your work. You'll have to live with it.

I edit like this: I hammer a chapter into shape until it looks and feels like a completed chapter. I spell check as I go, usually several times during each 2,000-word block of work. I do it as I write. I have the Check Spelling as You Type function working (in Microsoft Word, it's Tools, Options, Spelling and Grammar). I disable the Grammar Check because it's useless. As I said, a lot of good writing ignores the dusty old rules of grammar. And again, you should absolutely learn these rules before you break them. Break them because you want to, not because you don't know better. Your writing will be exponentially better because of it.

Here are three pages from the work in process from *$30 Music School*.

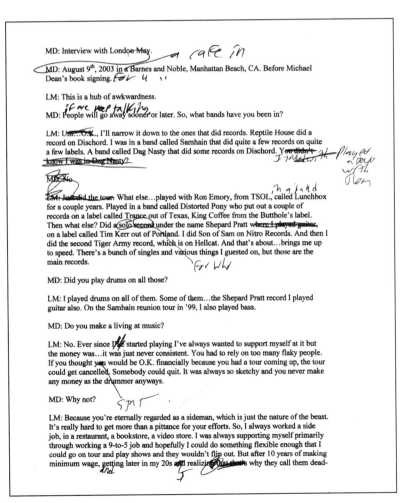

Figure 8.1 *Proofreading 1.*

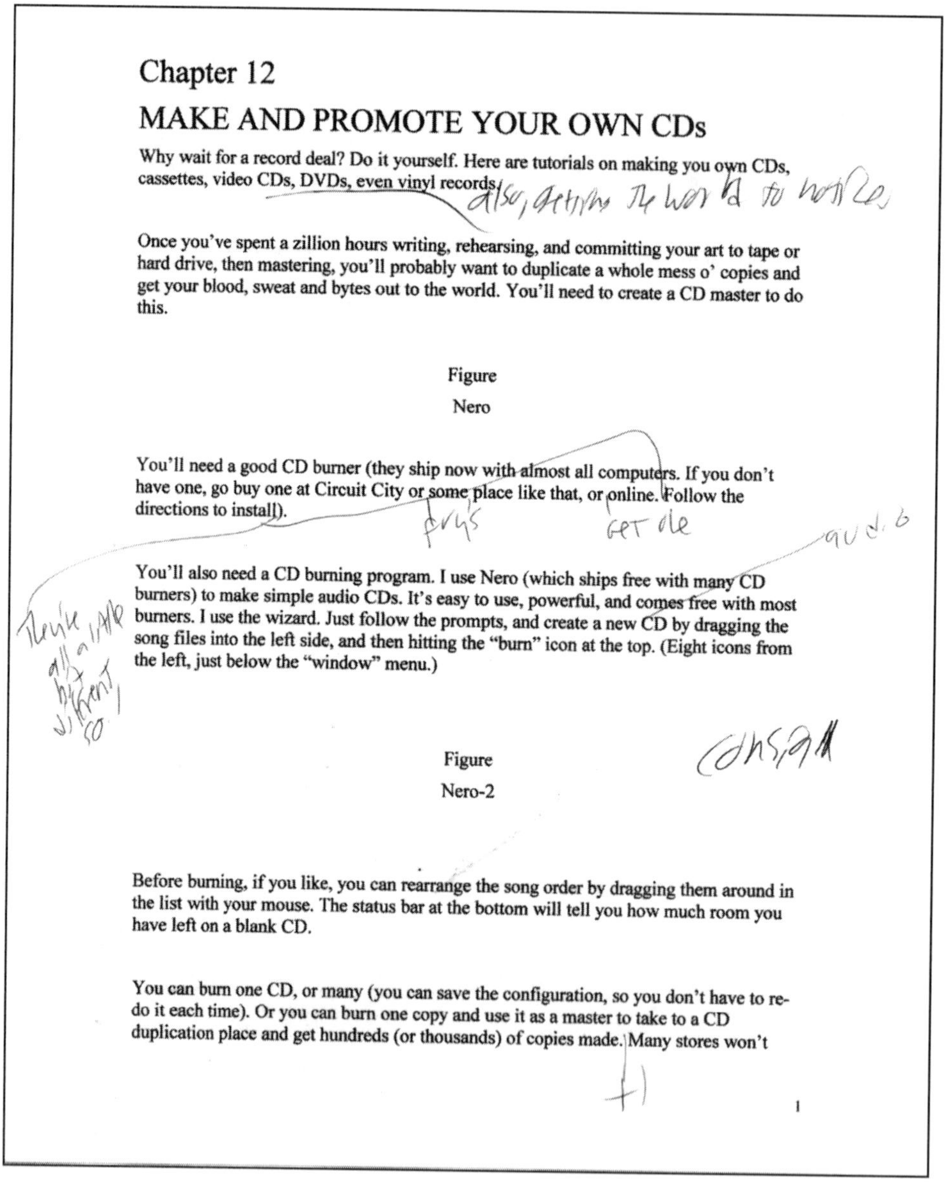

Chapter 12

MAKE AND PROMOTE YOUR OWN CDs

Why wait for a record deal? Do it yourself. Here are tutorials on making you own CDs, cassettes, video CDs, DVDs, even vinyl records. *also, getting the world to notice*

Once you've spent a zillion hours writing, rehearsing, and committing your art to tape or hard drive, then mastering, you'll probably want to duplicate a whole mess o' copies and get your blood, sweat and bytes out to the world. You'll need to create a CD master to do this.

Figure

Nero

You'll need a good CD burner (they ship now with almost all computers. If you don't have one, go buy one at Circuit City or some place like that, or online. Follow the directions to install). *prys* *GET ole* *aud. b*

You'll also need a CD burning program. I use Nero (which ships free with many CD burners) to make simple audio CDs. It's easy to use, powerful, and comes free with most burners. I use the wizard. Just follow the prompts, and create a new CD by dragging the song files into the left side, and then hitting the "burn" icon at the top. (Eight icons from the left, just below the "window" menu.) *They're all different so*

Figure

Nero-2

(dns,9d

Before burning, if you like, you can rearrange the song order by dragging them around in the list with your mouse. The status bar at the bottom will tell you how much room you have left on a blank CD.

You can burn one CD, or many (you can save the configuration, so you don't have to re-do it each time). Or you can burn one copy and use it as a master to take to a CD duplication place and get hundreds (or thousands) of copies made. Many stores won't *+)*

1

Figure 8.2 *Proofreading 2.*

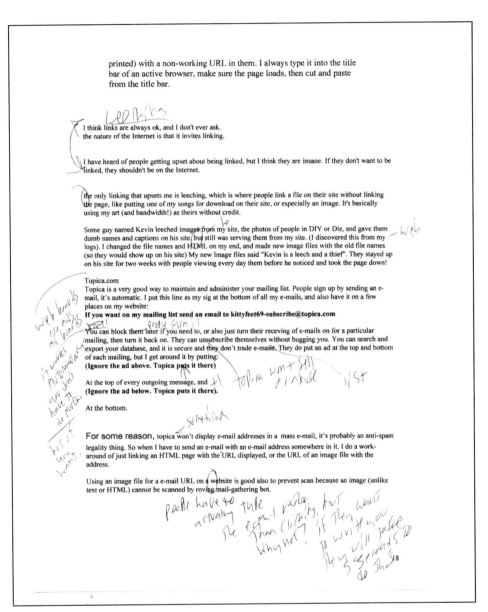

printed) with a non-working URL in them. I always type it into the title
bar of an active browser, make sure the page loads, then cut and paste
from the title bar.

I think links are always ok, and I don't ever ask.
the nature of the Internet is that it invites linking.

I have heard of people getting upset about being linked, but I think they are insane. If they don't want to be
linked, they shouldn't be on the Internet.

the only linking that upsets me is leeching, which is where people link a file on their site without linking
the page, like putting one of my songs for download on their site, or especially an image. It's basically
using my art (and bandwidth!) as theirs without credit.

Some guy named Kevin leeched images from my site, the photos of people in DIY or Die, and gave them
dumb names and captions on his site, but still was serving them from my site. (I discovered this from my
logs). I changed the file names and HTML on my end, and made new image files with the old file names
(so they would show up on his site) My new Image files said "Kevin is a leech and a thief". They stayed up
on his site for two weeks with people viewing every day them before he noticed and took the page down!

Topica.com
Topica is a very good way to maintain and administer your mailing list. People sign up by sending an e-
mail, it's automatic. I put this line as my sig at the bottom of all my e-mails, and also have it on a few
places on my website:
If you want on my mailing list send an email to kittyfeet69-subscribe@topica.com

You can block them later if you need to, or also just turn their receiving of e-mails on for a particular
mailing, then turn it back on. They can unsubscribe themselves without bugging you. You can search and
export your database, and it is secure and they don't trade e-mails. They do put an ad at the top and bottom
of each mailing, but I get around it by putting:
(Ignore the ad above. Topica puts it there)

At the top of every outgoing message, and
(Ignore the ad below. Topica puts it there).

At the bottom.

For some reason, topica won't display e-mail addresses in a mass e-mail, it's probably an anti-spam
legality thing. So when I have to send an e-mail with an e-mail address somewhere in it, I do a workaround of just linking an HTML page with the URL displayed, or the URL of an image file with the
address.

Using an image file for a e-mail URL on a website is good also to prevent scan because an image (unlike
text or HTML) cannot be scanned by roving mail-gathering bot.

Figure 8.3 *Proofreading 3.*

(Look on the CD-ROM in the Goodies folder for proofreading 1 LowREz, proofreading 2 LowREz, and proofreading 3 LowREz to see closeups of these scans.)

Sometimes I'll get a second set of eyes to help. Have people help proof (a person per chapter?). Get people who are good and keep them around. Help them. If they are smart and talented and interesting, keep them as interns/apprentices. (Finding these people gets easier as you get more books published. Eventually *they'll* find *you*.)

I usually type about three or four paragraphs and then, when I get a brain fart (writer's block that lasts about 30 seconds), I spell check that bit and then go back to typing. I also spell check the entire document when I'm done.

Then I print out the whole thing, and I look for stuff that spell check doesn't catch, like using "their" where I mean "there" or "they're," or using "here" when I mean "hear." (There's a term for words that sound the same but are spelled differently and have different meanings. But I can't remember it. And that doesn't matter. See what I mean about the rules? It's far more important to be able to write readable stuff than to be able to dissect it. Many English majors can diagram any sentence perfectly but can't write one worth reading. The same could be said of some English teachers, too.)

You can save ink by printing the document as draft grade output. In Word, it's under File, Print, Options, and check the box for Draft Output. Draft output looks almost as good as regular output and uses less ink. You can also pick Reverse

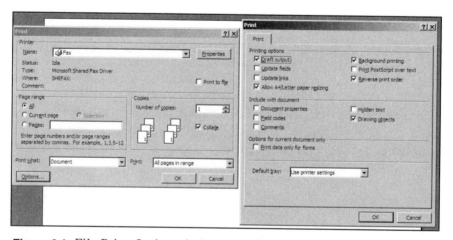

Figure 8.4 *File, Print, Options, check boxes for Draft Output and Reverse Print Order.*

Print Order if you want it to print the last page first and work backward to the first page. This is good because it makes them end up in the correct order (first page on the top).

I don't use standard proofreader's marks. I don't even know what they are. I use my own notation, and it makes sense to me. Sometimes I even use HTML, as I'm also a Web designer. I'll use <P> to mark a paragraph break, <BR> for a line break, and <I> to indicate italics.

I don't use a red pen; I use a normal blue pen, but I do circle mistakes after I notate them to make them easier to find for the next step.

TIP

Blue ink ballpoints work better than black pens for this, because you'll see it better in contrast to the black ink on the printout.

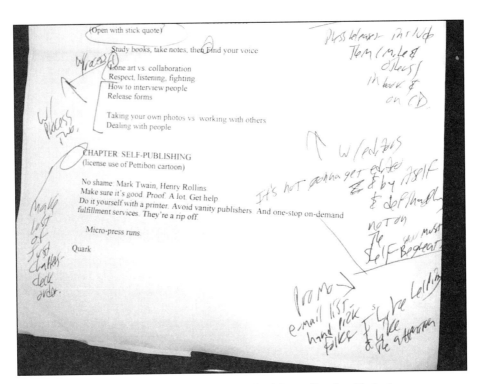

Figure 8.5 *My editing marks on the first draft of the outline for this book.*

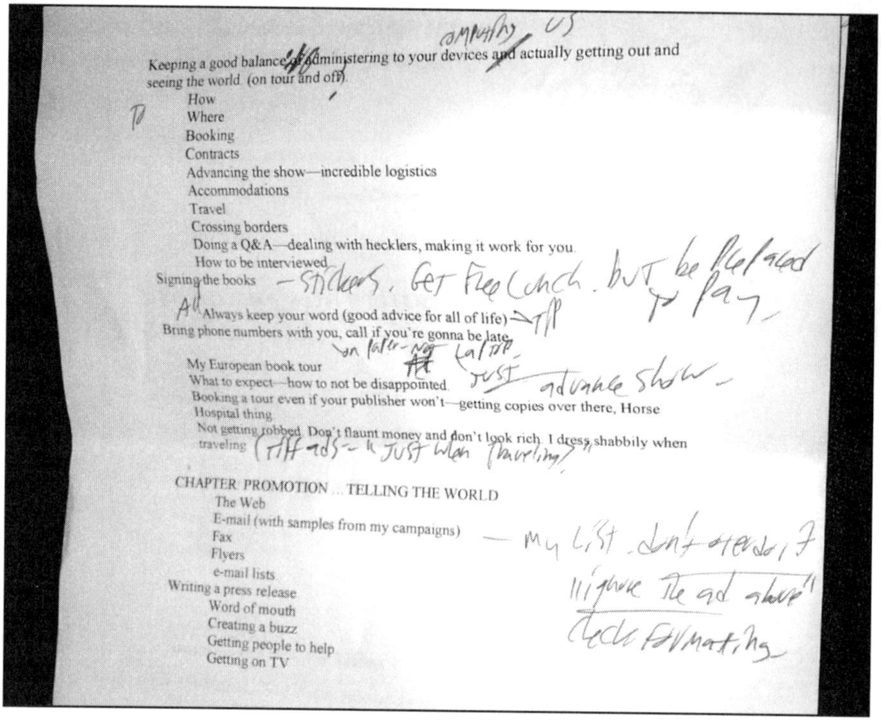

Keeping a good balance of administering to your devices and actually getting out and seeing the world (on tour and off)

How
Where
Booking
Contracts
Advancing the show—incredible logistics
Accommodations
Travel
Crossing borders
Doing a Q&A—dealing with hecklers, making it work for you.
How to be interviewed
Signing the books
Always keep your word (good advice for all of life)
Bring phone numbers with you, call if you're gonna be late
My European book tour
What to expect—how to not be disappointed.
Booking a tour even if your publisher won't—getting copies over there, Horse Hospital thing
Not getting robbed. Don't flaunt money and don't look rich. I dress shabbily when traveling

CHAPTER PROMOTION ... TELLING THE WORLD
The Web
E-mail (with samples from my campaigns)
Fax
Flyers
e-mail lists
Writing a press release
Word of mouth
Creating a buzz
Getting people to help
Getting on TV

Figure 8.6 *My editing marks on the first draft of the outline for this book 2.*

The next step is going through and entering my changes from the paper sheets into the electronic file. Then I back up the file (usually on my portable USB thumb drive) and put the pages in a drawer (I later sell all the rough draft copies with my proofreading scribbles on them on eBay).

TIP

It's far cheaper to get one of those ink cartridge-refilling kits and do it yourself. (And it's fun. They come with a big syringe to squirt the ink into the cartridge.) It works out to like five bucks per 500 pages printed rather than 30 bucks per 500 pages printed. And if you're a working writer, you're probably going to be printing out 500 pages about every two weeks.

So, over the weeks of working on a book, I go back and forth between chapters hammering this out. I have to turn in my progress at the 25 percent point, and at 50 percent, and 75 percent to my editor to get my checks, but I tell him not to start editing yet, because my process involves cutting and pasting from one chapter to another during the whole process right up to the end. So it would get very confusing and require *way* more work on his end if he were to begin editing before I turned in the final edits. Also, don't forget to move the associated images into the proper folders when you move part of a chapter.

TIP

You will have to turn in a CD-ROM of the final images to the editor with your book if your book has pictures. The editor will probably make copies for the copy editor and the tech editor so everyone's literally on the same page, i.e. all looking at the same stuff.

After I've done the whole book like this, I often print out the whole thing and take a second pass through to catch stuff I missed, usually more like fine-tuning. For instance, if it becomes apparent that something from Chapter 10 would go better into Chapter 3, I cut and paste it there. When I finish this, I send chapters off to my editor. At this point, it's pretty close to what finally gets printed in the actual book. I think the problem that a lot of writers have is assuming that an editor will do the first two parts of this process for them. It's a big mistake. First, publishers don't want to deal with anyone who can't self-edit. You are wasting your time if you cannot turn in a manuscript that's 98 percent there. Unless you're a rock star or the president's wife publishing a tell-all book. In that case, they may work with you more. (More on the *politics* of working with an editor and the publisher are covered in Chapter 12, "More on Business.")

When sending chapters to the editor, I zip the files using WinZip (shareware from www.winzip.com) to prevent any of the formatting and file integrity problems that can occur when sending files across the Internet.

To set a password in WinZip, click on the Password button to open the password prompt window and type your password and follow the prompts.

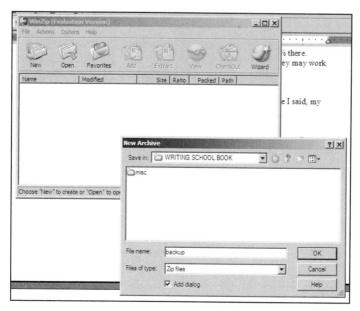

Figure 8.7 *WinZip in action.*

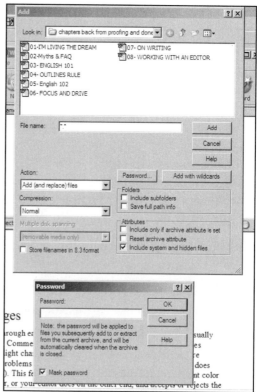

Figure 8.8 *Setting a password in WinZip.*

Tracking Changes

My project editor reads through each chapter and makes a few suggestions. He usually makes them via the Insert Comment feature (Insert, Comment) or the Track Changes feature (Tools, Track Changes, Highlight Changes) in Microsoft Word. (Here is where you're going to run into problems if you're using some other freeware utility that does not support these features.) This feature makes your changes show up as a different color (until you go through later, or your editor does on the other end, and accepts or rejects the changes. Then they turn black like the rest of the text).

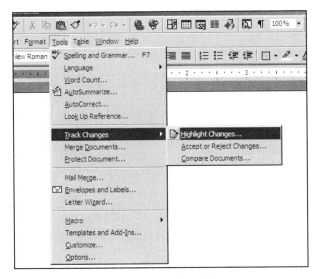

Figure 8.9 *Accessing the Highlight Changes feature.*

Figure 8.10 *Check all three options.*

He and I agree on the changes. And later when the editor is done and wants to accept or reject my changes before passing them on to the final page layout people, he uses the Accept or Reject Changes feature as needed.

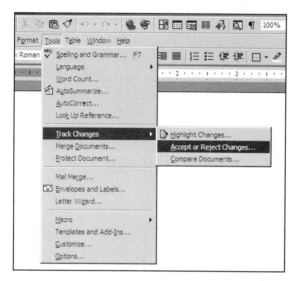

Figure 8.11 *Accessing the Accept or Reject Changes feature.*

Then he has the option to either accept all, reject all, or go through and accept one by one.

Figure 8.12 *Using the Accept or Reject Changes feature.*

When I'm working with non-editors, just friends proofing for me before I send to an editor, or sending a transcribed interview to the interviewee for final approval, I'll use this feature, too. A lot of people don't know what it is. So I tell them. Here's how I explain this easily in an e-mail to people when I need to use the feature with them.

> Do you know how to use the Track Changes feature in Word?
>
> Here's what I did on my end:
>
> Select Tools, Track Changes, Highlight Changes.
>
> Then put a tick mark on all three.

If more than two people are working on this, the computer will put each person's changes in a different color. You'll get a little tip balloon indicating the author of the change by hovering the mouse cursor over it. It will indicate the name of the person the computer is registered to, so if someone is using someone else's computer, it will have the name of the computer's owner, not the person making the changes.

Then on your end, you choose:

> Tools, Track Changes, Accept or Reject Changes.

Then you can accept all changes, reject all changes, or use the right-facing Find button to go down the document and accept or reject each one.

> Turn the feature off when you're done reviewing the changes.

I also usually add this when working with friends:

> I am just telling you how this all works so you can use it later in your own work with people. For what we're doing here, you'll just make your changes, and it will show what you've changed in color. Leave it up to me what to accept or reject later. Thank you.

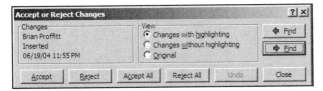

Figure 8.13 *The Accept or Reject Changes feature in action.*

Look at the documents on the CD-ROM in the folder called Showing Versions and Rewrites, in the Marika Stuff subfolder. They're all versions of me playing editor to Marika's interview of me that is in the first chapter of this book. You can see the automatically inserted underlining in the changes I made. That's the Highlight Changes feature in action. She and I did this via e-mail while she was in Prague, and I was on trains all over Europe with my film and my book.

Also check out Interview with Michael Dean by Cassidy Coon.doc in the Showing Versions and Rewrites folder. Then check out Interview with Michael Dean by Cassidy Coon for—The Offices of Max G. Arnold_final_all changes accepted.doc in the Interviews with Michael Dean folder. Compare the first version to the second for more on using the Track Changes feature.

Also, check out the file $30sd09TE_(3) in the Showing Versions and Rewrites folder. This is one of the chapters from *$30 Film School* after going to the copy editor and then to the tech editor and back to me. Note how each editor is assigned a different color by Word. Word knows when it's opened up on a different person's machine. Also in this document, notice the use of production directives like ***Insert Figure 9.42.jpg. Crop to SoundForge screen.***, and the fact that they are labeled Production Directive in the Style menu drop-down menu.

This particular style is not normally used in Word, but is inserted by the use of the Muska/Course standard template (included on the CD-ROM— Goodies/tech book template_Course Technology.doc).

Also note the filename, $30sd09TE_ (3).doc. We will talk about this in a minute.

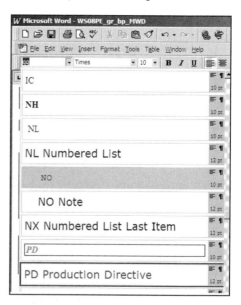

Figure 8.14 *Choosing Production Directive in the Style menu drop-down menu.*

Compare Documents Function

Another cool feature in Word is the Compare Documents function. This allows you to open one document, pick another document (for instance, another version of the same document), and compare the two files. Whatever text is different between the two will show up as underlined red text.

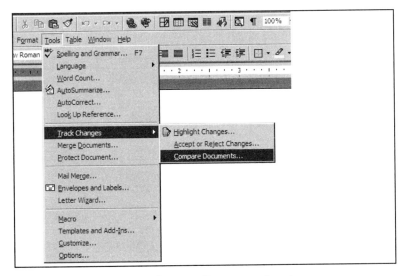

Figure 8.15 *Accessing the Compare Documents function.*

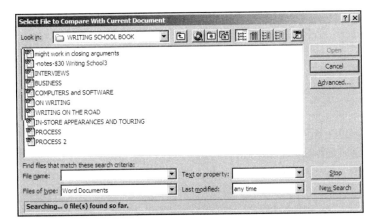

Figure 8.16 *Using the Compare Documents function.*

This is useful if you have two versions of the same file and you can't tell which one is newer by the date you made it. For instance, if you opened both and saved them, the Modified By date would be the same. Or perhaps you had two versions on two computers and forgot and were adding to both of them, and want to find out what to keep from both.

By the way, you can tell the date a file was made and modified (and more information) by right-clicking the mouse and accessing the Properties dialog box, as seen in Figures 8.17 and 8.18.

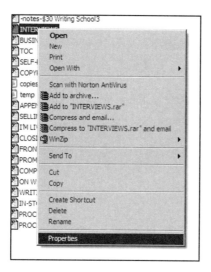

Figure 8.17 *Right-click on an icon to access the Properties dialog box.*

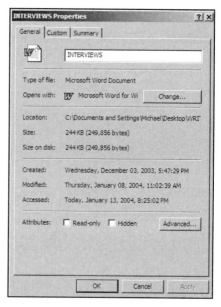

Figure 8.18 *Properties dialog box accessed.*

Windows XP makes this even easier. You can access this information merely by hovering the mouse cursor over the folder or file, and the info will appear (see Figures 8.19 and 8.20).

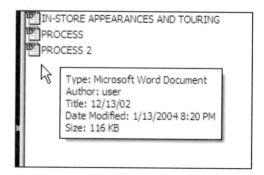

Figure 8.19 *XP hovering mouse trick.*

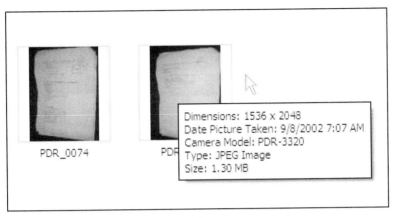

Figure 8.20 *XP hovering mouse trick 2.*

The only time I've ever used the Compare Documents function was as a last-ditch workaround because I lost track of Version Control.

Version Control

Version Control makes sure I am not working on a file and adding to it while my editor is working on the same file. If that happens, you lose changes or have a lot of trouble doing backtracking to fix things.

Basically you want a linear path: A chapter finished by you goes to the project editor. It goes from the project editor to the copy editor. From the copy editor back to you. From you to the project editor. From the project editor (to the tech editor if needed—if it's not a technical chapter, that step is skipped) to the proofreader. From the proofreader to the page layout person. From the page layout person to pre-press. From pre-press to the printer.

This seems straightforward, but it can get complicated under the duress of the deadline of author review. We're all working 10- or 12-hour days on the same project. The book is already listed on Amazon.com for sale, stores have taken orders, and advertising has been purchased. Stuff can get screwed up in this phase if you're not careful.

One thing you *should* do for sure is follow your company's convention for naming subsequent drafts for revisions. This will give you a good chance at preserving document integrity. In other words, this will make sure that you or your editor don't have to proof the same chapter twice.

In the example a few pages back, $30sd09TE_(3).doc means *$30 Film School* Chapter 9. Sandy Doell (sd) has proofed it, and the tech editor has, too. And it's in its third round of getting passed around.

After I look at it and act on Sandy's suggestions, I change the filename to $30sd09TE_(4).doc and send it back to my project editor, Kevin. The (4) at the end of the filename lets him know I've looked it over and made changes. This all saves time and effort, especially during AR where my copy editor, project editor, tech editor, and I are all working 12-hour days for about two weeks to get the thing done, and chapters are flying back and forth via e-mail at an astonishing rate.

TIP

Since I am almost nocturnal and my editor keeps 9-to-5 normal hours, and he is two time zones ahead of me, we almost always have to work asynchronously, via e-mail. We're rarely awake at the same time, so I talk to him on the phone probably only once or twice per book.

Most of the work in modern publishing is now done via e-mail. I didn't even meet anyone at my publishing company face to face until after my second book came out. In January 2004, I sent this out to my list:

I'm signing books this Saturday in Anaheim at NAMM, a music industry manufacturers trade show (part of The International Music Products Association). My publisher has a booth there. Cool! I'll finally get to meet some of the people from my publishing company! All this has been done via e-mail! Never met any of them!

www.thenammshow.com

It's at 800 W. Katella Ave. I'll be in booth 1116 in hall E.

Keep in mind that when you get a publishing deal that comes with an editor, that editor will probably have his own way of doing things, and you'll have to abide by this. They will send you a style guide, a Word document who tells you how they do certain things. If you're a kick-ass writer like me that comes up with a great series that makes them a bunch of money without a lot of stress, you probably can ignore certain stuff, but don't count on it.

My publisher tells me I have to do everything in 10-point text, and I use 12-point. They also tell me in my contract that I have to turn in the final manuscript on a floppy disc along with a printed-out version. I never have printed it out for them and also have never sent them a disc of the whole thing. (My new pooter doesn't even have a floppy drive.) I e-mail individual zipped chapter documents as I finish them.

The Rest of the Process

So . . . my editor makes more changes and e-mails the zipped, changed files back to me. I either make the changes he suggests or come up with compelling reasons why I shouldn't. I e-mail the changed, zipped file back to him to send on to the copy editor. She makes and suggests more changes and returns them to me. I make more changes and send them back. This can get into a high pressure situation at the end of the process when the book's about to go to print, a release date has been sent out in press releases, and it's already listed on Amazon and has been ordered by stores. It can turn into me working 12-hour days, even if I'm on vacation. That is one cool thing about this job: With a laptop I can work from anywhere.

There is one additional step to this process for the chapters that have technical stuff. The documents go through a tech editor, a person who's adept at finding mistakes or unclear explanations in descriptions of computer processes.

TIP

This whole back-and-forth process and protocol and might not work exactly the same with every company, but it will probably be some variation of the process I've outlined here.

Here's a sample of the e-mails going back and forth between my two editors and me:

Michael

Attached are chapters 1, 2, 3, 5, 6, 7 for author review . . . they have been CE'd by Sandy, the copy editor of the Film School book.

A few comments . . .

1. Sandy has made some very worthy points about some of the organization. She suggests some chapters be split up, some added to others, and so on. They are very good comments, and they should make you sit back again at look at the big picture of the book and the logic of some of the organization. Let me know what you think.

2. The first chapter, I think, could be a little stronger. Maybe the Intro should be the first chapter. Sandy has a comment about this also. Let me know what you think of that also.

3. Since this is now officially AR, you can go ahead and number the figures and figure references in the chapters, unless you see that there needs to be discussion of some major chapter reorganization. So, this is kind of like the Film School book, where the great content is all there, but as we go through the chapters, some things start to make more sense, you know?

Also, do you know anyone who might be a good candidate to Tech Edit your chapters? Do you have a musician friend who could review the technical content of software, hardware, equipment, and those types of things for complete accuracy? It would be a pretty easy way for someone to make a few bucks reviewing your content. Let me know what you think of that.

Hope everything's still going well for you . . . when do you return to the States?

Kevin

I told Kevin to get my friend Michael Woody to do the tech editing. It's nice to be able to get paid work for smart, cool friends.

Then I replied to the letter by writing Sandy and CCing Kevin:

```
a couple questions on chapter one:

what do the parts in [] mean here:

Talk about knowing your game. . . .

and

One of my groupies, (Grace—she asked to be mentioned)

------=

also, kevin sent me this:

"The first chapter, I think, could be a little stronger. Maybe
the Intro should be the first chapter. Sandy has a comment
about this also.

Let me know what you think of that also."

—

I don't have an intro. Do you want a separate chapter intro?

I asked Kevin if there was such a document, if he meant to add
to the chapter "band politics" or did he mean "make the intro
chapter one and make 'band politics' chapter two".

Any comments on this?

do you think the band politics chapter needs work other than
making the corrections you suggested? I really don't, but i'm
open to suggestion.
```

For one or two chapters, they will send me a PDF file if something has to be verified, but not for most of it. They did this for me in the *Music School* book, on the chapter that had my guitar and piano chord figures for me to make sure they didn't screw up and put the C chord where it said D chord and such. I guess this would take the place of the paper galleys used in old-school publishing. But things happen a lot faster these days.

NOTE

In old-school printing, and with big-budget books, after all the proofing is done, a "galley" copy is printed and sent to the author to read through and find small changes. With this series, I use the first printing as a galley. I mark it up with a pen and send it to the company, which uses it to make changes. (I also actually photocopy the whole thing before I send it back, in case the company or the overnight service loses it. It takes like 80 (unpaid) hours to proof the whole book, and that's something I don't wanna have to do over.) It makes sense to use the first printing as a galley in tech-type books, as the second pressing is more likely gonna have updates than with a novel anyway. Software has updates, Web addresses change, and so on.

Second printings are done more frequently than they used to be. Advances in printing technology have made it cheaper to do smaller runs. My books are done in print runs of 5,000. Twenty years ago, print runs were almost always 10,000 or more.

Once this is all done, it goes off to the page layout people, then to the printer. I usually get one copy of the book about two weeks before it hits stores, and then a box of 50 a few weeks after it's in stores.

TIP

An outline helps you not to overwrite. The other two books of this series I've overwritten and had to cut some interviews. I don't wanna do that this time. The interviews are what they cut because they're at the end, and the publisher does page layout chapter by chapter in order. They can't go back and cut previous stuff. It would cost way too much money and interrupt their process. It is sort of the book version of the inverted triangle approach used by newspaper writers. (Inverted triangle approach is the process of making an article start with the most important details and work down to the least important at the end. That way, if the editor has to cut text to fit in more ads or whatever, she can cut from the end without thinking very much.)

The publisher had me cut three good interviews from *$30 Music School*, and I had them cheat (widen) the margins and reduce the font size on that chapter to fit all the interviews in. They wanted to cut more. I'm so prolific that I tend to overwrite books these days, even if they are 500-page books I write in four months, and the bean counters won't go past 520 pages at a $30 retail price.

Many publishers will create a related Web site for a book containing errata. Errata can include technical errors, dead Web sites, and information that has changed. This is the nature of technical writing. Stuff changes. (I later sell the copy of my book with my corrections on eBay.)

You generally do this for free because it helps keep your book in print.

Conclusion

We've covered a whole lot really quickly, the stuff you'll need to know to get started writing. You've learned the basics of English, how to write an outline, how to write, how to edit, and how to work with an editor to polish your work even further. Now let's check out the gear you'll be writing with: computers and the software that loves them.

Chapter 9

Hardware

$30 WRITING SCHOOL

People wrote for thousands of years without computers, but I can't really fathom how they did it. I had a typewriter when I was a little kid, and I wrote and even got published (poems) years before I used a computer. But I didn't really get inspired to run with it until I got into computers.

Computer hardware makes the task of editing long, complex documents exponentially easier. Computers are machines to strengthen the brain. And computer software is the magic numerology of zeros and ones, a song written in invisible math that makes this magic possible.

NOTE

Go buy my other two books from this series, *$30 Film School* and *$30 Music School*, even if you only want to write. Both have tons of stuff that will be useful to writers or *any* type of artist. In fact, these books have more things in common than not. Art is art is art, no matter what the medium. The rest is just mechanics.

These three books have a lot that is universal for all artists. This is true not just for the computer information, but also for the promotional tips as well.

Anyway, go get those books and read them, even if you're not a musician and don't plan to ever make your stories into films. (But you should *especially* read the *Film School* book if you want to write for films, even if you don't want to make the film yourself.)

So I'm not going to repeat everything from both that would apply here, because if I did, this book would be over a thousand pages long. In fact, I sort of conceived of these three as a trilogy to be enjoyed together. (My friend Michael Woody suggested selling them together along with my movie, *D.I.Y. or Die: How to Survive as an Independent Artist*, and he jokingly called the proposed boxed set *$99 Loser Academy*. I like that. Because I'm a beautiful loser. Join me. . . .)

Computers are the ultimate sexy alchemy. You have a spinning loadstone sending shivers through gold hairs to crystallized sand into glowing phosphorus shocked with the controlled lightning of fast math.

I need a computer to write. But you don't need the top-of-the-line model. You really don't need that much. We'll cover it all here.

So, the usual thing I cover in this part is the Mac versus PC thing. But I think that in a writing book I should first cover typewriter versus computer (with some side forays into other, cheaper solutions), then laptop versus desktop, *then* Mac versus PC. That may seem backward, but it's not. I think for most people the whole *argument* is backward. Mac versus PC just ain't that important anymore, especially in writing. But be patient, grasshopper. We'll get there in a few flicks of a cat's tail.

Typewriter versus Computer

I say the computer wins. I guess there may still be some people who write on a typewriter, but I can't imagine it. Even Cubby (Hubert Selby, Jr.—see the interview on the CD-ROM), who started writing in the '50s on a manual typewriter, uses a computer.

I still see typewriters as icons of The Writer ill in movies and even books. The very cool movie *State and Main* has the writer of a film unable to complete the script until he finds a suitable manual typewriter on which to work. There's even a saying about the predictability of the film industry that says, "Hollywood: There's one typewriter in that town and a thousand Xerox machines." (Actually, this saying probably predates computers being common. The film industry has been predictable and bland for a long time. They even allude to this with the dustbowl Okie (as in Oklahoma) joke in the 1950 film *Sunset Boulevard.*) Regardless, I think you're a masochist if you insist on writing on a typewriter in this day and age. They hurt your hands and aren't very portable, and most importantly, if you write something brilliant that someone wants to publish, eventually you're going to have to pay someone to type it into a computer.

NOTE

The exception would be if you don't mind your final product *looking* like it was done on a typewriter. You could technically take your typed pages and have offset printing rolls photographically made from them. You can also photocopy the pages into a zine. I've seen this done, but not for a while. You'd better be good at spelling, though, or not care. Computers have spell check, typewriters don't.

The only reason I can see to use a typewriter, other than some insane romantic throwback to the good olde days you never experienced (and this would be all about image and not about pragmatism, which is antithetical to the $30 Way), is absolute poverty. You can probably get a typewriter at a yard sale or the Salvation Army now for 20 bucks. But then again, you can get an older computer that will swim circles around a typewriter for maybe 75 bucks. So there.

Okay, there is one reason that I could see favoring a typewriter over a computer: lack of distraction. I can't check my mail on a typewriter. I can't open an image editing program and mess around to kill time. I can't watch a movie on a typewriter. But then again, all the other functions of a computer help when I write these books. In fact, these days I've started working on *two* computers at the same time: one to write, and one to do the high-end stuff that I need for making these books—video editing and rendering, sound stuff, CD-ROM mastering, photo manipulation, even online research. It really helps to have two computers for this.

My next book is a novel. I may consider getting a third computer, another laptop, on which I would *only* work on that novel, because a novel does not require all that other crap. It seems liberating to me to have only one project (the novel) and one program (Microsoft Word) loaded on a virgin computer.

NOTE

And it would run *really* fast. The more crap you load on a hard drive, the more it bogs down. And a computer with no Internet connection wouldn't get a virus very easily.

But I doubt I will do this. I like access to all my toys in one place.

NOTE

Gently vacuum the dust out of all computers and peripherals (such as DSL modems and printers). Vacuum especially where there are fans or vents where air (and dust) gets sucked inside. Also, unplug and *carefully* vacuum inside once a month or so. Be careful and unplug it! Do not get shocked. Just because I'm willing to die for my art doesn't mean you should be.

Laptop versus Desktop

You get more computing power for your money if you sacrifice mobility. My new laptop cost 650 bucks new. I could have gotten twice the power and speed for that price in a generic desktop computer.

> **NOTE**
>
> Generic means non-branded. I *always* buy non-branded computers when I can. They are the one thing that you usually aren't screwing yourself with if you get them made locally. And they are *way* cheaper.
>
> Unfortunately, there are no generic laptops. This is because laptops are not modular the way desktop units are. Laptops have to have all the parts fit together in a tight area, so they have to be custom designed, and all the parts have to be made to work in concert with each other.
>
> There are cheaper, non-brand name laptops. Two sources are Eurocom (http://eurocom.com/) and AOpen (http://store.myaopen.com/index.html). But you will not get the huge differences in price you'd get between brand name and no-name desktops. And my brand name Toshiba laptop, with out-of-box discount and rebate, was cheaper than these non-discounted no-names. But check 'em out. My deal was uncommon, and you might do better at either of these sites.

I resisted getting a laptop for a long time. I had a clunky one a long time ago that couldn't even run Windows, and it weighed 22 pounds and ran only half an hour on a battery charge, so I don't count that.

Laptop Computers

Laptop computers (also called notebook computers or, if they're really fast, desktop replacement computers) are magic. These are dream machines. A laptop is, at minimum, an ultraportable typewriter with access to the world's libraries. I love mine. It makes me free to travel the world and work from anywhere.

> **NOTE**
>
> Laptops get stolen a lot. Guard yours well.

About four months ago, I got my first good laptop. I'm glad I waited this long. I usually do that—I wait until all the first-adopters work out the bugs and drive down the price, and then I buy *cheap* and catch up and pass them up, in terms of output, in a matter of months.

But I finally had to get a laptop. As I got more success in film and writing, I found myself traveling a lot. And traveling with a lot of downtime. In Europe I was spending up to six hours a day on trains, every day for two months. The vagabond, hippie lifestyle *demands* a laptop. So I broke down and got one.

> **NOTE**
>
> For a while I had two computers: the desktop and the laptop. But then I traded the desktop to Newt for a car (a Supra!). I like having just the laptop. It's kinda Zen. Simplifies my room and my life. And I don't need two computers because I'm almost done with this book. My next book is gonna be that novel written in the second person.

Most laptops have a touch pad built in that functions as a mouse. I don't use mine much. In fact, I'm so mouse-dependent that when I recently forgot my mouse when I went to the coffee shop to write, I got there, ate my bagel, and came home. Using the touch pad works for some (especially "writers" who write but never edit), but it's a lot more work for me than a mouse. I am constantly cutting and

pasting and moving stuff from chapter document to chapter document and taking screen-shots and cropping them in Photoshop in the course of a typical writing day (especially in the later stages of writing one of these books). So I *need* that mousie.

Figure 9.1 *Old photo of my laptop with my old e-mail address on it.*

NOTE

If you have a non-optical mouse, one of the old ones that actually has a rubber-covered steel ball inside, the rollers that touch the ball will become slow and hard to use with time. You can fix this by opening them up. (Push down on the small round covering on the bottom. You'll probably turn it counterclockwise about 45 degrees.) Clean the gunky scum and dust off the plastic rollers with the blade of a pair of scissors or a paperclip. Rollers turn, so it can be tricky. Or you can just buy a new mouse. This kind is about five bucks.

Write your name and e-mail address (an e-mail address you can check from other computers, not just this one) on all your computers, cameras, and other peripherals. If it gets lost, it may actually get found by an honest person. Maybe not, but maybe. Besides, what have you got to lose?

A silver pen (available at any stationery store) works well for this, except with Apple stuff that is often silver-colored. Use a black pen for this. You can also print stickers on your computer.

Don't worry about lowering the value of the gear. If you're a real writer, you'll run it into the *ground* before you have a chance to sell it.

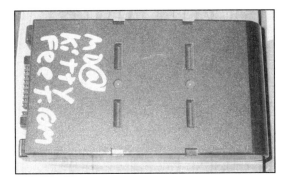

Figure 9.2 *My extra laptop battery with my e-mail address on it.*

Figure 9.3 *My laptop wireless card and FireWire card.*

Figure 9.4 *The back of my laptop wireless card and FireWire card with my e-mail address on it.*

Sent out to my e-mail list just before I went to Europe:

I'm excited! I'm leaving Saturday morning to fly to London for my "WORLD IN A BACKPACK" tour 2003.

I have a show almost every day for six weeks, in five countries, so don't be offended if I don't answer e-mail as much as usual. I'm mostly gonna be traveling and working. But I promise to take lots of photos.

Just bought a BITCHIN' new laptop, so I can do author review with my publisher via e-mail on "$30 Music School" while I spend every day sitting on a train. And write "$30 Writing School." (After that one, I hope to get back to some actual WRITING. I might even write another novel. . . .)

I got my laptop at a local MegaloMart-type place. I don't like to order computers on line. I need to check them out in person, because the most important feature for me is if I like the key click. And I like the key click on this one. Some high-end tricked-out laptops have clunky key clicks. Doesn't make me feel inspired at all. It's too much like WORK to use them.

It's a Toshiba Satellite A15-S127 Notebook PC with Intel Celeron Processor 2.0GHz. It was $990 with tax. (It was an open-box model, but fine and guaranteed. Someone bought it, assumed it had a floppy drive, and returned it when they discovered it didn't.) That took a hundred off the price. And it had a $250 rebate, so it was 650 bucks! What a kick-ass deal.

When buying a computer in a store, ask if they have any "out-of-box" or open-box models. This means someone bought it, and returned it in less than a week. They check it out 'cause it's still under warranty, it's just that someone else has already had it and returned it.

The computer also has one dead pixel. With many companies, up to six dead pixels is acceptable for sale. Six you'll notice. I barely notice the one dead one. Only when watching movies from DVD and it's completely black before the credits and I see the one tiny white dot.

And they have a deal you have to ask for sometimes; if it goes on sale within 30 days of buying it, they refund you the difference.

I added two 512-meg memory modules and sold the original 256-meg module it came with on eBay for 20 bucks.

Total cost with upgrade and cheap FireWire card: under 1100 bucks with tax after rebate.

NOTE

When searching for things on eBay, try searching misspellings. Sometimes people type something wrong and then no one bids on it. You can sometimes get stuff for a steal like that.

Later a guy at the MegaloMart here said they don't give the rebate on my computer for out-of-box items, but I got it anyway because I lost the box and sent a photocopy of the bottom of the computer showing the serial number instead. The store guy thought I did it intentionally. I didn't, but it's good to know. (Dude, this is an easy one. You're a working citizen of the only remaining Super Power on Earth! God Bless America! If you've demonstrated no dishonor, your word is honorable until it's not. The clerk must take you at face value (he should have been made to salute you at the start and conclusion of your transaction) or substantiate a cause for discrimination. In America, we think discrimination is bad. Evil, even. It is, after all, all for one and one for all, this being a union and all, because, if we don't stand together, we'll hang apart, divided and conquered. And so on. Well, at least that's the mood in San Francisco in 2004 for some of the more affluent. It's better than nothing, I'm told.)

I also bought one of those 128-meg USB key chain removable drives. It's equal to 80 floppy drives. It rocks. I also put a text file on it called "read me if found" that said,

> "read me if found:
>
> this device belongs to Michael dean, who
>
> is on tour of Europe with the DIY or DIE
>
> film. If found, please e-mail him at
>
> mwd@kittyfeet.com
>
> to get it back to him.
>
> thank you.
>
> Md."

Laptops pretty much rock. I love them. Once I got mine, I traded my desktop computer for a car. (1981 Supra. Pretty good deal.)

But the screws on laptops tend to get loose if you carry them around a lot. Gently tighten the screws on the back every few months if needed.

Also, you need to run them on batteries once a month until the battery is dead, even if you are not traveling and are home running on AC all the time. Cycling (fully depleting) the battery like this will extend the life of the battery a lot. If you have two batteries, do this with both of them once a month. Especially on long European train rides!

Be sure to save often if you're working while the battery is running down, as you will lose work if your pooter powers off without first saving it. Save often anyway. Make it a habit. And back up your files.

Desktop Computers

They're boring. But they work. I don't have much to say about them.

I buy mine from a local "screwdriver shop"—a place in the neighborhood that puts computers together from parts. About half the price of name brands and fully guaranteed. But no tech support in English usually, so not a good first computer. In San Francisco they are often made by Chinese families. In Los Angeles, Mexican families. It's usually mom, pop, and the teens doing the assembly, little kids running errands, and grandma answering the phone.

These units are cheap, and they work fine. I wrote much of *$30 Film School* and *$30 Music School* on one. (Until I traded it for the car.)

> **NOTE**
>
> You can also buy stuff refurbished. That means previously used, returned quickly, checked out by the manufacturer as good as new, fully guaranteed, and sold to you for 1/3–1/2 off.
>
> Try www.Refurbdepot.com.

Keyboards

Ergonomic keyboards take the strain off your wrists. I highly recommend them if you get any wrist pain at all. They're about 30 bucks.

(Hey . . . if any PC laptop manufacturers ever get it together to make a laptop with a built-in ergonomic keyboard, send me one. I'll talk it up for sure.)

> **TIP**
>
> Keep coffee and beer (and any other stuff you might drink) away from keyboards, computers, and other gear. When you lift a glass with liquids, lift it around the keyboard, not over it.

Figure 9.5 *Ergonomic keyboard.*

Backing Up

A writer I know in Los Angeles wrote a novel and lost the completed manuscript before it could be published. It was on her laptop, which was destroyed by an earthquake. She had worked on it for years and got very bummed out about it.

I am incredibly anal about backing up stuff. Some girl at a party once made fun of me for it. A week later her laptop with her novel on it got stolen out of her car. She had no backup.

(I know this all sounds like the beginning of a chain letter, but I swear it's true.)

In 12 years of non-stop all-day-every-day daily computing, I've only lost one file, and I think it was the universe playing a joke on me. It was the list of women I'd slept with.

My work, any work, on a computer is worth far more to me than the computer it's on. Every few minutes while working, I hit Ctrl+S to save the file in case the computer crashes or the power goes out (or the cat unplugs the computer, which does happen). Every day I back up the day's work to my thumb drive and keep it in my pocket. If I'm working a lot, I'll do it twice in a day. Once a week I back up to CDs (good in case your computer gets viralized. There will, at some point, be a unviral backup on a disc) and keep them at a friend's house.

I also make a zip file of what I've been working on, password protect it, and upload it to a server in another state, in case California is destroyed by an earthquake and I somehow live. (Since I travel a lot, there is a good chance I would. There's another reason I bring extra backups on

Figure 9.6 *Weekly backup.*

password-protected data DVDs of *everything* when I leave the state or country: so that when it all goes *down*, I will just stay wherever I am.)

TIP

All I ever need is a laptop and a pretty girl.

When I'm near the end of a project, where it could conceivably be finished without me, I send all the images on a CD-ROM to my editor and let him know where the backups are online and what the password is, so it can be finished in case I die.

My friend and I both lost everything on our laptops to viruses. (I was trying to install some downloaded stuff, and forgot to scan it.) She lost some data and spent a lot of money having a shop fix it for her. I sent her this:

> Thankfully I'm dating a total computer nurd programmer gal at the moment. Artist (design student), but she knows ten times as much about computers as me. She was here petting my cat when my pooter went down. An hour later she had it deviralized, up and running with a fresh install of Windows XP, literally good as new. Sans my data, which I'd backed up the night before.

> Now that I'm writing for a living, I burn CDs of my books in progress, and all the image files and all the time. And I back up the files for the book every day on a thumb drive that I take with me when I leave. And leave the CD backups at a girlfriend's house.

> I'm totally compulsive about this stuff lately. And if you think I'm spending too much time on this, just wait until you lose a lot of work. You'll see. . . .

> Use a good antiviral program. (I use Norton Antivirus by Symantec. It rocks. So does McAfee virus scan.) Download updates once a week and run a complete scan once a week (you can set it to do this automatically). Make sure you set it to check e-mail attachments. Even so, don't click on stuff you're not expecting. I delete most of the crap my friends send me that they think is cute. I ain't online to be cute or giggle. I'm trying to change the world. And your cute little game is, at worst, gonna wipe me out, and at best, gonna waste my time.

They say, "It's not *if* you'll have a crash, it's *when* you'll have a crash." I've had two (actually, one hard drive failure and one virus that wiped out a hard drive). And I didn't lose much with either because I back up nervously and regularly.

I hit Ctrl+S a lot to save as I'm typing, in case my computer crashes. I like doing this better than allowing AutoSave to do it, which takes a second to work and interrupts my flow. I'd rather do it myself. I disable AutoSave in the preferences of most programs.

At the end of a day when I've written a lot, I will usually back up the day's work on my thumb drive and keep it separate from my computer. You don't want it in the same place as the computer in case of fire or theft. When I had a car, I used to keep my weekly backups on password-protected CDs in the trunk of my car on the street so I'd still have my work in case my house burned down. My backups are worth more to me than the computer. Computers are expendable and infinitely replaceable. Work isn't. I could never type the same chapter the same way.

You can also back up stuff by e-mailing it to yourself on a Hotmail or Yahoo! mail account or burning backups on a CD or floppy disc, though more and more new laptops don't have a floppy drive. Floppies are becoming obsolete because they don't store that much, and media these days is increasingly robust, and the file sizes get larger and larger each year.

The full Word files for a book of mine probably would be only about 1 meg or a little more-and would fit on a floppy. The thing that wouldn't fit on that floppy would be all the high-rez image files for the book (all the files for *$30 Film School* totaled about one gig and required two CDs to back up). The files for the CD-ROMs that come with my books total another 700 megs and, of course, fit on one CD-ROM.

You can also back up projects on a rewriteable DVD, which holds 4.7 gigs, more than enough for *all* the files for all three of my books and the associated images and CD-ROM. I used to back up once a week and keep it in my car, in case my house gets hit by a meteor while I'm at the store.

TIP

Always have a pen with you. Don't leave the house without it. And if you find yourself in a situation with an idea and no pen, you can call yourself from a phone and leave the idea on your own voice mail.

Lydia adds, "Maybe mention about writers who've lost novels in progress due to house fires: Maxine Hong Kingston rewrote *The Fifth Book of Peace* because her first burned with her house."

TIP

Copy and paste, then delete. Don't just cut and paste—with text blocks as well as with files. That way you don't lose data if something crashes or you lose power during the operation.

I like doing CD-ROM and DVD backups at least once a week. They're more permanent than anything backed up on a hard drive or thumb drive. Magnetic drives like hard drives, thumb drives, floppy discs, iPods, and so on are all susceptible to magnetic fields. If terrorists develop pulse bombs or a UFO lands in your backyard, the electromagnetic radiation is probably gonna erase all magnetic drives, but optical storage mediums like CD-ROMs and DVDs will probably be cool.

Pocket USB drives for backup are great. They fit in your pocket and can hold between 16 megs and two gigs (gigabytes). Mine holds 128 megs and cost 50 bucks. I keep a backup of my current book on me most of the time (password protected in case I lose it) in case my house burns down. I don't leave my home without it. (Michael Woody adds, "Calamity befalling your domicile is a recurring theme. Your automobile is often considered a place of sanctuary. You've been in LA too long.") (Again with the house in peril!)

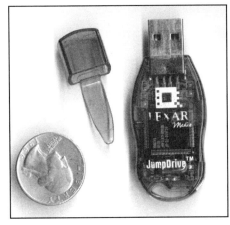

Figure 9.7 *Pocket 128-meg USB drive.*

Figure 9.8 *Pocket 128-meg USB drive, other side.*

You can use them for backup or to move stuff back and forth from one computer to the other without networking them.

They're pretty hardy. I don't recommend this, but mine accidentally went through the wash. It still worked fine afterward.

TIP

Often when you've using a network in a public place (like a university library), the admin has crippled certain privileges, like installing software. You can sometimes get around this by installing small programs on a USB drive and actually running them from the drive. I was able to use an FTP program (WS_FTP—it's small, simple, one of the oldest, and definitely the best, in my opinion) to update my Web site and back up some of my work from the library at the University of Manchester in England, even though I was unable to install my FTP program there.

In Windows XP, NT, or 2000, as soon as you plug a thumb drive into a USB port, it automatically assigns a new drive letter.

Then you can copy or paste to and from it as if it were a drive on your computer, remove it when you're done, and slip it into your pocket. (Some are even wearable!)

You can get ones that are password protected, and Linkyo and a few others even make ones that are thumbprint biometric protected! That way, if you lose it, you don't have someone in possession of your project.

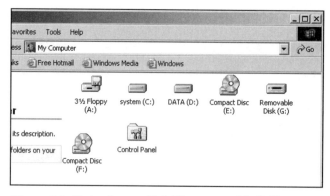

Figure 9.9 *Drive letter added (G—removable disk).*

> **TIP**
>
> If you travel a lot and are going to run into older Windows operating systems a lot, you can download the drivers for your USB drive from the manufacturer's Web site and keep them on a CD-ROM with you.

Pocket USB drives are made by lots of manufacturers (didn't anyone patent this thing?). The 128 and 256 meg ones are reasonably priced, like 50 and 75 bucks, respectively. You can back up a whole book on one, and then some.

> **TIP**
>
> If your USB drive stops being able to hold the capacity it's supposed to, simply reformat it. (Back up the info on it first, as formatting will delete the data.) Right-click on the drive letter from My Computer and select Format. Hit Start and wait until it's done.

Pocket USB drives that hold a gig and up are gonna set you back several hundred dollars. I backed up this whole book, all the high-rez images, and the stuff from the CD-ROM on one and kept it on my key chain the whole time I was writing this book. That way, even if my house was stolen by housejackers while I was out, I'd still be able to get the book out. And the book is worth more to me than everything in the apartment. (Except the cat, and she's usually outside when I'm gone.)

> **TIP**
>
> An iPod is basically just a hard drive. You can use one to for backing up any data, not just for storing and listening to MP3s. Same with a digital camera. I've used them to move non-photographic data from one computer to another. They just show up as a new drive letter, just like a USB drive.

Tweaking Windows to Do Your Bidding

Most new PC laptops come loaded with Windows XP. It's pretty good, but I hate the way it looks. I hate the fact that a company has to change a working and familiar interface just to justify the higher price, when the stuff behind the appearance justifies that price hike. I guess stupid people need to look at something different to figure they're getting their money's worth.

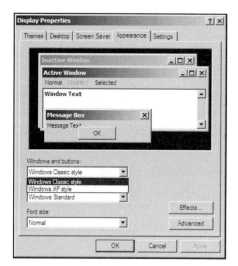

Figure 9.10 *Select Windows Classic Style from the drop-down menu.*

Figure 9.11 *Right-click the Start button and select Properties.*

I like the new functions, but the old look was fine. So I set it up to look like Windows 98. Go to Settings, Control Panel, Display, Appearance tab, Windows Classic Style, Apply, OK.

Then, right-click on the Start button (bottom left of screen), go to Properties, and select the Classic Start menu.

Figure 9.12 *Select the Classic Start menu.*

When I get a new computer, it takes me about a week to get it loaded up and set up the way I like. There are utilities that enable you to clone one hard drive to another, such as Norton Ghost, but I would be cloning all the problems I've acquired after a year of having and using a computer. The new cloned one will run slow, and will have all the broken shortcuts, registry problems, and so on. Cloning hard drives is most commonly used to create large numbers of identical laptop or desktop configurations for large numbers of drone employees performing identical droning tasks, as found in large corporations or the government.

I prefer cracking open a virgin machine and taking her for a spin and getting to know her. You know how it is: the joy of tweaking a new machine to do your bidding . . . like housebreaking a cat . . . or teaching a new lover what makes you purrrrrrr. . . .

I love getting a new computer. It makes me hot.

TIP

Donate your old computers to schools or other non-profits. (But format the hard drive first to eliminate all your data.) It's good karma, *and* you'll get a tax write-off.

Passwords

I put a password on my laptop so that if it's stolen, people can't get at my data. They could format the hard drive and resell it, but it would delete my data. Which is what I would want, as I would have it backed up, and I wouldn't want them to have it.

To put a password on a computer in Windows XP, go to Start, Settings, Control Panel, then double-click User Accounts.

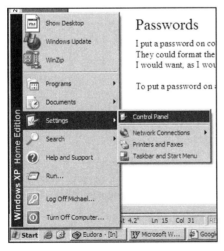

Figure 9.13 *Accessing the Control Panel.*

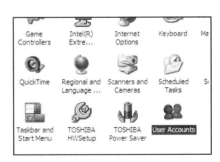

Figure 9.14 *Double-click on User Accounts.*

Pick a task...

- Change an account
- Create a new account
- Change the way users log on or off

or pick an account to change

Michael
Computer administrator

Guest
Guest account is off

Figure 9.15 *Pick the account to change.*

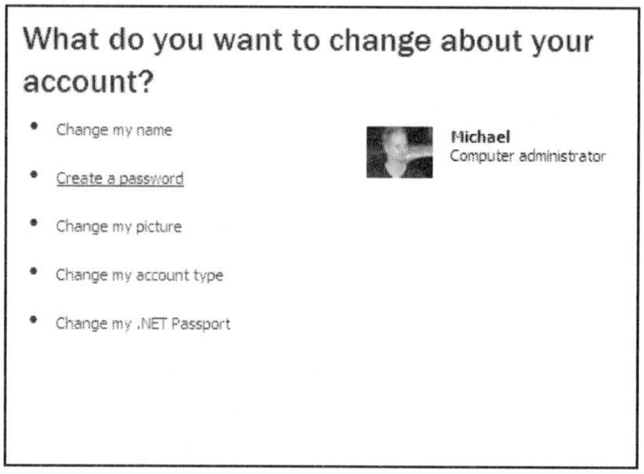

What do you want to change about your account?

- Change my name
- Create a password
- Change my picture
- Change my account type
- Change my .NET Passport

Michael
Computer administrator

Figure 9.16 *Click on Create a Password.*

Create a password for your account

Type a new password:

••••••••

Type the new password again to confirm:

••••••••

If your password contains capital letters, be sure to type them the same way every time you log on.

Type a word or phrase to use as a password hint:

The password hint will be visible to everyone who uses this computer.

[Create Password]   [Cancel]

Figure 9.17 *Follow the prompts to create a password.*

Short passwords are probably okay for this. You're going to be typing it a lot. And if someone really wants in, he will get in. This is just to keep the casual user out. Also, if it gets stolen by an idiot, he won't be able to hack your data or sell it easily.

Note that the password is masked as you're typing it, so if someone is looking over your shoulder, they won't see it. You can set a way to retrieve it if you fail, but don't make the password or hint so obvious that someone can guess it.

Wireless

Wireless is totally cool. I have it on my laptop and can go anywhere in my house or yard and work. If it's not too sunny, I go work on my second-story back porch with my feet up on the ledge, typing and answering e-mails. I love to do this and sip iced coffee as the sun is going down.

> Got my laptop wireless! Heck yeah!
>
> It's fun. Freedom, sort of.
>
> Hub: Netgear MR814 (802.11 a/b).
>
> Price: 70 dollars on Amazon.
>
> Card: Proxim model 8461-05.
>
> Price: 50 dollars from manufacturer.

By the way, with this setup, five people can share one DSL line with little noticeable speed loss. Cheap! Wire up your roommates. It will work wired or wireless and is easy to configure. And wireless works up to 150 feet (with line of site to antenna. More like 50 feet without).

TIP

If you have a DSL line, you often have a dial-up account for free. If you trust your friend, you could give her your dial-up number (available on the service provider's Web site), username, and password, and she could configure the Windows dialer (Start, Settings, Network Connections, New Connection Wizard) to get free dial-up at a different house than where you get your DSL.

Also, two people could split a simple dial-up account from two different locations, but they can't usually dial in at the same time.

Both of these tricks are probably not legal, so I'm just saying you *could* do this, not that you *should* do this. I would never recommend you do anything illegal.

I wonder about the safety of wireless laptops and other devices, though. They say it's safer and has less energy emission than a cell phone, but I don't know about the idea of having a little microwave transmitter sitting on your groin. Might make you sterile.

> **TIP**
>
> Again, I would never recommend that you do anything illegal, but I am told that when people install, um, "borrowed" software, it helps their chances of the installation working and also of them not getting caught if they turn off their Internet connection while installing. That way, the software can't "tattle" on you and abort the installation.

Mac versus PC

In the end, it's six of one, a half-dozen of the other. More or less.

I just don't like the contentious implication some have that "if you use PCs, you ain't a true artist," because I know so many great artists who use PCs.

I've done tons of art in many media using many computer programs on computers since 1992. All of them were PCs. And my art kicks ass.

(And for some reason, it seems like every wannabe screenwriter in every coffee shop in Los Angeles uses a Mac iBook.)

> **TIP**
>
> If you write in a coffee shop, do not leave your laptop unattended for any reason at all. I see idiots do this so often, I wanna rip them off and run out the door on my skateboard and skate around the block and then bring their laptop back just to make a point.
>
> When I'm at a coffee shop and even go to the bathroom, I take my laptop with me.

Macs used to be better than PCs. That's evened out so much that the only difference I can see (especially for writers) is that PCs are cheaper. I think that people who claim otherwise might be engaging in parroting, nostalgia, and chauvinism. If you're gonna do that, go all the way and just get a typewriter!

I think it can also depend on how your mind works. Some people just find one OS (operating system) more intuitive than another.

I think Apple sells their image and consciously markets it with a bit of snobbery. I feel like it's kind of like a cult, like Apple sees itself as fuzzy Berkeley hippies, but they seem to imply that Bill Gates is Satan.

In fact, Microsoft pulled Apple out from the brink of bankruptcy in the 80s, and Microsoft owns some stock in Apple. A lot, considering they are alleged rivals.

I think Microsoft allows Apple to continue to exist to keep itself from being a literal monopoly, which is a legal problem.

TIP

Michael Woody jokes that the My Computer icon on your desktop doesn't mean that it's *your* computer, it means that it's Bill Gates' computer. I replaced the icon on my system to reflect this. My My Computer icon is a little photo of Gates.

And Apple is just as satanic as Microsoft in my mind. They're both huge corporations that want to devour everything. And I think Apple hasn't been a bunch of fuzzy hippies since about 1981. I hate the whole argument.

I just love computers, all computers, and don't like to get into pissing contests.

I love the products of both these companies. Advances from both of these companies have literally allowed me to quit my day job.

I have absolutely no problem playing with the toys of aggressive multinational globalization. It's like dancing on the graves of the Mammon-worshiping living-dead devils in suits.

I'm fiddling while they burn.

TIP

Computers used to display text only. They were hard to use, requiring extensive knowledge of arcane and elaborate strings of commands. Xerox invented the first GUI (graphical user interface). Apple "borrowed" it from them. Then Microsoft "borrowed" it from Apple.

Interestingly, Xerox originally developed it only to teach programming to children. They didn't envision that adults would use it.

Linux

Linux is an open-source, free-of-charge operating system. It was put together via the Internet by thousands of very smart people worldwide. Unlike Windows or Mac, it's easy to "get under the hood" and change stuff you don't like, or add something you wish was there, if you know what you're doing. If you don't know what you're doing, there are easy-to-use Linux programs for everything from Web browsers to networking to video editing to word processing. (I included a Linux version of the word processor AbiWord on the CD-ROM in the Software folder.)

Many countries are pushing Linux, even at the government level. China is also going Linux for government agencies. (I heard they were just openly bootlegging Microsoft before.) Other countries that want to cut down reliance on Microsoft and the U.S. make location-specific versions, even naming word processors after local poets.

Many of the squats I stayed at in Europe were running Linux, and some people were very adamant about it, even getting mad at me when I would open my laptop running Windows. Whatever. I don't dig the self-righteousness. (They're still running that free hippie Linux OS on hardware made by heartless multinationals. The day I see a punk rocker make his own hard drive, chip, and motherboard, I'll consider their argument valid.) But I can see their point; Linux makes sense, and it's free. I'm just used to Windows, and when something ain't broke, I don't fix it.

I think that Microsoft actually considers Linux a threat, judging by the fact that the Microsoft Word spell check refuses to acknowledge the word "Linux" as a real word! Also, a Google check of the word "Linux" revealed 91 million results, whereas "Microsoft" had "only" 66 million!

NOTE

My friend C-Note says the best Linux distribution is Debian: www.debian.org.

Michael: Your friend C-Note is a Deb-Head. Debian is great, but for new users, I usually point people to Mandrakelinux or the new Xandros desktop (which actually runs some Windows apps). Love, Brian Proffitt, aka Managing Editor, Linux Today *:-)*

Good sources for free Linux programs are http://freshmeat.net and http://distrowatch.com.

Other Hardware Options

A laptop isn't as portable as you might think. Unless you want to spend several grand, at this point they're not that light. Generally over four pounds. Mine weights about six. And the battery life is only about two hours (more if you're only typing, less if you're editing video or listening to MP3s or running some other memory-intensive application), so I bring another battery with me on long trips. That adds a pound. And a hundred bucks to the price.

I shucked my laptop all around Europe for two months. Got a heck of a lot of stuff done. But it was still a burden to carry it and all my stuff. (And I packed light. Took all my clothes and *everything* in a student book bag-sized backpack. I packed so light that when I took the train from Belgium back to London, the lady at customs thought I was lying or trying to pull something. "This is *all* you're taking on a two-month trip??!") There are a few options for writing that are lighter and cheaper.

NOTE

My friend Gunter in Berlin says his girlfriend takes more baggage on an overnight trip than I take for two months in Europe.

One option would be one of those little palm-top computers (you know, computers that come with a little tiny keyboard and run the CE version of Windows), but I can't use them. The keyboards are too small. I need a full-size keyboard. Three cheap and easy solutions with real full-size keyboards are the AlphaSmart, the Dana, and a Palm or Handspring using a detachable, fold-out full-size keyboard.

AlphaSmart and Dana

A good compromise between the single-mindedness of a typewriter and the versatility and portability of a laptop is the AlphaSmart 3000 (www.AlphaSmart.com).

This is a dedicated word processor made for children. Looks like a toy. People have laughed at me for using what they think *is* a toy, but screw 'em. I write stuff on it that sells and moves the minds of adults.

The AlphaSmart does only text-based word processing and then only in ASCII (non-formatted) text. It's light enough (two pounds) that you don't have to wonder if you'll need it when leaving the house, you just take it with you. It's cheap ($199), lasts a year on two AA batteries, boots up and shuts down instantly, and saves text when you power it off. It is searchable, has spell check, and just plain *rocks*. You can easily upload the text to a computer (running any OS and any program) to be formatted and edited. I LOVE IT I LOVE IT I LOVE THE ALPHASMART!!! I wrote at least some of each of my four books on one.

My friend Steve Diet Goedde had a great comment. I put the AlphaSmart in his lap to take it for a test spin. He said, "It looks like something from the past. Or maybe from the future."

Or both at the same time.

I use the AlphaSmart incessantly. Nothing will ever replace it, though some might try.

Figure 9.18 *AlphaSmart (with Sarah Amstutz).*

Figure 9.19 *Dana (with Charlie).*

AlphaSmart also makes another fine tool called the Dana ($379). The Dana is somewhere between an AlphaSmart and a laptop. It weighs two pounds and boots and shuts down almost immediately (slightly slower than an AlphaSmart, but way faster than a laptop). It's basically an AlphaSmart with a Palm operating system, so you can do formatting, run spreadsheets, get e-mail, and even surf the Web (albeit slowly and without color). It runs 25 hours on a battery charge.

It does not replace a laptop, but is a unique and cool hybrid of its own. Try one if you can before you buy it. It might be perfect for some folks. (But I would recommend you buy the basic above-mentioned basic AlphaSmart without even trying it. It's that cool.)

They even have a wireless Dana ($429). Either Dana can run any program that will run on a Palm or Handspring, and there are literally thousands of cool programs available (many are freeware—check out www.freewarepalm.com). Dig it.

I like the key click on both of the Danas and the AlphaSmart. It makes my fingers fly. And like I said, that's important.

The AlphaSmart corporation also just came out with a new unit called the Neo. It's basically an AlphaSmart with more memory, a sleeker design, and a bigger display. It lists for $229.

Palm or Handspring

Another low-tech, low-weight solution for writing on the run is to just get a Handspring or Palm.

Figure 9.20 *Palm M505.*

You can use these with a detachable keyboard. The two together will be even lighter than an AlphaSmart (less than a pound for the Handspring with the keyboard), and the same price or less (the Handspring Visor Deluxe on Amazon is $149 new, $49 used). Palms are a little higher. I like the Handspring better anyway. The viewable area is larger, and it feels a little less fey, a little more rugged. The Targus Stowaway Portable Keyboard is $99 new and as low as $20 used. You can do formatting on it and upload to the computer.

This is not as convenient as the AlphaSmart, as you have to put the Handspring or Palm unit onto the keyboard, and you also need a flat surface, whereas you could use an AlphaSmart while whitewater rafting as long as you didn't get it wet. But the Handspring/Targus (or other foldable keyboard) combination, used, could get you set up as a real mobile writer for 60 bucks. Try to beat that! (You could use a computer at the library to do formatting and stuff.)

I like the key click on the Targus keyboard a lot.

Figure 9.21 *Cat Palm: Palm unit with Targus keyboard.* Photo by Lydia Lam

---

TIP

You can get MiniWord, a simple freeware word processor for Palm, at www.bitmaster.com.au/software/.

Conclusion

Okay. We've pretty much run the basic range of writer options. You don't need as much computing power as you would need for, say, editing video. But we've got you covered. Now let's move on to the magic zeros and ones that make your dream machines run . . . software!

Chapter 10

Software

$30

WRITING
SCHOOL

computer is just a tool to strengthen what you've already got. So I will reprise the most important lesson in this book and say it until it's a fact in your head: *nothing* is a replacement for good skills, good planning, good writing, and good editing.

Use software to augment, not replace, that.

Software is that sexy math I mentioned in the last chapter. I've oft conjectured that modern software is numerology delivered by aliens to mankind in 1954 at Area 51. But then again, I did a lot of acid in college.

I could be wrong, but hey, you got a better theory?

Word Processing

I *live* in Microsoft Word. Word is the *de facto* program that most writers use. I even use an old version of Word, Word 97. You can get old software very cheap. (Try eBay—but note that buying used software might violate the user agreement. Though this would probably only affect the person selling, not buying, I would *never* suggest that you, um, do anything that involves yourself in any part of anything illegal.) I got Word 97 free from a friend. And I like it better than the new version. There's nothing in the latest version of Word that I need that isn't in 97. And there's a whole lot of what I consider to be bloatware—dancing baloney that I *don't* need—in the latest version of Word. And I like the interface better in 97 than in the new one.

NOTE

Software is the ultimate in planned obsolescence. As I write this, my *$30 Music School* book came out last month, and I'm already making notes for the second printing on software I covered that's already out of date.

I don't buy into this business model. It's crap. I used to be addicted to heroin. I don't want to get addicted to software upgrades.

NOTE

If you need to share files with someone who does not have Word, save them from the drop-down menu in Word as Rich Text Format (.rtf) files rather than Word files (.doc). Rich Text Format files can be opened on almost any word processor.

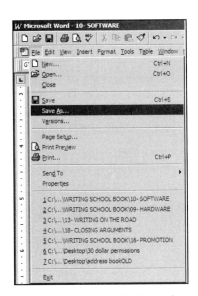

Figure 10.1 *Pick File, Save As.*

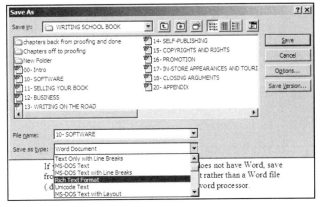

Figure 10.2 *Scroll down the drop-down menu to Rich Text Format.*

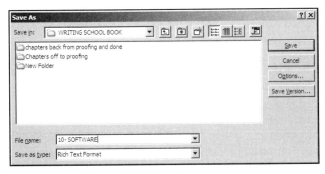

Figure 10.3 *Save as Rich Text Format.*

If you don't feel bad about the richest men in the world having a few less bucks, there are even freeware word processors, such as OpenOffice from www.openoffice.org or AbiWord from www.abisource.com, which can open and save as .doc files that will work in Word. They even look and act much like Word. They have many of the same keyboard commands and toolbars. They work great, though you may run into problems when working with your editor if she's using Word. A full working version of AbiWord for PC and one for Linux is included on the CD-ROM.

TIP

If you're writing tech books like this, you can sometimes get free software and hardware to review. It's tough and takes some cunning and attention. And it's better to call on the phone than to e-mail. Usually I try to find the number for the marketing department on its Web site. Failing that, I call the customer service number and ask for the number for the marketing department.

This will work *only* if you already have a deal with an established publisher, and they'll want to talk to your editor, too.

The more books you do, the easier this gets, though. Sometimes now, *they* send *me* stuff without me even asking for it.

Keyboard Shortcuts

You should get really fast and accurate at typing. It's easy. Just learn home row and such, then practice. Here's a good tutorial. It's from a middle school's Web site: http://www.crews.org/curriculum/ex/compsci/keyboarding/fingerkeys.htm and http://www.crews.org/curriculum/ex/compsci/keyboarding/index.htm. Very cool!

Also learn the keyboard shortcuts. Especially Ctrl+Z (undo last command) and the case functions. Keyboard shortcuts will make your experience as a writer easier, more powerful, and robust.

My friend Newt says it's scary watching me work on a computer because I'm so quick and deft with these commands. Here they are. They're on the CD-ROM also, as a printable document you can hang on your wall called Keyboard Shortcuts.doc. It's in the Goodies folder.

Keyboard Shortcuts in Word

PC: Ctrl+	Mac: Apple Key +	
a = select all	j = justify	s = save
b = bold	k = insert hyperlink	t = change margin
c = copy	l = align left	u = underline
d = font	m = change margin	v = paste
e = align center	n = create new document	w = close
f = find	o = open	x = cut
g = go to	p = print	y= repeat
h = replace	r = align right	z= undo
i = italicize		

Alt+1 (2, 3, etc.) = switch to different open Word document.

Alt+Tab = switch programs (good to use at your job to switch from your work to their work when you hear the boss coming)

F7 key = spell check

Shift and F7 = thesaurus

Shift and F3 = change case (highlight word or phrase and hit Shift and F3 more than once to toggle through title case, lowercase, uppercase, and sentence case)

Some of these are Microsoft Word-specific, and some work in any Windows program. Experiment.

These work in most programs: Select all, Copy, Find, Open, Print, Save, Paste, Cut, Undo.

Find Function and Search Function

I use this all the time. I click in a document and hit Ctrl+F to search for the phrase I am seeking.

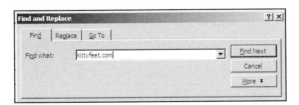

Figure 10.4 *Find function in Word.*

This works on most Web pages too. You have to click onto a non-linked part of the top of the page first.

Often, when working on a book, I use the Universal Document Search function in Windows, too. This is good if you can't remember what document you typed a certain text string in, or if you can't remember if you just thought something or actually wrote it.

Right-click on a folder or drive. If you're searching a drive, it will take a while. And other processes will slow down. You can narrow your search to speed it up using the Advanced Search function (click on More Advanced Search Options) to specify the file type and so forth.

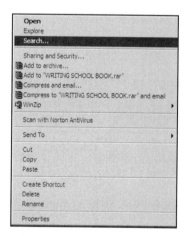

Figure 10.5 *Search folder function in Windows.*

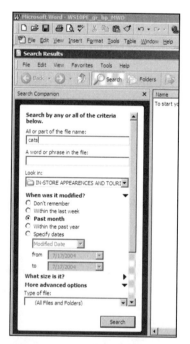

Figure 10.6 *Advanced Search in Search folder function in Windows.*

Keep in mind that this function will not work on any open files. Only closed ones.

I also often right-click in a folder and arrange documents by size, type, or especially date. This will put the most recently altered document at the top (or bottom).

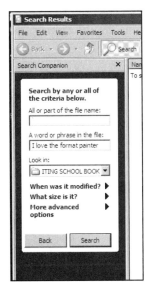

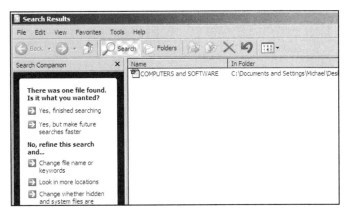

Figure 10.8 *Search results.*

Figure 10.7 *Searching for the phrase "I love the format painter."*

Format Painter

I love the Format Painter. I use it all the time. It's that little paintbrush icon on the toolbar in Word. Basically you use it to copy the formatting from one paragraph to another.

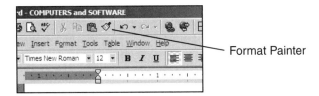

Figure 10.9 *Format Painter.*

I do a lot of cutting and pasting of Web addresses, quotes from Web sites, other documents I wrote, or e-mails I wrote, and the formatting often acts screwy in Word. (I always give credit and get permission for something I didn't write. But I do use a lot of stuff I write in an e-mail. I'll answer a friend's question, and if it pertains to something I'm working on. I'll cut and paste it into a book. A good example is the different city temperature chart a few chapters back.) Cutting and copying or pasting from another program or document at the end of a paragraph will sometimes reformat the entire paragraph.

TIP

On the subject of repurposing stuff I wrote once and using it again in a book: Whenever I do an interview by e-mail, I get permission from the interviewer to use it on the CD-ROM for a book or in the book itself, including the questions. That way, if I can't get permission from the magazine he sells it to, I still have the Word file to use. I work too hard on interviews not to own them. They're mine, ya know? Otherwise you're just doing free work for a writer that he gets paid for. (Michael Woody adds, "The same is true for reporters. You can pretend a larger purpose is being served, like the public's right to know the answers to *Trivial Pursuit*, but the truth is you're putting butter on their bread. If they forget, remind them to thank you.") (Albeit, you are spreading your thoughts and legend in the process.) See all the interviews in Word format on the CD-ROM with this book.

Basically, to use the Format Painter, you just click the cursor in the paragraph you want to copy, click the paintbrush icon from the Word toolbar, then "paint" the formatting from one paragraph to another. Everything—the indent, the font face, size, color, and style—will copy. Keep in mind that it will remove any bold, italics, and so on, so be careful.

A Note on Cutting and Pasting

When you copy something from a Web page and paste into Word, Word will bring the formatting and even the images from the Web page with it. It's one of those situations of Microsoft assuming that I want to do more than I want to do and making it hard not to do that.

You usually don't want this.

When cutting from a Web site, I often first paste the text into a Notepad document (or Simple Text on a Mac) to remove *all* formatting, Weblinks, photos, and such and reduce it to ASCII text. Then I copy from the Notepad document to Word. I keep a blank Notepad document on my desktop for this purpose.

You can also do this quicker by pasting text into a browser's address window and then copying that ASCII text to a document. However, this works only if there are no line or paragraph breaks. I often use it for short things, like book titles copied from a Web page.

TIP

Cassidy Coon asked me, "Hey, on Word, why does it do that really annoying thing where all of a sudden it decides that if you go back to correct something, it's going to type over everything preceding it as you make the correction?"

The answer:

Hit the Ins or Insert button again on the keyboard. You bumped it by accident. (This is true in any program, not just Word.) This key is useless. It is a throwback to when computers did not have a mouse.

I demand all manufacturers remove the Ins key immediately. It's a useless hassle.

Word Count

I use the Word Count function (Tools, Word Count), but not a lot. I use it to make sure I've done my daily minimum of 1,000 words. You can either check the total words in the document (I sometimes do that when I start and put it at the top of the document, then compare it to the count at the end of the writing session) or highlight a section and just count that.

NOTE

Sometimes I'll check all the folders and add it up to see how a project is going so I can gauge how much to write so I don't overwrite. Editing costs the publisher money. They sometimes pass it on to the author. Mine doesn't, but some do.

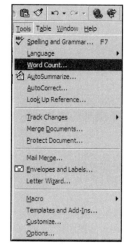

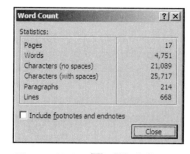

Figure 10.11 *The Word Count dialog box.*

Figure 10.10 *Accessing the Word Count dialog box.*

Sometimes, especially on your first book, it's good to overwrite and then trim down. (Hopefully you are doing some of that yourself, so as not to saddle your editor with it.) This makes for a stronger book. But this is my fourth book, and I have a good feel for the process. And I know that in this series, the book should be around 100,000 words and have 200–300 images.

Figure 10.12 *Right-click on a folder to count the number of file images inside.*

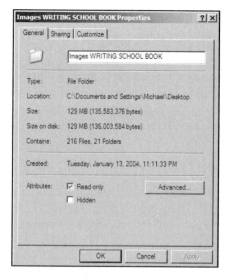

Figure 10.13 *Viewing the number of files (images) in a folder.*

Word Count is useful if you have a writing assignment for a magazine (or school) such as, "We need 5,000 words on the mating habits of the North American Flying Squirrel." But I try not to worry about it too much with books.

Keep in mind that your editor will probably cut a lot and may even ask you to expand certain parts. You aren't usually done when you think you're done, especially if you're working with a good editor who'll guide you a bit and see the bigger picture better than you (who are probably bogged down too much with the minutia to see that). Hopefully, your editor has a feel for the spirit of your project and is going to help you make it better, rather than just making changes to justify his job.

A novel is usually between 60,000 words and 125,000 words. A tech book can be more or less, but usually has a lot of illustrations. If you use the default margins in Word and use 12-point Times New Roman font as I do (which is a nice, readable way to work—the default is 10-point), it will work out to about 500 words per page. Published novels are usually about 325 or 350 words per page. Tech books are usually about 150–300 words per page. They have more illustrations and more whitespace than a novel.

As I said, don't get too hung up on this. Just know it exists and leave it at that.

Annoyances in Microsoft Office and Windows

I work alone partially because I don't have people being overly helpful. I hate all the Microsoft Office crap that pops up and disturbs me from being in the zone with my art.

Want to get rid of that awful people-pleasing, stalking, codependent animated help icon (paper clip, cat, dog, piece of paper, and so on) in Word? Right-click the icon and turn off Assistant. Then delete the folder called Actors in the Office folder.

To delete the Office toolbar, delete it from the Start menu, then right-click and exit.

Only the Tools You Need

A lot of crap gets foisted at writers to help them write. You really don't need many tools. I'm a professional writer and mainly use a non-fancy laptop and an old copy of Word. You really should ignore most of what people will try to sell you.

There are two exceptions, and that's only if you are a screenwriter or TV writer. Then you should check out Final Draft and Final Draft AV.

Final Draft and Final Draft AV

Final Draft (from a company also called Final Draft—www.FinalDraft.com) is a dedicated word processor for screenwriters. Final Draft AV (Audio Visual) is a similar program intended for producers who don't have a regular writing background but put together shows.

Final Draft is an elegant and beautiful program that does one thing only and one thing well: It formats scripts for movies, plays, and TV. It works great.

Final Draft is a pretty amazing company. They're very small, have only a few products, and have cornered the market in a powerful part of Hollywood. There are a couple of other screenwriting programs (Movie Magic is one), but Final Draft is way easier to use and in my opinion better, and it is the industry standard.

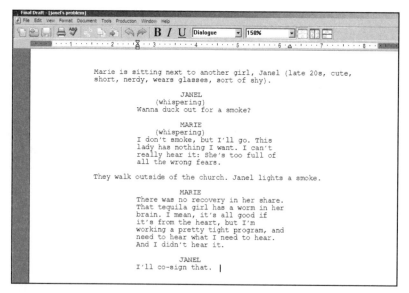

Figure 10.14 *Final Draft 7.0.*

It's easy to use. You just type, and it automatically formats when you hit Enter or Tab. Check it out. A free 15-day trial version is on the CD-ROM (one for PC and one for Mac). It gives you all the features and functionality of the full version. But the maximum document length is 15 pages, and the pages will be printed with a watermark.)

Final Draft AV is an even simpler program that makes two columns: one for video and one for audio. The new version has time code support, which makes it easier for a writer/producer to work with an editor.

TIP

Screenwriting itself is deceptively simple and simultaneously rather complex. See my book *$30 Film School* for a good overview on how to write a screenplay.

If you look in the Goodies folder on the CD-ROM, you'll find two documents (scripts.fdr and scripts.rtf). Both documents are the same first few pages from one of my scripts. scripts.fdr is native to Final Draft, so you'll need that program to open it. scripts.rtf can be opened in most word processing programs.

You could also save the RTF document as a new document, delete my words, and simply use the drop-down Style menu as formatting to use as a freeware script utility in Word or AbiWord. It might have some issues and require massaging, but it should work. But you wouldn't have a lot of the other stuff that makes Final Draft so cool. More on that stuff is covered in *$30 Film School*, but you would have the basic formatting for characters, action, dialogue, and so on.

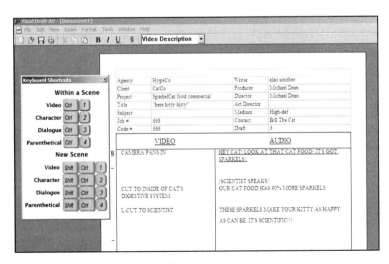

Figure 10.15 *Final Draft AV.*

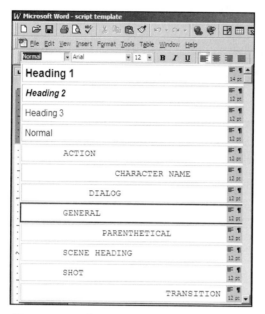

Figure 10.16 *Style drop-down menu in Script Template.*

Voice Recognition Software

Programs like Dragon Dictate and ViaVoice will take your spoken words, via a microphone, and turn them into printed text.

I tried Dragon Dictate about six years ago, and it was spotty at best. It had to be trained to your voice, which took a long time, and even then, if you didn't speak clearly and like a robot, it turned whatever you said into a poetic interpretation of what you meant.

I imagine the new version might work better, if simply because computers are far more powerful than they were six years ago. You probably still have to train it and check the results, but it probably works better.

Alas, I don't know firsthand, because my queries to the marketing departments of both companies to procure a working copy to review for this book were ignored. (Maybe for the second printing they'll send it to me? Hint, hint.)

Regardless, it might be worth trying.

The interview I did by phone with Cassidy Coon is on the CD-ROM in the Interviews folder. She transcribed it by hand, without voice recognition software. It took her 24 hours of work, spread out over a week. She did a great job. Then I proofed it to perfection as we worked back and forth, using the Track Changes feature in Word.

She and I hit it off really well and ended up being friends and even lovers later. Ahhhhh . . . such is the life of an artist.

It's cute. When I went through and proofed the interview, I could sorta see us falling for each other, something I hadn't seen clearly when it was happening. I joked that we should invent a Track Changes in Your Relationship feature for Word.

NOTE

Sometimes you end up dating people you collaborate with. There's nothing sleazy about it, if you do it right. Why *wouldn't* one be attracted to like-minded, really smart people in the same line of work with the same passion about life and art as yourself?

Anyway, this is the longest interview I've ever done. Cassidy and I talked for 100 minutes on the phone, and it's almost 15,000 words long. And it's totally coherent and a good read. That's pretty cool. A short novel is 60,000 words. So it makes me wonder if I could actually just speak complete books in a few two- or three-hour sessions. Maybe I'll try.

I told her that and she said, ". . . and then you could get people to transcribe it for you . . . in five different languages. You could crank out a few books a week. It'd be a factory."

We were joking, but it got me to thinking, there's really no reason one *couldn't* just dictate an entire book and have people or software transcribe it. It would probably still take some work, but if Dragon Dictate or ViaVoice is willing to take my calls, I'll give it a shot.

Show Desktop

Show Desktop is a very cool function in Windows that not everyone knows about. It's a little button in the bottom-left corner of the System Tray. Clicking once on it will instantly minimize all active windows and get you to the Desktop without having to minimize each one manually. It's great for people like me who constantly have eight or ten things going on at once. (You can also right-click on the bar at the bottom of XP and select Show the Desktop.)

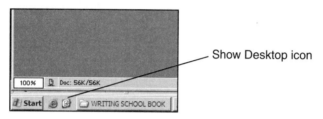

— Show Desktop icon

Figure 10.17 *Show Desktop icon in Windows XP.*

Screenshots

All the images of computer processes in this book are what are called "screenshots." Being able to take a screenshot is useful for writing books, for teaching something to someone else, or even showing a problem to anyone giving you tech help over the Internet.

TIP

I take the screenshots for these books by hitting the PrtSc (print screen) button at the top-left of my PC keyboard, then I paste the image into a new document in Photoshop. Then I save it as a .jpg at the highest possible quality (the slider all the way over to 12. If I were saving for the Web, where file size is an issue, I'd set the slider at 6 or 7).

To take a screenshot on a Mac, hold down the Apple key, the Shift key, and the 3 key. It is automatically saved to the hard disk as Picture 1, Picture 2, and Picture 3.

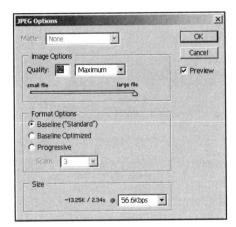

Figure 10.18 *The Photoshop slider all the way over to 12.*

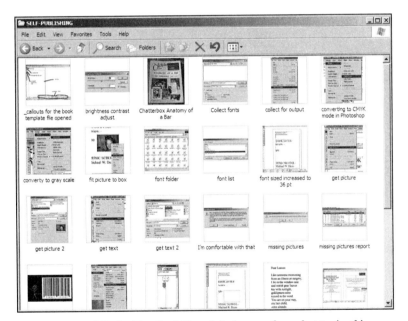

Figure 10.19 *The inside of a folder of the images for a chapter in this book.*

To make the thumbnail images appear in a folder, click on View, Thumbnails at the top of the folder.

Callouts

I often need *callouts* (the lines pointing to things in an image to emphasize the relevant parts of the picture). Most how-to books do. I don't make them myself; I leave it up to the page layout production people to do that. I just make two images: one clean image and one to show the production people where to make the callouts. The second one is a copy of the first one that I draw lines and type words on with Photoshop.

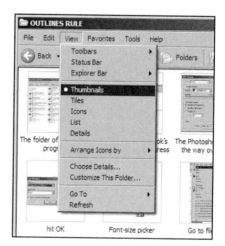

Figure 10.20 *Click on View, Thumbnails.*

I give the second figure a filename referring to the first figure, such as _callouts for MouseCount by Michael Dean.jpg.

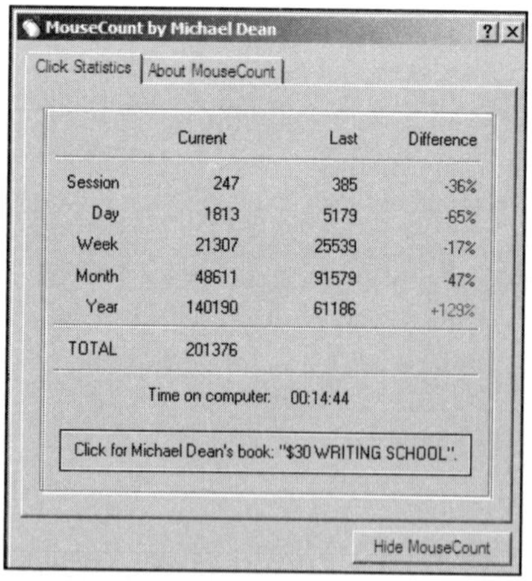

Figure 10.21 *The first figure, MouseCount by Michael Dean.jpg.*

Figure 10.22 *The figure I include for the page layout people.*

Then I put a production directive (highlighted in blue from the drop-down menu of my publisher's template) that says:

> ********production, please note _callouts for MouseCount by Michael Dean.jpg******

This line is later deleted during final production.

The production people never print the second image. My sloppy callout image just tells the layout people where to put their callouts on my first clean image.

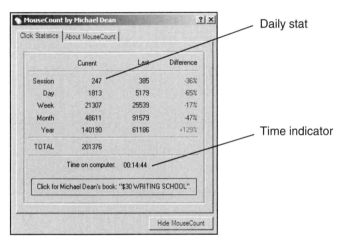

Figure 10.23 *Image with callouts produced by layout people.*

MouseCount

MouseCount is a program I invented and my friend Helmut Vogler programmed. It's on the CD-ROM in the Software folder. It counts your mouse clicks and time on the computer. It's fun and useful for monitoring your computer use, good stuff to consider if you end up with sore wrists.

MouseCount is tiny (108Kb). Feel free to e-mail it to friends or put it on your Web site as a download. If you want a custom version with your company info and logo on it, let me know.

PawSense

BitBoost Systems (www.bitboost.com/pawsense) sells PawSense, a program that detects "cat-like typing" from your cat and sets off an alarm. Probably not something you need, but how could I resist mentioning it? I'm a writer, my Web site is Kittyfeet.com, and my cats not only type with their kitty feet, but somehow they open files and cut and paste from the Clipboard sometimes.

(I trained my cat not to sit on the keyboard without using this software. Whenever she sits on the keyboard, I grab the canned air I keep on my desk to clean computers with and spray it into the air. She *hates* this sound for some reason.)

My cat typed this:

tfrrrrrrrr;;jhnvcsdfx Emws`675c7LNM

` +_GBHYuhgNJMKZ4 h

JMN[

Cats think laptops exist only as tummy and butt warmers.

Figure 10.24 *A kitty named Squeaky on her Mac iBook laptop.*

Figure 10.25 *Squeaky updates her Friendster profile.* Photos by Julie Peasley (www.juliepeasley.com)

TIP

Many help lines are open 24 hours. Often, the best time to call is very late at night. The wait is shorter, and since nerds are nocturnal, you're more likely to get someone who knows what he's doing. During the daytime, you'll probably get some idiot reading from a script who knows far less about computers than you and who was probably selling shoes last month.

Because of the time differences, this trick will not work with companies where you are getting routed overseas. Because of the low price of international calling and the low price of labor, a lot of tech calls get sent to India now. It makes sense. Many people speak English there and the education level is high.

Conclusion

So that pretty much covers all the tools I use as a writer. Hope this wasn't too much nurding around. I try to keep a good balance between computers and writing, tool and trade, science and art.

A good computer and a good, simple word processing program are all I need. A lot of companies and magazines and salesmen will try to sell you a whole lot more crap than that. But you really don't need a whole lot of crap. You need a simple basic setup. You need to be comfortable, calm, and confident, have some talent, drive, and maybe a tiny bit of that divine spark from the universe. That's all you need to be a writer.

Well, that and some luck and some business sense. Which brings us to selling your book.

Chapter 11

Selling Your Book

$30 WRITING SCHOOL

Everyone wants to be a writer. And it's quite a feat to actually finish a book. But sometimes an even bigger feat is to get someone to print it and sell it for you. I've done it, so I can tell you how I went about it and give some solutions I came up with to problems I encountered on my journey.

Fiction is hard to sell. Unless you're somebody famous, your fiction book has to be completely done and ready to go. Even then, and even with an agent, it's a hard sell, and if you do sell it, you likely won't get a large advance for it.

Non-fiction is easier to get a deal for, and it's often sold without having it all completed first. Most non-fiction is sold on a proposal and two sample chapters. It's easier to sell, and you'll get a larger advance.

But even so, you probably won't get a rockstar-size chunk of cash up front. If it's your first non-fiction book, you'll probably get less than $10,000, and not all at once. It's usually given in staggered amounts, such as 20 percent upon signing and turning in 25 percent of the book, 20 percent upon turning in half the book, 20 percent at 75 percent of the book, 20 percent upon turning in the whole book (chapters, images, and release forms), and the last 20 percent upon completing author review (working with the editor to make the final changes and readying the book for the printer). Sometimes the staggered payment schedule is four payments of 25 percent rather than five payments of 20 percent.

Advances from the publisher have to be paid back from book sales. If the book doesn't sell, you don't have to pay them back out of your pocket. They're taking a gamble on you. Any other deal is probably a scam. More on this later.

The point of an advance is not to make you set for life: it's simply to give you a McDonalds' wage for four or six months so you can work full-time to finish the book without actually *working* at McDonalds.

Being a success at fiction is often considered more interesting, as well as more spiritually, emotionally, and artistically fulfilling, to most writers (and readers). What I do is write non-fiction and put enough of myself into it to be rewarding to me and as interesting and unique to the reader as my fiction.

> **NOTE**
>
> A lot of people are unrealistic about what getting a publisher will do for their lives. Many writers think, "My life is a drag, but the minute I ink the *deal*, everything will change." Be realistic: A book deal ain't gonna "fix" you. It won't make your life perfect. It probably won't sweep you up sky-high in a tornado of adulation and money and fame and love and respect. And even if it does, you'll still be *you*, and still have most of the same problems you have now. And you'll even have new problems. And a deal doesn't include a suddenly increased capacity to deal with life. So work now at being as happy and sane as you can *without* the deal, so you can be happy and sane *with* a deal.

You sign a contract when you sign a book. Most publishing contracts are short and simple. For this book, the contract was five pages and written in simple English. When my band signed to Warner Brothers, the contract was 75 pages long and basically impossible for me to understand without paying a very expensive entertainment attorney to explain it to me.

I do most of my own lawyering. I would be remiss legally to advise you to do the same, but I'll just say I do. But I will add that I've heard that for most simple contracts, you are probably going to do just fine doing that, if you're smart and attentive to the details. If you must use a lawyer, the $150-an-hour family lawyer is probably just as good as a $400-an-hour entertainment attorney. Results may vary.

Nothing in this book constitutes legal or tax advice. All information is provided for entertainment purposes only.

Who Does What in the Publishing World?

You can produce, publish, and promote a whole book by yourself. I did this on my first novel. I not only wrote it and did most of the editing, but I also did the photography, design, page layout, and even designed some of my own fonts. And I got it into stores myself. In effect, I was my own editor, agent, designer, publisher, and distributor, as well as being the author.

But my later books all involved a team helping out on the editorial stuff and taking it to market.

You have probably heard some of these terms: writer, publisher, agent, acquisitions editor, project editor, copy editor, tech editor, proofreader, layout/design, marketing people, and publicist. Most people really know what only the first one does. Let's break it down.

Writer

That's you, the person who comes up with this stuff—the person who provides the actual content that drives the publishing industry. The writer is the person with the bad back hunched over a computer while all his friends are out playing and partying and dreaming.

Writers are sometimes underappreciated by the industry that depends on them. Expect this. It's not that farfetched in the movie *The Player* when Tim Robbins' character facetiously makes fun of his colleagues' motives by saying, "Yeah. Let's get rid of the writers. And while you're at it, if we can get rid of these actors and directors, we might be on to something." (Who would know that this line was also foreshadowing modern CGI animation techniques that may actually threaten the jobs of actors a bit? Not to mention the glut of horrible "reality TV" that eliminates writers, actors, and directors and keeps only the producer, the cameraman, and the editor?)

Publisher

The company. The organization that puts money into putting books out and hopes to make a good return on investment (ROI). Some publishers are into art and will take a risk on something that may not make big bucks, but most publishers exist to play it safe. They know it's easier to sell a fluffy coffee table book with photos of cats than it is to sell a powerful novel. Check out what a publisher typically publishes before you send a proposal. It could save you a few rejection letters by doing the obvious.

Many publishers got started in the business from their love of literature and art, but the realities at the end of the day stifled the art and made them care more about the bottom line. This is fine with me. I just make art and find a way to make it commercially viable without compromising one bit.

The term *publisher* is sometimes also loosely used as a name for a person, usually a high-level executive at a publishing company. Unless you sell a *lot* of books or your publishing company is very small, you probably won't be dealing much with this person.

Agent

Also called a "literary agent." This is the person (it's often a woman) who acts as a liaison between the artist and the industry. Agents are common in many artistic endeavors, like music and painting and acting. Artists are generally considered a little nutty, and the people running the industry don't love dealing with them, so a whole buffer layer of the "agent" job description was spawned to protect them. They also do the dirty work of the business: sifting out the wannabes, getting work for the talented artists, and negotiating a better deal for them. Many artistic types are not good at business—it's a left brain versus right brain thing, so it is often to the advantage of the writer to employ this person.

NOTE

Last year I was doing an in-store book signing at a Borders in Dallas, Texas, for *$30 Film School*. A woman came in with her daughter. They'd just bought my book. The mother said, "My daughter will be graduating high school next year and going to Los Angeles to go to film school. Please tell her what to do."

I was shocked that someone would give me that much credence, like, "Here—my child's fate is in your hands. Impart wisdom to her." (See? *That's* the power of being a published author.) I gave her the best advice I could. I said, "Read my book, get together with your friends, and make films. Get good at it. Then, don't go to film school. Go to business school."

I don't know if she did it, but I think it was great advice. If that girl is reading this, and you did move to LA, drop me an e-mail and I'll buy you lunch on the coast.

Agents work on commission. If any agent ever tries to charge you money for *anything* up front, hang up the phone and delete the e-mail. They ain't legit. Same if they say something like, "I might take you on as a client if you had a 'book doctor' work with you," and then they recommend a book doctor by name. A book doctor is, in my opinion, a scam artist who charges money to make the unreadable readable. The fake agent gets a kickback for each writer he recommends. Some "agents" recommend a book doctor for *everything* they receive. These agents have usually never sold a single project to a real publisher.

Acquisitions Editor

There are several types of editors, but when I say "editor" without an adjective in front of it (like "copy editor" or "tech editor"), I am basically talking about an acquisitions editor. The acquisitions editor is kind of like an A&R person in music (what used to be called a "talent scout."). He works for the publisher and signs the writers. The acquisitions editor is the person the literary agent pitches a project to, and the acquisitions editor then goes to his boss and gets the deal. The acquisitions editor is the liaison between the agent and the publisher. He finds talent, negotiates contracts, and after the deal is signed, he also acts as the intermediary between the writer and the publisher. He works with the writer (usually via e-mail) on all the big picture type stuff, guiding the overall project. (In this capacity, he is probably also analogous to the producer on a music project or the director in film.) He works with the writer on fine-tuning the outline and then usually passes the work on to the project editor.

> **NOTE**
>
> If you do get a book deal, you'll be e-mailing a lot of your work in electronic form back and forth between the publisher and the editors. Don't post your stuff online or even e-mail to anyone outside the book company (except your agent) without permission from the publisher, and even then be careful. There's probably something in your publishing contract that the content must all be "previously unpublished material." Putting it on the Internet (or allowing someone else to do so) may be considered "publishing" and may violate the terms of your contract.

Project Editor

The project editor is sometimes the same person as the acquisitions editor, sometimes not. It depends on the size of the company, and how busy they are. Kevin Harreld was both for my first two books in this series, and he got very busy, so Brian Proffitt is the project editor on this book.

The project editor is the person that the writer sends the completed drafts of each chapter to. Invariably, the project editor suggests changes to be made by the writer (hopefully reaching a mutually amicable compromise). He also sometimes does some proofreading, catching obvious stuff before it gets passed on to others. He usually sends the chapters back to the writer for another pass, then routes the revised chapters on to the copy editor. The project editor will also handle what is known as development editing, a sort of macro editing that checks for consistency and flow.

Copy Editor

The copy editor basically catches mistakes that the writer and editor don't catch: grammar, spelling, syntax, stilted (hard to read and/or unnatural) language, and text that lacks continuity, doesn't make sense, or presents non-facts as facts. He marks changes for the writer to approve or decline. (If a recommended change is declined, the writer usually has to have a good reason.)

> Diary entry, 10/13/2003, being driven by Tobi on the autobahn on tour in Germany:
>
> > Sandy Doell, the copy editor at Muska & Lipman, sent me a fan letter today! That made my day. She's editing my finished book, *$30 Music School*, and she loves it. Wow. It's so cool to work with someone who totally "gets" my work.
> >
> > With her it feels more like collaboration than correction. I love that. I always resisted being "worked with" because I felt it was "tainting my purity." But I'm digging this.
> >
> > She worked on *$30 Film School*, too, and really helped me improve it. I'm going to get her to work on *$30 Writing School*.

Tech Editor

If the book is a technical book (like *UNIX Unleashed* or *Web Design for Dummies*), all chapters are probably sent to the tech editor after going to the project editor and before the copy editor. If it's a non-tech book with a few technical chapters (like *$30 Film School*), only the technical chapters go to the tech editor. A tech editor is a person who is very adept with the technology relevant to the book and who can find mistakes in any technical writing. In the case of computer programs, often he will download a demo and go through the steps described in the chapters and see if it all works like it's supposed to. He will also notify the writer if the screenshots are not from the latest available version (though the writer should take care of this himself).

Proofreader

Usually after all this copy and tech and project editing, it will go through one more pass by a proofreader. A proofreader is a person who catches (hopefully) any mistakes all the other folks involved didn't.

Layout/Design

These are the folks who work in Quark and Illustrator and Photoshop to make the cover and lay out the text for the inside of the book in a pleasing, readable, and artistic manner. They rock. They are often the difference between a book looking professional and a book looking crappy.

Marketing Department

The people who know how to get the biggest ROI for the company. They usually have MBAs (business degrees) and could sell deodorant to a Deadhead. Live to sell, sell to live. Geniuses in their own odd little world.

I try to stay out of their way and just let them do their job, though sometimes I'm asked by the company to offer suggestions to them (like on what magazines to advertise in and stuff like that), and I do. I guess I know some stuff about marketing to the "Gen-X hipster contingent" that they don't teach in college. Probably because I'm in the "Gen-X hipster contingent" (or at least I was at one point, back when I wore a thinner man's clothes).

Publicist

This is a person or firm employed by the publisher to push your book and get it into the public eye. Sometimes it's a full-time employee or even a department at the publisher, and sometimes this is farmed out to a third party. A publicist is basically a person who is very good at calling up writers at magazines and getting them to pay attention (as opposed to the marketing department, which mainly targets other marketers at bookstores, buys ads, whatever). They might not be any better at this than you. But they probably are. They also have a Rolodex of these numbers, and you don't. But most importantly, they have *relationships* with the people at the other end of the phone.

All business is based on relationships. Know this early on, and don't forget it. Ever. Someone at a publishing company once asked me if I had any friends in high places that could help promote my book. I replied, "All my friends are in medium places."

Remember the first rule of show business (and writing *is* show business): "Be fair to everyone. You meet the same people on the way up that you meet on the way down."

NOTE

Writing a book about writing was a little harder than writing a book about music or film-making. First of all, it was a harder sell to my publisher, even though I already had two successful books through them. When I proposed *$30 Film School* and then later *$30 Music School*, I was basically saying, "I'm an expert in both these fields." I wasn't bluffing, but I was certainly not an expert in the conventional sense of the word. I had a lot of scattered experience in both fields and enough brains and moxie to pull off making it work. Somehow the synergy (combined with my cool project editor, Kevin Harreld, pairing me with an exceptional copy editor, Sandy Doell, the one who totally "got me") worked. And we had two really good, really popular books out fairly quickly.

But these two fields were easier to sell to the company because no one there was an expert at filmmaking or music.

(Interestingly enough, while I consider being a writer the coolest job in the world, many writers use it as an "in" to work up the rungs of the publishing world. Being an editor usually pays a lot more and has health benefits, while being a writer usually does not.)

Secondly, writing a comprehensive writing book is harder because it covers more. There is more variation. Believe it or not, writing and recording a punk rock song and writing and recording a country song have far more in common than writing non-fiction, writing novels, and writing magazine articles have in common. In fact, most aspects of creating, disseminating, and administrating almost all aspects of any type of Western music are almost identical. The only noteworthy differences are the volume and intensity. It's all the same chords and song structures. But writing text for different venues of consumption is far different, and I have limited experience: I wrote two tech books and self-published a novel. But my writing book couldn't just be a *$30 $30 School* book (a book only about how to write a *$30 School* book). I had to expand. Luckily, I still have a lot of moxie, so I believed in myself enough to talk my way into the deal and write this book. It seems to be working, since other folks seem to like it.

Book Proposals

As this book goes to print, I have four other books out for submission: A completed novel (*The Simple Pleasures of a Complex Girl*), and two collaborations with Cassidy Coon: an illustrated children's book called *Newberry and the Milk Cats*, and an illustrated self-help gift book called *My Thinking Cap*. I also have a proposal for a new motivational book called *Get Off Your Lazy Ass!* I'm making my agent very busy. And that's a good thing.

As I said, most non-fiction is sold on a proposal and two sample chapters. There is a pretty standard way to write a proposal. This sums it up well (courtesy of my agent, Kimberly Valentini, at Waterside Productions, Inc.):

NON-FICTION SUBMISSION GUIDELINES

These guidelines are designed to assist you in the preparation of your book proposal. With the information you provide, we should be able to clearly:

Distinguish your project from other books on the same subject.

Identify the audience for which you are writing.

Determine the marketability of your finished book.

Credentials: List your previous publishing credits and credentials that are pertinent.

Proposal: This should be at least four or five typed pages, explaining: (a) what your book is about; (b) the problems, reasons, or situations which prompted you to write your book; (c) why your book is needed; (d) what are the unique features; anything that makes your book different from all other books in the same area; any new or fresh approach you offer; any special features you will include.

Market: Describe the audience at which your book will be aimed and your level of expertise, (no experience, beginner, intermediate, advanced). What are some specific applications or uses for your book (e.g. small business management; health; entertainment; education)? Who would be the most likely candidates for purchasing your book and why should they buy, use, keep and talk about it?

Competition: List three to four books which compete directly with the project you are proposing. Briefly discuss how they compare to your book in length, depth and spectrum of topics covered, format, visual appeal. If there is no available book for the market you are addressing, cite any which seems remotely comparable, and indicate the differences among your approaches.

Outline: Present a brief capsule of about 100 words of the contents of each chapter. A detailed list of the key concepts to be included per chapter is also acceptable.

Sample Chapters: Please submit one or two sample chapters, preferably not the first one, which will provide an example of your writing style and the actual content of the book.

Publishing Details: (a) Proposed *book length* (an average book contains about 70,000 words; this size manuscript makes a 250 page book); (b) if there are *photographs* and/or *illustrations*, how many are there; and, (c) what amount of *time* you will need to complete the finished manuscript?

I followed this very closely. Look in the CD-ROM in the folder called Book Proposals. It shows the proposal and sample chapters (and several drafts of each) for all three of these books.

And yes, after you've had success with one, you still have to write proposals for the next ones. Just know that it gets easier and that the company is far more likely to accept them if you've already had some success. For this book, I just told my publisher the title idea, and they told me they'd pick it. But then I had to write the proposal before they sent me the contract.

Have a good description (for example, for the *$30* series I used, "The punk rock *Artist's Way*").

For competition, consider this letter I sent to a friend who was considering writing a book on a very narrow field of heavy metal music and heard there was another book like that coming out soon. I wrote him:

> That's a tough one. It's not so huge a subject that a small publisher will likely take a chance on one book when another one's out. I mean, there can be 300 cat books, 50 "How to do eBay" books, 20 "I knew Kurt Cobain" books, but I really don't know about (that sub-sub-sub-genre of heavy metal) books.
>
> You might want to pick a more general subject for your first book.

Then again, what do I know? I've had a bunch of ideas turned down.

Publishers are fickle. They ain't into art. They're into commerce, and that's OK. You want them to be. Then you can just concentrate on the art.

If the other book was out and selling like hotcakes, they might consider another.

Search books on Amazon and look at their rankings. A book has to be in the top 10,000, or better yet top 5,000, to be a book worth putting as "competition" on a book proposal.

After I wrote the outline, proposal, and two sample letters, I wrote a query, which is just a short letter asking agents if they want to read the proposal. The query should be about a page long. It doesn't need to be the whole proposal; it's just a teaser to get the agent to want to see the proposal. It should contain the title, a *little* about the book, a *little* about you, and you asking the agent if he wants to see the full proposal. That's it.

Here's the e-mail I copied and pasted and sent out to about 50 agents that led to my book deal:

SUBJECT: "TWENTY-DOLLAR FILM SCHOOL." Query for non-fiction book

Hello Kimberly

NOTE

I changed the first name for each agent, obviously.

Are you interested in seeing the full proposal and two sample chapters of this?

"TWENTY-DOLLAR FILM SCHOOL." Query for non-fiction book by Michael W. Dean

NOTE

I wanted the book to cost 20 bucks. When I finally got a publisher, their bean counters said I'd have to ditch the CD to do it for 20, and I insisted on the CD being in there. Then their spreadsheets upped the retail price to 30 bucks, which determined the final title.

"Twenty-Dollar Film School" is a quick-start course on how to jump into digital filmmaking. Whereas traditional film schools cost 100,000 dollars and take four years, this book will have you up and running in a week.

UCLA and NYU prepare people to work in tiny capacities on huge projects for other creative people. Their film school grads are more likely to end up bringing coffee to the guy who brings coffee to the guy who brings coffee to Steven Spielberg than they are to replace Steven Spielberg. This is a frustrating problem for many creative people.

"Twenty-Dollar Film School" is the antidote.

Based on the author's Website, 99CentFilmSchool.com, "Twenty-Dollar Film School" is a book for anyone who ever wanted to make movies but thought it was completely out of their reach. Michael refused to buy into the lie that filmmaking is for educated professionals and took matters into his own hands. In this book, he shares in simple terms and interesting angles his experiences with you.

Michael W. Dean has taken his films on tour and shows you how to make your own, how to promote them, and a whole range of issues the aspiring filmmaker may encounter.

Dean has been reviewed and interviewed for NPR, in Filmmaker magazine, Film Threat, and on the front page of the San Francisco Examiner.

Digital D.I.Y. (Do-it-yourself) filmmaking is the new folk music, the new punk rock, the new medium where anyone can tell their story, and tell it in a powerful way, to millions. The learning curve is low, and there is an exponentially unlimited potential for reaching an audience. "Twenty-Dollar Film School" is your ticket in.

The six sections of the book, PURPOSE, INTEGRITY, COMMERCE, SELF-DEFINITION, DEALING WITH ADVERSITY, and GIVING BACK, are named after the six sections of Dean's groundbreaking documentary "D.I.Y. OR DIE: How To Survive as an Independent Artist." (www.diyod.org)

This book is different from others in the genre:

> The "how" is covered clearly and briefly, as that's all it takes. The "why" is considered more. Even though the author lives in Los Angeles, this not a "Hollywood" book. It is about cutting through the star-system BS and getting to the heart of art, and making powerful films on no budget that can reach the world.

> Michael W. Dean is the author of the critically acclaimed "Starving in the Company of Beautiful Women" (Kittyfeet Press, 2000, ISBN 0-9705392-0-7) and the director of the documentary "D.I.Y. OR DIE: How To Survive as an Independent Artist." He is self-taught, and progressed quickly in film-making based on his background in the related fields of photography, music, and writing. He was the singer in a band on Warner Brothers, and has written articles for many commercial Internet sites.

> The six sections of the book are all approximately 1/3 written.

> "Twenty-Dollar Film School. You'll get your money's worth."

Quick pointers for proposals:

- ◆ Don't cuss in the outline, even if there's cussin' in the books.
- ◆ Don't insult or make fun of your target audience. Or the publishing industry. Or yourself. Conversely, don't brag about yourself. List your accomplishments and be confident but not cocky. I'm a little more cocky even than you should be, and I'm probably the exception.

  Follow the dumb directions the agent gives you on their Website. Jump through the hoops they present to you. They're basically giving you an intelligence test and also seeing how well you follow directions, which basically tests how easy you'll be to work with.

- ◆ The first two graphs should present:
  - • The cause or problem, i.e. what is missing in the publishing world.
  - • The benefit (how the reader will overcome the problem presented in the first graph).
- ◆ In some cases, the problem and benefit could be two paragraphs each, but get to the problem and your solution quickly.

NOTE

My buddy Saby Reyes-Kulkarni asked me, "Is publishing like the music business, where you're signed to exclusive contracts with labels? I'm thinking no, because it behooves the publisher to sign new writers to one-offs or at least one book with options or they'd want right of first refusal on your next idea on a handshake or something. Obviously, that's a bit ambitious. A new, unpublished writer (the audience for *$30 Writing School*) just wants to get his first book published. BUT . . . is it advisable to work on multiple books at once? I would think not, as it's a severe time commitment. But I know in my case I've got a few ideas that wouldn't all work for the same publisher."

My answers to him were:

Most agents ask for exclusive contracts. I don't have one, and as we saw a few chapters back, try to get people to negotiate it down to a book-by-book basis.

Most publishers are not monogamous like this, unless it's on books in a series. For instance, it would have been at least a serious breach of decorum, if not law, for me to offer a book in this series to another publisher without first asking the people who'd already put out the first two. My next book will be a novel, and I will seek a different publisher because this publisher doesn't do fiction.

But in general, writers are free to be promiscuous with unrelated projects. The hope would be that you can find a publisher who will fulfill all your needs and you wouldn't consider going elsewhere. And many writers will write for many publishers in a lifetime. Many writers, if they're prolific, will work on more than one project for more than one publisher at once. Generally, you'd want to offer the idea to your current publisher first if it's the type of stuff they do, unless you have a good reason not to.

It is also worth noting that I went through my agent on all three of these books and paid her the 15% commission even though she technically only got me the first one. I could possibly have pitched the other two directly to the publisher, because after *Film School* was out, I had a direct daily e-mail and phone relationship with him. I never considered the legality of not going through her and cutting her out of that loop. I have no idea if it would have been legal because I wouldn't do it. I wouldn't have the deal without her, so I considered her directly entitled to the others through the same company in my same invented series. I even sent the proposals to her to send to my editor, just because that is how the first one was done.

If something ain't broke, don't fix it.

Selling Fiction

I've never done it. I'm gonna do it soon. (I basically do everything I set out to do. So look for it. As I said, it's called *The Simple Pleasures of a Complex Girl.*) But I did write a book that got a very high-end agent. (Jeff Hermann. He wasn't able to sell it though, so I ended up self-publishing it.)

Selling fiction is usually done through an agent. Here's the query that got me the agent:

> "*Starving in the Company of Beautiful Women* is an inventively voiced *Go Ask Alice* for the millennium."
>
> —author (Random House, Prentice Hall)
> and online columnist, Debra DeSalvo

> "Michael W. Dean is a talented and dedicated writer with a steadfast work ethic . . . I'm sure that he will be read for years to come."
>
> —author (2.13.61 Press) Don Bajema

> "Michael Dean is part brilliant visionary, and part annoying child."
>
> —author (Masquerade Press)
> Charles Gatewood

> "His tenacious nature defies his age, but he needs better teeth."
>
> —"Singer" in Gwar, Oderus Urungus

NOTE

My friend asked me, "How did you get reviews for a then-unpublished book to use in your query?" My answer: I sent it to people I knew and asked them to read it. Any testimonials by even marginally famous people will always help your cause, before *and* after publishing.

Starving in the Company of Beautiful Women is 89,000 words of taut, steady fiction centered mostly in the underground rock world of San Francisco. The book would appeal to fans of Tom Robbins, Charles Bukowski, William S. Burroughs, and Jim Carroll. The angle is unique, however; one-third of the story was written while I was using drugs. The remainder of the writing, and all of the editing, occurred during the last three years of drug-free living. This mixture lends a credible attraction as well as a shimmering clarity to the adventures.

Starving in the Company of Beautiful Women is poetic, carnal, and spiritual. It chronicles the adventures of independent pop legend, Cash Newmann, in his pursuit of and musings around God, sex, drugs, and purpose. Cash is good-looking, smart, talented, and basically kind, but a little bit evil. He is a very believable character. Several short selections from the book have already been published on the Internet in literary magazines. Many Internet publications have printed excerpts, and all have asked me to become a regular contributor.

My home page has received an extra 20-30 hits per day as a result of links from these publications. E-mail has ranged from fan-like devotion to abject hatred.

The protagonist was culled from my experiences, observations, and imagination. I am a 34-year-old musician, clean and sober for four years. As the singer in the rock group Bomb, I was a recording artist on Warner Brothers with a loyal cult following. I toured the dives of America and Europe, slept with everyone, drank anything, felt, saw, and lapped life to the inside of my skull, died a few times and lived to tell the tale.

Cash dies. After two-hundred-and-fifty pages of very personal yet universal first-person narration come two pages of a third-person account of the finding of Cash's body. I had to kill the character—not out of any didactic need to evangelize, but merely to balance the reality of my drug-using past with the viewpoint of my substance-free present. Given the subplot of the dirty city worming its way into his spirit and tainting his very beautiful and very human soul, Cash's death is the end of a natural progression.

This book is different from others in the genre for several reasons:

The book neither condemns nor champions drugs.

It does not admonish, does not brag, and has no moral.

It is very honest.

It is based on the unique viewpoint of a person in recovery writing as a person on drugs.

This combination fuses the depravity of one extreme with the self-knowledge of another. *Starving in the Company of Beautiful Women* is a bedtime story for the jaded, fueled by an uncommon amazement with the ordinary.

When the protagonist dies, he is simply gone. Game over. I have had 44 friends die. I feel numbed and bewildered by this, but try to keep living and laughing and feeling. I have poured some of their stories, some of my stories, and some of my obsessions into this book. It yields captivating results. As I said in a recent college-radio interview, "Everything that can be done has been done. Being a great artist consists simply of being a great editor."

I am open to touring, and I am willing to work very hard to promote this book.

If you'd like to see the completed manuscript, please let me know.

Cheers,

Michael W. Dean

Selling Screenplays

I've never done it. But a good book that I've read and know to be read by people who've done it is *Screenwriter's Survival Guide* by Max Adams (Warner Books, 2001).

It's sometimes done through an agent. Sometimes done through hustling. Hollywood is based on hustling.

I had a screenplay that was being pitched by an entertainment attorney in Los Angeles, but he didn't sell it. The same screenplay is currently being considered by a director. It was shown to him by his girlfriend, who has been a friend of mine. Things often work that way in Hollywood.

There's more on screenplays in my book *$30 Film School*. In particular, read the interviews with Josh Leonard and Daryl Haney.

Selling Articles to Magazines

I've never done it. But pretty much everything you need to know is covered in the interview with Jackie Cohen in the chapter on interviews included on the CD with this book.

It's usually not done through an agent. It doesn't pay enough to be worth his effort. So you have to hustle, again. One key to doing it is to look at the magazines you're trying to pitch to. You will be wasting your time to send articles out randomly without seeing what they want.

Agent: Pros and Cons

A problem with doing art for a living is that the people who are the best at creating art are usually *not* the best at selling and promoting it. That's one reason we get agents. Agents are people who do the selling for us so that we can just do the work.

Should you get an agent? It's a toss-up. You end up paying a percentage, but they probably get you more work than you could on your own. They take between 10 and 20 percent of your fee. Your publisher sends checks directly to the agent; the agent takes her cut and sends you the balance.

I have an agent. If you're good (and you work at it for years), you can probably get an agent.

Finding an Agent and a Publisher

I found my choices for agents from a Web site called Preditors and Editors. (They intentionally misspell "predators" for trademark reasons.)

They have a list of agents they recommend, a list of agents they do *not* recommend, stuff on how to submit, and more.

Main Site: http://www.invirtuo.cc/prededitors/

List of Agents: http://www.invirtuo.cc/prededitors/pubagent.htm

This is also mirrored here:

Main Site: http://www.anotherealm.com/prededitors

List of Agents: http://www.anotherealm.com/prededitors/pubagent.htm

This is a great site overall. There's tons of useful stuff here. Check it out. Here are some other good ones too:

http://everyonewhosanyone.com/

http://www.writersservices.com/

www.publishersmarketplace.com

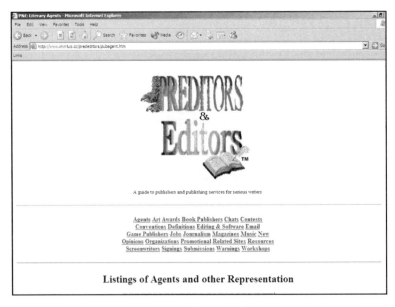

Figure 11.1 *The Preditors and Editors Web site.*

http://www.geocities.com/ebyame/warning.html is another list of agents who are *not* recommended.

NOTE

My publisher, my agent, my cat, and I are not responsible for the content of any Web site listed in this book. They're all just listed for grins and giggles. Do with them what you may. That's the whole of **my** law.

I went to the alphabetical listing of agents and contacted all that accepted non-fiction that the site didn't consider predators. As I said, the ones that charge are predators.

So are those that recommend a "book doctor." As I've said, a book doctor is a scam. An editor or agent says, "Your book is good, but you need a book doctor to fix it up." Then they refer you to someone who charges you between 500 and 5,000 bucks to help you critique or rewrite your book. Real writers never do this. They do it themselves, until it's good enough for an editor to want to sign it and clean up the rough spots. (Reputable publishers don't usually charge for this, and if they do, it's taken out later from royalties, not charged up front.)

The agent has never even sold anything, and he refers *everything* that comes in to a book doctor. He gets a cut. Sometimes he *is* the book doctor, using a different address and identity. It is my understanding that book doctors are always a scam.

Reputable companies do not solicit the public. Reputable companies have employees whose job is to *weed out* unsolicited stuff!

Reputable agents do not charge you up front. They charge a percentage only if they sell your stuff.

Reputable publishers also do not charge you up front. They pay you a percentage if they sell your stuff.

Keep in mind that when your publisher has a paycheck for you, they pay it to your *agent*. Your agent takes out her percentage and then pays you the remainder. This is how it works. Always. In some cases, as with my agent, the pay is immediate. Kimberly sends me my 85% the next day. With some agents it can take a month or longer.

NOTE

Don't ask for your advances early. It won't work. I've done it only once, and it worked. It was for my second book; the agent knew the check was coming from the publisher and sent me my share a week early so that I could buy this new laptop to take on tour in Europe.

If you ever have to do anything like that, put it in terms of the benefit to the company, not how it will help you or how broke and hungry you are. Say, "If you send it to me early, I'll be able to work on my next book on tour with a new laptop, and you'll get more money from that investment a lot sooner." That works. "I'm starving and about to get evicted!" doesn't usually work.

Some scammy agents even search the copyright office and contact everyone who copyrights anything. As soon as you file a copyright, the agents find you.

Your stuff is good. Don't pay to throw it away.

Check out http://www.sfwa.org/beware/cases.html for info on an agency called Edit Ink that got shut down by the feds. And also check out the scan on the CD-ROM in the rejection letters folder called "Edit Ink." It was a company participating in the scheme, trying to get me to pay Edit Ink.

Go with a reputable agent who has sold books in your genre. Also check out Jeff Herman's *Guide to Book Publishers, Editors and Literary Agents 2004: Who They Are! What They Want! and How to Win Them Over! (Writer's Guide to Book Editors, Publishers, and Literary Agents)*. This is pretty much the industry standard for this kind of thing.

Jeff Herman used to be my agent. He tried to sell *Starving in the Company of Beautiful Women* and didn't succeed. He's a very successful agent but almost always in non-fiction. I'm guessing he took my fiction novel as an experiment. The experiment apparently didn't work.

When I finally got Kimberly as my agent for the non-fiction *$30 Film School* project, she got me a deal very quickly.

I will explain more on negotiation in the next chapter.

Series Editorship

If you come up with a series and the publisher uses your title and format to write other books, you are said to be the series creator and get a credit called *series editorship*. (At least you should. I would write this into your contract if it's not there.) If you develop something cool and they run with it, you get a (smaller) royalty on each book sold, even if you don't write it. For example, if my publisher gets someone else to write *$30 Business School*, *$30 Law School*, or *$30 Med School*, I would get a little bit on each one sold. I would probably ask to have some input on it, to maintain the integrity of what I created. I would probably ask to write the foreword and also write a style guide for the subsequent authors to follow. They'd probably let me.

> **NOTE**
>
> I conceived these three books as a trilogy and wrote them as such. Any other books in this series will likely be written by someone else. I'm ready to write another novel anyway. My brain hurts from all this left-brain work. I need to do some right-brain stuff for a while.

To that end, I have written such a guide. I will use it if this turns into a series, and I could also use it to help me establish a trademark of the series name. Look in the CD-ROM in the folder called Book Proposals. There is also a document in there called Series Outline. In it, I describe what is unique about this series and my invention of it.

Rejection Letters

They're part of life. You will get some before you get published. I've included some of the more interesting ones I've received. (I marked out the names to protect the guilty.) Look on the CD-ROM in the Rejection Letters folder. Some of them are pretty funny. Have a good time.

Conclusion

All right. That's a bit on the biz.

Again, you really should read the other two books in this series, *$30 Film School* and *$30 Music School*, even if you don't plan to make films or music. I promise there is enough information in there that you will find applicable to writing to make it worth your while. The three books are really one thing, one collection, and they endlessly reference and reinforce each other, especially on business.

Speaking of business, let's move on to the next chapter, "More on Business."

Chapter 12

More on Business

$30 WRITING SCHOOL

Writing is the dream. We've already established that. If you're reading this book, you probably understand the magic of typing something up and eventually getting people to read it. It's almost voodoo. But the even higher voodoo comes into play when it comes time to get paid. Can you write what you like *and* pay your rent with it?

Can I Make a Living?

I started my first novel, *Starving in the Company of Beautiful Women*, before I could even type. (I learned to type when I was 29.) I made rough notes for it by mumbling into a Dictaphone while on tour with my band, Bomb. But the bulk of it, the *work* of hammering it into a coherent document, mostly occurred while I was at work as a temp receptionist or administrative assistant at law firms in the financial district of San Francisco.

Over the last couple of nights, I've listened to the commentary tracks on the DVD for *Fight Club*, which is my favorite movie. The author of the book, Chuck Palahniuk, said he wrote much of the novel *Fight Club* the same way. He wrote while working in offices, allegedly getting paid to do something else. (Which is probably why the book is about an extremely pissed-off office drone.)

The point is, you don't always make money writing, at least *while* you're writing.

NOTE

This commentary is good proof that amazing writers aren't always compelling talkers. The commentary from the director is astonishing, the actors' commentaries are very interesting, but the track of the novelist and screenwriter sound like two frat boys who weren't even involved in the film watching and going, "Dude! Check out this part! This part is so cool!!!!"

Most writers have day jobs of some sort. The hardest thing to do, and make a living doing it, is to write novels (and screenplays), which is often considered the sexiest of writing jobs. It's just damn hard to sell a novel.

TIP

If you get to the point of quitting your day job, don't tell them to "take this job and shove it." Making a living at art is such that you may have to ask for that job back someday!

$30 Film School has sold 11,413 copies since it came out last year. *$30 Music School* came out this year and has already sold 2,866 copies. This means I've put $428,370 into a sluggish economy. And people like it and dig it, and I'm helping them, basically without leaving my bedroom.

I made about $13,000 writing last year. I'll probably make a little more than that this year. And I don't write full time. I do *art* full time, but I probably write 25 hours a week. That works out to a little over ten bucks an hour—not spectacular. I could certainly be making more in the corporate sector. I have. But ten bucks an hour for changing lives, helping people, traveling the world on promotional tours, being loved for your art, *and* not having to get up to an alarm clock is pretty damn huge. I dig it.

I will probably make a little more this year as advances get paid back and royalties start rolling in from these three books. But I won't be rich from it. Not yet. And if I ever did get rich, it wouldn't mean I'm a bad man.

I spent most of my youth proud of my poverty, wearing it like a badge to prove I was "down" and cool and not part of the system. As I get older, I realize that some of that is false pride, and that making money (even a *lot* of money) is not inherently evil. It is more what you do to make it, and what you do with it. I know a couple of millionaires who are damn fine people, filled with integrity. And I've certainly seen people lie and sell out their friends for 20 bucks.

It's all context, intent, and action, ya know?

Job Security

There really isn't any security in most jobs these days, especially in the world of writing. Most book writing is at-will employment. You can be fired at any time and not get unemployment. And it isn't technically getting fired. Most book writing is legally in a gray area somewhere between being self-employed and being a day laborer.

But the way to be in demand and irreplaceable is to create your own niche, like how I combined tech, how-to, pop culture, and spirituality.

If you create your own niche, one that is uniquely *you*, then you are writing the book or series that only *you* can write. There are plenty of books out there on filmmaking, music-making, and writing. But no one but me could have started the *$30 School* series. It is a combination of a basic tech book with stuff about spirituality and drive and desire and purpose, combined with a conversational tone ("write like you talk") that is uniquely Michael W. Dean. If you can, create your own series that is uniquely you.

My editor actually wanted me to tone down the affirmation stuff when we were first editing *$30 Film School,* but I fought him on it. And later, when people ended up loving that stuff specifically and buying lots of copies to prove it, he let me do what I wanted in the next two books.

Some projects will allow you more control than others. It's often hard to do something that is truly in your own voice and make a lot of money. I've hit a good combination with this series because it allows me to teach, make some money, and put a lot of myself into it, too.

I did make one compromise on the first book. For the *$30 Film School* book, about halfway through the project, I was asked to cut out the swearing. I felt like saying "FU*% YOU!!!!!" Note that the swearing crept back into one book, starting with my refusal to cut the swearing in Henry Rollins' interview in the *$30 Music School* book.

Interestingly enough, Rollins does not swear in his own music, because he wants to make—I forget his exact wording, but something like—"totally subversive records no one can ever put a sticker on." I did not say "screw you," however, and I am glad. They wanted to make the book for everyone, including young teens, and they did.

NOTE

My band Bomb did one record (*Love Fed Hate*) on a major label (Warner/Reprise) in 1990. It was one of the first records that had to have the "parental warning" sticker on it. About that same time, Warner released Ice T's "Cop Killer" song that caused so much controversy. People were actually making daily bomb threats to the Warner Brothers offices in Burbank because of this. It didn't help our cause to be in a band called Bomb on a label that was getting threatened with the specter of actual bombs. I don't know why, but my life is full of interesting coincidences like this.

I took the cussing out of this book without being asked to, because I saw no reason to put any in, and I wanted them to be able to more easily sell these books to youngsters I wish I'd had these books when I was a youngster.

NOTE

I'm learning that you can change more people and be more subversive by not being vulgar. A PG rating reaches more prime minds than an R rating. And a PG-rated book or movie can contain far more dangerous ideas than a lot of the boring and unspectacular R-rated ones.

The other thing that conceding to dropping the cussin' did help, however, was that since I gave them that, it gave me more power to fight for something else that mattered a lot more. They wanted me to trim the "spiritual pep talk" stuff down, or take it out. They were mainly into writing tech books and didn't really know how to market my books, because my type of book did not yet exist. There are no other books that tell you some of everything about film, music, or writing, from how to pick out the tools to how to sell the final product, *and* do it with an anti-corporate, "do it yourself" mentality. They just do not exist. So I had to fight to keep the "closing argument" chapter and all the other such stuff so strong in the book. I felt it was important enough to be insistent about it. And I was able to because I'd compromised on snipping the "F-bombs" in the language.

If you go look at the *$30 School* reviews on Amazon.com, most of them glowingly mention the friendly tone and anti-corporate pep talks first, and the technical stuff second, if at all. So there.

I've been writing since I could read (I'm 40 and started reading and writing at age 5). I was first published at 12. I've written every day for over 10 years and only made a living as a writer for about two years. And I don't pretend that it will last forever. I know I may have to go temp again someday. I still have a suit and some ties in the back of my closet.

Being Realistic

To make a living, you must be great, driven, and lucky, and have good people skills. And it may still take 10 years to make half your living writing. Or you may never get there. Some great writers wrote only one good novel in their lives and never made much money on it, such as Harper Lee with *To Kill a Mockingbird*. Like Fyodor Dostoevsky with *Crime and Punishment*. Or Djuna Barnes with *Nightwood*.

You shouldn't dismiss the idea of doing writing jobs that are not the sexy, high-profile stuff. Not all writing jobs entail writing the Great American Novel.

The most money I ever made writing was a job that I felt was really stupid. It was writing descriptions of consumer electronics and catalogs for a Web site. I made 30 bucks an hour working in an office.

I worked in jeans and a T-shirt with my feet up on the table and the keyboard on my lap, chatting up my friends on the phone, in full view of my boss while I worked. And I worked there full time for six months, and I was one of 25 writers they had. The company went under before the Web site even went live! (Ahhh . . . the dot-com boom in San Francisco. Good times, good times. . . .)

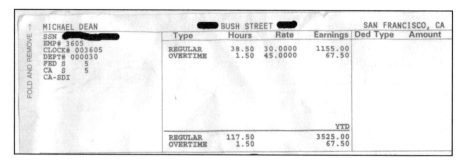

Figure 12.1 *Dot-com pay stub. (And this is what the temp agency was paying me. God only knows what they were charging!)*

My friend Tracy Hatfield in Houston writes for the local NBC affiliate. People don't recognize her on the street, but five days a week she writes copy in the afternoon that is heard that same evening by over a million people. Her writing is really good. And it's a secure job, with health benefits.

Jackie Cohen in San Francisco writes freelance for many different magazines. It's tough work, takes a strong will, and requires a lot of hustling, but she makes a living. (See her section in the Interviews chapter on the CD-ROM.)

My friend Stephen Elliott (see his interview in my film *D.I.Y. or Die*) worked for years teaching law school test reviewing, and worked as a manager in the writing department of a dot-com, before landing his paid job writing the novels he wants to write. (Okay, *he* was the boss at the feet-up-on-the-table dot-com job I mentioned above.)

Keep an open mind. All writing helps you with all other writing. My first book was a novel. It was good, but scattered. You can bet my next book (a novel I'm writing called *The Simple Pleasures of a Complex Girl*) is gonna kick ass. I've learned a lot writing three 520-page non-fiction books (including this one).

Alternate writing jobs:

- Technical writing
- Web stuff
- Ad copy
- Proofreading/editing
- Band promo
- Magazines
- Newspapers
- Writing press releases
- Computer game scenarios
- Journalism
- Music reviews/interviews and scene reports
- Editorial/social commentary
- Script writing
- Zines
- Online journals and travel writing

NOTE

Consider working for free to get experience and build a resume.

Contracts

Get things in writing, but don't get into a hostage situation with a company. Don't be controlled. Don't sign a horrible contract that makes someone practically own you. We write to be free.

As I said in the previous chapter, be willing to ask for changes. Don't be a creep, but ask for what you're worth. Or maybe a little more, because most of the time they'll bring you down to a little less than what you ask for. But if you have something someone wants, in any world, not just publishing, they usually try to lowball you at least a little with the first offer.

NOTE

In contracts, make sure that you don't end up paying for promotional costs. That is part of the normal operating expenses of running a company. It shouldn't come out of your pocket.

I repurposed *very* little material from the first book for the second book, or from the second for the third. What follows is the only part to be found in all three, as I feel it is of paramount importance. And since it is specifically writing-oriented (I sort of retrofitted it as a parable in the film book and the music book), it belongs here even more:

Negotiation made easy:

How a "nobody" negotiated without a lawyer to get a good literary agent, on his own terms (a parable for any negotiation):

When I was finishing up my first movie, some kid heard about it. He wrote me an e-mail and said, "I wanna make movies too. How do you do it?" I spent about an hour writing everything I could think of and sent it to him. I kept a copy of it.

A few weeks later, someone else wrote me and asked me how to promote a movie. I spent about two hours writing everything I could think of and sent it to her. I kept a copy of it. I expanded it into a Web site called 99CentFilmSchool.com. People read it, but no one went to PayPal to pay the 99-cent tip I asked for.

I decided to expand it into a book with a CD-ROM. I expanded the Web site into the first two chapters of the book, and then took the Web site down once I realized what I had going. I called the book-in-progress *$30 Film School*.

I studied online how non-fiction is sold. I realized that it is often sold with only a proposal and a sample chapter or two written. I wrote a 28-page proposal following this format exactly. It included my "credentials," which basically were nothing more than an interview on the front page of the *San Francisco Examiner*, and the fact that I had made one film, had booked a shoestring tour, and I had a lot of moxie.

I wrote a one- or two-page query and e-mailed it to 40 agents that I found from online research. Most never wrote back. Ten wrote back and said, "Not for us." Six wrote back and said, "Please send us your proposal." I wrote back and said, "E-mail or snail mail?" Four said e-mail, two said snail mail. I sent them all out that day.

Two days later, one e-mailed back and said, "We love it and want to represent you." They attached a contract. I checked them out online. They didn't have much of a track record, and I considered them a last resort in case the other five said "no."

I e-mailed the other five agents looking at my query and said, "So-and-so sent me a contract, but I wanted to talk to you before I signed it. Have you had a chance to look at my proposal yet?" The ones who had opted for e-mail all said, "No, but I'll look at it tonight." Apparently, knowing that someone else was interested lit a fire under them.

I looked at the last-resort agent's contract and noticed that they wanted me to sign over my entire literary career, forever non-fiction, fiction, screenplays, articles, and so on. I e-mailed them back: "I have a lawyer who is acting as my agent for screenplays, so those rights are not available to sign over. As for everything else, I would be much more likely to consider this if we did this on a project-by-project basis, rather than for everything I write. My old agent did this for my novel." (This is true. But he never sold my novel and we went our separate ways. I self-published my novel, D.I.Y. style. I didn't tell them that he didn't sell my book, but I wasn't lying.)

They agreed to represent me on a project-by-project basis.

Three of the five other agents wrote back, and *all* said, "We are interested in representing you." All three sent contracts. The two who didn't reply were the two who had insisted that I send it by snail mail rather than e-mail. They had just gotten my stuff and were not operating at Internet speed . . . a common problem with people in the publishing industry who are still stuck in an all-paper mindset. They lost out because of it. One did later send me a contract, two weeks *after* I'd already signed with my agent.

All three of the contracts wanted me to sign over my entire literary career forever: non-fiction, fiction, screenplays, articles, and so on. But two of the agencies were heavy hitters with huge batting records. One was my absolute number-one choice of all—Waterside. They are one of the most powerful agents for non-fiction how-to tech books in the world. They even agented *HTML for Dummies*, which I bought in 1996 and learned Web design from.

I wrote back to all three and again said, "I have a lawyer who is acting as my agent for screenplays, so those rights are not available to sign over. As for everything else, I would be much more likely to consider this if we did this on a project-by-project basis, rather than for everything I write. My old agent did this for my novel. And right now you and three other agencies (I named them all) have all sent me contracts, and one has agreed to do it only for this project. If you did that also, it would likely sway me in your direction."

Even if you don't have an agent for your screenplays, you should be able to skip that line and maybe still pull off this negotiation. I'd love to be mildly responsible for making a change in this industry, because I don't like the idea of any agent getting everything. The idea of the agent owning people is not fair. And if no one gives into it, it may go away.

My number-one choice wrote back and said okay. And sent an amended contract. (I wanted them so badly I would have signed their original contract, but I played my cards right and everyone came out ahead.) I read the contract for a day, thought about it, signed it, and faxed it to them on a Saturday, e-mailed them confirmation, and snail-mailed them the signed contract.

So, this is how I got a great agent, on my terms, in a week. In all of this, I was humble and calm, not cocky, and I didn't lie. Everything I told everyone was true, and I got what I wanted. This is a good working model for negotiations. But the only way you can do this is if you have some kick-ass art to back it up.

Keep in mind that negotiations aren't always events. They are sometimes conversations. And these conversations can happen in one sitting, but usually they happen over a period of time. People are more into negotiating with people who respect them than with people who are trying to "play them." Always go for win/win, my friend, win/win. (That is, they win, and you win. Everyone's happy.)

> **NOTE**
>
> By the way, I think that if all contracts were signed in crayon, the world would be a better place. People take stuff waaay too seriously. I don't like to deal with people who do.

Taxes

Keep receipts and serial numbers of everything you buy. Often you can write off tools of the trade, like computers, software, printers, ink, and such (including "instruction," like this book). If you devote a certain percentage of your apartment to work only, you can sometimes write that off, too. If you do verifiable in-store appearances in different cities, you might be able to write off some of the travel, accommodation, and food for that. Keep a poster from the event and the phone number of the person who booked you, along with your receipts. (And what's to stop you from having fun in that city once you get there, before and after your appearance?)

> **NOTE**
>
> Sometimes it's worth *not* doing this. In Los Angeles they consider you a small business if you do this, and they make you buy a business license and pay local business taxes!

You can also sometimes lose money at a "hobby" for a year or two and write that off. Check with a tax preparation professional, because laws vary and change from state to state and from time to time.

You can sometimes amortize the price of a computer or other large purchase over more than one year of taxes. And when it's outmoded, you can donate it to a non-profit educational institution for a tax write-off *and some good karma!*

NOTE

Nothing here constitutes legal or business advice. It is merely the experience of one person and is provided for entertainment purposes only.

Money for Writing

Money for writing is inconsistent. It's hard. I've had helpful landlords who let me pay three months at a time and then be a month or two late. It helps if you can show them a contract so they know you ain't jiving them.

Sometimes you have to rob Peter to pay Paul, let bills go late, and do a lot of what I call "justifinancing"—you know, sort of using a junkie mentality to work stuff out. Juggling bills. Maybe playing a few credit cards off each other. (There're a lot of tips on making money stretch in both my other books in this series.)

Dealing with the Company

Be low maintenance with your publisher and your editor. I know you're excited to finally be working, but keep the e-mails short and very to the point. It is their job to guide, and they work with a lot of people. Don't overinvolve them in your home life. Let them add personal touches and mention non-work stuff before you do it. Study the main character in the book *Bright Lights Big City*. His behavior as a writer is an excellent example of what *not* to do when working with an editor.

Also, it's easy to misunderstand people via e-mail, and people get upset in ways they never would in a face-to-face conversation. With business or personal stuff, when something starts to spiral outta control from e-mail, nip it in the bud. Place a phone call and straighten it out, even if it's long distance.

You don't wanna get dropped because of a misunderstanding. I try not to turn on the junkie charm at the first sign of stuff not going my way. (Junkie charm is the skill set I acquired back when I was using drugs. It basically means whining and bitching until I get my way.) If you must do that, it works better after you have a bit of success. It could have gotten me dropped if I'd done it on my first deal, before making a few hundred thousand dollars for the company.

A little of me (especially in sober-guy-behaving-like-a-junkie mode) goes a long way. An old roommate said, "A day without Michael is like a day without glass in your food."

Once, a check I was owed was late coming from the publisher. I went ballistic. Told him how I needed it to buy Christmas presents and pay December rent. I said, "Should I write my daughter now and tell her that her X-mas present is not coming by X-mas?"

It got done. But it's very difficult. The work and time it takes to get money for work we do as writers is frustrating to me. I kick ass and turn down other work to get this stuff done on time, then it gets lost in the loop when it's time to pay me. And you end up wanting to yell at your project editor when you should really be yelling at his boss, but you don't know his boss. And his boss probably doesn't want to know you. It's not his boss's job to know you.

How do you get angry at a large company? Stand outside HQ and yell at the bricks? Suck it up. You have to remember to play the game a bit.

It is usually better to get your agent to take care of this stuff anyway. It's his job. Your job is to write.

Most corporations are really aggressive when it comes to getting you to meet deadlines, and very lax when it comes to paying you for your effort. Not just lax, but forgetful even. Expect this. You want security, go work in an office.

NOTE

Anger will make you old.

Keeping Your Friends

If you ever have to cut someone from a book that you said you'd include, or if someone's name gets cut, let him know. I had to send this e-mail out once:

> Don't kill me, but due to an error at my publisher, they took the credits off the names for the photos.
>
> There are several cool pix of you in my new book, but your name is not in it.

I apologize.

Your name is on the Web site though.

Also, any time you need a letter of recommendation, I'm there.

I'll have a book for you in mid-January some time. I'll let you know.

— md.

Mail Boxes

You need an address to do business from. I used to think that it looked cheap to have a P.O. box rather than a physical address. To this end, I went to one of those places where you rent boxes and got what looked like a non-P.O. box address. It was a camera shop that also had a side business renting boxes. You know, you get an address like 666666 Sunset Blvd., Suite 258, Hollywood, CA 90026, and it's really *box* 258, but the people you're doing business with think you are big enough to have an office. Well, it may or may not have helped me get my movie and writing career off the ground. (I think, if anything, that just having an address—*any* address—in Los Angeles helped, because my stuff really took off after I moved here from San Francisco. But it might just have been the time in my life, too.)

Well, that place went out of business. It was a *huge* inconvenience. I lost mail. The post office will not forward mail from those places. I had to update all my Web sites. I had to spend hours on the phone changing info for my credit cards, my gas bill and both phone bills, people I work with, people who owed me money, domain registrations, and so on. I had to reprint my business cards and checks. It cost money to do all this.

Well, I got another place up the street. It had been in business 14 years. It *only* offered mail boxes. That was all they did. I figured I was secure. Well, after nine months, *they* went out of business, too! Allegedly, someone there started a fake online escrow company and was committing mail fraud. I don't know if it was a box holder or the owner. (I had noticed one day that the owner suddenly started staring at three computer screens all day every day, whereas he had had no computers before that.) The FBI closed the place down. Not even a note on the door. Had to ask a neighbor. And again, it was a *huge* inconvenience. I lost mail. I had to update all my Web sites . . . a second time. It cost yet more money to do all this.

This was actually the third time this had happened. Years earlier, my band Bomb got a box at a U-Haul rental place in San Francisco. They discontinued their box service. So if anyone writes a fan letter to the address listed on our first record, it gets returned to sender.

So now I just use a box at a United States Post Office. There're a few drawbacks:

♦ There is often a waiting list. You can get around this by signing up at two post offices near you and telling them you're willing to take the smallest or the next-smallest size box. The prices vary, but not by much. And they're still cheaper than those mail drop places. The advantage of a bigger box is you won't have to get a slip and go wait in line if the box fills up. Take the first one that opens up—they'll contact you, though it can't hurt to go in and check after two weeks.

♦ They won't take FedEx or UPS deliveries, only U.S. postal mail.

♦ They don't seem as impressive as a street address. And you can't disguise your address, such as making P.O. Box 29704 into *physical address of post office* Suite 29704. You used to be able to do this, but now the post office will send stuff back. Sometimes (not often, but sometimes), they'll even send it back if it says Box 29704 instead of P.O. Box 29704. They don't want anyone disguising the fact that it's a U.S. Postal Service P.O. box in any way.

♦ You can't call ahead and see if you have mail. You often can at those non-Post Office mail box places.

But they're actually cheaper than those mail places, and they will not go out of business. (My friend said, "Don't bet on it.") So I'm gonna stick with the Post Office from now on.

NOTE

There is a subplot in the movie *Barfly* where the writer has moved so many times that his editor hires a private detective to find him. This is romantic, yet unlikely. Chances are your check would just get returned to sender and forgotten.

Three Last Ways to Make Money

Writing is, in my mind, bigger than the money. But there's nothing wrong with making some. Here are three ways you might not have thought of:

Amazon Advantage

This is the program Amazon has for you to sell your books on their site. They charge $29.95 per year and also take a 55% commission, but they also pay shipping and provide fulfillment. That is, they keep a few copies of your book on hand in their warehouse (or more than a few if they're selling quickly) and ship them directly to people who order them. They keep track of record-keeping and send you a check if you sell enough to cover the yearly fee. It's not a great deal, but it is an okay deal, and they actually get your name out there and get your stuff available. It's a resource to have: When someone asks where to get your book, they're more likely to remember it and buy it if you just say, "It's on Amazon.com" than if you say, "Um, go to www dot fluffykittybooksandstuff dot com backslash tilde new book dot html" or whatever.

It's easy to get on Amazon Advantage. Just go to Amazon.com and click on the "Advantage" link on the bottom left side under "make money." Then follow the prompts, submit it and if you're approved (most people are), they'll tell you where to send copies and how many to send.

Amazon Associates

Be sure to go on Amazon.com and join the Associates program. This is free. You can get a link to put on your Web site and in e-mails where you get money on each copy sold. You can get it in cash or credit.

I actually get a little more money per book sold doing this than the royalty I get from the publisher for selling the book! There's no agent's fee taken out, and I get the publisher royalty on top of the Amazon payment.

Be sure to go on there and put links to *my* books on *your* Web site. They seem to be selling pretty well, and there's no reason you can't promote something you like *and* get paid to do it.

Again, it's on the bottom-left of Amazon.com under Make Money.

eBay

I sell my rough drafts on eBay. And people buy them. I list them in the Books: Antiquarian & Collectible: Other category and also send the URL out to my list.

Here's a typical post:

http://cgi.ebay.com/ws/eBayISAPI.dll?ViewItem&item=3588829010&ssPageName=ADME:B:LC:US:1

"$30 Film School" rough draft.

OWN A PIECE OF HISTORY

Unbound rough draft, with handwritten proofreading marks by the author, of book "$30 Film School" by Michael W. Dean. (Cutting-edge book on do-it-yourself no-budget filmmaking with an independent attitude.)

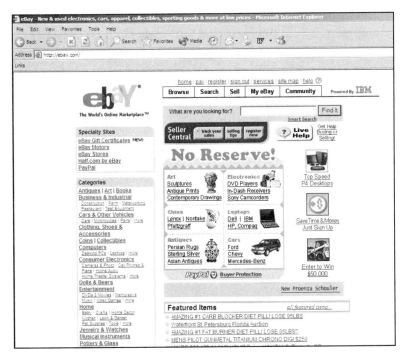

Figure 12.2 *eBay—a published writer's friend.*

This is one of three drafts for this book that will be offered for sale (this is the second of three drafts), all signed by author. This is somewhere between 300 and 500 pages printed out on his computer, gone through by author with a pen in the process of writing the book. First page is signed to you if you wish.

See inside the mind of this well-known writer and understand his process.

Web site for book: http://www.30dollarfilmschool.com

Press for book: http://www.kittyfeet.com/30bucks/press.htm and http://www.filmthreat.com/News.asp?Id=1221

Amazon site for book: http://www.amazon.com/exec/obidos/tg/detail/-/1592000673/ref=ase_www30dollarfi-20/002-6447922-7280868?v=glance&s=books

DETAILS: Purchaser does not own the copyright to the contents of the book. Only the pages themselves.

Purchaser agrees not to publish or print the pages. (There is some matter in it that did not go in the book and may be used in a later book or article.) Copyright is retained by author.

Purchaser may scan up to ten pages for his Web site, provided they are pages that ended up in the book, not the pages of new matter described above.

Purchaser will pay shipping and insurance. Shipping will be 10 extra dollars US for shipping out of US. Purchaser will pay via PayPal within 24 hours.

Thank You.

Typical rave about this book (see Amazon.com for 30 more!):

Posted by Jeff Irvin (205.188.208.133) on December 06, 2003, at 18:00:27:

$30 Film School, a great book. A must have for any novice or amateur con-templating making a movie. Especially if the artists' have little or no money or no idea where to start from. Chock full of info (technical, artistic & movie biz-wise), it provides a great launching pad. Most importantly, it kicks you the REAL DEAL on the challenges novice filmmakers may face and offers creative ways around those challenges.

In general, what I liked most about the book is its fiercely independent atti-tude and "Do-It-Yourself" resourcefulness . . .

Bare-boned, stripped down, aggressive, and unflinchingly honest are some adjectives that come to mind. Obviously written by someone "In the Belly of the Beast," making art on his terms, for himself, and sharing his knowledge and experience. Who can't respect that?

Plus it's entertaining as all hell, and like I said, INFORMATIVE (I don't want to understate the TECHNICAL VALUE - camera types, specific shooting angles, working with actors, etc.) Go buy the book, you know you will anyway . . .

— Jeff Irvin

I also sold copies of my book drafts, for even more money, directly to several different people on my e-mail list.

Conclusion

So, you still wanna be a writer? Okay, now you know how to write. You know a little of what it takes to sell a book, and how the industry works. If you're still reading this far, you're probably ready to move on and learn more. How about something damn fun for a little while—writing on the road.

Chapter 13

Writing on the Road

$30 WRITING SCHOOL

PCs are the ultimate in corporate technology, so it's ironic that they've become the required accessories for modern bohemian gypsy hippie freedom. I wrote much of *$30 Film School* in cafés and friends' houses while on tour with my film around the U.S. I wrote much of *$30 Writing School* in cafes and friend's houses while on tour around Europe with my film and *$30 Film School*. I like this cycle. I'll tell you how I pulled it off.

Equipment

I'm putting this in a separate place from the general equipment chapter because it's stuff that's specific to living and working on the road.

Figure 13.1 *Working on* $30 Film School *on tour in Seattle on my friend Clint's kitchen table. I'm using a laptop borrowed from my friend Christian. I liked it so much I later got the same model.*

Voltage Converters

Most countries in the world run everything on 220 volts. The U.S. runs everything on 110. So if you have stuff made in the U.S., you will probably need adapters and converters to run it in another country.

Before I went to Europe, I went to my local Mega-Lo Mart-type consumer electronics store and bought a generic universal adapter set. I paid a little extra for the

lighter model. It was about 40 bucks for the kit, which all fit in one little plastic box. It consisted of a step-down transformer (a device to turn 220 volts into 110) and an array of color-coded adapters for different regions and countries. One was just for England, another for Germany and France, one for Asia and Australia, and so on. There are seven or eight in all. They all have different plug configurations for the different wall sockets in the different regions.

Figure 13.2 *Power plug in England.*

Figure 13.3 *Wall socket in England.*

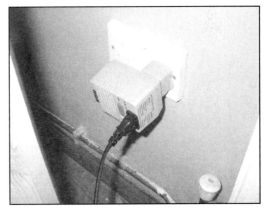

Figure 13.4 *Transformer and adapters in England.*

In England, about halfway through my European tour, when I was *very* tired, I accidentally plugged my laptop into the adapter and straight into the wall without the step-down transformer. After a few minutes, I noticed and violently yanked it out of the wall, thinking, "Holy cats! I just fried my computer!" I booted it up from the battery, and it was fine. I thought it was a miracle until I read the small print on the power adapter that came with my computer, the thing that goes between the wall and the laptop. It says that it can take an input of anywhere from 100 to 240 volts! Damn, I love new technology.

Figure 13.5 *The small print on the power adapter that came with my computer.*

Turns out that many (but not all—check or you might fry yours) new laptops have this feature.

Figure 13.6 *Front of same power adapter.*

As soon as I figured this out, I gave my transformer to an American kid living in Paris. He needed it, and I didn't wanna carry it. It added a few pounds to my backpack, and I'm all about light travel.

Cables

There are a few wires you'll need to get up and running and writing anywhere in the world.

Phone

In some countries (England, for one), you'll need a different phone cable to do dial-up. The end that goes into the computer is the same, but the end that goes into the wall is different. It will cost you about 20 bucks if you get it at the airport and about two dollars if you get it locally in a shop in the country you're gonna use it in.

Network

If you have a network-capable laptop, bring a CAT-5 (network) cable.

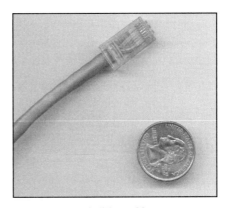

Figure 13.7 *CAT-5 cable.*

More and more Internet cafés, hotels, and even squats have high-speed Internet access and a place to plug in. You'll be much happier using your own computer to send and receive e-mail from your e-mail program than having to use someone else's computer and use some Web mail service, like Hotmail or Yahoo!. Those are fine in a pinch, and you can even configure them to collect your own mail from any POP3 mail server, but it's much more convenient to do everything on your machine.

Also, keyboards in other countries have some keys in different places than on American keyboards. The worst, for me, are French keyboards. On them, I go from 90 words a minute to about 5 words a minute.

Most mail programs (like Outlook, Netscape, and Eudora — I use Eudora) are set up by default to be able to read and write e-mail offline. You simply go online, download all your mail, then get on the plane, train, boat, or pack mule, or in your freezing darkened squat with no electricity, and answer your e-mail offline. You

Figure 13.8 *French keyboard. Look at the letters.* You *try typing on this!*

Figure 13.9 *German keyboard. Notice that the "2" and "3" keys have different symbols above them than those you find on an American keyboard.*

hit "Send" when you're done with each one, and it queues it to send and receive automatically whenever it senses an Internet connection again. Pretty cool, no? (This is also good for me, who *way* more than once has sent an e-mail I wish I could unsend. This gives me a few hours to think about it before it actually goes out.)

This is what all businessmen and women do on planes, and it's what all writers can and should do. Nothing could be more simple. (Some trains, including the Eurostar and some others in England and Germany, have AC outlets.)

Figure 13.10 *Eudora mail queue.*

Getting Online

From my mailing list, July 30, 2003:

> Today I did something I never thought I would do. I'm not proud of it either. Yes folks, I signed up for a free trial AOL account.
>
> It is my opinion that AOL sucks. They make it hard to even save an image in a format that can be used outside their system. AOL is like having your Christian Republican grandfather lookin' over your shoulder and monitoring where you go on the Internet. They seem to want to keep you in their closed system, only talking to other, approved people in the same system. I think they don't want you talking to outsiders where you might learn something!

But like Henry Rollins told me: AOL is the only way to get online in every single country . . . and don't worry, I didn't have an AOL e-mail account. I send and receive from the Kittyfeet account via Eudora—which is faster and safer (less susceptible to viruses) than Outlook—and answer the messages offline on the train to send from the next stop. I only use AOL for connectivity.

I have this, um, friend who claims, "When I went to cancel AOL from the free two months, I put on a redneck voice and told them, 'I wanna cancel 'cause I don't git this interweb stuff. I jest dun get it. I'm tryin' to look at football scores and can't get my durned football scores on your interweb.'

"They offered me two extra months free and also took off the 80 bucks of connection charges I logged while I was in Europe. So I ended up with four months, two of it all over Europe, for free."

Keep note of two things: First, dial-up charges may occur in Europe for local charges on AOL. So maybe if you're using it from someone's house while you're there, go online, download your e-mail, go offline. Answer your e-mail and then go back online to send. Also, maybe give them a pound or a couple of Euros for their trouble. (More on currency in a minute.)

Second, after you finally do cancel from AOL, make sure you get a confirmation transaction number, and make sure you check your next credit card bill. You have to give your credit card info to sign up for the free account. AOL has been known to charge people after they cancel. I just saw a thing on the news about it tonight.

See http://www.msnbc.com/news/986024.asp?0si=-&cp1=1

and

http://www.glendale-online.com/news/20031201ispregulationscancel.html

and

http://consumeraffairs.com/internet/aol_double_bill.html

When doing dial-up from someone's house, if they have an answering machine, you often have to bypass it to get online. Ever though the other side of the answering machine has a dial tone, you won't usually be able to get online. Just plug directly into the phone jack in the wall.

Internet Cafés

They're everywhere, or they're coming your way. You go in, pay, and use a computer. Usually about five dollars an hour in the U.S. Usually has high-speed Internet access. Usually filled with a bunch of cool 20-year-olds from all over the world. They're mostly answering e-mail and doing chat.

I use them a lot. Watch out for viruses, and be wary of entering passwords over them. Someone could easily load a key logger (a program that surreptitiously logs all keystrokes and can be viewed later from that machine or at the same time over the Internet from another location). I wouldn't use a credit card over these machines. Too many chances to get ripped off with key loggers or such. Internet cafés are a favorite launch pad for hackers for what must be obvious reasons.

Call Centres

Europe is full of call centres, basically Internet cafés that also have a number of poorly built little phone booths with a phone in each one. They are not coin operated. You just go up to the counter and get a login. These people all speak some English, regardless of the country. You log in and can make cheap calls anywhere in the world. It's a good deal, and it's also a hangout and hub of youth culture. Most of them allow smoking and even drinking.

Internet connectivity is very cheap at these places, usually a couple of Euros an hour. (Euros are the new currency that many countries in Europe have gotten together and produced, to help spread a global, or at least Europe-wide, economy. Euros are accepted in most of the countries in Europe *except* England. Last I checked, a Euro was about $1.10 U.S. I call Euros "superbucks" because the mental conversion is so easy: They buy as much as a U.S. dollar with a little bit more punch packed in. No need to do the math when you've got Euros. Just think dollars, but have your chin a little higher, because you're a little wealthier than you think. I love a pocket full of Euros. And they're stunningly beautiful. They were designed by a committee made of the most artistic countries in the world. Interestingly, there are no people on them, because they couldn't decide who to put so they put buildings. And they invented all the buildings because they couldn't agree on which country's buildings to feature.)

Here is a currency converter so you can keep current: http://www.xe.com/ucc/.

Figure 13.11 *Seven hundred Euros and a cat.*

> **NOTE**
>
> I was sending some editorial notes back and forth via e-mail with Michael Woody about this, and we got into a discussion on globalization. In it he referred to European people as "Euros" for short. I wrote back, "If you call Europeans 'Euros', can I call Americans 'Dollars'?

College Networks

Most colleges have computer labs. Most of them require a logon to use, but it's pretty easy to get around that.

First, you have to walk in and act like you belong there. I can do this. I'm 40, but I look like a college student. Or maybe a young, hip teacher. (At least I'd like to think so. LOL.) I just walk into any college anywhere in the world and ask where the computer lab is. There are often tons of machines online at high speed in these rooms. I will either walk around and find a computer that someone forgot to log off of, or ask a student if I can get on and check e-mail. Sometimes the library has computers. I've even told the librarian the truth, said I'm a visiting author (it helps if they've heard of you, but it's still possible if they haven't), and asked very nicely to get on and check e-mail.

Once I'm in, I do more than just check e-mail. I don't harm anything, of course, but I have a bit of a hacker's ethic fueling my "I'll do what I damn well please on any computer in the world" attitude. And I'll do any amount of "human engineering" that seems justified to get there. And I don't feel bad about fibbing to people to get this done, as these people are just enforcing a moderately arbitrary bureaucracy for reasons that don't apply to me. At that point, they are not humans, they are impediments to the free flow of my information. I will not treat them poorly or rudely, but I look at their attempts to block me the same way I would look at a piece of hardware or software that is attempting to block me: as a hindrance to be routed around.

Business Centers

I love business centers (or "centres" in England). They're like Internet cafés for yuppies. Almost every airport has one. They're usually out of the way, so you have to ask at the ticket counter or information booth for directions.

Basically they have high-speed Internet access, photocopy machines, fax, and more. And they're reasonably priced and not full of loud kids.

The Dublin airport in Ireland has one of the best. For fifteen Euros, you get free coffee and drinks, can put your feet up on the table, print for free, and even use your own laptop with their CAT-5 cable and access. And you can stay as long as you want.

> **NOTE**
>
> They don't have Internet access, but if you just need a place to chill out, most airports have a chapel. And in these godless times, they're usually empty. You can hang out there quietly as long as you want. This is great for long layovers. And they usually have inspirational non-denominational posters to stare at, and sometimes a bubbling fountain to encourage serenity. Just ask at the information desk. They'll know where the chapel room is.

Public Libraries

Gotta love 'em. Books, records, and free Internet access, the world over.

Wireless

Wireless access so far is a crapshoot. It's only usually available at airports, nicer hotels, a few Starbucks, and a few squats. At most places (except the squats) it's probably coded, and you'll have to enter a credit card number and surrender some demographic information to get online.

Different countries have different wireless protocols for connectivity. So your card here may not work there.

These issues may be solved in a year or two. I would love to be able to take a laptop anywhere and get high-speed access all the time. Cheap. Let's hope so.

If any manufacturers want me to beta test this stuff, I'm your man.

Travel Tips

You will bond with your laptop. It's your friend and the way you'll interface with the world while traveling. I had to protect mine like a baby in squats and such. I was in places where it was worth more than the combined property of all 20 people living there. They were basically all honest, but they are also very trusting, and who knows who is hanging out there?

Don't lose your computer or let harm come to it. Here are some tips:

◆ Carry a plastic bag in your laptop bag. It will be useful to put over the laptop bag if you ever get caught in the rain.

◆ Get a travel mouse. I got a small travel mouse that works fine and takes up less space in my bag and on a plane or train foldout desk.

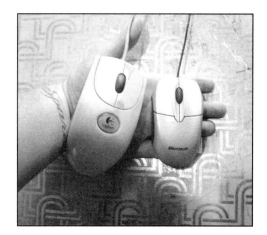

Figure 13.12 *Normal mouse on left, travel mouse on right.*

Here's some more tips that are not computer-specific, but might really help you on your way:

◆ Always take your bags with you when you leave a place. You never know if you're gonna find a better place or if your plans are going to change quickly, and you don't want your stuff on the other side of town or the other side of the country. Wherever you are, keep your stuff in one pile. Do an "idiot check" before you leave anywhere. That is, take a second look to see if you left anything. Look under and around things. Then look again.

◆ Do a newsletter to keep people in touch. You are living the dream. Don't be cocky, but let people know what you're up to. Some of them will be inspired to action. Others will never do anything great, but they get to live vicariously though you. You're traveling for the whole scene, not just for you. It's like when a poor kid joins the major leagues playing ball. He's playing for the whole neighborhood. See European Tour Diary.doc in the Goodies folder on the CD-ROM. It's all my postings from my tour in one document.

◆ Be malleable. People really do drive and even walk on the left in England. You can get hit by a car if you look the wrong way crossing the street. Be good at quickly adapting to the proclivities of different countries. The more you do it, the better you get at it. It's a good feeling to be able to transfer money and deal with customs, directions, driving, trains, and so on effortlessly.

◆ If people are going to meet you at the train or anywhere else and you haven't met them, e-mail them a clear and recent photo of you so they'll know who to look for. Ask them to do the same. I usually ask them to have a sign with my name or the name of my book or movie. That makes it easier.

◆ Don't get robbed. Don't flaunt money. Don't pull it out in public. Don't look or dress rich. I even remove my airplane tags from my backpack so I look like I came in on a bus rather than a plane. I dress shabbily when traveling. (Tiffany read this and added, "Just when traveling, Michael?") Put your money in a wallet with a chain. Put it in your front pocket when in a crowd. If you somehow make money while traveling, get it as money orders and mail them home to yourself. Keep the receipts.

Be careful. Don't be an ugly American. Travel with respect for others and be a good citizen of the planet Earth. Don't be an ass.

Conversely, don't be terrorized. Travel where you like. In most places, people are nice and helpful. But there are a few creeps everywhere. I even ran into two people (two in England, one in Germany) who treated me poorly because I'm American. There are some people who don't like foreigners, especially if you're from America. (And especially if you're from Los Angeles. After a while, when a drunk stranger heard me talking and asked in an aggressive tone, "Where are you FROM???" I'd answer, "Vancouver." (Michael Woody adds: "Tell them you're from San Francisco. Many EuroPeons think S.F. is the only humane city in America. If they only knew.")

Pack light, you'll be happier. Stuff gets damn heavy after a few weeks of shucking it around. Roll things to pack—socks, underwear, and such.

Someone told me I take less for seven weeks in Europe than his girlfriend takes for one night.

Figure 13.13 *Anti-American graffiti on a door in Berlin. ("Ami" is slang there for "American.")*

I had fun at Customs when I got off the train in London. They said that I packed light. They implied that I packed *too* light, like I was hiding something about my motives for being there. They searched my bags, asked a million questions. Then they did something I've never seen—they used a little vacuum cleaner to suck dust and residue out of my bag and ran it through a chromatograph. They do something like that with swabs on airplanes now, but this was to test for drug residue. And they asked me if I've been anywhere that drugs were used. I said "no" and tested negative, but I was a little worried. I don't smoke it, but I'd spent a lot of days in the previous six weeks in rooms with people smoking hash. But I tested clean.

I'm on a Virgin train to Manchester. Virgin, as in the airline and record store. All the trains in Europe are privatized now. That's why they don't run on time anymore. But the coach section in this train is really nice, better than first class on some trains in Germany. Which is odd, because most other trains in the U.K. and Ireland are dreadful.

It is *really* nice to be listening to English again. My brain likes it.

I've *loved* having the laptop on the trains. It's made the trips a lot easier. It does require some care and feeding, but I think it's worth it.

Trains

Trains are the way to get around in Europe. They're cheaper than in the U.S. and very comfortable.

The German train schedule site www.Bahn.de is the best place ever for checking train reservations. You can't always order the tickets from there, but the listings are so accurate that travel agents in England use this site rather than the official English site run by British Rail!

You can click on the English tab (on the left) on the first page and view it in English (other language options also are available).

Trains in the U.K., except Eurostar, are generally slow. The trains in Germany no longer run on time (you know the horrible saying, "At least Hitler made the trains run on time"). The trains are privatized now and tend to run 10 or 15 minutes late. But not always, so be early.

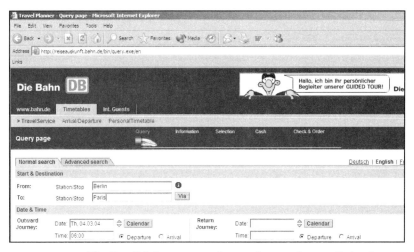

Figure 13.14 *The English language train search part of www.Bahn.de.*

NOTE

You can buy an ID card called a Bahncard at any rail station in Germany. It costs 200 Euros and gets you half off on all train tickets—worth it for sure if you're going for more than two weeks and traveling a lot. You need to bring a recent photo (I got one done at a shop next door to the ticket office for five Euros). They'll give you a temp card that you have to show when you buy a ticket and also on the train to the ticket taker. They mail you a really cool card back to your home to use next time. It's good for a year. This was waiting for me when I got back:

Figure 13.15 *My Bahncard from Germany.*

They will also try to sell you a Railplus card. I paid extra for this. It's supposed to get you discounts in all other countries in Europe. I bought it in Germany and then learned it does *not* work in all the other countries. Just get the Bahncard.

Here are some more train tips:

- Keep receipts for taxes. I put all the receipts and tickets from a given trip in one envelope.

- Sleeping on trains is tough. Get earplugs and eye shades. Master being curled up in two seats without your legs hanging over. Sleep on your stuff so you won't get robbed. Be especially watchful at stops when people are getting on and off.

- Get good at getting people *not* to sit next to you so you'll have more room. When people are getting on the train, I blast my computer speaker headphones and pick my nose so they won't sit by me. Also, setting up camp, hanging dirty shirts over seats, and so on will help achieve this goal. (Michael Woody adds, "So much for *not* being an ugly American.")

- Get there early. Go second class but get reservations. Note that just because there's a seat number and car number doesn't always mean that it's a reserved seat, particularly on Virgin trains in England. If you don't get on 10 or 15 minutes early, you might end up sitting on the floor between cars. Get on trains early if they don't have reserved seating. Take first class only if you're rich or if it's a long trip, like longer than nine hours.

- Learn how to read your ticket. It's not hard. But it's different in every country. Ask someone.

Phone Cards

You can buy them anywhere. (Usually liquor stores in the U.S., and usually call centers or train stations in Europe. The post office in England.) You punch in a bunch of numbers, and you can make a call. You will get sick of punching in the numbers—it's something like 15 numbers plus the number you're calling. But they're cheap. In England and Germany, calling the U.S. with a calling card can be cheaper per minute than calling Los Angeles from Seattle. In France they're incredibly expensive, like a dollar a minute for local calls. And in France, you can't use coins in a payphone. You *have* to use a calling card. What a racket. Another example of why it's hard to love France. (Though I still do.)

Teaching English in Foreign Countries

This is an opportunity that's available to everyone, but it's especially great for a writer. You get to live somewhere else, have adventures to write about, your money goes way further, you get to teach (which is fun), and you have lots of free time to write. You don't even need to know a second language. You're teaching people who already know some English.

If you're a published writer, you are then an "expert" and can get more gigs and more money per gig.

Check out:

> www.eslcafe.com/joblist/Jobs
>
> www.eslcafe.com
>
> www.escapeartist.com has a link on writing from overseas.
>
> http://www.passportvisaexpress.com/travel_visas2.php3 has info on getting quick visas.

Here's an e-mail exchange between me and my friend Skip Lunch (skip80802001@yahoo.com—reprinted with permission), who is going to teach in China soon.

> Skip: Well in China, businessmen buy drinks and . . . usual stuff. All-nite Karaoke and easy love!
>
> You just get invited out by all the Chinese girls for free. They love Americans. My friend Mike did this for several years.
>
> I'm leaving next week, and maybe not coming back. I told them I had a friend interested, just to schoozem, so if I get the job and it's cool, I will hook it up for you too. I was reading about ex-pat (expatriate) writers too— you can live cheaper in a weird country, that's the thing my other friend

Mike that speaks Chinese is hooking me up. We plan on travelling to all the out-of-the-way exotic places—Tibet, Thailand, Laos, Prague, where love and rent and food R Cheap! Why pay USA rent?

$60/mo for a Luxury APT, or free if you teach 15-20 hrs a week. Its seems all my adult friends are all over the world now, you were Mr. Euro, Howie Mr. Africa, I got a Russian connection, Hawaiian, several Chinese connections etc. . . . etc. . . . It's time to leave this culture behind, and live like the middle-aged white devils that we were born to be! We rule, and America is a rip off. (but nice to be American, ironically). I'll show ya, and good! call me before I go. Cool gig, free apartment, good pay and language lessons. No experience necessary for native English speaker. If you wanna you can do it for the summer

—USA Skip

Michael Dean: Could I get a better paying job since I'm a published writer?

Skip: Yes the pay scale changes according to your degree mainly, or experience in your case. show them the books, they'll be impressed. You would be a "foreign expert" they would pay more. You don't have a masters degree but the "experts" get better apts and more $.

Standard operating procedure . . . reimbursement on airfare, sometimes half. You get about $600- 750 a month, yet you live great on 100 there. Search "ESL", "teaching in China", etc. . . . lots of ex-pat pages with people talking about how to do it.

Michael Dean: Maybe I could teach English, music, filmmaking and writing!

Skip: Maybe! The thing is that Chinese are English-language CRAZY . . . they can write it, but still speak Chinglish. And for business with the US (the dream), they need to sound good. It's insane, as a westerner, if you stand on the corner for awhile people will offer you $$ to tutor them and their families. The Kids, they all hang out in the park and "practice English" everyday.

These people—http://www.minriver.org/employment_opportunities.htm—told me they lost teachers who went on holiday to party in Thailand and didn't come back They need them now. The other place is like that. Big turnover.

You can teach in Thailand, Korea, China and Philippines are faves, also western Europe. Just travel and teach and get paid. ESL and TOEFL certification helps. ESL you can get online for 295 bucks. It's needed in some places, China no, but it helps with the pay scale.

Love, Skip.

NOTE

Be careful with what you say and do in some countries. China recently jailed a bunch of Internet café owners for allowing people to access banned Web sites (mostly unmediated political forums where anyone can post).

Anyone interested in traveling the world and sleeping on exotic couches for free should get on over to www.couchsurfing.com.

www.tribe.net has a board for overseas jobs.

NOTE

Read Edmund J. Pankau's *Hide Your Assets and Disappear (A Step-by-Step Guide to Vanishing Without a Trace)*. This book is incredibly useful, especially for anyone wanting to become what he calls a PT (permanent traveler). You don't have to be committing fraud to be a PT, but with today's mobility, a writer with a laptop can, and probably should, have no fixed address.

I'm sort of a PT, even thought I maintain a residence. The best PTs have a lover in every port. That makes it easier.

Here's more on becoming a permanent traveler: "100 Ways To Disappear And Live Free": http://www.textfiles.com/survival/livefree.txt

Check out the other cool text stuff at http://www.textfiles.com.

Conclusion

Well, I hope that whets your wanderlust. I love travel as much as I love getting home and working hard in my apartment.

Also, there is a lot of information in Chapter 17, "In-Store Appearances and Touring," that will be helpful with writing on the road.

But for now, let's work on what we do if we *don't* get that book deal: self-publishing.

Chapter 14

Self-Publishing

$30
WRITING
SCHOOL

What do you do if you've written a book and can't find an agent or a publisher? Should you self-publish? Can you get 10 people who aren't in your family to read and love your whole book? If you can, it means you're both good enough and have enough hustle to make self-publishing work for you.

This chapter includes a lot on when to self-publish and how to do it. Also, some of this information is going to be germane to writing in general (especially the information on editing), so go ahead and read this, even if you plan to get a publisher.

Most Self-Published Writing Stinks

As I said before, the problem with the fact that anyone can make a record is that everyone does. The same is true with writing. Most self-published books are self-published for a reason. They stink. They are self-published because the writing is too poor to attract a publisher.

In his interview in the back of this book, Dan Gookin, who has sold 15 million books, says "Do not self-publish. Avoid the vanity presses."

Check out the scan on the CD-ROM in "Rejection Letters" called "Publisher Wanted Money." It was a company I submitted to that turned out not to be a real publisher. They were trying to get me to pay them to print my book. Real publishers pay *you*.

If your stuff isn't ready for a real publisher, then it's not ready to be published. Keep working at your craft until what you write is ready for real publication. There are exceptions, but not enough to be mathematically significant. Trust me.

Yes. There are exceptions. And good reasons to self-publish. There is no shame in being self-published if you're great: Mark Twain and Ernest Hemingway were self-published at first. Henry Rollins still publishes his own books. And I like his books a lot. (Not many people know this, but Rollins won a Grammy for the audio book of one of his self-published works, *Get in the Van,* which is basically his diary. I heard on NPR that the book *Alcoholics Anonymous* (the handbook of the fellowship of the same name) was self-published by a committee put together by early members in the 1930s. It has sold over 20 million copies over the years, and since the fellowship self-published, they kept all the control of the copyrights.

Also the book's primary author, Bill Wilson, wrote on the road, as I encouraged you to do in the last chapter. Even though he was several years sober at the time, he had spent so much energy working with others in developing and spreading the program that he didn't have a job other than developing and spreading the program. He was basically homeless and couch surfing, traveling and staying with friends while he wrote it.

So there are good self-published books. Some are great and positively affect the lives of millions. Most books in this category are ahead of their time. Publishers don't "get" them yet. (Of course, publishers have the exact reaction to rubbish, which can be confusing to the young writer.)

The exception that makes you self-publish shouldn't be based on impatience. You will end up publishing junk at worst, and (if you don't mind me mincing some metaphors) unpolished diamonds in the rough that no one will wade through to find the gold at best.

Some writers are desperate, and desperation is not cute. Unabomber Ted Kaczynski and the Zodiac Killer were both people who murdered innocents to get newspapers to publish their manifestos. You don't need to do this.

NOTE

A manifesto is just an essay written while angry.

I have run into several desperate unpublished writers in my day—people who feel their hearts are going to explode if they don't get an agent/publisher/following NOW! And they're often not good enough or experienced enough to have any of those things.

A cogent argument can be made for self-publishing. There is a good chance that self-publishing my novel helped me, directly or indirectly, to get other book deals.

Writing is a long, strange trip. It really is a lifelong journey. I mean, my third book just came out, and it's still trickling out to the public. I'm just starting to get some e-mails and reviews. Books have a long life. It's not overnight like with other stuff.

Don't panic. Try to have less desperation, more inspiration, and more determination, and work steady over a long timeline.

And once you have a book and/or a deal, remember: A book *can* be successful, on several levels, without being on the *New York Times* bestsellers list.

Eager is good. Impatient is bad.

I self-published my novel, *Starving in the Company of Beautiful Women*. But I had good reasons. It was a damn good book. It had attracted the attention of a major agent. The agent was unable to sell it because his expertise was non-fiction. Also, the book was pretty raw in subject matter (sex and drugs), and the market was in a lull for that. I think it would have sold easily had it been making the rounds two years earlier or later.

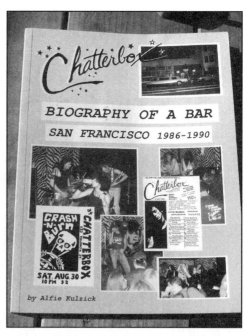

Figure 14.1 Starving in the Company of Beautiful Women. *A good book that I wrote and self-published.*

Figure 14.2 Chatterbox: Anatomy of a Bar. *A good book my friend Alfie Kulzick self-published. (She's at alfiek@sbcglobal.net.)*

> **NOTE**
>
> *Chatterbox: Anatomy of a Bar* is a cool book. A sort of yearbook for drunks. It's all about one scene at one bar 10 years ago. It rocks. A photo of me is on page 53.
>
> Every bar in the world should do this. (And thank "Alfie from the Chatterbox" in the book for the idea!)

So I self-published it. But I didn't go to one of those cheesy vanity presses that advertise in the back of writing magazines. Or God forbid, one of those on-demand vanity presses. (You pay a set-up fee and then they print them one at a time as you get orders for them.) (Okay, my buddy Rev. Keith A. Gordon castigated me for this. He prints on-demand and does well with it, and his books are good. Check out his Rev. Keith A. Gordon on Self-Publishing.doc in the Goodies folder on the CD-ROM.)

All that stuff makes books that *look* self-published. If you're gonna put the book out yourself, start a publishing company (even if you publish only your one book) and make it look great.

First, your book has to be great. Make sure your work's *tight*. Have several people help proof it and offer feedback. (I lovingly call these people "helper monkeys.")

One reason to have more than one helper monkey is so they don't get burned out as much. Also, if their computers get stolen or hacked or they end up hating you and post your stuff to the Internet, they have only several chapters, not the whole thing.

> **NOTE**
>
> I know this book isn't self-published, but I did get a bunch of good proofers to proof several chapters each because they wanted a sneak preview of what was in it. I got five writers who were all trying to figure out how to get published to proof this book quickly and for free. (Michael Woody did most of it, by far. He is smart as heck and generous as all get out. I am trying to help him—I wanna see him write his own books.)

Get reliable people so that you don't have to end up sending letters like this:

Dear _____

It is polite to let someone know you aren't gonna be doing work for them that you said you'd do.

I ain't pissed, just letting you know. You should treat unpaid work (especially work you asked to do) the same as paid work in that sense.

I'm not in a pinch, I can get someone else to do it, but If I hadn't asked you the follow-up "how's your progress?" question and I'd just waited several days until you told me, it would have put me in a pinch.

Just a heads up.

Thank you.

m.d.

Get rid of all the typos you find. Enter the corrections into the Word documents. Then print it out and go through it again. (You'll catch mistakes the second time around you didn't catch the first time around, because you've gotten rid of a bunch. The eye really can't catch *everything*, and it's easier to find the mistakes when there are fewer mistakes to wade through.) Maybe do this a third and fourth time. (If you have to do more than that, you probably aren't ready to be published.) It helps to get other eyes on it, because other people will find stuff you won't find. You know when you typed "their are" you meant "there are," and "lose" when you meant "loose." Your mind corrects it, so you don't see the mistake. Your friend's mind's eye will catch it.

Good proofreaders who understand your incongruities are priceless. Sometimes the process has to be explained. One friend wanted to correct the grammar when we did the checking for the second printing of *$30 Music School*. I sent her this:

Please leave the grammar as is, i.e., in an informal, conversational tone. That's my style, and even a selling point of the book/series.

Let me know if a word is brazenly misspelled (such as "their" when I meant "there") or the name of a drum company (I already caught "Sonar" where I meant "Sonor"), and so on.

If I spell *rocking* as *rockin'*, that's obviously stylistic choice and shouldn't be corrected.

There's no need to over edit. It's mostly done. I'm mainly looking for stuff that is out and out wrong, like the thing about a fourth being eight semitones and such, or if I spelled "semitones" as "semitomes." Stuff like that.

Thank you!

Also, have someone look over the whole thing after you're done having everyone proof all the chapters. Hopefully he will catch continuity issues, such as if you do something that contradicts something you wrote earlier, or don't tie up a loose end that needs tying up, or do what I do a lot: write about the same thing the same way a few hundred pages apart. I do this because I think so much all the time that I can't remember if I wrote something or just thought it.

Make sure the people proofing for you are smart. I usually give a chapter each to a few different folks, and pretty quickly I'll get a feel for who helps and who doesn't. Get an e-mail agreement that they agree to do the editing for free in exchange only for thanks and a copy of the book. Or pay them if you can. Regardless, get your terms in writing (always, with everything). I once had a friend (a good friend, even!) offer to take a look at a script. He made a few small, good suggestions. Then he tried to tell me I owed him 10% if the script sold!

Make sure that the people who help are thanked somewhere in the book and that they get a free copy without having to ask for it—a few free copies if they do a lot of work. I keep a text file on my desktop that says "copies for" and just keep adding to it until the book is out. Then I track them all down and send each one a copy. It can't hurt, if you are mailing them, to send them an e-mail right before you send the book out to make sure they haven't moved and you have their current address.

NOTE

Thanking people is important from a karma standpoint, but also, not thanking people can work against you. I know a guy who self-published a pretty good novel based on his punk rock life on the street when he was younger. I probably would have included a photo of it in here but didn't because he didn't thank me in the book. I had helped him a *lot* with advice via e-mail on how to write and how to make his book. He thanked all his buddies, a bunch of dead rock stars he never even met, and ex-lovers who don't talk to him any more, but he didn't thank me.

Getting Ready for the Printer

This involves doing professional layout and design (or getting someone else to do it) and taking it to a real printer.

I used Quark 4.0 (also called QuarkXPress) for my page layout. There are other programs available—In-Design, PageMaker, and others—but I prefer Quark. It is elegant, powerful, and easy to use.

Quark is up to version 6.0 as of this printing. That's what our screenshots will be, except as indicated.

You will probably want to have only black and white in your book, because color pages inside a book are *way* more expensive than B&W. The cover can be color or B&W. I opted for color and paid a bit more for it.

If you are (or you have) a good designer, you can make a compelling cover in B&W.

NOTE

After you choose a printer, ask if they have any technical issues specific to their own process that you need to know about. Also, ask if they have book templates to use, or if you should use the ones that come with this book's CD-ROM. Mention this book to them by name. If printers become familiar with it, it will save you effort when you mention it. They'll know exactly what you know and what else they need to tell you.

The cover is designed as a document separate from the book itself. You will be bringing the printer one of two things: either the files in electronic format (on a CD or several CDs, or data DVDs) or the camera-ready art, all set to go. This means that for the book itself, you'll bring laser-printed page spreads and four-color separations for the cover. Four-color separations are four big separate pieces of B&W film negatives, one for each of the four different colors used in printing color on a book. To print color, they have to separate the color images (using Photoshop) into the four different plates, one for each ink color that makes up each printed picture. Then they make a separate print run for each ink and send the cover through the printing press four times, allowing it to dry between each. This is time consuming and adds to the expense.

If the printer asks you to also bring a printed-out version of the book, ask him what it's for. I was told this with *Starving in the Company of Beautiful Women* and figured it was to check stuff. But they actually made the film and printed the book by making plates from photographing what I brought them. I'd printed it on an inkjet printer. If I'd known they needed it for production, not for proofing, I would have paid to have it printed on a laser printer.

NOTE

Get something in writing from your printer, at least a one-page agreement, about what he's doing for you and what it costs, and something about quality. I did my first novel on a hand-shake, and the printer screwed up about 10% of the copies. There were some pages out of order—I didn't notice that until I was doing a reading on the radio. It messed me up in mid-read and was pretty horrifying. Also, books were already out to a lot of stores and mailed to people who had ordered them. I ended up having to look through about 900 copies by hand, find the messed-up ones, and then almost sue to get some of my money back. (And I almost got sued myself by an overzealous and stressed-out printer.) Yuck.

If you have to print it out for them, you should print it one-up and add registration marks. These are the circles with lines through them in the corners that are used to make sure each page is lined up.

I will cover Quark more in-depth later in this chapter, but for now, go to File, Print to open the Print dialog box. Select the Document tab and then Registration. Select the drop-down value of Registration/Centered.

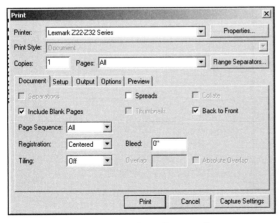

Figure 14.3 *Adding registration marks.*

Figure 14.4 *Close-up of a registration mark on the side of a printed output page.*

You won't be doing this for the cover if it's in color. The printer will do the four-color separations. You've probably noticed that when color is used inside the pages of a book, it's usually all in one section. You can have a lot of black and white photos throughout the book—it costs the same to print a page with just words as to print with words and black and white pix on the same page. When there are color photos, it's often 4, 8, or 16 pages with all the color photos together in the middle somewhere. Or maybe the end. But regardless, the pages are usually all in the same place.

This is because books are printed in spreads (also called *printer's spreads*). Books are printed with the pages 4-up, 8-up, 16-up, or 32-up. This means 4, 8, 16, or 32 pages on one huge sheet. This large page is later folded into one section and added to the other sections that comprise the book, and the top fold is literally chopped off by a giant machine that puts the book together. Look closely at the top of a book (or sometimes the bottom, sometimes both), and you will see what look like knife serration marks. Check it out on the book you're holding right now.

Printer's spreads are not done in order. The way that the book parts are folded over and put together prevents this. Here's how it's done for a 4-up book:

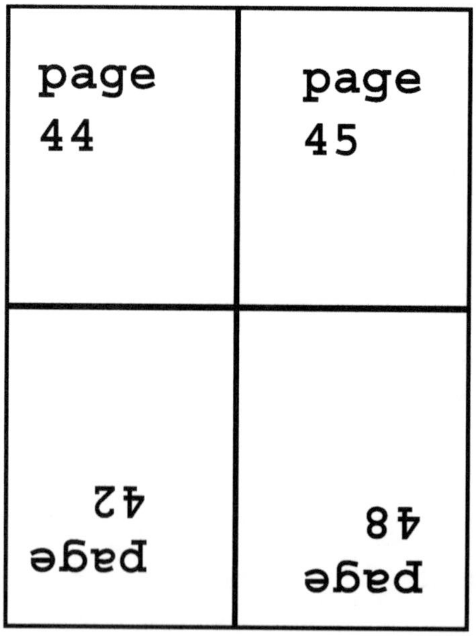

Figure 14.5 *Layout of a 4-up printer spread.*

The fact that books are done 4-up, 8-up, or 16-up is the reason books always have unusual numbers of pages (and always an even number), like 304 pages. It's always a number divisible by 4, 8, 16, or 32 (4-up is an 8-page spread, because it's printed on both sides of the spread). This is also the reason there will be several blank pages at the end of a book.

You don't really need to know this; your printer will probably prepare the printer's spreads. But it is a good look into the craft of bookmaking. My whole thing is that the more you know about anything, the better you are at everything.

NOTE

Your goal is to kill a lot of trees. If you sell a lot of books, you're killing a lot of trees. We need trees to live. They make oxygen. I like oxygen.

100%-recycled paper is prohibitively expensive. Consider using paper that is part post-consumer waste. 10 or 20% post-consumer contains that much recycled material and is basically the same price as paper containing no recycled matter. Ask your printer. Consider going to another printer if they do not provide this option.

You might also consider planting some trees yourself if you expect to be doing a lot of publishing, regardless if it's self-publishing or through a publisher. Give back what you take away. Always.

Shop around when looking for printers. Ask to see stuff they've done. And talk to people they've done books for and see if the people are happy. Also, see if they do their own binding or have someone else do it. If they have someone else do it, check the work of the people they outsource to. If they do it themselves, check out work they've done. Check books they've done, not just pamphlets or posters.

You might be able to get printing done cheaper by going out of town (or even out of the country), but I prefer to be able to drive over and look at the proofs in person. Out of town/state/country will have various advantages and disadvantages. Out of town might be cheaper, but you'll need to pay shipping. Out of state you might not pay tax, and out of the country might be really cheap but you might pay a tariff.

> **NOTE**
>
> As with anything in life, the rule is, "You can have something done fast, good, or cheap. Pick any two." Nowhere is this more true than with printers.

Cost and Expectations

I had my printer make 1,000 copies of my 304-page novel. It looked good, looked like a real book, and cost about 4,000 dollars. It took me four years to get rid of the books. I sold about half (for between 5 and 13 dollars each) and gave away the rest or traded them for favors or other people's art. (Alternately, my first book with a major publisher, *$30 Film School*, has sold 8,000 copies, at 30 bucks a pop, in eight months.)

I sent copies of my novel out to magazines. They took up to a year to get reviewed. *$30 Film School* started getting reviewed a month after it came out. Part of this is that it's easier to grok the idea of a tech book without reading the whole thing. Also, people take stuff more seriously when it comes from a major publisher.

CMYK

Computer monitors display all of their colors using only the three primary colors (red/green/blue). The three-color model is called RGB.

Color in books is typically done as a four-color process. The four-color model is called CMYK, and it's what you get in printers you buy at the Mega-Lo Mart. (Cyan/magenta/yellow/black. Black is abbreviated as a K to avoid confusion with blue.)

There are more than four colors of ink you can print with, but that doesn't matter here. What does matter is that, typically, all images used in color printing must be converted from the computer standard of RGB to the print standard of CMYK. This is done in Photoshop (select Image, Mode, CMYK Color).

Don't be surprised when colors that used to be vibrant appear to be faded or desaturated. There's a difference between making new colors by adding light (a computer monitor) and by adding pigment (a printed page), and the computer will try to simulate that difference. Be prepared to compensate and to make more than a few test prints.

Figure 14.6 *Converting to CMYK mode in Photoshop.*

Adjusting Saturation

Go to Image, Adjustments, Hue/Saturation.

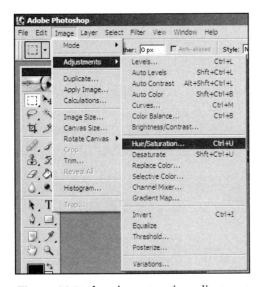

Figure 14.7 *Accessing saturation adjustment.*

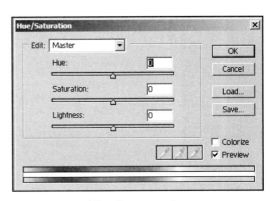

Figure 14.8 *Adjusting saturation.*

Move the sliders until the desired effect is achieved. Then hit OK and save.

You might want to practice with a copy of your image until you get good at this so you don't screw up something you can't undo. (One more reason to make periodic backups of everything.)

Adjusting Contrast and Brightness

To adjust contrast and brightness, go to Image, Adjustments, Brightness/Contrast.

You can move the sliders either way to change the settings. Keep in mind that stuff looks different on the screen than it will printed. The only way to really get a good view of how stuff looks printed is to go to a Kinko's-type shop and have a test printed on the Fiery brand printer. This will cost 8 or 10 bucks a page. I did it for the cover of the novel. You should, too.

Make the black colors on the cover "superblack." This is a richer black that prints better. It's added as one of the colors on the drop-down menu on the book cover template. I included it on the CD-ROM.

For the inside of the book, the text part, unless you're rich, you'll probably want it all black and white, in which case you'll want to convert your images to grayscale (Image, Mode, Grayscale).

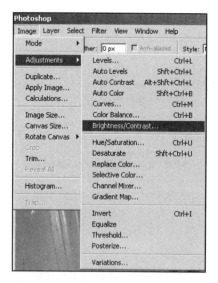

Figure 14.9 *Opening the brightness/ contrast adjustment.*

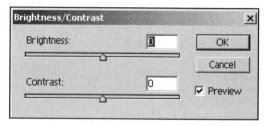

Figure 14.10 *Brightness/contrast adjustment.*

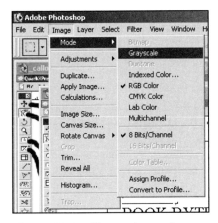

Figure 14.11 *Converting an image to grayscale.*

You can also automate this as a batch process in Photoshop, but that's outside the scope of this book. In fact, there are a multitude of ways to perfect photos for prepress, and a detailed examination is, again, beyond the scope of this book.

You might want to find a friend who is experienced with working with prepress. (Prepress is the term for the process of making stuff ready for the printer.) It's an art unto itself, and people who do it well get paid really well. If you aren't ready to do it yourself, see if you have a friend (or look on craigslist.org, an excellent resource) or someone to do it for resume experience or trade. And don't forget to credit them in the book. (And give them copies.)

PANTONE

There is a six-color process called PANTONE. It looks more vivid than CMYK, but it's very expensive and complex to use. It is outside the scope of this book.

NOTE

Technology has changed to the point where it's easier to make a profit on fewer books. So books are not as elitist as they used to be, whether self-published or through a publisher.

Image Resolution

I *hate* how many people now use Web-rez (Web-resolution) images for print. This is becoming very common as more idiots get computers.

Photos in books need to be at least 300 dots per inch (dpi), and Web-rez is 72 dpi. (Even dot-matrix newspaper photos are 150 dpi.) There are *way* too many people who do not comprehend this. Just look at all the crappy pixilated band flyers and even mainstream business ads in newspapers and magazines.

You can set your digital camera to either take print-rez or Web-rez photos. (It's different on each camera. Read the manual.) If you take print-rez (which will result in larger file sizes—you can't fit as many per card), you'll have more versatility. That is, you can downsample print-rez to Web-rez, but you can't upsample Web-rez to print rez. However, if you only do stuff in Web-rez, you might want to leave your camera set for Web-rez so that you don't have to take the time to downsample.

NOTE

With most digital cameras, you have to push the button down halfway, wait a second for it to focus, then push it down all the way. Try that while looking at the monitor and you'll get it.

For the really close shots (less than a foot), you wanna put it on the macro setting. On many models, the icon is a flower. If not, check the manual.

Using Quark

I'm not gonna go into Quark in depth. There are other books, longer than this book, that do that. But I'll teach you enough of what I know to self-publish a good-looking book.

A demo of Quark is available at www.quark.com, but it does not allow you to save. Get the real deal somehow.

You'll be doing the book and the cover as separate documents.

First, open Quark. Go into the Page Layout Quark Stuff folder and click on the book template.qxd Quark file on the CD-ROM.

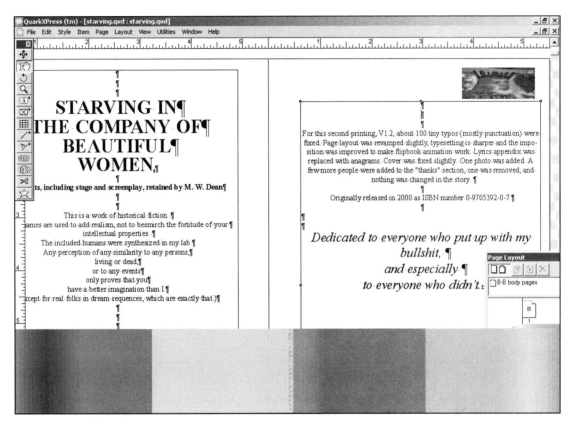

Figure 14.12 *Quark 6.*

You will probably get an error message that the project uses different project settings.

Figure 14.13 *Quark settings error dialog box.*

Hit Keep Project Settings. The file will open.

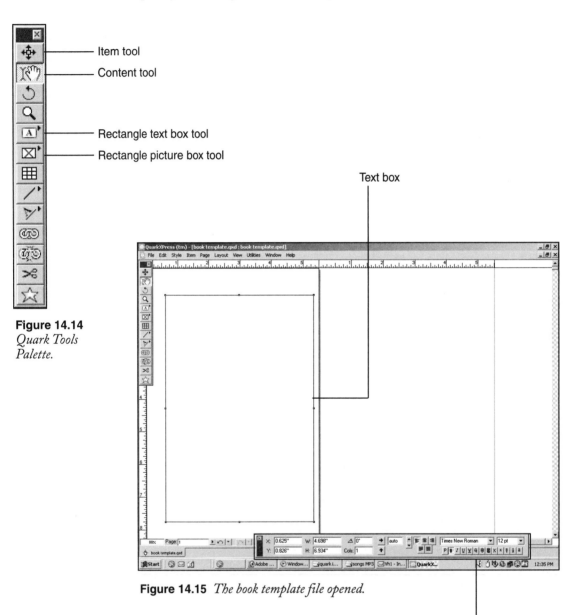

Item tool

Content tool

Rectangle text box tool

Rectangle picture box tool

Text box

Typography tool

Figure 14.14
*Quark Tools
Palette.*

Figure 14.15 *The book template file opened.*

NOTE

If you get a little icon that looks like a lock, the file is locked. Hit the F6 button on your computer to unlock the file. Locking preserves your items in place. You can lock individual items when you have them where you want by clicking once on them with your mouse to select and then hitting F6 again. Or you can hit Ctrl+A to Select All and hit F6 to lock the entire document.

The only five tools I really used for making my book were the Item tool, the Content tool, the Rectangle Text Box tool, the Rectangle Picture Box tool, and the Typography tools.

Click on the Content tool, then click inside the text box. The Content tool is always used to select or move the contents inside a box. The Item tool is always used to select or move a box.

NOTE

Quark does everything in boxes. It simplifies design immensely. Just think of everything as boxes.

Get Text

Click once inside the text box and then go to File, Get Text.

Figure 14.16 *Get Text.*

Click on the Word file that contains your brilliant novel (or a chapter of it).

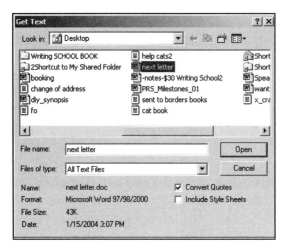

Figure 14.17 *Get Text 2.*

The text will come into Quark, maintaining most or all of the formatting of the original document. The text box will flow over as many pages as are needed to fit the text.

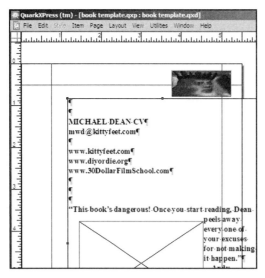

Figure 14.18 *Imported text in Quark.*

If you hit F4, it will pull up the Page Layout Navigator. You move pages around or delete unused pages at the end by right-clicking on them and clicking Delete Pages, or add pages by right-clicking and then clicking on Insert Pages. You can even do advanced things here such as setting universal styles. (Again, get a dedicated Quark book for that.)

Once you've got your text imported, you can click on any of the text and use the Typography tools to alter all the aspects of the formatting: font face, font size, left/center/right alignment, bolding, italics, kerning (how far the letters are from each other), leading (how far apart the lines of text are vertically), and other stuff.

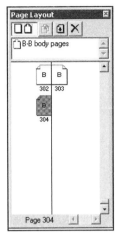

Figure 14.19 *Page Layout Navigator.*

Figure 14.20 *Font size increased to 36 points.*

NOTE

The Help menu can answer a lot of your questions. This is true in most computer programs.

Go through and format all your text the way you want. Get creative, but don't forget to keep it readable. A lot of people make the mistake, when they first discover all the bells and whistles in a new program, of getting whacked trying to do too much, just because they can.

Good designers know to keep things simple, balance white space with text, photos, and graphics, and keep it cool.

Move a Text Box or Picture Box

Click on the Item tool and use it to move the box. You can also right-click with the Item tool selected to get more options to format and alter the box.

NOTE

Don't move the boxes (or any items) too close to the inside margins, or you won't be able to see them when the book is printed. They will be squished down into the binding.

To Add a Picture

Click on the Rectangle Picture Box tool, hold down the mouse button, and draw a box wherever you want it.

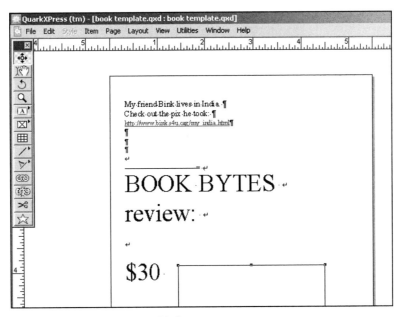

Figure 14.21 *Picture box added.*

Go to File, Get Picture to select a high-rez image.

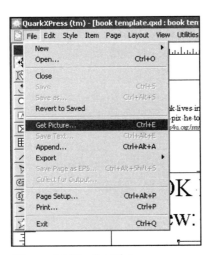

Figure 14.22 *Get Picture.*

Select the image you want.

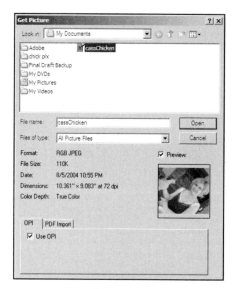

Figure 14.23 *Get Picture 2.*

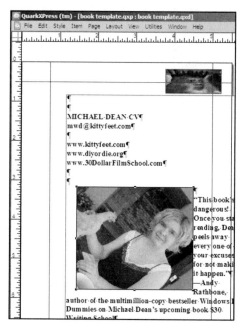

Figure 14.24 *Picture in place.*

Once the picture is imported, you will have to right-click on it and use Fit Picture to Box to get it the right size. You can do the same thing by left-clicking once on it and using the three-key keyboard command, Ctrl+Shift+F.

Collect for Output

Go through your whole document, import all your text and photos, and make them look the way you want to make them look. Print a copy, go over it, and check everything. Make notes, and make changes as needed in the file.

Then you'll save the document and all of the associated photos with it using a special command called Collect for Output.

Go to File, Collect for Output.

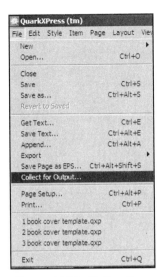

Figure 14.25 *Collect for Output.*

To collect the fonts, you will have to check the box at the bottom labeled Fonts.

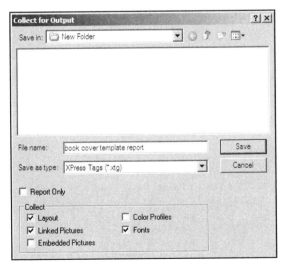

Figure 14.26 *Collect Fonts.*

You will get a warning box that tells you that you are taking the law into your own hands by collecting these fonts. If you are the sort of person who doesn't mind taking the law into her own hands, you could click OK. (Though I would never recommend you do anything illegal.)

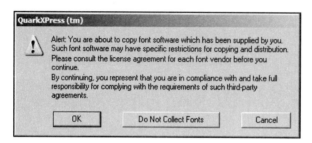

Figure 14.27 *I'm comfortable with that.*

If any items are missing, you will get this dialog box:

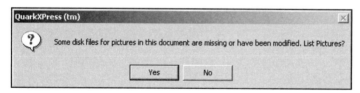

Figure 14.28 *Missing pictures.*

Hit Yes.

This will give you a report of the missing images.

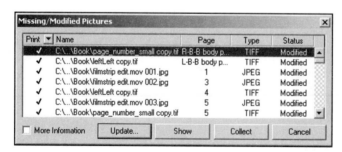

Figure 14.29 *Missing pictures report.*

If any need updating, click Update and indicate where they are. Then hit Collect. Save to a new folder. The folder will fill with copies of all the associated images and the Xpress tag template. This is everything you need to take to the printer on CD.

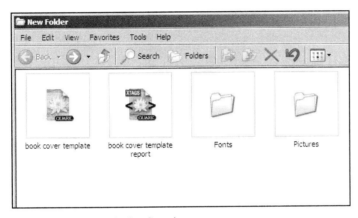

Figure 14.30 *Ready for the printer.*

If you have an older version of Quark, it will collect everything except the fonts. Quark didn't used to collect the fonts because the Quark company was afraid of getting sued. Fonts might be copyrighted. So if you have an old version, you'll have to collect them yourself. (I have to add that if they were copyrighted, you would be remiss to collect them. So this is for illustrative purposes only. I would never advise you to do anything illegal.)

Go under utilities and hit Usage.

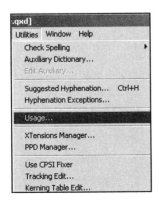

Figure 14.31 *Utilities, Usage.*

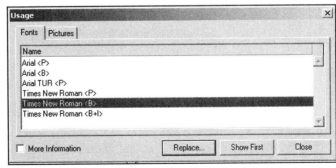

Figure 14.32 *Font list.*

You will find a list of the fonts here. Then go into your Fonts folder. In Windows 2000 or NT, it's C:/WINNT/Fonts. In XP, it's C:/Windows/Fonts. On a Mac, it's in the font folder in the system folder.

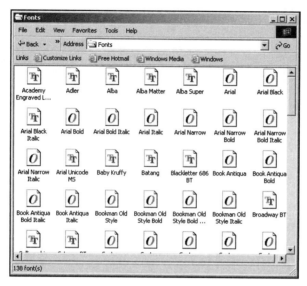

Figure 14.33 *Font folder.*

Select and copy (don't cut!) the listed fonts into the same folder with your images and output.

Repeat all the above steps for the book cover, except don't convert the photos to grayscale if you're using color.

Then save both the Book and the Cover folders with all Quark output documents, all the images, and the fonts on a CD. That's what you'll give your printer.

The printer may need to do a little touching up of stuff to get it ready and do the printer spreads and such. Ask up front what they'll charge for this.

They should provide laser-printed proofs (galleys) before actually doing the print job. Take a good look at them, because the book isn't gonna correct itself on the shelf. This is your *last chance* to get it right.

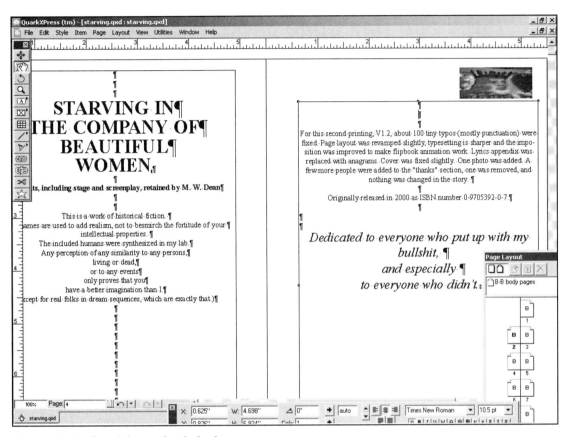

Figure 14.34 *Quark layout for the book cover.*

You don't have to publish a long novel to make all this work worthwhile. You can print 16- or 32-page chapbooks ("chapbooks" means "cheap books"—small self-published books, usually of poetry) or even zines (short magazines, usually about music, but sometimes about personal thoughts) this way. Anything you make more than 1,000 copies of is gonna be cheaper if you go to a printer than if you photocopy it, and it will look better.

See Dame Darcy's interview in the Interview chapter on the CD-ROM for how she used self-publishing comics as a way to get her thoughts out as a teenager, and how it worked as a gateway to her current publishing deal with the prestigious Fantagraphics company.

ISBN and Bar Code

The ISBN and the bar code are sort of indirectly related to copyrights, in that you should take care of them when you're about to self-publish a book.

ISBN

An ISBN is a number unique to each book that's published. For instance, the ISBN for *$30 Music School* is 1-59200-171-8.

Having an ISBN makes it easier for stores and libraries to search for your book within their databases. In short, it makes you more accessible to people all over the world. I highly recommend getting one. Also, having one makes a self-published book seem more like a "real" book, even to people who don't know what an ISBN number is. It's just something they're used to seeing on a book.

You have to buy ISBN numbers. They are purchased in minimum lots of 10 from www.bowker.com. It's $225 for 10. If you start a small company with a friend, you can split the cost.

Then you have to register your ISBN. Go to http://www.isbn.org/standards/home/isbn/us/application.asp. This is free.

Bar Code

You need a bar code to sell your book in most stores. The bar code is the thing that they scan to get the price to show up automatically on the cash register. They are also used for inventory and tracking purposes. I would highly recommend you get one if you self-publish. If you have a publisher, they will take care of the ISBN and the bar code for you. Many stores will not take a book (or any product) that does not have a bar code.

You can get high-rez bar codes made for about 10 or 20 bucks from a number of vendors, including Bowker at http://www.isbn.org/standards/home/isbn/us/barcode.asp.

They will need the following information to code into the bars:

+ Title
+ Author
+ Publisher (your company if you start one)

- ◆ Retail price of book
- ◆ ISBN number

These five things all get coded into that little bar and can be read by any store scanner worldwide. Pretty cool, huh?

You pay them via credit card, and they'll e-mail you the final file or send it to you on a disc. Then you just drop it into the Quark template in the appropriate place.

NOTE

Some people think that the bar code is the "mark of the beast" spoken of in the Book of Revelation in the Bible. You know, that mark of the Antichrist that everyone will have to accept before they can buy or sell anything. I don't believe this, but I certainly do agree that all the tracking we put up with nowadays in the name of security and convenience and stuff is a Big Brotherly invasion of privacy.

Here's an interesting religious site with lots of links to digital invasion of privacy stuff:

http://www.bible-prophecy.com/mark.htm

Anyway, I sell my stuff easily even if I don't put a bar code on my books and movies, so I drew a little image of a guy peeing and just put it next to the bar code in the Quark template. I've included two versions of this in the Page Layout Quark stuff folder (one white on black—BarCodeppBoy.tif—and one black on white—ppBoy–Reverse.tif—to match different cover designs) on the CD-ROM. Feel free to use them for free if you credit me. You can also flip or color them in Photoshop or Quark if you need to.

Figure 14.35 *My art of a guy peeing on the bar code, used on the DVD of my movie,* D.I.Y. or Die.

Chapbooks, Zines, Ezines, Blogs, and More

These are the ultimate in no-budget self-publishing. A good way to get past that first million not-so-great words, so you can really fly and write that great American novel.

Also, it's my opinion that while there are some good 20-year-old writers, most 20-year-olds haven't lived enough to write a novel. So write anywhere you can until you get good enough *and* have enough experience to write something long and amazing.

Chapbooks

I love them. They are small, pure, sweet, and full of zest. You make them yourself and give them away, trade them with other writers, or sell them if you can.

My cousin Kathleen Tenpas has published them since before I was born. She gave me a book like this when I was about six, and it's one of the things that made me want to be a writer.

You can print them on a photocopy machine or your computer printer.

Figure 14.36 *"Weeds."*

Pear Leaves

Like someone recovering
from an illness or surgery,
I lie in the window seat
and watch pear leaves
toy with sunlight,
gold/green coins
tossed in the wind.
You are on your way,
my last child,
gone already.

Figure 14.37 *Poem from "Weeds." "Weeds" is a cool self-published, 60-page chapbook of poems by Kathleen Tenpas. Handmade and individually numbered, number 24 of 50 produced.*

She added a note for me on a bookmark: "Dear Michael. Typed on a Compaq Presario 5020 with Win 98, CopyMaxed, cover done in Print Shop 5.0, printed using same computer and an Epson 640 stylus printer. An $8^{1}/_{2}$ x 11 inch sheet equals four pages. I used Weldbond PVA glue to hold it all together. Cottage industry in a big old farm house."

Contact her at hillfarm@cecomet.net.

Figure 14.38 *A self-published comic book by Becky Stark and Ron Regé, Jr.*

Becky has it all. She's beautiful, talented, smart, and amazing, and her spirit is bigger than a house. She rules.

Zines

Zine stands for "fanzine"(which stands for "magazine for fanatics"). They are those little photocopied, hand-stapled magazines put out sporadically, usually by young people, usually in short print runs (between 50 and 1,000 copies). Usually short on proofreading and respect for grammar, spelling, and copyrights but looooooong on moxie, humor, zeal, zest, and spunk. (It is a long-standing zine tradition to appropriate artwork from any source you like. This might fall under Fair Use, but more likely falls under "too few copies are printed for anyone who would care to ever notice.")

In the past, they were usually about local bands but now are usually about a mish-mash of subjects, usually leftist culture of some sort. There are feminist zines, punk zines, gay zines, biker zines, feminist punk gay biker zines, and so on. Zines are the voices of the millions for the ears of a few, and there are probably a million zines. That's quite a few ears.

The zine shown in Figure 14.39, called "Damn You, Drunk Rooster!," is put together by Travis Patrick Ritter and Cassidy Coon. The cover is by Jonathan Wing (wing@thebeatunion.org).

Figure 14.39 *"Damn You, Drunk Rooster!"*

Zines are easy to put together and tons of fun. I used to do them, pre-computer, with a typewriter, pen, razor blade, blank paper, and rubber cement. (Don't inhale the rubber cement. It *will* make you permanently stoooopid!)

Now people sometimes use computers rather than scissors and paste for their cutting and pasting (Quark would be fine, but I've seen ones done in Microsoft Word). Some zines are still put together the old-skool way, even set on a typewriter, or even written with a pen!

NOTE

If you use a computer to lay out your zine and print the master copy (the copy you make copies from), use a laser printer if you can. It will look better than an inkjet printer. Then take what you print out and copy it on a Xerox machine.

Zines are usually short (8–32 pages) and will sometimes print anything. It's not a bad idea to do one yourself or write for free for someone else's zine to get experience. Get local businesses to buy cheap ads (20 bucks? 50 bucks?) to offset printing costs (if you're making more than 1,000 copies, it's gonna be cheaper and easier to get them printed at a printer than to photocopy them). If you do them yourself, have a monthly collating party with all your friends to put them together and staple them and mail them out. You can also get your friends' bands to do a benefit to help defray costs.

NOTE

It's easier to get businesses to donate goods (like food) or services (like a DJ) to a magazine than to get them to give up cash. No matter what, make sure you thank them in the zine and onstage at the benefit.

Zines don't usually make money, at least not for a long time. They sometimes lose money but are good experience. In the punk rock '80s, working on a zine in some capacity was almost a required rite of passage. If you weren't in a band, running a label, or putting on shows, you almost surely were doing a zine.

NOTE

I've heard of people doing photocopying at work for their zines when the boss ain't looking. Keep in mind that the new generation of really high-end copiers (the ones that are huge and cost like ten grand) often keep digital thumbnails of everything they copy.

Also, if one was to do one's own work on the company's time and on their computers, keep in mind that if the computers are networked, they have a copy of everything. A good friend lost her job this way when they found some risqué photos she took of herself for her zine.

Some places, especially big corporations, go even further and install programs that log all your keystrokes and take periodic screenshots to see what you're up to.

E-Zines

This is exactly what it sounds like: a zine on the Internet instead of on paper. Cost? Basically zero. And it will likely be seen by more people than all but the most established paper zines.

The process is the same as a paper zine. Write your articles, get your pictures, and put it all together in an interesting way, except that you do it all on your computer and then publish it to the Internet.

NOTE

Get a catchy URL that people will remember. And don't use Geocities or any of those places that are gonna put up pop-up ads every time someone views a page. I think these ads (and Web communities that use them) stink, and nothing makes me wanna leave a site more quickly. These sites have outlived their welcome as a business model. You don't need them. Server space is cheap or free now.

Blogs

Blog is short for "Web log." Basically a blog is a cross between a diary and an e-zine done by one person.

Does anyone read these things? Many I've perused seem ranting, unfocused, and repetitively redundant, with poor writing, grammar, and spelling.

But why not? At the least, it's going to get some of those million words out of the way. I look at blogs as more therapy and purging of the soul than as actual publishing of quality work. And therapy is a good thing.

> You can set up a free blog site at www.livejournal.com.

> English professor and published author Michael Bérubé (see the interview in Chapter 19) has a great blog.

He says, "I get about 500–1,000 viewers a day, apparently. Completely weird—My first book sold 500 copies, mostly to libraries. As my site administrator said to me, 'You basically have a full auditorium of people every day now'—as compared with last year when maybe 10–20 people stopped by per day."

Alternate Multimedia Publishing Models

Think beyond the paper box. Think beyond crushed, bleached trees.

You can put out books with pictures on CDs, DVDs, or split-session CDs. You can do a photo book on DVD. You can do a CD+ (a CD that plays music and video).

You can make a CD that includes a browser-based piece of multimedia art. You can make a photo book on DVD.

The split-session CD (now called CD-Extra) is a forgotten medium that should be revitalized. You should make sure your CD is readable a cross browsers, a cross platforms, and backward compatible. I cover how to make these in *$30 Music School*.

There are ideas and tutorials on how to do all of this in *$30 Film School* and *$30 Music School*.

Conclusion

When your book is finally done and in your hands, whether you've done it yourself or with a publisher, relish it. Sit with it, hold it, fondle a pile of them. Relax and see that what you have done is good. Rest on your laurels for a moment. Not longer than a night, but give yourself some satisfaction.

I love reading my book for the first time when published. I enjoy writing, but I get so bogged down in minutia that when I'm done and it's out, I'll just hold if for a while like I did with other people's books when I was a kid. I'll pet my book.

I read it once for enjoyment and once for typos, and then I move on. Occasionally I'll take it off the shelf as a reference, but I'm so busy with life I rarely look back.

Chapter 15

Copyrights and Rights

B ooks are worth money. People get paid to write them, and people make money printing them. How do these people protect themselves from getting their ideas ripped off? Keep reading and I'll tell you. (Some of this is reprinted from *$30 Film School.*)

Copyrights are registered by the United States Copyright Office, which is a division of the Library of Congress (www.loc.gov/copyright). Copyrights are granted to one's self; the Copyright Office merely registers them in case of dispute. That makes it easier to sue in case of infringement.

You copyright your work simply by putting "Copyright" (or the little © symbol), then the year and your name, like this:

Copyright 2004 Michael W. Dean

©2004 Michael W. Dean

[Michael Woody adds, "Now you can distribute that work to the public with some assurance that it will always be knowable in the marketplace as having been yours."]

It costs very little money to register, about 30 bucks, depending, and is easy to do. Some say you can do a "Poor man's copyright" by mailing it to yourself and using the postmark to establish the date in a dispute. This is not recommended. It's too easy to open or alter a letter.

According to the U.S. Copyright Office Web site (http://www.copyright.gov/circs/circ1.html#hlc), a copyright is good for the life of the author plus 70 years. That's a long time.

The following excerpt is used under the provisions of Fair Use (more on that later in this chapter), although much government stuff is by nature copyright free if credited. (I always check the "legal" or "copyright" link on a site before citing it elsewhere.) If taxes paid for its existence and maintenance, it belongs to the American people. And that might include you.

"Copyright, a form of intellectual property law, protects original works of authorship including literary, dramatic, musical, and artistic works such as poetry, novels, movies, songs, computer software, and architecture. Copyright does not protect facts, ideas, systems, or methods of operation, although it may protect the way these things are expressed."—From the U.S. government copyright site (www.loc.gov/copyright).

I have never registered a copyright. I get a work done, put my notice on it, and then make at least a thousand copies and sell them. This is, for me, proof enough. I've made a lot of good art, albums, books, and movies, and no one has ever claimed my work as their own that I'm aware of.

When I do a book like this one, through a publisher other than myself, they register the copyright. Look in the beginning of the book (the copyright page is usually the page after the title page, which is where you should put yours if you're self-publishing), and you'll see that the copyright is in the name of the publisher, not me.

Many people get too hung up on worrying about copyrights. They spend too much time working on this and not enough on the art itself. Complete or partial works are rarely stolen. (Ideas, which are not copyrightable, sometimes are.) I know a budding novelist who paid to consult with an attorney on how to copyright that novel he has big plans on writing someday.

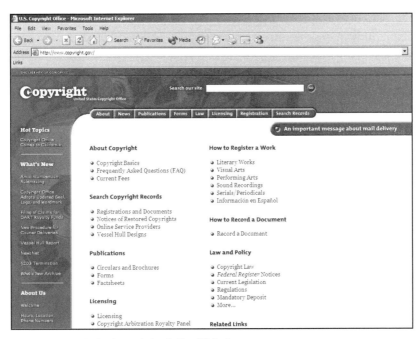

Figure 15.1 *U.S. Copyright Office Web site.*

Permission

I use content by other people in my projects *all the time.* I usually don't pay them, but I credit them and make sure they get a copy of the book without asking, *the minute I get copies.* (I have it in my contract that I get 50 free copies of each book, and my publisher is also good at sending out promo copies on top of that. For *$30 Music School,* I sent them a list of 140 magazines and people to send stuff out to, on top of Course's usual press list.)

I love collaborating with people and consider a work *way* stronger if it has opinions and input from people other than just me. And most people are honored to be included in something cool.

I always get permission to use other people's contributions. In fact, my editor rides me pretty hard to make sure I send the permissions from each project before we go to press. This protects him and the company, as well as me, from lawsuits. You must get permission in writing, even if it's from your best friend. People can change, especially if they see you getting some success and they aren't doing so well.

If I'm filming someone, I get him to sign a release form (one is included on the CD-ROM in the file goodies/ interviewee_and_actor_release). Sometimes I film him signing it. If it's something else, like a quote or a cartoon, I just get an e-mail release. I just send an e-mail like this:

> Hey Joe. How are you? Remember we talked about using your cartoons in my book? I'm working on it now and would love to include the cartoon series that starts on your site here:
>
> http://www.allstarpowerup.com/index.pl?node_id=1007&i=1
>
> in my new book *$30 Music School.* I can't pay you, but I'll credit you and send you a copy when it comes out. Thanks!

Then Joe writes back and says, "Sure," or something like that. He has to leave my original text intact in his reply. If he doesn't, I write back and ask him to please reply in the affirmative again without deleting my question. I explain why. They almost always do it, no problem—at least most of my friends, because most of my friends, like me, are into art.

That e-mail reply is good enough for me and my editor. I save all the release e-mails for a particular project in one folder, and then I save it as one long text document (with the full e-mail headers intact) and e-mail it to the editor. I always keep a copy for myself.

When interviewing people by e-mail, I usually preface the interview with something like this:

> By answering, you consent to have your answers used free in a new book by Michael W. Dean, tentatively entitled, *$30 Writing School*. Michael is not required to use the interview but probably will. He may edit for length and continuity. He will run his final draft by you for approval if you ask.
>
> (Michael doesn't know you but he loves you and promises to use your words for good, never for evil.)
>
> I will also need a high-rez photo. E-mail or snail mail a photo; I can scan it and mail it back. And a bio.

(This is also in the goodies folder as permission.txt so you won't have to re-type it.)

Note this wording above:

> Michael is not required to use the interview but probably will.

In the other contract on the CD-ROM, I word this as:

> I will be credited in the book if I am used. However, the author is under no obligation to use the interview with me.

and

> I hereby irrevocably grant _____ the right (but not the obligation) to use these photographs.

In these forms, the *not the obligation* part is so that, if you have to cut the interview for one reason or another, the person won't sue you.

However, do tell them before the book comes out if it turns out their part won't be used, so that they don't have expectations and then resentments. Offer to help them write a reference for jobs in the future (if they were good to work with).

NOTE

Nothing here constitutes legal advice. This is for educational info only. If in doubt, consult a lawyer and give them all your money. (Though no one has ever sued me.)

NOTE

Archive your old e-mail to CD once in a while. You may need it for legal reasons at some point, and hard drives do fail sometimes.

Fair Use

Fair Use is the use of excerpts of copyrighted material for review, news, research, and educational use.

An example of journalistic use would be someone quoting short passages from a book when reviewing the book in a magazine. An example of educational use would be me quoting the lyrics to the song "Long Black Veil" as an illustration of a songwriting technique I was explaining in *$30 Music School*. That was completely legal, required no permission, and no royalty had to be paid.

Fair Use can also include using existing art to create completely new works of art, like a collage. (This is *sampling*, whether in music, photography, video production, or any other medium.) This is probably the place where people most often cry "foul" and get a lawyer. These laws are complex and open to interpretation. The Web site www.loc.gov/copyright says, "The distinction between fair use and infringement may be unclear and not easily defined."

NOTE

Michael Woody adds: "I know you won't have a section on writing for the stage, it being a dead art and all, so you probably won't be interested in this famous playwright I've worked with by the name of Charles Mee, Jr. (http://www.panix.com/~meejr/html/about.html). Many of his works consist entirely of repurposed texts, including other plays, essays, articles, manifestos, court transcripts, and so on. He conjures a theme and a setting, assigns speeches to characters, and calls the work his own. He's quite shameless about it and routinely releases his works back into the public domain. After staging a world premiere and publishing it online himself, naturally."

NOTE

For a good overview of libel and slander laws, see Chapter 14 in *$30 Film School*.

BookCrossing: A Defense

BookCrossing.com is a very cool site. It's a non-profit, free, virtual library. Basically people are encouraged to take books they've read (or in my case, written), mark them with a unique number, and register the book on the site. Then you print or write out a label such as this:

"I've registered this book at BookCrossing.com so that I can track its journey through this world. Please go to www.BookCrossing.com/*book number here* to let me know you found it, then read it and/or pass it on for someone else to enjoy. Thank you!"

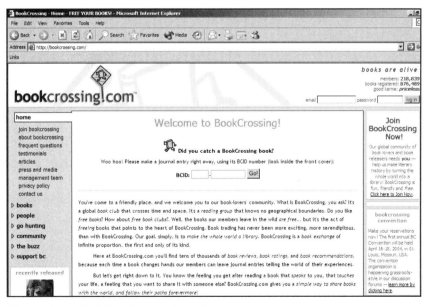

Figure 15.2 *BookCrossing.com Web site.*

Then you just leave the book on a street, in a café, in a park, and so forth. People find the books, read them, do a diary entry on the site about where they found it, and then rerelease the book. It's kind of combining the information-wants-to-be-free hacker ethic of the Internet with the real world of paper books. It's making people have to take a new look at copyrights but I think that's a good thing. I love BookCrossing and I participate in it.

Some writers and publishers have denigrated BookCrossing.com, saying it takes money away from them. I think they are tightwad old farts with no imagination. Here's my response to these old dum-dums:

In Defense Of Bookcrossing

I make my living as an author and I love the idea of BookCrossing. In fact, I've been crossing books my whole life. I can't keep a book in my house after I've read it. The idea seems wrong to me. I have read thousands of books in my life and only own perhaps six or eight at any one time. I read them and pass them on, usually to friends, but sometimes by leaving the books in public places.

While I've never thought to trace their journey, I love the idea. A big inspiration to me was writer Phil Sudo, who wrote the book *Zen Guitar*. I met him and interviewed him three weeks before he died of cancer last year, and one of the coolest things he said was, "Writing a book is like sending a message in a bottle, and you never know who's going to get that message." I love that spirit, and it is one of the main reasons I write.

There is a new shift in how things are done in this digital world, and I love it. I write, I make music and films, and I encourage all of my works to be spread by non-commercial sharing and sometimes even copying. Sure, if you bootleg my movie and sell thousands of copies, I'm gonna come after you, lawyers blazing, with the tenacity of a bulldog. But if you burn five copies of the DVD and give them to your friends, I will thank you.

The big record companies going after file sharers are fighting a losing battle. It would be like if the horse buggy manufacturers had sued the first car drivers for putting an old business model out to pasture.

Books printed on paper are currently the only medium *not* worth bootlegging in the West (though a friend who just came back from labor-cheap Thailand said they do photocopy and hand-bind travel books and best-sellers written in English and sell them on blankets on the sidewalk there). So writers have the least to worry about. Why are a few unknown authors and a few known publishers getting uppity about what basically amounts to a new way of running a library?

I grew up hanging out in libraries. But the Internet has virtually rendered the brick-and-mortar library obsolete. Their main function now is, in fact, often just to be a place where people who don't own computers go to get on the Internet. A lot of people walking in the door of a library never pick up a book, unless it's a book on how to use the Internet.

BookCrossing is the open-air library of the millennium.

I spend many hours of every day on a computer. When stuck waiting somewhere, I sometimes read e-books on my handheld. But I also still love the physicality of an actual book printed on paper. I love to hold it in my hands. I love the feel of the object, as well as the high-resolution, easy-to-read text. Ya can't get any of that on a computer.

I believe that BookCrossing is encouraging, not diminishing, the spread of books printed on paper. BookCrossing won't put publishers out of business. It will help them by rekindling the public's lost love of books.

The American library system was founded by social architect and author (and publisher) Benjamin Franklin. He felt that books were magical, and the fact that they share information is one of the things that drew him to writing.

I'm willing to bet he'd have loved the idea of BookCrossing.

Rights

You need to know a bit about rights. You'd be amazed at how little some writers know about what's legal. I've even heard horribly naïve things that could land you in the lurch, or even the clink. Like one cat told me, "Don't ever ask people for permission when you reprint something. Just do it. That way you can't get in trouble."

Don't be a dum dum—Know your rights.

Using Real-Life Events

Some novels are basically real-life events with the names changed and some embellishing. Of course, I did not do this in my novel. My lawyer has suggested that I let you know that I made it all up. And I am a Republican, a Christian, and a virgin, too, and I never took drugs.

For some reason, though, shortly after the book came out, a girl I know ran over the book several times in her car. Then she tried to run me over in her car.

Another gal I dated recently told me that if I include her in any way in the novel I'm writing now, she'll use her kung fu skills on me.

The Woody Allen movie *Deconstructing Harry* shows a character who is a novelist about to be shot by his ex-wife. She's mad because he not only based a character on her in his book, he made money on it. (In a line only Allen could have penned, the writer begs to be spared, claiming, "I spent all the money. On psychiatrists, antiques, lawyers, and prostitutes.")

A lot of writers do a lot of automythologizing. I guess we have to. If you don't believe your own hype, how can you ever get others to believe your hype?

Anyway, basing books on real people is a mixed bag. They might sue you. They might kill you. Or they might just run your book over with their cars.

I tend (now) to ask people permission. Most will give it. I get it in writing, in an e-mail at least.

And when saying things about people or companies, I've heard that it's easy to avoid being sued for slander or libel if you state things as opinion, not fact. Don't write things like, "The Willem Farnsworth Music Corporation rips off bands." That's libel, which is illegal.

Say, "In my opinion, the Willem Farnsworth Music Corporation rips off bands." Or, "I've heard that the Willem Farnsworth Music Corporation rips off bands," or, "An argument could be made that the Willem Farnsworth Music Corporation rips off bands."

Plagiarism

Plagiarism is the act of stealing someone else's writing and calling it your own. Don't do it. It's sleazy and evil, and you will get caught.

If you must use something word for word in your work to prove your point, put it in quotes and give credit. *Cite* the author, publisher, year, and page like this:

> The best thing to do is to create something cool that people want and then find a distributor who wants it and will mass-manufacture it. You don't owe them your soul or even your next project. With a deal like this, you can often get between 10 and 25 percent of the retail sales price. I did.
>
> —Michael W. Dean, *$30 Film School.*
> Page 380. Muska & Lipman, 2003.

You can probably skip the page number and maybe the publisher and year if it's in an informal setting. But in an academic or scientific paper, all are required.

For more on media law, see the great article made just for this book, "Jackie Cohen on Media Law," in the goodies folder on the CD-ROM.

NOTE

Nothing in this book or on the CD-ROM constitutes legal advice. This is for information purposes only.

Freedom Of Speech And Freedom Of The Press

The Freedom of Speech and Freedom of the Press enjoyed in the United States are pretty darned cool. They don't have that everywhere. I really do take 'em for granted to the point where this section was literally an afterthought that I put into this book as it was going to press.

But current events and political climates are threatening Freedom of Speech, Freedom of the Press, and other fundamental rights guaranteed by the Constitution. The erroneously named "Patriot Act" was slipped in the back door to take these away. We need to be vigilant before politicians, corporations, and vested interests erase our rights.

Check out these online (and other) resources for more on how we can protect our inalienable rights:

www.firstamendmentcenter.org

www.pen.org\www.aclu.org/FreeSpeech/

www.ifea.net

www.freedomforum.org

www.eff.org/

(Thanks to L'il Mike for links.)

Conclusion

We've written our book, we've published it, and we've protected it. Now let's get out there in the world and promote it.

Chapter 16

Promotion . . .
Telling the World

$30 WRITING SCHOOL

The German word for a publicist is *Presspreacher*. I love that. It totally tells it like it is. A publicist is a person who preaches to the press for you.

But a publicist can cost 5,000 dollars a month or more. I've never hired one, and I get tons of press. This basically means I have to be my own crafty and relentless publicist, with a religious fervor, preaching my own fantasterrificness with a humble but unstoppable zeal.

> It doesn't matter what they say about you as long as they spell your name right.
>
> —Attributed to Tallulah Bankhead

Rule One: Be Willing to Get Your Hands Dirty

If I could ever *just make art* like other folks and have a full-time promo person who really kicked ass, what would I do? So much!

In his film *The Big One*, Michael Moore remarks that his was the lowest-budget book tour ever. Yet he's got publicists picking him up at every turn, and he's staying in economical three-star hotels. On my book tour, I was walking from the train station to the squat. And sleeping at the squat.

He's speaking to 1,000 people in universities. I'm standing up on a chair, talking with no microphone to 60 kids in an unheated, abandoned building liberated by punk rockers with a pair of bolt cutters. I'm holding up a copy of my book. It was published by a large corporation, and I'm telling people who want to destroy large corporations about the book and telling them they should buy it. And they're thanking me for coming.[1]

---

[1] I am not the only person ever to do a no-budget book tour. There are a few of them. Carissa Clark, author of *Yours for the Revolution*, did. Jim Monroe from No Media Kings has done several. He's even toured Africa. I don't know anyone else who has, even with a band. (His site, www.nomediakings.org, is a great resource for more info on DIY publishing and promotion and touring.)

Some people would say that a book tour like this is not worth doing. I say those people are insane. Most people who say that sit at home and dream of stuff bigger than what Michael Moore does; they will never do what he does or even what I do because they aren't willing to get their hands dirty. They want it all handed to them. Most of these people will spend their days writing in coffee shops and spend their nights eating cheese and watching TV.

Figure 16.1 *Cool flyer for my tour from Magdeburg, Germany by Lars-Olle Richter.*

Figure 16.2 *Cool flyer for my tour from Magdeburg, Germany by Lars-Olle Richter 2.*

NOTE

Making it economically as an artist basically means being able to soar with your mind "outside the box" and rock out in ways a marketing person never would, but being able to switch gears from time to time and actually *think in little boxes*.

How I Got On VH1, NBC, NPR, BBC, Connie Martinson, and So On

I've been interviewed in hundreds of zines, scores of newspapers, and dozens of magazines. To get those sort of things, you contact them. Or they contact you. Taking your act on the road makes it easier to get interviewed, hands down. You writing a book is not necessarily news, but it might be news if you're coming to the town where the paper is to promote it. And it's news even more if there is some sort of angle, especially if it's a local angle. You always want to hand the angle to the reporter. It makes his job easier, because you've done half the job already.

Figure 16.3 *Michael Dean on* Connie Martinson Talks Books.

Figure 16.4 *Michael Dean and Sarah Amstutz on* Connie Martinson Talks Books.

Look here:

www.kittyfeet.com/promo.htm

for the segment VH1 Classic did on my book *$30 Music School*.

The feature NBC news did on the benefit I helped organize for cats (www.RockForCats.com is the site for that if you want to organize a cat benefit and show my film). I'm in the piece. Also at this page is an NPR interview I did.

Each of these happened for different reasons. I got on VH1 by sending them a press release. I got on NBC by pitching them a good story. NPR contacted me. I was staying with a guy who happened to do a show on the BBC while I was showing my film in Belfast, Northern Ireland. I got on the *Connie Martinson Talks Books* show (her interview of me is on the CD-ROM) by sending her an e-mail from her Web site. I am a fan of her show, and that helped because I knew something about it.

NOTE

The video I put of the *Connie Martinson Talks Books* thing on the CD-ROM is a good example of something you'd want to use on a CD for an electronic press kit. I taped it off TV onto a VCR, transferred it to my DV camera, imported it into my laptop, and encoded it with Adobe Premiere. Information on how to do this is covered extensively in *$30 Film School.*

Basically, an edge to getting any kind of press for yourself is to understand the specific needs of the job description of the writer you are trying to contact. (And it doesn't hurt to compliment them. Don't flatter them, of course. Rather, fulfill their needs, as best you can.) Too many people miss this entirely and send out identical faxes or e-mails to everyone they can get contact info for, without tailoring the pitch at all. This is basically spam and will make enemies in this game. You're looking for friends, not enemies.

If you feed an interested writer a pitch that he can use, you are basically doing quite the opposite of spam: You are helping him do his job. Writers appreciate this, and they will not only write about you, but you will also be on your way to building a professional relationship with these people, a win/win symbiosis that can last the rest of your life.

Getting Contacts

You can get contacts directly off the Web site of a paper, magazine, TV station, and such. They usually have the job descriptions of the writers and sometimes their contact info directly on the site, especially with smaller papers.

Now that you know this secret, you must promise to use it for good and never for evil.

Smaller Papers Rule

Don't overlook smaller, independent papers, TV stations, and so forth. The small-city hometown newspapers will probably have someone who will review your book and be thankful for the opportunity to do so. When I had my publisher send out review copies of *$30 Music School,* some of the small papers wrote about it in a favorable light almost immediately. They did so way before the big-city papers and magazines got around to it.

NOTE

Can't find someone's e-mail? Often, the convention for e-mail addresses at a corporation is firstname.lastname@company.com.

Thus, if there were a person named Lydia Lam who worked at the Kittyfeet Company, her e-mail would probably be lydia.lam@kittyfeet.com.

You can test it by sending a message to the possible address, then sending a second, blank e-mail with the subject "test" to a made-up and improbable name at the same company (like ronald.raygun@kittyfeet.com). If the first one goes through and the second one bounces, chances are you're golden.

Sometimes the convention is the first initial and then the last name, like llam@kittyfeet.com. And don't forget the reverse (lydial@kittyfeet.com). I've seen it.

Neither convention is the case in my company, but you get the idea.

This was good. It got the word out, generated sales, built up the press kit, and let my publisher, as well as the public, know that stuff was getting done. This kind of press stuff is also helpful in building your own press kit, which you can use later for booking speaking engagements and such. If you publish a non-fiction book and it does well, you become an *expert*. Experts can charge money for their time.

NOTE

I don't believe you need permission to use a clipping in a press kit, because it is not going out to the public and is not being sold. I think this would be covered by Fair Use.

Mainstream Media

How do you get attention from the bigger people? You need the direct contacts, which you probably won't find on a Web site. The way I did it was by trading my list with someone for his list. This is sort of a catch-22, as you need your own list to begin with, and you also need some standing in the community to be trusted and have a name. But you can build this on a small level and work up.

Don't ever give your contacts to idiots. Make sure you tell people they can't post them on the Web, and insist that they be very cool with how they use the contacts. Having high-end contacts and getting to use them successfully puts you in an elite fraternity. Membership in this fraternity is tenuous and conditional, so don't blow it.

NOTE

If you get a list like this (or any list), do not abuse it. Don't post it online. Don't send those on the list e-mail about everything you do. You'll drive them nuts and dilute the list for yourself and everyone, and they will start sending your e-mails to the trash. Act like a professional. I write people on lists like this only once or twice a year, when I have something very good that is very in keeping with what they write about.

The way I got these high-level U.S. press contacts was by amassing a really bitchin' list of contacts in Europe for booking my film. I handpicked and researched it, and then I took my movie on a small but important tour of England, Ireland, Germany, France, Holland, and Belgium. I was approached by many people who asked me for these contacts, and I turned them down because they were people I felt would dilute the power of the list, basically idiots who would hassle my friends and associates and give me, and the scene, a bad name. Conversely, I actually gave them to several filmmakers I liked who had nothing to offer me in return. I would never sell them. But I did trade them to two people I really liked and trusted in exchange for their lists. One was a powerful indie record label who had direct contacts at VH1, NBC, *Spin*, and so on.

NOTE

When you change e-mail addresses, make sure that you change it on your Return To e-mail in the preferences on your mail program.

I got a great list in exchange for my European tour contacts from a cool person who wouldn't spam my people or sell or post the list.

Writing Press Releases

In addition to understanding the job description of the person you're sending promotional materials to, it's important to sum up the story quickly in the headline and then a little more completely in the first few lines of the letter. Basically you want to hand them the hook. People who get 200 e-mailed press releases a day (and another 50 on the fax machine) are gonna hit Delete pretty damn fast if you make them look for it. Keep your press releases short and to the point!

The book title *$30 Music School* pretty much says what it is, and the elaboration is in the second line ("a 520-page textbook on D.I.Y. music production and distribution").

I sent the people on my new contact list an e-mail that read:

> Subject: Do you want a review copy of *$30 Music School?*

> Let me know if you want a review copy, and your address.

Coming in January from Course Technology Professional Trade Reference (http://www.courseptr.com):

Michael W. Dean's *$30 Music School*, a 520-page textbook on D.I.Y. music production and distribution.

http://www.30dollarmusicschool.com

Everything from picking a guitar to writing a song to recording to booking a tour. All with sensible goals and an easy, fun, conversational tone. Over 300 illustrations. Also exclusive interviews with Henry Rollins, Joan Jett, Jonathan Richman, and more.

The book also comes with a CD-ROM of software, song examples, videos, press information, and goodies.

This book is the follow up to *$30 Film School.*

http://www.30dollarfilmschool.com

Author Michael W. Dean played in the band Bomb, toured the world, made 12 records (most indie, one on Warner Brothers), and made the documentary film *D.I.Y. or Die: How to Survive as an Independent Artist.*

http://www.diyordie.org

"Michael Dean is definitely one of the most powerful, knowledgeable, and experienced living legends still around from the heyday. If anybody knows real rock, it's Michael Dean."

— Peter DiStefano
(Porno for Pyros, Peter Murphy)

"A living underground legend, Michael Dean is one of the few integral rock 'n' roll spokesmen we have left of our generation."

> —Eric McFadden
> (Parliament-Funkadelic, Eric McFadden Trio)

———————

"Get your slacker ass in gear with Michael W. Dean's latest alternative textbook, *$30 Music School*."

> —London May (Samhain, Tiger Army, Dag Nasty)

———————

"Michael Dean is the epitome of super charged and always active. He's always up to something that, if good, is very good and, if bad, it's even better."

> —Janis Tanaka, bass player
> (L7, Pink, Fireball Ministry)

The only difference between what I wrote to the big media places and the small ones was that on the small ones, I added this line after the subject line:

> I'm tracking the copies with a number. Please don't ask for it if you're gonna sell it without reading it. If I see your copy sold used, with no review, ya won't get the follow-up book, *$30 Writing School*. Play nice, please! We ain't rich, and it's an expensive book.

I took a chance by adding that, and it angered a few people. But most people understood that I had to do it. Too many people accept free books just to sell them. Writers are a poor lot who depend on the kindness of strangers.

I cut and pasted the letters, but addressed each e-mail to "Dear _____" with their name. I did not send them out anonymously as a Cc or Bcc.

Some didn't write back. A few said, "No thank you." One said, "You're an ass for telling me I have to review your book or I don't get one. I won't be pushed around like that." But most said, "Sure. Send it to me."

Doing this rather than just mailing the book out first does three things:

- Plants the idea in their head.
- Saves you or your company money. A small percentage of the people will say, "I no longer review books," or, "That's not something we'd cover." By querying first, you save the price of a book and shipping.
- Raises the level of the submission from "unsolicited" to "requested material." You can even mark the package "requested material" or "requested matter" (but only if they did respond favorably). This may get the stuff looked at sooner if they have a high-volume office.

A lot of the people who received a copy reviewed it. VH1 did a 30-second featurette that they showed six times in one day. That's three minutes of airtime on a *huge* station. That's worth like 100,000 dollars. For free. Actually it's worth more, because the 100,000 dollars would buy you that much *ad* time, which is not taken as seriously as an actual part of a program.

NOTE

Please don't ask me for my contacts. Thank you.

When you're dealing with press people, you need to approach them as peers, but in a businesslike way. They are not your minions, and conversely, they are not gods many rungs above you. You are doing each other a favor. Press people need good stories.

NOTE

Never send an attachment with an e-mail without first being asked to. Because of virus problems, many workers in corporate environments are trained to hit Delete whenever there's a questionable attachment. Sometimes the company's server does it for them, and they never even see your e-mail if there's an attachment. While you're at it, make sure your anti-virus software and definitions are up to date, and run a scan once a week at least. Set your program up to autoscan both incoming and outgoing e-mails.

Being Proactive

I hate the term "proactive" because most people who use it are idiots. But it isn't a bad idea to be proactive if that's what you're really doing and it's not just a buzzword.

I ego surf for my name and the names of my projects on Google once or twice a week (in quotes to get only instances of the exact phrase) and send the URL of any new reviews to my editor and the publicity person at my publisher. They appreciate this, and they can use it to help get stuff done. It also shows that you're proactive about doing some of your own footwork. They appreciate this. The best situation is when you have a good publicity department at your publisher, and they do some work, and you also do some work on your own.

Don't be pushy, but be willing to help out.

When a new book comes out, and I'm getting a lot of reviews, I wait until I have two or three at once before sending them in, so I'm not inundating my company with e-mail.

Search *$30 Music School* and *$30 Film School* on Google and check out the results. I've been quite busy.

I like the publicity people at Course. They pay for and get in-store displays in bookstores. (These are called "end caps." They cost money and require connections I don't have). They do some ads and have direct connections at a lot of music and tech magazines, getting me press I couldn't get on my own.

They also work with me a lot to augment my press-preaching efforts. They're very on top of sending out promo copies when I ask them to. Contrast this with when my band was on Warner Brothers records. We actually had to get someone who worked there to "borrow" copies for us to send out, and we had to pay out of our own pockets to send them!

It's good to negotiate in your contract that you do not have to pay for promo copies. You shouldn't have to. My company sends out up to 200 copies of a book to people I request, as well as whatever they usually send out. They also give me 50 copies, so I can give them personally to people who helped me out with different things over the months.

NOTE

Say "thank you" and mean it at the end of every e-mail you send people at your company. Say "thank you" and mean it at the end of every e-mail you send to press folks you deal with, especially if they cover you, but even if they can't but are nice to you.

If people are mean, ignore them. Don't get pulled into that crap. Have enough confidence in your art to know you are good, and just move on. A lot of magazine writers are unpublished book writers who are jealous that you got a book out. Leave them alone.

NOTE

Sometimes fax numbers are listed instead of or in addition to e-mail addresses for press contacts. I haven't had the best luck with faxes, and I use them only if no e-mail address is offered. If you do use faxes, use the same rules as with e-mail: keep it simple, hand them the headline, be respectful, use their name, and keep it short. You can add a graphic to a fax, but it has to be high-contrast and simple and look good in black and white, because fax machines butcher detail on the other end.

Don't blow it. If you get on VH1, NBC, the BBC or in *Rolling Stone* or any other big media, don't act like a little tittering schoolgirl and freak out the person. Don't hassle them, demand a copy, stuff like that. Pros don't do that.

Same goes if you get to interview a famous person. Don't bug them with a dozen follow-up e-mails, send them all your art, and so on. It's tacky and may preclude them working with you in the future. Show them a tiny bit and walk away. Let them pursue you if they want.

I just got back from walking around Los Angeles hanging flyers on poles. (The flyer is on the CD-ROM as Music School Flyer.doc.) Does it help? Who knows? (Note that flyering is not a legal activity in a few cities.)

Even though copies of my books are available at every chain store in the country, I take a few copies one by one and put them on consignment or sell them outright to small stores in my neighborhood. Is that useful? I don't know. I also personally fax press releases (found on the CD-ROM in /goodies as music school fax press release.doc) to the book buyers at stores that already have the book, just so they would maybe notice it a little more. Advantageous? I don't know. But I do it anyway. It's back to that old argument of "I'd rather do that than watch TV and eat cheese."

Figure 16.5 *Me hanging flyers on Vermont Ave in Los Angeles.* Photo by Dattner (www.monkpunk.org).

We're on this planet for only a few years. Make them great. And know that greatness doesn't always mean winning a Pulitzer or making a million dollars. It's great to make something good and then devote your time to spreading it, even if you're spreading it slowly to a few people at a time.

NOTE

There is a flyer for this book on the CD-ROM in the goodies folder. It's Writing School Flyer.doc. If you dig this book, feel free to make copies and put them up in your town (check local flyer laws). You can also give them to bookstores, teachers, and libraries. The flyer is also available at http://www.kittyfeet.com/writingflyer.doc.

More on Writing Press Releases

My friend Tracy Hatfield is a TV news producer and deals with press releases all day long. She knows what works and what doesn't. Here's what she suggests:

> When sending to newspapers, put all the appropriate information in it. The written media can actually create articles from a press release without having a copy of your book or movie in front of them. But for TV, the press release is simply bait. They will need visuals. Give them the story ideas, something more than "I wrote a book so talk to me."

> When sending to news media (and that term can be used loosely), you must have an angle for your story, something they can use to hook the viewers. To come up with that angle, watch the show you want to be on. See what the stories are about and write your press release to push that button. Also, don't peg just one show. Morning newscasts are different from those on nights and weekends.

> TV press releases, and I would say releases in general, need to be shorter with more bullet points. A catchy caption-like title is helpful.

> If the station doesn't interview authors, and many don't, especially if there is not a local angle, they probably aren't going to interview you.

> Almost all local public access shows interview local people, so that is almost a given to get on your local PBS station.

> If you want to be on a station that is not where you live or will visit, you can do a satellite interview or send them tape (professional beta or better) of an interview with you.

> If that doesn't work, you can offer contacts of interview-savvy artists in their area—people who have read your book or are covered in your book or have said your book saved their lives or inspired blah blah blah . . . you get the idea. That makes their job much easier. And to be honest, news people have to turn over so much stuff a day. Making it easier sometimes gets it done.

> Ask them to include a reference to your book in the story and a link to your Web site on their sites. Do this in a way such as, "Since I can't be there and I *am* giving you these great people to talk to, do you think you can sneak a mention of the book in there?" They may or may not do it, but most will try

to if they can. (Keep in mind that they aren't gonna link your site if there's anything remotely obscene on it.)

The side benefit of offering up interesting interviews in place of yourself or your story ideas is that you become a source of information. You begin a relationship so that the next time you are in town, maybe you can get that interview about yourself and *your* stuff.

An example of this is medical stories. It is a common practice that a doctor or a particular hospital that gives us a patient relevant to the story will appear in the story. That's why you see "Doctor Expert" and "Ailing Patient" come from the same facility in the same story.

The biggest thing, and obviously I am speaking for TV, but it translates to all media, is that you shouldn't just shotgun-fax anything. Have a name. Call the station. You can get their information from www.tvjobs.com, and NAPTE has a book with contact information for every station in the country.

Ask who produces the show you want to be on or who is in charge of special projects (these people do more difficult, more preproduced stories). You can also ask who takes information about news ideas. Sometimes you can send it to them.

Another thing—skip faxes and use e-mail. The fax machine is 15 steps from the desk, but it is the Bermuda Triangle. I hardly ever get the things.

Web sites are great resources. Ours, www.click2houston.com, has a section for viewers to write in with information or questions. I get stuff forwarded to me all the time from viewers and people with ideas.

If you see a story on local musicians, send an e-mail about the story with another story idea.

Ask for that to be forwarded to the reporter or producer of the story. You might try to request a response to make sure they received it. Complimenting their show or a particular story doesn't hurt, but try not to make it sound overtly like kissing up. Almost everyone responds to questions about stories or ideas if they are good.

If you build a relationship with a reporter or producer, provide him with information or ideas. He becomes a fan and will let you know the best way to promote yourself and may have some ideas for you.

Having a tough time coming up with a news angle? Anything you can add with more specifics helps. For instance, if you are pitching your music book, talk about the number of artists making independent records nationwide or the amount of money they are generating or any facts about how the movement (call it a *movement* or something like that) has grown. The idea that they may be able to report on a trend or show people something they didn't know makes their mouths water.

Everyone promises the media they are giving them the next great thing. But numbers help make it seem more real.

You might throw in something about how artists or those who dream of being artists no longer have to be tied to Los Angeles or New York. This adds to the idea that the story could have relevance to national audiences. If you have examples of some Tom, Dick, or Harry in Middle America making a living, you could throw that in. Just remember that you are trying to sell a book, but they are trying to tell and sell stories. Try to give them real angles to create stories.

Talk less about how fabulous you are (though you are) and more about the movement, about how easy it is to do this, how this ideal will change the way the world works.

I would try a slightly different approach with MTV... younger - more HIP and story driven - keep with the movement idea.. just make it sound more fun... more young teen artists taking over the world... play up the aspect of doing things this way keeps thing cheaper for consumers.. less about trying to control what kids buy and more about the message.

VH1 . . . same as MTV, but I think you might go with something about artists making a real living without anyone having to know their names . . . artists sticking with their ideals and beliefs . . . how they do it . . . and how younger artists are learning from them and from your books how to do it . . . be sure to include the technology thing again.

This is all based on the assumption Network works somewhat like we do . . .

Hope this helps.

Here's a sample e-mail Tracy wrote for me to send out (follow-up to their reply after my first contact):

Thanks for your interest. I will send the book *$30 Music School*.

I am also going to send a documentary I did called *D.I.Y. or Die . . . How to Survive as an Independent Artist*.

DIY, which stands for "do it yourself," is a philosophy of creating art and putting it in the world without compromising for corporations or getting caught up in pursuit of "star system" BS. It's why I wrote the book.

The documentary turned out more to be about why people choose DIY over signing record deals and contracts. Some have even turned down major label deals to stay in control and do it in their own small companies. So I wrote a book to explain how.

What was a trend in the 80s and 90s has taken on new legs as better and cheaper technology allows anyone to make, produce, distribute, and sell their art.

It goes along with so many stories of the problems facing record companies as they battle to keep hold of their control.

This book is a step-by-step guide for musicians to show them how to do it themselves.

I also wrote *$30 Film School*, which does the same thing for aspiring movie and documentary filmmakers. I can send this one along upon request.

Let me know if I can put you in contact with local DIY artists. They are everywhere. You'll see in the documentary that they make great interviews and provide plenty of visuals.

Thanks again,

Michael Dean

Living Vicariously Through Michael Dean

When you are promoting your art, you are promoting yourself. There are two sides to this. One is what I've said over and over in the first two books of this series: Be a champion for the art, all art, including yours. That way you can be a pulpit-pounder and not seem like an egomaniac. You're a friend of the *art*, and you just get to go along for the ride.

This isn't something to do to trick people. It's a way of looking at things that makes you saner after rejection and nicer after success and just overall more effective at promoting.

The second thing to consider is that you are selling your *name*. The more people know and value your name, the more you are a commodity that can make a living doing cool stuff. It's a nice position to find yourself in.

The other way of looking at this is to know that people live vicariously through their favorite artists. I said before that people want to live through the heroes in the stories they create. It is worth noting that they also want to live through the people creating those stories.

I called my solo record *Living Vicariously Through Michael Dean*. It was kind of a joke name, but it kind of wasn't. People do live vicariously through me.

Like I said in my novel, *Starving in the Company of Beautiful Women*:

> The world is fond of the image of the starving artist. People love the archetype of the struggling, brilliant young man or woman, garrisoned away in a garret, slowly going insane while producing a dazzling body of work, and then dying or being consigned to the madhouse or skid row.

> The rock fan who works in a gas station cannot afford to trash hotel rooms and snort coke off of a supermodel's breasts, so he pays Mötley Crüe or 2-Live Crew to do it for him. The yuppie consultant cannot leave his job to pursue madness, so he finances madness in another by purchasing a powerful painting.

> We pay our artists to live these lives that we daren't live. When you buy a great rock record, you are acquiring more than music; you are procuring a lifestyle.

Word of Mouth

One way to get word of mouth is to involve lots of people from the start. When you collaborate with people (like I do in my movie and these books—not just the interviews, but quoting people, plugging their bands and books and movies, and so on), you can bet everyone involved will talk it up to all their friends. A guy interviewed in *$30 Film School* took a copy with him everywhere he went in Europe and showed his interview to everyone he met. You can't *buy* publicity like that.

Collaborating with people is just a good idea overall. All artists, especially writers, tend to isolate themselves, and involving others gets you out, or at least talking to others. By collaborating, you get a wider viewpoint and the credibility of experts, and it's just good karma to plug others. Riffin' with your friends and such is a grand idea. It's like jammin' with different musicians. It's win/win all around.

A friend of mine just got back from the Sundance Film Festival and said someone on a panel discussion there mentioned to the audience that *$30 Film School* is a great book for filmmakers. Again, you *really* can't buy publicity like that. You get it from making something good and from collaborating. (Lloyd, who runs Troma, did the blurb for me for the front of that book.)

Just don't forget to get release forms signed, thank and credit everyone in the book, and again, send them a copy without being asked *as soon as it comes out.*

Getting Interviewed

Getting interviewed is part of promoting art. Published authors get interviewed a lot. You can set interviews up yourself or have someone do it for you. When you get better known, people will come to you. Regardless, it's a chance to really shine. Here are some thoughts on the art of the interview.

How

Either you contact people or they contact you. It's usually tough to ask people to interview you when you're starting out. You can befriend people at local papers or radio stations or college radio. You can just send them a press release and offer. It's odd. . . . It can come off as a little desperate when no one's heard of you. Just find it in your heart to do it for the art, and then if you're rejected, it isn't you, it's the art.

It gets easier as you get more recognition. People come to *you* and ask to interview you. About half the interviews I do come this way. Another third come from me offering. For instance, I'm going to be in the Pacific Northwest on a book tour next month, so I contacted some radio stations there and set stuff up.

If you do something great, people will want to talk to you eventually. In the meantime, you might have to give them a heads-up. Adding the line "available for interviews" into a press release can't hurt.

What to Do

Same as with anything else. Talk from the heart. Don't try to blow their minds, just be yourself and talk like you'd talk to a friend. (Michael Woody adds, "Because you're really talking *through* them to a potential fan base that may as well be your friends.")

Watch and read interviews you like by people you like (and even good ones by people you don't). Look at what works and what doesn't.

I actually practiced being interviewed when I was a kid . . . stood in front of the mirror with a tape recorder. It can't hurt, and I recommend it. Get together with your friends and practice interviewing each other and videotape it. Then watch it and take notes.

What to Ask for in Return

When someone wants to interview me, I usually ask for two things.

One is permission to reprint the interview or article in a book or on a CD-ROM after it comes out. Sometimes they can't offer to let me use the actual scanned article out of the magazine or newspaper, as that is sold to the paper and belongs to them. (Sometimes I also get reprint permission from the newspaper. Only one publication ever said no. It was *Time Out NY.*)

But I can usually get permission to at least get the Word file from the writer and publish that myself (after his article comes out, of course). If they won't grant that, I probably won't do the interview. So far no one has said no, and they are usually honored to be included in a book.

The second thing I ask for is a chance to look the thing over before they send it to press, especially if it is mostly an interview and not a straight-up article—that is, if most of the words in the piece are mine and not the other person's. Either way, people usually agree, if only because they usually know my writing and respect me as an artist first. I often end up even doing some free proofreading on the thing, which makes them look better. It makes me look better, too. And I also want to check stuff for accuracy. I consider this jamming. It's collaboration. It's different than what some big bands that sell millions of records request. They demand final viewing and veto power over anything published about them. My M.O. is more peer to peer. I'm not dictating, I'm riffing. I make my changes with the Track Changes tool in Word, so they can see what I change and then accept or reject the changes. With writers at smaller magazines and zines, I often have to tell them how to use that feature. But it's all worth it. It makes anything to do with me look better.

If someone won't grant me both of these rights, I will probably not do the interview. I am not that needy for press or ego stroking. Anyone who knows my stuff can tell that I'm doing it out of mutual respect for both people's art, and if they can't respect me or my love of art, they should go interview someone else.

I don't usually ask big magazines to do this if I trust them, because they usually have good editors and are usually on tighter deadlines and might not understand that I work at high speed. But sometimes I do. *Spin* magazine, for instance, has blatantly misquoted me. They printed a retraction at my request two issues later, but it could have been avoided if they'd let me see the piece first.

When this goes right, good things start to happen, such as when Saby Reyes-Kulkarni voluntarily sent me his review of *$30 Music School* before it was published (in *Rockpile* magazine) and invited my feedback. That amazed me. Here's the first draft:

> Michael Dean—
>
> *$30 Music School* (Muska & Lipman/Course Technology)
>
> Attitude goes a long way in this how-to manual for all aspects of starting and maintaining a band. Its DIY musician/filmmaker author (not the same guy from Corrosion of Conformity) uses breezy, flippant narration that's easy to get through but in spots obscures his true wisdom. For instance, did you know you can tune instruments to a telephone dial tone? Or that instrument retailers will often settle for 50% of list price? That Craig's List is a good place to find band mates? Or that you can use soap to get a window

unstuck? Opinionated to a fault (but always entertaining), Dean's perspective feels like sitting with a good friend whom you take with a grain of salt but can nonetheless eke some sense from. The cutesy irreverence gets cloying but is also quite effective when aimed at major record labels (the "Fuck Getting Signed" band mate ad sample was my favorite). Some more thorough info would have been nice (like an out of town booking section), but Dean's spirit is inspiring enough to get you thinking, and that's what counts—and makes *Music School* a great complement to other well-known how-to's by Donald Passman and Tim Sweeney. Whether it's worth thirty bucks is up to you, but the accompanying CD-ROM might swing your vote.

—Saby Reyes-Kulkarni

I sent him this:

You said something about changing things. Were you actually giving me the chance to offer suggestions? If so, that's unprecedented cool!

Here's what I would change:

>"not the same guy from Corrosion of Conformity,"

add:

this Dean was the singer in Bomb.)

>"but in spots obscures his true wisdom."

Really? That feels kinda mean. And most people that read it are telling me the opposite.

Is there any way to say that kinder?

>"Some more thorough info would have been nice (like an out of town booking section),"

Like what? There is a whole chapter on Touring.

that's all.

Thanks for listening.

much respect,

—md.

And he made the changes! I loved this because it was collaboration. All great art is. Even if just on a 200-word review. It shows a lot of respect on his part.

Quotes

Quoting people who like your work is a good thing to help sell yourself. It's you tooting your horn by reprinting someone else tooting your horn for you. And this looks a lot cooler to people than you simply tooting alone as you play with yourself.

So . . . Put a statement on your Web board so that you can use anything anyone posts there anywhere else. If you look on my board at http://www.kittyfeet.com/board/wwwboard.html, you'll see this:

> And anything posted here becomes property of Michael Dean and may be used in any way he sees fit. And he thanks you.

So I can use cool stuff like this anywhere. Like in this post, for instance:

> Greets.
>
> Subject: A Sacred/Gnostic Text
>
> I just found Michael's (Your) book on the same shelf I have searched at the bookstore around 15 times for books on Filmmaking and the ilk (at least at this one particular bookstore) and after reading about 5 or so of them I had exceptions of more of the same. I went ahead and got this one because it had something none of the rest had . . . and then when I read it it had more than I could have ever hoped for . . . the most positive and human delivery of heart and knowledge through the printed media I have taken in in years. I found it to be one of the finest spiritual self help books hidden inside a package that would reach a wide variety of very specific types of people that needed a wide variety of very specific itches that need scratching.
>
> It is impossible to tell on what level the communications inside this book will effect our Universe, and I've got quite and imagination! (the Han Solo meaning is inferred here).
>
> Thank goodness I got this book when I did! I was about to go nuts without it!
>
> —Daniel Runyon

and

Posted by Cavanaugh Rhodes on November 08, 2003 at 16:17:26:

$30 Film School has not only given me the advice I need to promote and get all the legal crap out of the way to make sure my first film, "No Movement" goes somewhere, but Michael Dean's writing is helping me conclude that I want to lead a life that never sells out, and one that never burns out.

Thank you so much Michael for writing this book! If I was a chick I would totally do you every single second!

NOTE

Send an e-mail to kittyfeet69-subscribe@topica.com to join my weekly list.

If your publisher won't send you on tour, it can't hurt to ask for a few hundred bucks per book to cover stuff like flyers, gas, and parking to do in-store interviews and things like that.

Getting Your Books into Stores

It's tough. But basically you go and politely ask them to take the books on consignment. You get an invoice and come back later and hope they've sold some. This is covered in depth in the first two books of this series, and the process is basically identical for books as it is for DVDs and CDs.

You can also go through distributors. There is a list under Promotional on the Preditors & Editors site at http://www.anotherealm.com/prededitors/.

There's always the danger of companies going out of business while still owing you money. That's happened to me with records and also a little with books. (Such as Destroy All Music in Los Angeles. They went out of business still holding some copies of my novel.)

Undoing Bad Press

You don't want to write angry letters to people who pan your art if they are mean-natured jerks. But if they write something that seems *off*, sometimes I write them and enter into a reasonable discourse. James Wright reviewed my film *D.I.Y. or DIE: How to Survive as an Independent Artist* in *Modern Fix* magazine and basically said that it didn't live up to the name. That it was more "why to survive" than "how to survive." I wrote him that it was a precursor to the three *$30 School* books and sent him the *Music School* and *Film School* books. He became one of my fiercest defenders and wrote more than one review championing both books in several venues.

Miscellaneous

Promoting via the Web, e-mail, flyers, stickers, word of mouth, e-mail lists, and more is covered in depth in *$30 Film School* and *$30 Music School*. I couldn't fit it all here, though most all of it would be applicable to writing. Take a look through those books, even if you can't afford to buy them. Read 'em in the store.

Here are some more things that might help you:

Street Teams

Bands and record labels have "street teams" of kids who go out in each city and pass out info on upcoming releases. There is no reason you couldn't do that for books if you had a following.

You have to give them something in return. Music people give the street teams concert tickets and CDs. Maybe you could give away free, signed advance copies of your next book or your rough drafts.

NOTE

Answer your e-mail and fan mail. When people tell you they like you, ask them to post a review on Amazon. See if they'll hang flyers in their town.

Keep records of all your contacts and fans. Invite your fans and friends to join your e-mail list. (I use topica.com. The URL for starting a free list is http://lists.topica.com.)

I like having my list . . . I like answering them on an ongoing basis. I enjoy helping people, I enjoy the attention, and we also help each other. It's win/win. Sometimes I even end up collaborating with them or making them an intern or apprentice. Or art slave/helper monkey/love slave (think of the stories you've heard about the Naropa Institute and the Beats and the college freshman they had doing stuff when they started). Or assistant. Or a girlfriend. Or collaborator. Or all of the above. I *always* handpick my friends *and* my fans.

Don't overdo postings to your e-mail list. Don't over-post. And stay fascinating.

Devotion and Lack of Fear

My friend Beau Brashares read *$30 Music School* and basically called it *$30 Dean School*. It reminded him of what his dad said, 20 years earlier when we first met: "Michael Dean will succeed someday. Because he has absolutely no fear of rejection."

Beau said that my book succeeds partially because so much of it is "How to Be Michael Dean." It's a hard balance to achieve, putting so much of yourself into a non-fiction book. But if you rock, I encourage it. If you don't believe in yourself with this much intensity, how do you plan to inspire others to believe in you?

I will never forget cartoonist Keith Knight (one of the interviewees in *D.I.Y. or DIE*) at a free outdoor concert in San Francisco. It was a Fugazi/Sleater-Kinney show in Dolores Park. He was promoting one of his books by walking around wearing a sandwich board with his drawings on it. He looked pretty silly. And it totally made me respect him.

He now has a syndicated strip that appears in many newspapers as well as Salon.com. And it's his tenacity and unrelenting moxie that got him that far.

(I was trying to remember what it said on the sign. I asked him about it recently. He said, "It had a strip on either side of it. That was it. People would have to get close to read it, and I would be holding books and pitch 'em after they read and laughed at the strip. I would make sure the strips were my best ones, so they'd immediately get hooked. Like crack, actually . . .")

Conclusion

I hope I've put a fire under your butt to get you wanting to spread your ideas like a virus. And I hope I've given you some tools that will act as kindling to start that fire and even pour some nitro on top. Because we'll be extending our ability to extend our spirit out into the world more in the next chapter, "In-Store Appearances and Touring."

Chapter 17

In-Store Appearances and Touring

$30 WRITING SCHOOL

So, you wanna get out and shake some hands and meet the folks who read your books? Or better yet, get some new folks to buy them? This is the place. We'll cover touring and booking and in-store appearances here. There is a lot of information in Chapter 13, "Writing on the Road," that will be helpful with in-store appearances and touring.

Also, check out *$30 Film School* and *$30 Film School* for more on touring. Much of it will apply to books, too.

Touring with a book is tough but good. And it will not always feel fair.

Have you ever been in some big chain bookstore and seen some unfortunate man or woman sitting at the "meet the author" table with a pile of unsold copies of his book and a sad look on his face, wishing *someone* would come talk to him? That could be you. Sometimes it's me.

NOTE

Actually, when I do in-stores, I never have *nobody* show up. There are usually 10 or 20 people at them because I promote the hell out of myself, and I have a few fans in every city. I get my stuff in the paper and on TV (see Chapter 16, "Promotion . . . Telling the World"). At the one or two stores where no one showed up for the first hour, I brought a laptop and sat there *writing* my next book until someone came up and asked me, "Are you writing your next book?", and we struck up a conversation. Then other people start talking to you, too.

Bring a few good friends with you to a book signing. Sit them at the table or in the chairs and talk to them. People are more likely to start talking to someone who looks like people want to talk to him than someone sitting alone at a table with a hound-dog look of "Someone please talk to me!"

For the first *$30 Music School* book tour, I did "singing signings." I set up stuff at Borders Books, where I brought my friend Sarah Amstutz (an excellent singer and the gal on the cover of that book), and we sang six songs, then I talked about the book for 20 minutes, then I signed books.

NOTE

Don't bug famous authors to try to get them to read your stuff. They're barely making a living themselves and can't make you famous. The only exception is if you think they might turn you on to their agent. But don't bug them. Just ask nicely. Don't ask them to recommend you unless they know you.

Conversely, do talk to authors doing an in-store if there aren't many people. It's a lonely gig, and you'll make their day, even if you don't buy a book.

If you are playing music and are supposed to have a PA system through a prior arrangement, and they say you don't need one (because they don't feel like setting it up), politely tell them that you *do* need a PA and you're expecting one. Have them set it up. You aren't going to get anyone coming over to hear you sing without a PA. Bookstores soak up a lot of sound.

Don't be obnoxiously loud, but it does help to have a mike. And the PA that most stores have kinda stinks. Be prepared to tweak it quickly and set it up. (More on this in *$30 Music School*.)

There are several types of books I could see being written that justify playing music at the book signing. From books like mine to a tell-all by a musician to just any book by a musician.

If you do music stuff in bookstores, find out ahead of time exactly what they have as far as PA stuff. Bring a couple of extra mikes and cords and some duct tape, too. You'll probably need it. And they often have only one mike stand, so be prepared to use that one for your voice and tape a mike to a table for your guitar.

Basically, you don't want to have unrealistic expectations. I don't. And I convey this to the people booking me. I actually heard of one idiot who did a book signing and then tried to sue the store because no one showed up. What a deluded loser.

I have four books out, three with a somewhat large publisher, and I do not get mobbed at book signings. It's not a *Harry Potter*-type thing. There're usually two or three people there who've already bought the book, five or eight who just happened to be there, and the other three to five people are just being entertained. A few might end up buying the book.

One reason it's worth it to do in-store appearances is that you get to meet the people who work in the store and make a good impression on them. (Another reason to be on your best behavior; they might even buy your book!)

Meeting them and having them like you is huge, as these are the people who make recommendations all day to people who are looking for books. Introduce yourself and be nice to them.

It's worth it no matter what. Even if only to take home the big poster that they make for the in-stores.

NOTE

Don't steal the poster. Ask for it, and they'll give it to you. If you just take it, it is stealing. This will not get you invited back, and you actually could get arrested.

Figure 17.1 *Poster from a Borders in-store appearance in Pasadena.*

Figure 17.2 *Michael Dean and Sarah Amstutz at Borders in Hollywood.*
Photo by Lydia Lam.

Figure 17.3 *Michael Dean and Sarah Amstutz at Borders in Glendale.*
Photo by Lydia Lam.

Figure 17.4 *Michael Dean and Sarah Amstutz at Borders in Glendale 2.*
Photo by Lydia Lam.

It's also worth it to me because everything that I do is cross pollinating. I'll reuse an interview on the CD-ROM of a book. Same with reviews (I have to get permission for that). I will do an in-store for 10 people one day and then use recent recollections on it to write 2,500 words the next day in this chapter. I will show my film to 30 people in Germany and use it in a press kit to book myself a speaking engagement for 200 people at a college in Madison, Wisconsin. It all helps everything else. That's the *nature* of being a modern Renaissance cat.

My publisher does not send me on tour. I go myself, in conjunction with another tour, usually film, music, or speaking at a college. A lot of publishers don't encourage you to go do in-stores. They aren't that important at a non-rock star sales level. But I do them anyway because I am an egomaniac, and I *love* talking to people about my stuff. That's the difference between me and the people who write just for the money. I feel like I'm on a mission from God, like my stuff has the power to change people's lives for the better, that every copy sold is more than a unit on a spreadsheet. It's a better *life* for someone. And it is this unfailing conviction that makes me succeed. But keep in mind, if you're this cocky, you better have the chops to back it up, or you're just like the horrible and deluded also-ran singers who get the virtual gong on *American Idol*.

I don't mind leaving the house to do small stuff. It beats watching TV and eating cheese. I'd rather be the main attraction for 20 people than sit home and watch someone *else* perform for 2,000,000 people.

Another reason that it's cool to do in-store appearances is that it is a feather in your cap for your press kit. If you do a store thing and six people show up, that's not just six more people who've heard your message and will tell two friends. It's your name and the book's name in the paper, on the bookstore's Web site, and so on.

It is something to add to your press kit. And that's huge. That cannot be taken away from you.

See *$30 Music School* and *$30 Writing School* for complete info on making a press kit.

NOTE

I have heard from another writer that whenever he goes on vacation and flies somewhere, he sets up a book signing at the destination city. Then it becomes a business trip, and he says he writes it all off. He saves all the receipts and newspaper clippings to prove it and keeps them with his tax records.

Figure 17.5 *Photo of me and Sarah doing a singing signing at Borders in Pasadena, February 7, 2004.* Photo by Lydia Lam.

How to Get Booked

This comes back to the press kit. What else you can throw into the mix? In Europe, I booked showings of my film, but I also passed around a copy of *$30 Film School* at each squat, bar, and youth center that I showed at. You can piggyback your book stuff on other stuff if you are a modern multitasking Renaissance Jack-of-all-trades, such as myself.

A healthy press kit, and especially a few non-fiction books like mine, make you an *expert*. Experts get paid for their time. If you're professional, punctual, polite, low-maintenance, humble, and compelling, you get asked back.

Bookstores

To speak at Borders, B. Dalton, or Barnes and Noble, they'll have to already be carrying your book. Once they do, it's not a very hard sell. Call the store in the cities you wanna go to and ask for the Area Marketing Manager's number. Often, one person is the Area Marketing Manager for a region or even a state. That one person, if he likes you and your book, can book you at all the stores for his jurisdiction. This makes it easier.

If you can't get your stuff into chain stores, you can do in-stores at smaller independent stores. This is actually harder, but it can be done. More or less, the rule is, if you can get people into a store, any store, and the people are cool and have a good time and buy something, the store is usually into it. You have to be crafty, though. Make it an *event*. Make it more than just a signing. A signing is boring. It's just star worship, and we ain't stars. Make it informative. Teach something for free and have your book be the bonus.

Don't call it a signing. Call it "free in-store book signing and conversation with the author." Or, "The author will be doing a free course on independent filmmaking and signing his new book," or something like that. That's more egalitarian, less intimidating. Fosters exchange rather than star worship.

NOTE

Once you've done an appearance at a chain bookstore in one town (like maybe your own town), if you've been polite and nice, it is easier to get booked at the same store in a different city if you mention the first showing.

You can check online with most chain bookstores to find the main number for the store in each city, and also sometimes check the individual stores to see if they have your book in stock. This will help when you contact them.

Here's an e-mail I sent out that got me booked at some Borders stores in the Pacific Northwest:

> Hi. I'm Michael Dean, the author of *$30 Film School* and *$30 Music School*. I would love to come do an in-store author event at your Eugene and Portland stores. You carry both of my books at both stores.
>
> I will play guitar, sing, and then talk a bit at the event if you book it. I have done many of these already. Feel free to contact Peggy at 213-zzz-zzzz in Los Angeles, who booked the Southern California Borders events for me— Hollywood, Pasadena, Glendale, and Montclair.
>
> I have no large expectations for the event and will perform, speak, and conduct myself in a professional manner.

Book/event info that we used for promo at the Southern California stores:

$30 Music School from Thomson Course Technology.

Author Michael W. Dean was the lead singer in the Warner Brothers band BOMB. He is the author of *$30 Film School*, *$30 Music School*, and *Starving in the Company of Beautiful Women*, as well as being the director of the documentary *D.I.Y. or Die: How to Survive as an Independent Artist*. He will be speaking, signing books, and maybe singing a few songs at this event.

$30 Music School is a 520-page book (w/ CD-ROM) on how to make and promote music with essentially no money. Everything is covered, from picking a guitar to writing a song, recording your own CD, or booking a tour. All with an easy, fun, conversational tone.

Dean brings a D.I.Y. attitude and a hacker ethic to making rock and roll with attainable goals. Why wait for a record deal that may never come? DO IT YOURSELF! Reach the world, spread quality music to the masses, and make a living. All without compromising to the whims of the entertainment industry.

Over 300 illustrations. It also includes exclusive interviews with Henry Rollins, Joan Jett, Jonathan Richman, and more.

Here is production material you may need to promote the event:

High-rez zip of cover:

> http://www.kittyfeet.com/30music/musicCover.ZIP

High-rez of author:

> http://www.kittyfeet.com/30music/backCoverB&W.jpg

(photo credit, Nick Plotquin)

Writer bio:

> http://www.kittyfeet.com/30music/Speaking%20bio_
> michael_Dean%20.doc

Thank you!

Feel free to contact me at Mwd@kittyfeet.com or 213-zzz-zzzz.

Much respect,

Michael Dean

BORDERS TOUR DATES:

SOUTHERN CALIFORNIA TOUR FOR *$30 MUSIC SCHOOL*

Free in-store book signing and conversation (and I'll play a few tunes at all of 'em):

> PASADENA
> Saturday, February 7 at Borders Books
> 475 South Lake Avenue, Pasadena, CA
> 4 P.M.

> GLENDALE
> Saturday, February 14 at Borders Books
> 100 S. Brand Blvd., Glendale, CA 91204
> 4 P.M.

> HOLLYWOOD
> Saturday, February 21, 2004 p.m.
> 1501 Vine Street, Hollywood, CA
> 3 P.M.

MONTCLAIR
Saturday, February 28, 2004, 3 p.m.
4 P.M.

NOTE

Get a telephone with speakerphone option. If you get busy with bookings, interviews, public appearances, airline and rental car reservations, and just being in the business of being a low-budget public figure like me, you'll be spending a lot of time on hold. A speakerphone will make this a lot easier. Having a fax machine, as old as that technology is, isn't a bad bet, either. Sometimes people will want you to fax something or fax something to you.

There are ways of sending faxes to a fax machine from a computer. But they are always problematic to me. Fax machines are cheap, and they work. And I kinda like the retro charm.

Once you've made initial contact with the marketing manager, offer to have your publisher send him a copy of your book. Don't say, "You carry it in your store, go get it off the shelf yourself." Big *faux pas*. Send a copy. They'll appreciate it.

Your publisher should pay for stuff like this and send it out promptly without charging you for the book or the postage. If they don't, certainly consider finding a different publisher for your next book, or at least negotiate to get this stuff in your contract for your second book.

NOTE

Don't just cut and paste my booking and query letters and plug in your own info. It won't work. The people who get them will start to recognize them. You should use the spirit of my letters as your template and tailor it to your own art, in your own voice and your own words. You're a writer. So write.

Also, be sure to tailor it to each specific audience. Don't just use the same one over and over. Like, for an indie venue, I'm more informal and play up my indie accomplishments. For Borders, I play up more of my professional-sounding stuff. This isn't lying, and I don't hide my bigger stuff from the indie folk and vice versa. I just know what each crowd will be interested in and play to that. When you start out, you probably won't have as much to choose from, so you'll have to drop your whole load each time.

Colleges

Sometimes they ask you, but feel free to ask them. I've spoken at a few, and sometimes they asked me, and sometimes I contacted them. It can be a long and convoluted process to find the professor whose class you would be appropriate speaking to. It's good if you know someone at the college and can ask. I've done that, but I've also just looked on the Web site and sent a few e-mails to track down the right teacher.

Museums

You can't ask them. They always ask you, and it's usually in conjunction with something else you've done, like showing a film. I spoke once at the Los Angeles Museum of Contemporary Art. I was recommended by someone else who knew someone there.

Museums are fun, a wonderful gig, and a high honor. Speaking at one looks great on a resume or CV. And it feels really good to do. It really feels like you've "arrived." (Even if you come home to a note that says you're about to get evicted, like the first time I did it!)

Alternative Events

Here is a letter I sent a Zine Fest in Portland.

> Howdy . . . you all showed my film there two years ago:
>
> > http://www.diyordie.org
>
> but it was shown away from the main space across the river, and not many people made it.
>
> Would you like to show it again this year in the main building? I think it's something a lot of people would dig.
>
> I would also love to do a workshop if you could bring me there. The workshop would be called "How to get international press for ANYTHING."
> In the past year I've written and had published two 520-page books
> (*$30 Film School*: http://www.30dollarfilmschool.com, *$30 Music School*:
> http://www.30dollarmusicschool.com), done a self-booked film/book/
> music tour of Europe, gotten press in over 100 zines and on VH1

(http://www.kittyfeet.com/woody/Vh1.mpg), and been interviewed on the BBC, NPR (http://www.kittyfeet.com/woody/wcpn.mp3), NBC (http://www.kittyfeet.com/woody/rockFurCats.mpg), and a lot of radio stations and cable TV shows.

D.I.Y. or Die is being shown next month as a benefit to raise money for the Texas Ladyfest.

I also do the Rock for Cats (http://www.rockforcats.com) cat benefit site.

I'm gonna be in Portland on April 4, showing at The Know and doing a book signing and speaking April 8th in Eugene at a class at U of O.

Much respect,

Michael Dean

Events You Set Up Yourself

This is a letter I used to set up an event at the DIVA arts center in Eugene, OR.

Thanks for contacting me. In addition to showing my film there, how about I do two one-day workshops at $15–20 per person sliding-scale.

I'll call the first one "$20 Film School" and the second one "How to get press for ANYTHING, worldwide."

Also, do you have any press contacts for Eugene that I might not have?

Respectfully,

Michael W. Dean

Don't forget to ask for press info, as I did in the last paragraph. It's all about building the contacts.

What to Do When You Get There

Get there at least a half hour before you're supposed to speak. Go to the front desk and tell someone, "I'm _____. I'm doing a book signing today." Don't interrupt them and don't hassle them. If you're nervous, or late, or tired, don't take it out on them. If there's an exceptionally long line, you might come up to the side of it, but if there's just one or two people, wait.

They will call a manager, who'll come get you, take you to where you're supposed to be, and get a few people to help set up. It won't hurt to offer to help them set up and move the table, PA system, and so on. Like I said, you want them on your side.

They'll get you all set up and then go make an announcement over the PA. A few people may or may not amble over. As I've said, if it's in your own town, try to bring a few friends. People are more likely to come over and listen if they're not the only ones there.

If you are playing music and you're good, people will amble over and listen to you. I usually play one song to check the mikes and bring people in, then introduce myself. "Hi. I'm Michael Dean, and I wrote this book, *$30 Music School.* I'm gonna be playing a few songs and then talking about the book and about my take on music. Then I'll be answering any questions you have and also signing books."

I play about five more songs and then start talking a little over the microphone. I usually talk for about five minutes about how and why I wrote the book, what my background is, you know, just introducing myself and my whole trip in a friendly, down-to-earth manner. I'll try to drop in a few asides about why my thing is different from the usual "you're gonna be a star if you buy this book" thing. Then I'll say, "If anyone has any questions, I'll answer them." If someone asks a question, I talk. If no one does, I talk about five more minutes. By then, when I ask for questions, people usually have them.

Don't talk down to people, but keep in mind that they may know *nothing* about what you're lecturing on. (If they were experts, they wouldn't need your book!) If someone asks a question that seems completely ignorant, I do my best to answer it. Once, a youngster asked the same question I'd just answered for someone else. I guess he was spacing out when I answered it. Instead of saying, "I already answered that question," I just talked more about it and added things to the subject that I didn't get to the first time around.

NOTE

Don't forget to get your parking validated. And find out if the store provides that for everyone. If so, announce it. You don't want your friends and fans to have to pay to hear you talk.

I'll do Q&A like this for between 15 and 45 minutes more, depending on how it's going. Usually a few people will want to keep listening to you, and the others will feel trapped if you talk longer. I usually stop before I feel people getting bored. I say, "Well, I'm gonna wrap it up and sign some books. If anyone has any questions, feel free to stick around and chat. Thank you very much."

> **NOTE**
>
> The Q&A is often better with small crowds than with big ones. It's more intimate, and the few who participate will get more out of it.

Then I start signing the books, even before people ask me to sign them. Sometimes no one buys a book. (At most stores, people have to go to the register and buy it first and bring it back to get you to sign it to them, with their name in it.) Usually I sell between five and ten at one of these events (though I sell more than that in the long run from increased exposure and people talking about the book and the event).

Usually a few people will stay and talk. Talk with them, answer questions, be polite, but don't stay forever. It's fine at any point to say, "Well, I've got to go now. Thank you."

You might just be alone at a table with no microphone and a sign that says "Meet the Author." It can be lonely. And sometimes people don't come by at first. But when people come by, be polite and say hello. Draw them in. It can be cool to have a friend come interview you, too, with a tape recorder or a video camera, so when people come up, you are doing something. Break from the interview and invite them in.

> **NOTE**
>
> I do what I call a "punk-rock end cap" sometimes. When I'm in a store, even if I don't have an end cap, I'll put a copy of my book in a more prominent place, like on a table display.

Autographs

I don't feel weird anymore about signing autographs. I used to, but now I'm honored. And I don't feel like it's a rock star thing at all. I look it as more like when I buy a book by someone else and give it to a friend and write something to my friend in the beginning.

I write a note in the beginning and thank them. It's just a special little thing. It doesn't elevate you above the person requesting it. It's just a special little fun honor. Treat it as such.

With touring and just writing in general: Don't try to be treated like a star. Ain't gonna happen. And even if it does, don't *act* like a star. Really. Treat people the way you'd like to be treated. Period.

NOTE

If you sign all the copies, they can't return them, and they have to sell them. Bring your own pen and sign them when there's a lull. This seems prickly, but they've never gotten mad at me for this. Or maybe they just sell all of them. Or maybe they can return them. I dunno. They usually have a roll of stickers that say "Signed Author Copy" that they put on the front cover after you sign them. You can even ask someone for the stickers and put them on yourself. I like this. I like to have something to do with my hands while I talk.

Signed books actually do sell more easily. And if you become any sort of cult hero, they might actually be worth more on eBay if they're signed. People know this.

Lodging

I usually stay with friends.

You can check out www.couchsurfing.com also. It's a free network of couch surfing places around the world.

If you're making a lot of money, your publisher may put you up in hotel rooms. Check and see if they've charged it back to you. If so, pick cheaper ones or stay with friends!

> **NOTE**
>
> One note on logistics: Don't forget to advance all showings. That is, call a month, week, and day ahead of time to let them know you're still coming. Check their Web site to make sure it's listed. Politely ask them to list it if it's not. Ask them for promo contacts and offer any poster info, bios, or materials they may need.

Time

Keep the signing open ended. Generally you're there for two hours total including set up, but don't make people feel trapped. And say at the beginning and once again in the middle of your talk that people are free to interrupt to get a book signed if they have to leave.

> **NOTE**
>
> Peggy from Borders, who booked my Southern California Borders tour, sez:
>
> I never schedule an ending time, I just list the start time in all the promotional materials. I would say that most people's attention spans don't last much longer than a hour and a half, and we don't want them wandering away without buying the book! Let's play it by ear, but after an hour, you might offer to sign a few books quickly for people who have to leave before the event is over.

How to Get Paid

Book signings at bookstores don't pay, even if you perform music. If you're lucky, they might buy you lunch. Feel it out, if it seems worth asking. I usually let them offer. It happens less than half the time. They should at least validate your parking. It shouldn't *cost* you to do an event.

> **NOTE**
>
> It's okay to ask your publisher to give you a couple of hundred dollars per book contract to pay for flyers and gas to in-stores and stuff like that. You shouldn't have to pay that out of your pocket.

Colleges and museums usually pay an *honorarium*, also called a stipend. This is a non-rock star amount that is pretty cool anyway. It's to cover your expenses and then some. It's to make you feel *honored* instead of put out. It's usually between 75 and 150 dollars. You'll have to give your Social Security number, fill out a form, and you might not get it for a month. They'll usually send it to you.

I remember the first time I was paid to speak. It was at an art class at a college near Los Angeles. When I was done, the teacher handed me a check for 150 bucks. This blew me away! I totally would have done this for free, but I got paid, too! Best 90 minutes of work in my life.

Zine symposiums and other indie events usually pay travel expenses and food and get you a place to stay. Sometimes it's a floor in some punk rock house. At the Underground Publishers Conference in Bowling Green, Ohio, one summer, I had an empty dorm room. That was pretty cool.

If you can draw people, events in bars or galleries typically pay half or two-thirds of the door money to you. And you usually get a few drinks and maybe dinner. Find out ahead of time and get it in writing. At least in an e-mail. I recommend printing it out and taking it to the gig.

Don't expect to make a lot of money speaking, at first. It's like writing. It takes years or decades of steady work to build the value of your name. And remember; every bit of press helps. Don't look at it as working toward a payoff. Look at it as part of living the dream, every step of the way.

If you become an expert in something or become a cult hero, you can make a lot of money doing speaking stuff. Henry Rollins charges 30 bucks a head to speak, and several hundred people show up. (His stuff is cool. It's sort of a cross between social commentary and stand-up comedy.) Jello Biafra does the same thing. A lot of us old punkers do. I do, and so does Dave from MDC. We don't make nearly as much as Rollins and Biafra, but we do all right, and have fun.

What to Do When You Speak at a College or Give a Speech

Sometimes I freestyle and just talk from the heart. I can do this, and it works. I did this when I spoke at Cal State Art College in Valencia, and I often do this when I talk in a bar.

I used to make a page of notes and freestyle from there. Now, I don't need the notes.

One thing that helps me is that no matter how convoluted the structure of my progression of story telling, no matter how many hypertextural tangents within concentric parentheticals I link in my speech, I come back to resolve the main points. There's one spoken-word recording I've heard by someone I really respect in which he talks mad science for an hour and goes down a million cool points, but I finished listening feeling unsatisfied. I listened again and noticed that he never finished the story he started. I didn't know that the first time through, but I felt that something was missing.

Sometimes I talk for 10 minutes and then say, "Are there any questions?" and go off of those. If no one has any, I keep talking. I never make people feel bad for not having a question, especially in Europe.

Be gentle. One time in Germany, I showed my film to 75 people and afterward got up and said, "Does anyone have a question?" Not one hand went up. I said, "Come on people, no one here has a question? I came a long way to not talk." Finally, one guy asked me an accusatory query about my punk rock credibility and said that my film wasn't really D.I.Y. because I put some people in it that make a decent living. I spoke to his question for 25 minutes straight. Then I said, "Any more questions?" No one asked me a follow up.

If people actually heckle you, deal with it with grace. Insult them only if you can make them look stupid and get the crowd on your side. Once in a bar in Sheffield, England, a drunk was calling me a wanker because I was a Yankee. He was blaming me for George Bush. I said, "I didn't vote for the motherfluffer. Don't blame me, sir." Everyone laughed with me, at him, and the guy sat down.

When you're talking in a country where English (or *your* first language) is not the first language, speak slowly! They will understand you a lot better. I started writing "SLOW" on my hand in Europe to remind me of this every day. (Watch the French TV interview I did. It's on the CD-ROM. Notice how much more slowly I talk compared the Connie Martinson interview I did in America.)

Figure 17.6 *My slow hand in Europe.*

Speaking Abroad

Most publishers won't pay for a tour for most books. They don't think it's worth their while, based on past experiences. I think they are probably right, from a spreadsheet viewpoint. But that didn't stop me from booking showings and even tours for my books. And my publisher was helpful, once I had stuff booked, by sending out promo copies and additional copies for me and such.

I did a tour of Europe in the fall of 2003. It was mainly a tour for my movie, but I also brought copies of my book, *$30 Film School,* and passed them around at every showing. And I actually sold some. This is another variation of what I call "the punk-rock drop ship."

I had my publisher drop-ship three or four copies every three or four stops on the tour. That way, I could be sure to always have copies waiting for me when I got there.

You can also sell them, which helps with pocket change and travel expenses. I also got it mentioned in a lot of fanzines, as well as a few mainstream magazines and newspapers. And I mentioned the book every time I did a radio interview. All the flyers for the film had a line at the bottom that said

> The director has a new book out on filmmaking: *$30 Film School*
>
> www.30DollarFilmSchool.com

I made the flyer template myself and e-mailed it ahead to all stops.

If you're in a band or have some other way of booking the tour, making the book piggyback on that is a smart move. Sell your book at the merch (merchandise) table.

I did 36 shows in 50 days in six countries (England, Ireland, France, Germany, Holland, and Belgium). I flew into and out of London, flew from England to Ireland, and took the train all the rest of the time and had a blast.

NOTE

Be sure to check out the 77-page European Tour Diary in the goodies folder on the CD-ROM. It's all of the thrice-weekly dispatches I sent out to my e-mail list while in Europe.

When I'm home, I send the list out about once a week. It's easy to sign up and easy to get off, if you ever need to. And I never sell, trade, or give the list away. To sign up, send an e-mail to kittyfeet69-subscribe@topica.com.

General tour tips:

- Archive all your press. Getting press makes any stop worthwhile, even if attendance is low.
- Thank *everyone* for everything (in life, too).
- Always keep your word (good advice for all of life).
- Bring phone numbers with you, not just on the laptop, but on paper for the next few days' worth of appointments. That way, if the laptop fails, you're not screwed. And archive the info on a Web site or with a friend so you're not out of luck if you lose the laptop.
- Call if you're gonna be late.
- Get a good sleeping bag when you go on tour.

Figure 17.7 *Small sleeping bag.*

- If you're in a country that doesn't have Euros, spend your coins before you leave; most places won't change coins.
- Banks or AFAX give a better exchange rate than airports or railroad stations.
- No one speaks English in France. Well, a few do (but they won't!), and not as many as in Germany and other countries.
- Don't carry lots of cash. If you're making money, PayPal some home or get travelers checks and keep the receipt and mail the checks home.

PayPal

PayPal is an online service for sending money. Anyone can set up an account for free and use it to send and receive money to anyone anywhere in the world (even if they don't have a PayPal account, but it's a lot easier if they do). There are over 40 million people with accounts, and PayPal doesn't take out much per transaction.

NOTE

If you ever receive an e-mail that looks like it's from PayPal asking you to enter your password or credit information, DELETE IT. IT IS A SCAM. PayPal never sends e-mails like this. Unscrupulous people send fake e-mails asking for this information and then use it for identity theft when people reply. Access the site or service only from www.paypal.com, never from an e-mail.

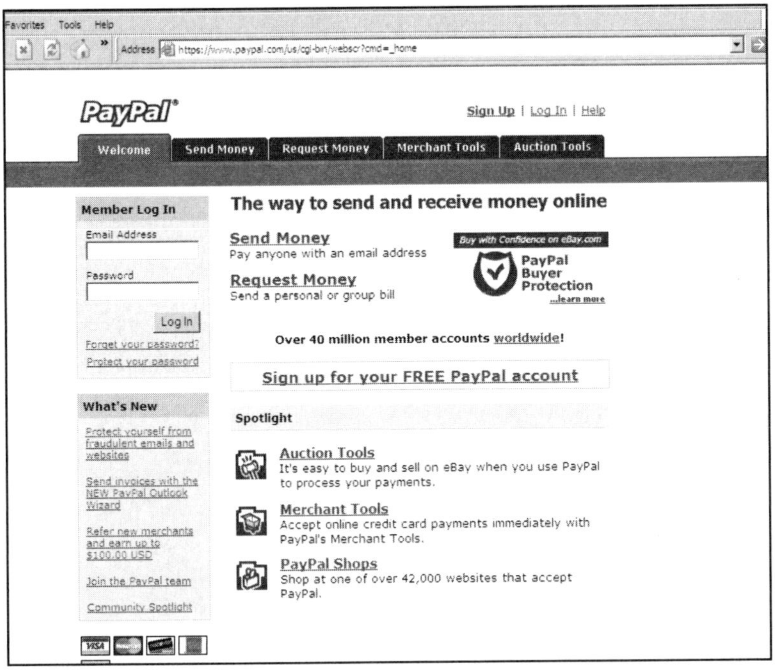

Figure 17.8 *PayPal.com.*

Crossing Borders

It's a lot easier than it used to be. Some people in high places in Europe are basically trying to make Europe into one big country, so the borders are a lot more open than they were 10 years ago. It's easier to travel around with impunity.

Just make sure you have no contraband. You probably don't want to say, "I'm here making money" if you are, because that's "working," and for that you need work permits. (I'm not telling you to break the law, I'm just saying how it works, ya know?) Basically, they want you over there *spending* money, not *taking* money.

Passports

You'll need a passport. They take a few months to get unless you're rich. Look in the phonebook under "Passport Office." You can actually get the applications at most U.S. Post Offices.

Figure 17.9 *U.S. passport.*

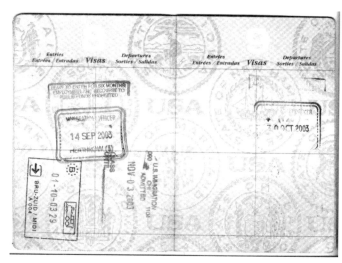

Figure 17.10 *Country stamps in a passport.*

You have to fill out a customs landing card in some countries.

Figure 17.11 *Customs landing card from England.*

How to Get Interviewed

If you do cool stuff some people know about, other people will contact you. What I also do when I send out a press release by e-mail is add a line such as this:

> The author is available for interviews. Contact him at interview@kittyfeet.com

> Click here to see recent press.

> http://www.kittyfeet.com/vh1.htm

NOTE

When you put URLs (Web addresses and e-mail addresses) in print and especially in e-mails, don't put a period at the end, even if it is the end of a sentence. Don't put any other characters or punctuation, either. People make assumptions, and computers are very literal.

These are valid URLs:

mwd@kittyfeet.com
http://www.kittyfeet.com/vh1.htm

These are not:

mwd@kittyfeet.com.
http://www.kittyfeet.com/vh1.htm.

The period will make them not work if they're in an e-mail or if someone clicks on the link. If they are in print, some people do not know this and will type them anyway. Make especially sure you never hyphenate one in a book, because people will type the hyphen, and the link won't work. Just hit Return before the URL and put it all on one line. And check for this in proofreading and/or set up your page layout program's hyphenation preferences to not do this. It's different for each program. Check the Help menu under "Hyphenation."

Don't bug people to be interviewed. Pros don't do it. Just put yourself out there and follow through, maybe a month later, with an e-mail that says, "Hi. Did you get the book I sent? I'm just following up. Let me know if I can do anything for you." If they think you're interesting, they might interview you. If they don't, leave them alone.

> **NOTE**
>
> If you do an interview with someone, write a thank you afterward. Same with someone booking you for an in-store or a lecture. And keep his contact info so you can tell him personally when your next project comes out. Don't bug him in it is between. Don't send non-new stuff. The less you send, the more impact you'll have when you want to have impact.

How to Be Interviewed

As I said earlier, I interview people a lot. I also get interviewed a lot. If you do something really cool, you will probably end up in that chair, too.

Being interviewed comes really easily to me. I actually practiced interviewing myself as a teenager with a Dictaphone in front of the mirror. This seemed kinda insane at the time. My friends thought it was pathetic and disturbed. But I'd calmly say, "No, I'm going to do important things, and people are going to want to interview me."

Basically, being interviewed isn't a scary thing. It isn't an occasion to worry about making a grand statement and saying it in a brilliant way (though that can't hurt). I have a friend who got interviewed on a small local radio station about her film, and she went nuts worrying about it. She lost sleep for three days. She made pages of notes to prepare. And when she got on there, she sounded like a self-important idiot. All her hard work on her *real* work got lost in the mix.

This needn't be the case. I do about three interviews a week, and it ain't no big thing. I don't lose sleep over it. I just show up and do it. Sometimes I have to *wake* up to do it. About the only time I ever use my alarm clock anymore is when I have to get up at 8 a.m. to do a telephone interview with a morning show on some radio station somewhere.

Be yourself in an interview. Don't try to sound wise or deep or outrageous. Just talk. Just say what's on your mind.

Before he died of cancer, my pal Phil Sudo said something to the effect that, if you never lie, you never have to remember which lies you told and tailor your new lies to cover the old lies. In the same way, if you live a life of integrity, you will always have the appropriate answer and action in any given situation.

Don't overplan. It gets *way* easier to be interviewed the more you do it. If you have something to say to the Universe, the Universe will give you the power and ability and words to say it. Hustle to set stuff up, do the stuff, and then move on to other stuff, without caring about the results of the last stuff. That's how you stay sane as an artist.

Tie Up Loose Ends

I tend to talk for a long time when I'm asked a decent question by an interviewer. I tend to talk in parenthetical, hypertextural concentrics. I talk in stories within stories within stories. In interviews, as with public speaking, make sure you come back to the original point. Tie up your loose ends. This gets easier with time, the more interviews you do, and especially the more you write in this style. I write in this style. If you write in a different style, you will probably do interviews in a different style. I tend to write the way I talk. Most good writers do.

NOTE

If you're going to be interviewed, make sure you have the phone number of the person responsible for the interview. Make sure he has yours. E-mail him a photo so he knows what you look like, and ask for one of his so you know what he looks like. (That way you don't have to ask, "Are you Bob?" to everyone who walks through the door.)

Get good directions and get there early. Get to that end of town and have lunch or something so you won't get caught in traffic. Show up for the interview between five and ten minutes early. No earlier, no later.

It's important to be on time. Someone thinks you're important enough to publish or broadcast your thoughts, so you should regard them as important enough to be on time.

There are two kinds of interviews. One is where they ask questions and then print your answers pretty much verbatim. The other is where they interview you and then use it as research to write an article about you and your art. There will be excerpts of what you said in it, but it will mostly be their words. The former type of interviewer will often use a Dictaphone. The latter will often just take notes.

NOTE

Whenever you're dealing with a person, try to learn his name before you meet him or remember it as soon as you meet him, and then use his first name several times when you're talking to him. For instance, "Thank you Bob. I'm really honored to be interviewed by your zine. Blah blah blah blah blah, well yes, Bob. That rocks." It will make him pay a lot more attention to you and feel special. Treat everyone well. They are special.

I could have probably learned this from *How to Win Friends and Influence People* or *The Seven Habits of Highly Successful People*. But I didn't. I learned it from Henry Rollins. (I wonder if he read those books?) He does this with everyone he meets, and it works.

Don't overdo it, or it will be obviously insincere. And *never* assume the familiarity to give a nickname to someone else. (G.W. Bush does it, and that alone should be reason enough not to do it!) If someone introduces himself as "David," don't shorten it to "Dave." You don't know him. A lot of people do this. A lot of people call me Mike. I correct them. My name is not Mike. It's Michael.

Study Good Interviews

All the interviews in the Chapter 19, "Interviews" are really good. Check them out, and then think about how you would respond to the same questions.

Be sure to check out the 35-page document Interview with Michael Dean by Cassidy Coon for—The Office.doc in the Interviews with or articles about Michael Dean folder on the CD.

Also, check out the video titled *Michael Dean on TV on the Connie Martinson Talks Books show* on the CD-ROM. It's a half-hour of me on a syndicated cable show produced by the Los Angeles Public Library. It's a really good show, and I was honored to be on it. I think it's a pretty good example of a good interview and being confident but not cocky. I had a lot of fun doing it, and a lot of people saw it.

And the interview with Cubby is amazing. It's the video on the CD-ROM called *Hubert Selby, Jr. Interview.*

Be Available

Don't turn down anything. And give it your all.

I will take the same care and time to do an interview for a fanzine that two kids do in their bedroom and photocopy 100 copies of as I will for NBC or *Entertainment Today* or the BBC. I've done all of these and always give them my full attention.

I give the same interview to both small and big venues. I don't censor or tailor myself to impress one type of reader over another. There are two things I will consider during the interview but it doesn't mean compromising in any way. One is the readership—I usually ask the interviewer to bring me a copy of the magazine to look at, and I ask about who reads it and where it's distributed. If the interview is via e-mail, I'll check out their Web site if they have one. The reason is that I don't like to repeat myself to the same audience in the same week. I get asked the same questions a lot, and I have pretty well-thought-out policies on many things. So I end up saying variations of the same things over and over. If two punk rock magazines from the same town interview me the same week, I try not to repeat myself much, answering with a different facet of the same idea or even see if I can respectfully steer the interviewer in a different direction. Same thing if I do two mainstream media outlets in the same town in the same week. But if it's a punk outlet and a mainstream outlet in the same town the same week, I don't mind so much talking about the same stuff.

The second reason I like to know the readership of the magazine or viewership of the TV or listenership of the radio station interviewing me is that I might wanna steer the interview to talk about something I think they'll be interested in. Conversely, I might want to steer it to a place they might *not* want to go but that I think they might *need* to go! I don't like to preach to the converted. I'm as likely to talk to punk rockers about how sometimes I feel it's totally okay to deal with major corporations (they hate this) as I am to tell mainstream people why anarchy is cool. I like to stir up trouble sometimes.

NOTE

A really fun way to stir up trouble is to tell a group of losers directly that they are losers and why, but do it in a way that they all think you're talking about the other guy, the guy a few seats or cubicles over. I can't really tell you how I do this, but read my stuff and watch my stuff and I think you'll get it. It's loads of fun.

So, I stay available. Sometimes I'll even put writing on hold for a day to get three interviews done by e-mail at once. The only reason I would ever turn down an interview that I can think of is if I got too busy to meet their deadlines. If it got to the point where I were getting dozens of requests a week, it would seriously impair my ability to get any work done if I were to take them all.

I recently contacted J.K. Rowling (I had my agent contact her agent via mail) to see if I could interview her for this book. I got a letter back that she was too busy to do it. I can't blame her. She probably gets 500 interview requests a week and has to temper her promotional life with her creative life. (And also, the *Harry Potter* series is such a money minter that it would seriously cost her tens of thousands of dollars to take time out of writing to spend an hour being interviewed by me.) I also tried to get Judy Blume, but her agent contacted me and said she was also too busy.

(It was interesting. The rejection reply did not come from her agent: It came from her agent's assistant's assistant. I guess at that level, an agent would not only devote full time to one client, but would probably have a huge support staff.)

I do the interview in Word, spell check, and then print out my answers and go through it with a pen before I make corrections and send the document back to the person.

NOTE

If the person does not have Word and sends you the interview in the body of an e-mail, you can copy and paste it into the working program on the CD-ROM (in the software folder) called emailfwdthing. It is a cool and tiny little program that will strip all the e-mail formatting and >>>> characters and line breaks. Just be sure to clip out the last line:

This email was cleaned by emailStripper, available for free from http://www.papercut.biz/emailStripper.htm

before you put it into your interview. (This program is great for doing any cutting and pasting from e-mails.)

Plan Ahead

Book ahead and don't stress. I booked an early April 2004 book tour of the Pacific NW starting in January.

People booking you are doing you a favor. Don't hassle them or hustle them. Gently hammer away, but the operative word is *gently*. When something really seems like it's not gonna happen, move on.

"Poor planning on your part does not constitute an emergency on our part." This is a common saying. Remember it. I remember it from a sign hanging on the wall at the dosing window at the Methadone clinic I used to go to when I was a junkie. It's especially funny there because junkies plan poorly and, by definition, are always pretty close to a state of emergency.

Conclusion

Again, so I don't have to reinvent the wheel, get my book *$30 Music School*. It has a lot on the specifics of booking a tour; enough that it will be worth getting even if you don't play music. The same is true of *$30 Film School*. Remember people, these two books plus the one in your hand comprise a trilogy and are meant to be enjoyed together, along with the supplement of my movie, *D.I.Y. or Die: How to Survive as an Independent Artist*. All together, the three books along with the movie comprise *$99 Art Academy*.

Chapter 18

Closing Arguments (a.k.a. "The $30 Manifesto")

$30 WRITING SCHOOL

This will deal with the *why*, rather than the *how*. The reasons we writers get up in the morning (or afternoon). What drives us. What could drive you. What *will* drive you. And how to see the world more consciously.

And *seeing* the world for others is what being a writer is actually about.

This book is the last in my trilogy. As I said earlier in this book, "You will see a conclusion at the end of this book in the 'Closing Arguments' chapter that not only sums up this book, but all three books." (This is also always the most fun chapter in these books to write!)

The series may carry on, but this chapter closes not only this book, but all of them. . . . So I'd better make this good . . .

Wrap Up

I am a published and known writer. I make a living, but I'm not rich. I live in a crappy studio apartment by myself. There are cracks in the ceiling, and the paint is peeling.

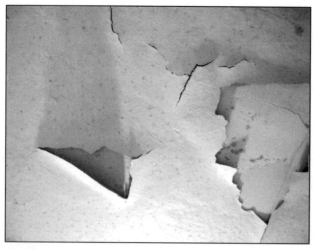

Figure 18.1 *My ceiling.*

But I love being a writer. I can get up when I want, I don't have to leave the house and talk to idiots every day. I do what I want when I want, and people dig what I do. I set my own hours, travel the world, change people's lives for the better, and get to date two girls at the same time who are both really cute, smart, creative, and in their 20s. And I'm 40. And they both know about each other. And I'm short, a little out of shape, have messed-up teeth, and don't have much money to spend on them. And I don't buy them diamonds or crap like that. I just treat them well, love them well, listen well, and tell good stories.

Tell me one other profession besides being an artist where you could live like that?

When I have money, I spend freely on my friends. But I won't have friends who consider money a prerequisite. I don't buy into the common ideas of time, money, career, all that. I don't even own a watch. I don't need to, because I have no boss. I don't want a boss. I'm working naked right now in my room because it's 95 degrees out. And I'm about to take my afternoon nap. You can't pay me enough to not be able to do those things.

Writing is better than sex. Anyone can have sex, but not everyone can create a cool book.

Direction

I need to write about 1,000 words (about three pages in a novel, about five pages in one of these books) a day to feel like I'm earning my keep on the planet. Not from a money standpoint, but from an art standpoint. I won't even usually go out to dinner with friends unless I've done my 1,000 words. There are exceptions, but otherwise, 1,000 words a day is a rhythm, if not a rule. When I'm editing or in author review, I often don't write. After a book ships to the printer, I may take a few days off and just go to the country with a gal and make out, space out, take walks, shoot guns, watch TV, sleep, and drink way too much coffee.

Flow

People see I'm doing pretty well career-wise and ask me, "At what single moment did it turn around for you?"

There is no single moment, except maybe getting off drugs. And even that took a while. My life is a series of small, beautiful baby steps and constant daily work.

Figure 18.2 *Me on New Year's Day, 2004, blowing off steam in rural Texas right after finishing* $30 Music School. Photo by Tracy Hatfield.

I like my life, I like what I do, and I like where I live. Living in Los Angeles drives you. Everyone here is working in "the biz" or at least trying (or pretending) to. I used to be turned off by this. It all seemed really phony. But after three years I realized it helps you keep working. Everyone everywhere here is trying to make something that gets seen on a large level. I don't look at it as competition. I feel pushed along by the vibe. I ride the wave.

But a lot of people want more than they deserve. They have big expectations, but things don't always work out. The *LA Times* classified section has more late-model BMWs and Mercedes Benzes for sale at "must sell" prices than anywhere I've ever lived.

I got sick of seeing people in Hollywood trying to come off as more important than they are. I went the other way: My new business card says, "Michael Dean. Nobody." And then my phone number.

NOTE

Just make art. No need to hustle or hate. Don't be piggy. Just let it all flow through you . . . money, art, life, love.

I have a friend who is a well-known artist who gets panicked about money and career from time to time. She'll call me, and I'll talk to her and calm her down. Mostly I just tell her not to panic. Try to have less desperation and more inspiration. Work steady over a long timeline. When life comes at you with challenges, don't freak out. Embrace the trouble. Turn *into* the skid.

I also tell her this: When you go to take a meeting with someone, don't cut right to your needs and demands. It's okay to talk about the weather for a few minutes. Or just make any kind of honest, fun small talk. Because any negotiation should be partly fun. It's all about relationships. It's part of the job. If you don't like your job, find a different job. (Or get a good agent to do all that for you, and give her a percentage of *everything* you do, not just part of what you do, like me.)

> **NOTE**
>
> Leave the house once in a while. My first two years in Los Angeles I sat in my room most of the time and had my computer on every minute I was awake. After I finished *$30 Music School*, I figured two 520-page books and a world-changing movie in two years had earned me a break. I went to Texas with Tracy and went out to the country for two weeks. I spent a week of that with no Internet access, and I didn't die. In fact, I had a blast. I'd never done more than two days without the Net before.
>
> Use computers to express life, but get off them occasionally to have a life worth expressing.

Don't Take Yourself Too Seriously

If you get some recognition, don't let it go to your head. It sure is nice to get fan letters. It sure is nice to have people think you're really cool. But not everyone is gonna think that you rock. It's easy to convince yourself that you're famous when you're not. If you get 10 fan letters a week, it sure feels like the whole world loves you. But the guy in line in front of you at the store where you buy your eggs may have missed that memo. He doesn't know you're a god to a tiny faction of the world. And you're sure gonna look like a jackass if you assume he does or should.

Most of the artists I like are popular in the way I am. A lot of people know who I am, but I'm not *famous*. I actually do get recognized on the street, all over the world (well, all over the U.S. and Europe), but not every time I step out of the house. Maybe three times a week. Even someone like Henry Rollins, who is many rungs above me on the fame ladder and does get recognized every day, anywhere he goes, isn't famous in the "mobbed on the street" sense like a huge movie star. My dad wouldn't recognize Rollins. My dad would recognize Sean Connery or Mick Jagger. Those people are famous.

There are only about three writers in the world who are that famous. Maybe fewer.

If you do become even mildly well recognized for your work, some people will *hate* you. It takes a strong heart to make art and get known. When I think about the amount of crazy, bitter mail I get and the number of people I've blocked from my e-mail server, I can only imagine what it's like if you're huge. I don't want it. I used to, but no longer.

Don't worry about recognition. Writers are some of the most anonymous people there are. If you wanna be recognized on the street, pick a different path. Writing is about solitary artists working in a solitary way, speaking to a solitary audience. That audience can number in the millions, but people enjoy books alone. It's not like music or movies. And even big writers can walk down the street relatively unmobbed. I can't think of any writers other than Stephen King who would be universally recognized. And maybe not even him.

Recognition is a Zen riddle: The harder I chased it, the more it ran from me. Once I got my life together and just *worked*, some tiny little fame started to chase *me*.

Living the dream as a writer is extraordinarily ordinary, spiked with tiny shivers and slivers and glimmers of transcendent cool.

Go Beyond the Dream

I try to be nice to people and try not to get too cranky. Sometimes I forget that I *am* living the dream, and I get as stressed about work (and life) as I would if a boss were standing over me. I have no boss. I have to remember that. I have to be vigilant about not getting too cranky and taking time to stop and sniff at stuff along the way. Life is a blast. I need to remember that.

Living the dream is different than simply dreaming. *Living* the dream requires constant work. This is a most axiomatic fact of facts.

On tour in Paris, I met a really cool, really cute girl who liked me, and I was very interested in her until she smoked a bunch of pot and then said, "Dreaming is better than doing." That *really* turned me off.[1]

Oh well, I was young once. But dreams alone are nothing. Action is all.

I even started writing a simplified word processing manual, a year before the first *Dummies* book came out. I called it *Compudum*. But I was on drugs and not able to bring the project to fruition. It never got published. And now it's too hopelessly out of date to publish.

So much for dreams.

Don't Follow Trends—Make Trends

In 1976, when I was 12, I pierced my ear. Not many males did that back then. I used to get beaten up for it. Today, the same people who used to beat me up now pierce their ears. I have no interest in it anymore.

My band, Bomb, was underground for a long time. We put out some really good records. We pressed the first one ourselves. The next two were on a tiny Berkeley punk label, Boner Records (even though we weren't really punk in sound, just attitude and energy). The fourth record was on Warner Brothers. Funny. . . . We never thought we could ever be on a major label when we started out. *We* didn't change (other than getting much better); the *industry* changed. Jane's Addiction got big, and Nirvana's major debut came out six months before ours. Scrappy garage bands with a few indie records under their belts were suddenly going multi-platinum. So of course the industry did what it always does in such a feeding frenzy—it signed every band that remotely resembled the one that just hit.

This is stupid, but not as stupid as all the bands that change their sound and dress to match the new big thing. First of all, they're selling out their souls and their soulfulness. Second, the lag time for a band to make it is such that the world will have moved on to the *next* next big thing by the time anyone notices them.

---

[1] My cat believes that dreaming is not only better than doing, but perhaps even dreaming is a little too much work. Kitty thinks that *being* is better than doing. Then again, she doesn't write many books. She does, however, chew and pee on books.

We didn't imitate Jane's Addiction and Nirvana. Considering that they had our records and came to our shows, there is a better chance that they were influenced by us than we them. Probably more likely is that we were just contemporaries and, as such, had the same influences: Bauhaus and Led Zeppelin in the case of Jane's Addiction, and the Beatles and punk rock in the case of Nirvana.

Longevity and Friends

I am an artist. Everything I do is part of my work. I've never been on a non-working vacation. All my travel is work related. And it's all very pleasurable. I love my life. You can do this, too.

I admire people who do a lot of things well. I want to be good at *everything*. I write, sing, play, make films, and do multimedia production, and I am not a dilettante. I do it all well, and that's me. I'm turning 40 this year and don't feel old. I really do feel like my life has just begun.

Pick your people well. In art, love, and work. I can't work with people I don't like. If I could, I'd get a normal job.

And I don't usually like people I cannot collaborate with. I'd like to like them, but work is too important to me. Art is *all*. So if someone isn't creating, I honestly have trouble making time for him.

I do a lot of small work projects with different people. I love to mix business with pleasure. My lovers and friends are my partners, and my partners are my lovers and friends. That's one reason I decided to be an artist when I was about five.

People want to feel useful. Give them something important to be a part of, and they will help and commit to you and your projects with a fierce determination. You will teach them, and they will teach you. It's win/win.

There is a posting on my Web board where a fellow called Attaboy writes:

> Michael Dean is a Verb.

> His movie is needed, and I watch it when my independent self is heartbroken from missing packages, people with nonexistent work ethics, and the often miserable state of things. It's like a blood transfusion during those times.

Michael Dean is a VERB. And that's my highest compliment. People who are verbs cannot be pigeonholed, stopped or let down. Surround yourselves with Verbs. They're the only people who matter.

There is a huge drop-off rate with artists. About the age of 30, most "I'm in it for life" artists give up and go straight. And there is a lot of fleetingness to employment in art, even if you make it past 30. There's nothing wrong with giving up, but I encourage you not to. I didn't, and I'm happy.

Attaboy is in it for life. So am I. Most of my friends are. If you pick good people and treat them well, the artistic life will go easier, even with the knocks and pricks.

The 30-Dollar Way

I always stick by my heart. St. Martin's Press wanted to publish the film school book, but I turned them down because they wouldn't do it with the CD-ROM. They offered a bigger advance, and they might have sold more copies, but I really thought the CD-ROM should be part of the package. So I said no.

Writing is work. I actually sweat when I write. It might be the coffee overdose I'm usually suffering, but I like to think it's my work ethic in action.

I like people who create. I used to date a girl who writes for television. I remember being in a log cabin with her out in the country. Most people would be like, "Michael, get in here and entertain me." She was in her room, totally self-entertaining. I could even hear her giggle from time through the closed door. And she wasn't in there watching TV, like most people would be. She was in there writing TV. I love that in a woman.

NOTE

Do it yourself. Don't wait for permission. Create your own history. If you don't, no one will.

Purpose

Think about why you want to write a book. Does it need to be written or are you just indulging in the fantasy of putting on the drag of playing the image of the writer?

Sure, that's fine. Sit in the coffee shop and pretend to be a writer. Or be a writer, but just write stuff that makes money and doesn't change anything. Neither thing really harms me or mine in any way. But it's not my way.

I want to write *important* books. They say that the Sex Pistols and the Velvet Underground didn't sell that many records, but everyone who bought one of their records started a band. I want to write books like that. I would rather sell 50,000 books that start a movement than sell 500,000 books about nothing. I don't even need to lead the movement. I would be happy to be the catalyst (or one of several catalysts) to get it rolling to the point where I am obsolete. My dream is to start things that run themselves.

> **NOTE**
>
> I have heard that all human endeavors are based either in fear or in love. (Yeah, I know a cool movie makes fun of this, but it's still true.) I will continue to hone my art into a sharp, pretty stick of love aimed directly at the throat of the consumer.

Book ideas are copied, especially tech books. When one company has a hit with a title, another company often quickly comes out with another book about the same subject. Tech books are easy to copy in style and content because the author doesn't usually put a lot of himself in them. One well-written book on using Photoshop or ProTools is pretty much like the next. They usually read like they were written by a computer. With tech books, often the more of himself the author puts in, the less he helps the reader.

My books are not copyable.[2] You could photocopy them or scan them, but you can't imitate them. They are too *me*. No one else in the world writes like I do, has

---

[2] I wonder if it's a coincidence that the leading "how to" book company came out with a filmmaking book six months after my filmmaking book came out. Let's see if they come out with a music book and a writing book that are similar to mine soon after. And start creeping some anti-corporate mentality into them. I'm gonna be watching. I hope they do. I don't mind influencing popular thought, even if I don't get credited for it. I've already done it with music. Now maybe I'll get to do it with writing.

the experiences, and can put himself into a tech work in the same way I can. Not many people can write a tech manual with a built-in self-help book. And not many people can write a single book that can take you from square one to touring the world. (Though Lloyd Kaufman can!) If someone else can, I'd love to see it. And it wouldn't be an imitation of me, because it would totally have to *ooze* the author's soul to work.

Computer wizard and founder of Sun Microsystems Bill Joy says, "I try to work on things that won't happen unless I do them."

Strive to make art that is uniquely your own, something that is not copyable. The world can't steal *you*.

The best great ideas cannot be ripped off because they involve yourself as a crucial ingredient.

Art versus Commerce—
Art and Commerce

The world is cursed. Corporations have more power than ever and are violating human rights worldwide in ways that only dictators used to. But I still have a lot of faith in humans. I just don't buy into nationalism. I'm not proud of my nation. I am proud of myself and my family and my friends, but a nation is too vast of an entity for me to blindly co-sign all its actions.

Screw nationalism. It's a cloak for the weak.

I am a citizen of the planet Earth. It sounds hippie, but it's true. I do enjoy the colorful differences in cultures and races, the beauty of all, but screw borders. The more I travel, the more I resent arbitrary schoolyard lines in the mud and the lies rich folk tell the poor to keep us ignorant.

Some of these divisions are artificially set up by nasty rich men (and yes, it's usually males) as a smokescreen to deny us the truth: that it ain't about race, sex, politics, or imaginary lines in the dirt set up before you were born. It's really about money. (And power. Don't forget power. "They" don't.)

I don't think that money (or power) is intrinsically evil. It's how you get it and what you do with it. I know millionaires with integrity, and I know people who have sold out their friends for 10 dollars. But too much piggy money, grabbed blindly for its own sake, is evil.

It's okay to make money. It's okay to be comfortable. To provide for your family. To have tools for your trade, health care, and a few toys. Maybe take a vacation.

But I'm sure it's not okay to amass unbelievable wealth to the point that it takes away from others. I guess I'm a capitalist with socialist leanings.

We don't need more laws, more cops, and more prisons. We need to teach ourselves to have less burning self-will. Self-will is why most people are unhappy. It is possible to have a perfectly formed ego, get things done, and advance in your chosen field without being a power-driven lunatic paving over everyone in your way. The universe wants you happy, healthy, and productive. But you need to quit demanding it to get it. Still work for it, but don't get caught up in the results.

It's that old Zen "give up to get" thing, and it really works. It's working for me. I'm less of an egomaniac than I used to be and my career is in a higher gear than ever.

> **NOTE**
>
> When you have to really talk yourself into doing something, your heart isn't in it, and you shouldn't do it.

Live for Art

I love feeling *useful*. I love feeling that I'm working on something *important*. This literally gives me a reason to get up each day.

I have to stay busy. *Busy* is what artists do best. It gives me something to do, somewhere to go each day (even if that place to go sometimes doesn't involve leaving the house).

I'm too busy to proof or critique your writing. Feel free to mail me a copy of your book after it's finished (though I can't guarantee I'll have time to read it), but please don't e-mail me works in progress.

Seinfeld co-creator Larry David could easily retire. He's 56 years old and has over 200 million dollars. Yet he keeps working (currently on my favorite current show, *Curb Your Enthusiasm*).

Why does he still work? To keep busy. He told *The New Yorker*, "You need a place to go. A place to go—that's what my mother always instilled in me. You need a place to go. And you're worthless unless you have a place to go. So I needed a place to go."

NOTE

Be on a mission. Make art that inspires other people to fight for you.

Last year I spent 5,000 dollars on art supplies and 60 dollars on clothes. I don't care about the external, only the eternal.

Artists have different priorities than most people. I recently saw a commercial for a diamond company showing a woman with a bullhorn outside her lover's apartment *screeeeching* for him to come down and buy her a diamond. The same company had another ad out right before Christmas showing a different woman in front of a Christmas tree yelling at her boyfriend on Christmas morn. She's waving a CD-ROM in his face and screeching, "You got me *software??!!* What were you *thinking??!!*" The implication of both seemed to be that if you get your gal anything but diamonds, you were going to find yourself very single very quickly.

If I gave my lover software and she bellowed, "What were you *thinking??!!*", I would calmly say, "I was thinking you were an interesting person who would rather have useful artistic tools than a dead lump of squished coal, you insensitive carbon blob."

I would then quietly walk out of her life forever.

My old girlfriend Maggie McEleney (she's in *D.I.Y. or Die*—check her out), who is still a good friend, used to tell me, "Diamonds are a girl's best friend. Dog is man's best friend. I must be a man because I'd rather have a good dog than a diamond."

I couldn't agree more. And I date only ladies who are as smart as Maggie. And if someone gave me a diamond, I'd sell it to some idiot and spend the money on another computer or some airline tickets.

I'd rather have a good cheap, digital camera than two dozen roses. (And they cost the same.) Ya wanna give me a gift? Someone recently gave me an expensive, ornate blank book to "chronicle my thoughts." Screw it. I'll never use it. Give me a backrub and a pad of Post-Its. Give me a gift certificate to Amazon.com or OfficeMax.

I would rather squat in a Unabomber-style shack with DSL than own a swanky townhouse with all the trimmin's if I couldn't create. It's not about what you own, wear, or save up in this world. Like they say in *Fight Club*, "You are not your bank account or the car you drive. You are not the contents of your wallet."

It's not about what you own, it's the about the effect you have on the world.

What did you do today? Did you make the world a better place than you found it? On your deathbed, can you say you made a difference? Think about all the great artists who died penniless. Any one of them made a bigger difference than the fat, complacent corporate drone sitting next to you.

It's not even about money. You don't have to be poor to be good. Some great artists live comfortably. If you're talented, driven, and have good people skills (a rare combination indeed) or have talent, a good agent, and some luck, you can even make the same wage a middle-management blob makes, not compromise yourself, improve the world, and make a name for yourself—a name that will outlive your earthly body.

I have a friend who is a well-known photographer. People in the realm he works in all know his name. A Web search on his name reveals about 4,000 results. (How many does your name return? If you have a unique name that will return unique results, try your name on Google, in quotes, and see.) But this photographer has a day job. And he told me last year he made a profit of only 70 dollars on photography for the entire year!

I have another friend who is a well-known painter. He recently lost his Web site URL (which is his name followed by .com) because he didn't have the 30 bucks to pay the annual fee.

Those two cats don't make much money. And they are changing the world for the better and will be remembered.

It's not even so much about being remembered. A lot of my heroes are not household names. They just quietly have their act together and quietly help others.

This is an excerpt from my novel, *Starving in the Company of Beautiful Women*:

> I have this feeling that rock 'n' roll is not all I am going to do with my life. I feel that it's just a stepping stone to something bigger, something more

along the importance of the invention of the electric light bulb. I want to be the next Thomas Edison. No, screw that . . . I wanna be the next Nikola Tesla. That's who Edison stole a lot of his ideas from.

I don't know what this next thing is, but I do know a few things about it: One is that I might not invent it, maybe I'll just pioneer it, the same way that Ford didn't invent the car, but he put one in every carriage house and barn. I also know that it will involve bringing people together. That is my strongest . . . far more important than rock 'n' roll. I have match-made a lot of . . . lovers, musicians and friends. I have an intuition about it; I don't just randomly try one person with another, and try them with someone else if the first attempt fails. Naw, I just get these feelings that person X must meet person Y, and I will try very hard to get them together in the same room. If I do and the magic don't take, I have done my part and usually don't try with them again. But it often works. There are couples that have been together for years because of me, bands that wouldn't have happened without my help and lifelong friends I've introduced. You could say I want to be a professional catalyst.

I'm not talking matchmaking in the conventional sense of the word. I'm talking about some brave new art-science spiritual-service that hasn't been invented yet. I know I have to keep my eye out for it, but that I can't look too hard, or it will evade me. I almost know that I could start doing this thing today and that when I finally find it, I'll hit myself in the head for not thinking of it sooner.

I want to find something to do that only I can do, and then do it really well.

I know that this process will involve computers, which is odd, because I've always said that I would never learn to use a computer. But I guess that being open-minded means being teachable.

I wrote that 14 years ago, before I even started using computers.

I feel that with *$30 Film School*, *$30 Music School*, and *$30 Writing School* and my film *D.I.Y. or Die: How to Survive as an Independent Artist*, I have begun to be a professional catalyst. Something I wrote as fantasy over a dozen years ago has actually manifested in my life. I'm writing my future.

I'm living the dream. Through writing. . . .

NOW GO WRITE
YOUR OWN BOOK.

Chapter 19

Interviews

$30 WRITING SCHOOL

I love the idea of having words by people other than me in my book. The viewpoints strengthen the arguments I present, and they sometimes even contradict me. But mainly they just make for a much stronger overview.

I picked people whose writing I like . . . I interviewed them because I'm a fan . . . I've read books by all these people. And I think they all have a lot of really good things to say. And they're funny as heck. So enjoy.

Hubert Selby, Jr.

Hubert Selby, Jr. (known to friends as "Cubby") wrote *The Room, The Demon, Song of the Silent Snow, The Willow Tree,* and *Waiting Period,* as well as *Last Exit to Brooklyn* and *Requiem for a Dream,* two of my favorite books, both of which were made into two of my favorite big Hollywood movies.

Figure 19.1 *Hubert Selby, Jr.* Photo by Lydia Lam.

Lydia Lam and I did a 35-minute videotaped interview with Cubby on December 3, 2003. It's an amazing interview. The audio from the videotape is on the CD-ROM. I could have just transcribed it, but I really wanted you to hear his *voice.* It's part of the magic.

4½ months after the interview, Cubby died of ongoing lung ailments. We're very sad. He was pretty amazing.

I'm making a documentary about him right now. I started it as this book was going to print. The film's working title is: "It/ll be better tomorrow" (www.CubbyMovie.com).

Last Exit to Brooklyn came out in 1964, was banned in England and considered obscene in the U.S. and helped pave the way for us to be able to say what we want.

I really appreciated Cubby. He was funny, smart, deep, irreverent, and spunky. Had beaucoup lust for life. This dude was on an oxygen tank and literally struggling for each breath as we did this interview, but he gave it his all anyway. Most people in his condition would give up and just rest, but Cubby was relentless. The man was 75 years old and had serious health problems, yet he was getting up and working every day almost right up to his death. And had a better attitude about life than many—no make that *most*—healthy young people I know.

Cubby is also a good reality check for anyone who thinks writing is gonna make them rich. He did not die rich, though he lived a rich life.

In some small but very real way, the few times I met this man changed me for the better, forever.

Andy Rathbone

Andy Rathbone has sold more than 15 million books in the *For Dummies* series, including *Windows for Dummies* and *Upgrading and Fixing PCs for Dummies*. He's currently writing *TiVo for Dummies*.

Fun tidbit: Cameron Crowe based the *Fast Times at Ridgemont High* character Mark "Rat" Ratner on Andy.

Michael Dean: Hi, Andy. What's your URL?

Andy Rathbone: www.andyrathbone.com.

Figure 19.2 *Photo of Andy Rathbone by Tina Rathbone.*

MD: Why did you start writing how-to and tech books? When? How?

AR: I never set out to be a tech writer; it just happened. I graduated from college in the late '80s, looking for a writing career. Back then, scientists, technicians, and nerds used computers the most, and they wrote mostly for each other. Nobody wrote for the small but growing number of consumers who were buying personal computers.

I'd bought a computer for word processing while earning my Comp Lit degree, and I'd written features for a variety of newspapers and magazines. So I combined my skills and began writing consumer-level articles for a local computer magazine.

There was very little competition back then, the PC field was taking off, and I found it the easiest way to earn money for writing.

A few months after I began writing for the magazine, the publisher tried his hand at book publishing. My girlfriend (now my wife) was editing both the magazine and the book division, and she suggested I parlay some of my countless hours spent playing computer games into a book proposal for *The Computer Gamer's Bible*. Stung by distribution problems, the publisher decided to stick with the magazine business shortly after publishing my second book, *PC Secrets*.

I wanted to stick with books for two reasons. First, published books magically elevate any writer's status, so they're a great ego boost. Even better, book deadlines are much longer than the daily grind of newspapers or magazines. I found that I preferred spending months on a single project.

MD: Do you write articles or tour or do speaking or lecturing? How do you get that work, and what do you like about it? Tell us a little bit about it, please.

AR: When the *For Dummies* books took off in the mid-90s, my marketing-savvy publisher arranged several tours and lots of promo work. The computer book market, like many others, has died recently—nobody's buying computers. The marketing budgets dried up, as did the promo work. Most successful writers now arrange their own publicity work. Luckily, after keeping a successful title going for a decade, I don't need to do much promotion to make sales.

I prefer newspaper and magazine interviews because the writer kindly edits out any "uhs," grunts, and head scratching; radio and TV [don't] offer that luxury. TV is the worst. You must be able to fake bubbling enthusiasm on demand to catch a viewer's attention.

MD: You've sold millions of books. Are you rich? What sort of lifestyle do you live? What do you spend money on?

AR: I certainly live comfortably, but I don't consider myself rich. I work perhaps three to five months out of the year, packing those months with 18-hour days. When writing about software, writers must finish their books several months before the software hits the stores. Since publishers schedule marketing budgets far in advance, a missed deadline can easily kill a book's sales.

When not writing, I keep up with computing news on the Internet, play my guitar and ukulele, work in the garden, paint watercolors, cook, work on the house, and spend time with my wife.

MD: How did you find an agent and a publisher?

AR: Coincidentally, the computer industry's largest agent worked in a nearby city, so I arranged to write him up for the local computer magazine. Just before leaving the interview, I nervously showed him my two small books, and everything fell into place. The Internet field was booming, he needed writers, I had proof that I could write, and I quickly began ghostwriting computer books for his more famous writers.

MD: Have you authored a series? How does that work differently versus just writing single books?

AR: I've never started my own new series of books. Instead, I've written proposals for new books that fit within an existing series. Those books stand the best chance of seeing print.

Almost every writer thinks up a new series, but very few publishers bite. Most new series start by accident: Publishers notice one book in their stable that sells surprisingly well, so they tailor a new series that mimics its style.

A new series is a huge financial investment; publishers rarely like taking risks, so they follow proven successes, molding new books after them.

MD: Have you written any fiction? Is it financially rewarding? Is it personally rewarding? What do you like about it?

AR: I've written fiction but never tried to sell any. Writing fiction is more frustrating than rewarding, I've found, and fiction rarely makes money. I'd rather play guitar in my free time.

MD: What is your work schedule like? What's a typical day for Andy?

AR: When I'm writing a book, I work long days and nights, constantly adjusting my schedule to meet the deadline. When not writing a book, I hover over the Internet, keeping abreast of new trends.

MD: How much freedom do you get to put "yourself" into the books you write?

Although the *For Dummies* series adheres to surprisingly rigid style guidelines, it allows many creative liberties. The books use a conversational tone, making it easy to add personal anecdotes. I'll sprinkle in pictures of my cat, for instance, or describe how my friends use scissors to cut their pizza.

MD: Do you consider what you do to be art?

AR: That depends on my definition of "art" at the time. Sometimes I think my writing is art. By choosing words, I'm framing a creation that inspires some sort of introspective thought by its audience. Other times I see myself merely creating functional objects. But that can be an art, as well. Just watch Norm Abram crank out an elaborate pie chest on *New Yankee Workshop*.

MD: Do you ever feel torn between being artistic and being commercial, or do you see them as interconnected? How?

AR: They're usually so widely separated that I rarely feel torn between the two. Artists rarely earn a living exclusively through their art. So they work within commercial guidelines to produce art that sells, sprinkling in as much of "themselves" as they can get away with.

Since I enjoy writing, I just write and don't worry about whether it's art. When my inner soul bursts with the urge for artistic creation, I play guitar or paint landscapes for a while. Actually, I keep a guitar by my side while writing books. Installing a new version of Windows can be time-consuming, leaving me plenty of time for quick licks.

MD: Do you use a laptop? What kind? Do you like writing at home or out of the house (like in a local coffee shop), or out on the road?

AR: I rarely write while in the field; it's too distracting. It might work for novelists, who feed off the meandering conversations around them. When writing computer books, however, it's a fine balancing act between clearly explaining a technical subject and boring the reader. It's difficult to hit that balance with a lot of chatter around.

Plus, I need two computers to write computer books: one to run the software, and the other to write about that software. That's too much to carry around. So I write at home on a desktop computer. I wrote my first few books in the garage at our condo. Now I have a small office in the house.

MD: Do you get fan letters? Has anyone ever said, "You changed my life"?

AR: Nobody's ever sent me that particular phrase. I just searched for it. However, almost all of my mail is positive; users are thankful for finally understanding why their computers are screwing up. I don't think I've had more than a dozen pieces of hate mail.

MD: What was the hate mail like, about, and so forth?

AR: In December 2001, somebody sent me an extremely rude letter about their problems with e-mail attachments. They said they'd just bought my book, and since they couldn't find an answer, my book was "a waste of money." I politely wrote back, telling them to please return my book and instead purchase a book that covered their particular e-mail program. They were using a third-party e-mail program not included with Windows. I even recommended a specific title for them to purchase.

They wrote back saying my "attitude stinks." Unfortunately, I let myself be dragged into the pit, and it quickly escalated. I finally threatened to turn on my e-mail's twit filter. On retrospect, I'm quite sorry to have responded to fire with fire. We must show compassion for our fellow man, even the twits.

MD: Do you consider yourself to be a nerd?

AR: On a scale of one to ten, I'd probably range between six and seven.

MD: What were you like as a kid?

AR: I spent a lot of time in the library, reading just about anything, from biographies to fiction. I hated PE classes, probably because I was always chosen last in dodgeball. When in high school, I worked on the student newspaper, which taught me plenty about the power of the printed word.

MD: Have you ever had an editor change something you were very unhappy about?

AR: Editors constantly change things, sometimes just to prove to themselves that they're needed. Changes used to bother me a lot more than now, so I rarely protest.

Besides, when you see the final proof, it's easy to adjust the settings so you can sneak your own stuff back in, undetected.

MD: How?

AR: I'm talking about the final proof before the files go to production for layout. Anyone can turn off the Track Changes area in Microsoft Word, make a change, and turn Track Changes back on. Please don't get me wrong on this one, though. I've never abused this privilege, and I've probably only done it once or twice in my career, mainly to see if the trick actually worked. For instance, a copy editor might change my phrasing so it's grammatically correct but awkward, so I'll change it back. Sometimes a copy editor will accidentally change something so it's grammatically incorrect, and I'll correct it.

But when somebody makes an edit that I don't agree with, it's a much more strategic career move simply to raise the issue face to face. This serves several important purposes: First, it tells the editors that I care a great deal about my work. Second, they won't be as liberal when making future corrections. Third, when I'm right and I've explained my reasons in detail, they've agreed and retracted the change. Finally, discussing the matter occasionally convinces me that I was wrong in the first place, and the editor was indeed correct. A backdoor edit simply provides a "hacker's thrill" and doesn't solve issues productively.

Taken as a whole, though, I've been happy with my editors. It's important to have an outsider explain what they don't understand, and why.

MD: Do you have groupies?

AR: Just the cat, and he prefers my wife.

MD: What operating system do you have on your computers? What program do you write in?

AR: Because most of my books focus on Microsoft Windows, all my computers run some version of that operating system. Some run older versions, others use the latest. One computer always serves as the test computer, running whatever version I happen to be writing about at the time.

I wrote with an early CP/M and DOS word processor called WordStar throughout college and in my early freelancing. While working at a newspaper, I replaced their awful program with a DOS editor called "VDE." I've been using Microsoft Word for the past ten years, mostly because that's the format the publishers wanted. I currently use Word 2000, and see no need to upgrade.

MD: How important is an outline to your writing?

AR: An outline is essential. The computer book market is tough, and only a convincing outline gives a publisher the confidence to approve the title and give you an advance. (Computer book publishers pay very slowly, by the way, so I've usually finished the book before I see any of the advance.)

Even after the outline's been approved, I usually keep adding information to the outline until it becomes unmanageably large, forcing me to break each chapter into its own file.

MD: How do you work with your editor?

AR: In the early days, I'd send the entire book to the editor in one chunk. Now they speed up the process by requiring each chapter immediately after it's finished. The editor edits them and ships them off to the technical editor, who verifies accuracy and sends them back to me for final changes. Finally, the chapters go to the production staff. After they're done, I see the page proofs of how they'll look when printed. When I give the final approval—usually required within 24 hours—they go to the printer.

Writers rarely get to write their own cover blurbs. The marketing department cranks that out, stuffing it with exclamation points.

MD: How do you feel about Kazaa?

AR: I've never used it, but file sharing will change several businesses. Musicians will treat recordings as advertisements, earn their living through performances. Some now auction off front row seats, reclaiming money that once went to scalpers. File sharing won't harm the movie industry as much, because people enjoy the social aspect of a movie theater.

The book industry is partially immune because most people prefer paper to pixels. Currently, only computer nerds scan in books and share the files, so the science fiction/fantasy and advanced computing markets are hit the hardest.

Luckily for me, file sharing won't affect the beginning computer book market much, if at all, simply because that audience still lacks the skills to share files. Plus, my readers need a printed book when their computers misbehave.

MD: What's it like being you?

AR: I was lucky enough to be on the field at the right time and place to catch *Windows for Dummies* when that book was thrown to me. However, I was a good enough writer to know how to run when I caught it.

I peaked early, made my money, and I'm typecast as a *Dummies* book writer. Looking at the industry realistically, I know I'll never repeat my success to such a large degree in any other field.

MD: What did you think of the *Simpsons* characterization of the *Dummies* book writer as an actual moron slurring, "Me go to bank now," while carrying a big sack with a dollar sign on it?

AR: I missed that one. *Dummies* books are an easy target. They made a lot of money in the early days, they have a distinctive look, and they've flooded the market. The publishers make more money than the authors, believe me.

Dame Darcy

www.damedarcy.com

Darcy is a good friend of mine and quite an amazing Renaissance Gal. She totally looks and acts like she just walked out of the 1800s but is very down to earth and has no pretense or affectation.

She inspires a rabid cult following all over the world. I went to a book signing she did once and there was a line out the door and down the block of people wanting to meet her and talk to her and give her stuff.

Figure 19.3 *Dame Darcy with Isabelle.* Photo by Michael Dean. Taken at 33 1/3 Books in Echo Park.

She writes and draws excellent, really intelligent comic books and graphic novels for the Fantagraphics imprint, makes music, sells the Darcy dolls she makes, and tours the world. Basically, she is just a very, very cool lady.

We both live in Los Angeles, and she and I sometimes commiserate about how we get fan mail and love offers from around the world but still somehow end up scrambling for the rent from time to time. I sat down with her at the Down Beat Café in Echo Park to chat with her about life, writing, art, and low-rent stardom.

MD: Hi, Darcy. So tell me about stalkers.

DD: Ummm . . . well, I had a stalker in New York for a really long time. His name was Dionysus. *(Michael laughs)* And . . . ummm . . . he would send me the most fucked-up crap, like, I'd beg him not to send me stuff anymore. And every time I did, he would just send me even more. He sent me a giant box that used to have a big-screen color TV, but instead it would have his version of romance in it, like this creepy fur coat. And cheap champagne wrapped up in the fur coat. *(laughs)* And then a box of candy hearts or something. But the hearts would come open inside the box that he'd sent me, and all the candy would be stuck in the fur. It's just disgusting! And then he'd send me these letters that he'd written in his own blood and stuff like that. But then eventually, he did send me this one package that was about 40 or 50 letters that he'd begun to me but hadn't finished, just all together in a little book. It was really horrifying. Another time he sent me a giant box of all of his videos from . . . he had a public access show. I had a public access show called *Turn of the Century* in New York and . . . ummm . . . he had one, too, apparently. And he sent me all of his originals and then after that begged me to send them back over, and over and over again. And I was just like, "I didn't fucking want them in the first place. I'm gonna throw these out," you know. But I sent them back. But I didn't wanna deal with this crap. But anyway, he's like, he not around. I'm not living in New York anymore. So my current . . . I don't have a stalker right now, really, and I don't want one. Knock on wood. (*Knocks on the wall of the coffee shop.*) What I do have is a guy who writes me from prison, and he just takes *a lot* of time. He's got a lot of time on his hands to write me the most elaborate prison letters. And I'm just like, "Wow." You know, he's in prison and he's writing me these novels. He tells me all this stuff but he never tells me what he's in for. He apparently has a goth girlfriend that he found out about me through.

MD: Are you a goth?

DD: I don't call myself goth. I don't think I am goth. However, maybe I am. I don't really know because *(laughs)* I'm popular with that scene, and my new band is the most goth *(laughs)* band I've ever had.

MD: What's it called?

DD: Death by Doll.

MD: You're, you're . . .

DD: Everyone in my band is kind of goth.

MD: Your books seem gothic to me in the original sense of the word, not like in the death-rock sense of the word. But in Victorian, you know, eighteenth century, seventeenth century, nineteenth century imagery. Uh, yeah, that's what I think of when I think of gothic. When I first heard the word.

DD: Yeah, I was a real purist for a while. I lived in the eighteen hundreds for about a decade. Now, I'm becoming a little more modern, and my band has keyboards and a drum machine, and we're very death rock, I think.

MD: And you have a computer but you only check e-mail like every six months.

DD: That's like a nightmare. I hate my computer.

MD: (laughs)

DD: I hate the e-mail! I do have to do it, though because I have to coordinate my career and the tours and the products and the art galleries and blah, blah, blah. That's the way people deal now. I wish they used the phone, but they don't anymore.

MD: Do people fax?

DD: Yeah, I do fax.

MD: Fax is kinda like old-school e-mail. Takes a little longer. You have to think about it more.

DD: Well, I do fax because I send my illustrations by fax to get approved by people.

MD: Who's approving them?

DD: The art directors or the people who hired me to do design.

MD: Have you ever met lovers or really good friends through your art?

DD: Yeah, all the time. I meet the most awesome people. *(laughs)* So, yes, definitely.

MD: Tell me about a lover and a friend. One of each.

DD: My best friend, Patrick Hambrecht, first found out about me when he was 19 because he worked for some comics distribution place in San Diego. And I went to the Comics Con when I was, like, 23. And I met him there, and he was 19. And after that he became my friend who, like, called me on a regular basis and stuff. But then I kind of convinced him to move to New York, and he became my assistant. And he moved his wife there as well. And he's been my best friend for, I guess almost 10 years now.

MD: And lovers?

DD: Ummm . . . I've had a lot of them that I've met through my comic books or through my records. And it didn't necessarily start out like that. Like, "Oh, I'm gonna score with the hot babes," you know, "Bring it on, guys," or whatever. It wasn't like that. It was more like they'd write me letters or they drew their own art or they had their own thing. They'd make me compilation tapes, and they just sounded cool. But then when I saw them, they were, like, hot. Like, young, hot guys. So I was like, "Oh, he's kinda hot." (laughs) And if I was single then I'd date them.

I actually like dating people who already know who I am in a way because they like me for my art and my soul and my personality first. Whereas if I just meet some guy at a bar or a party or something, it's just like, "Oh, she's pretty," or whatever. But they don't like me for who I really am. They like me just for the physicality first. And also when I haven't seen them and I just know them through letters or something like that, then I get to know them through their soul first.

Although it's kinda weird because there's a lot of people that I've met and know really well, for years even, like . . . ummm . . . I had this assistant, Dyslexia *(MD laughs because he loves the name)*, who is also a really good friend of mine . . . I knew her for four years. I felt like I knew her really well. And I'd never met her in person.

MD: I've got friends like that.

DD: And I met her after not even seeing her for four years, and it was really strange and cool finally knowing her in person. It's such a different experience.
I feel like it's kinda cool because you can't judge it on what they look like. However, I oftentimes feel like I'm behind a one-way mirror. Where I can see my face and they can see me but I can't see them because my photo's out there, my writing, my comics, my Web site, whatever it is. They know all that about me. They can read interviews, they can find out whatever they want. But there's nothing for me to look at. There's

no other reference. That's why I don't go jumping into anything with anyone. I really get to know them for several months to figure it out.

MD: Do you ever have problems with lovers being jealous of your career?

DD: Yeah, I've definitely had that before. But my current boyfriend isn't like that at all. He's very supportive.

MD: How about friends getting jealous of your career?

DD: Ummm . . . I don't really have that anymore, either. Or at least if I do, I don't know about it. I'm oblivious to it. *(laughs)*

MD: Are you pickier with your friends now?

DD: Ummm . . . partly that. And partly that I've been an established artist for my entire adult life now. Like, I started when I was 17 and became known like four years after that. I was published and had my books out and been on tour a lot by the time I was 21. So now it's been a while, and anybody who knows me knows that's what I am and that's what I do. So I don't particularly find them being jealous. They kind of just accept that's what happens because that's who I am. Whereas before, when I was in art school, when I first started, the jealousy was just insane. Like all these girls from my art school started wearing striped tights and trying to play the banjo and making their own zines and dying their hair blond and wearing Victorian dresses. And when I met them, they all had different looks. But then by the time I'd known them six months, a year, they would all copy me. And then start to hang out with each other and leave me out. And, like, ditch me. And try to hurt me.

    They were all from San Francisco or known each other a while. And I was this outsider kid who had come from the middle of nowhere just trying to live my life. And they were hurting me on purpose and being totally vindictive and mean. I didn't know that that would happen because it didn't even happen in high school. And I had to live in a really harsh world, and I was just trying to survive. And this was stupid kid bullshit. After I left San Francisco, though . . .

MD: That was my next question. What's San Francisco versus LA?

DD: Oh, well, I went from San Francisco to New York. And in New York . . .

MD: Compare all three cities for me. Pros and cons.

DD: Okay. *(pauses)* Well, after I left San Francisco for New York, nothing like that ever goes down in New York because everybody in New York is really serious. It's a serious place, and you really have to get your shit together to live there. And that's what I liked about it. People are not flaky in New York. What I like about New York is that the stakes are really high. Everybody's there to either be famous or make a lot of money. The rent's really high.

MD: It kinda weeds out the wannabes?

Figure 19.4 *Writing and art by Dame Darcy (from* Meatcake*).*

DD: Yeah. It definitely weeds out the weak, you know? It makes you strong. It makes you tough. It makes you really hardcore. It makes you have to be focused. You have to be a hustler. You know what I mean? And everybody there is, like, 23, 24 and making a hundred thousand a year. Nobody's a slacker. Everybody says what they're gonna do. They do what they say they're gonna do. They show up on time. They don't flake. And if they are gonna be late, they call you and tell you. They don't just not show up. And I couldn't even believe that kind of behavior when I first moved here. I find it absolutely. . . .

MD: You mean here or San Francisco? It's worse in San Francisco.

DD: Here, in Los Angeles.

MD: I think they're flakier in San Francisco.

DD: They are, yeah, they are.

MD: There's a little more of that New York edge here of competitiveness and people come here to make it. Whatever that means.

DD: Yeah, yeah, but they're creepy and fake and lame in Los Angeles . . .

MD: (laughs)

DD: . . . and in New York, nobody's creepy and fake and lame. They're all really for real. They don't have *time* to be creepy and fake and lame.

MD: I've never lived in New York City, but I lived in San Francisco for a long time, and one thing I've noticed different from here to there is, and it might just be me, but I think it's the city a little bit, too. When I was in San Francisco everyone I knew was crazy. Everyone was, like just out of rehab, on their way to a mental hospital, on parole, broke, getting evicted . . . you know, fucked up.

DD: Or on S.S.I.

MD: Or on S.S.I. And everyone here is doing their life. And they don't have as many personal problems, or so it seems.

DD: Well, I think that's for two reasons. And there's two reasons I left San Francisco. And one of the reasons is because I was with my boyfriend and I was in a band for four years. And then when I was broken up with my boyfriend and out of the band, I couldn't find a new scene. I just kept running into the same people over and over again. I couldn't start a new life. It kept haunting me. And that's the thing about San Francisco. It's a fucking awesome place to live. I love it there, and I wanna live there again. I feel like it's really my home more than anywhere. However, I don't wanna live there until I've got my career made and I've got my money made and I don't have to worry about looking for jobs and I don't have to worry about if people are flaky, because I've got my own thing. But when you're there and you're trying to get somewhere and you're trying to hustle and you're trying to get your life and you're trying to get ahead . . . nobody there kinda really is.

MD: It's too easy to just *hang out*. It's OK in San Francisco to just *be there*, you know. Or kinda just be pretending you're doing something. It's a city of dilettantes.

DD: Right, and we're not that.

MD: Right, and when everyone around you is, it's not very inspiring. I kinda hate the fact that in LA everyone in every café is talking about their alleged career and the deal or big break that's right around the corner and all this bullshit. But then I realize that it's not a competition thing for me but it's kind of inspiring. I hear people around me and they're all doing something, you know.

DD: Well, for cryin' out loud, I didn't move here for the culture! I moved here 'cause I wanna make a feature film and get on television. And the chances by just living here, being talented, combined with the proximity to all the industry people is why I think it will happen. And I've . . . because of the industry people I've met in the three years that I've lived here, I really think that I even have enough resources to maybe even start, you know?

MD: I think people also take you more seriously being from here. Like last week, my music book was featured on VH1. I mean the people that did it are in New York . . .

but I think that the fact that I was from LA maybe made them take my e-mail a little more seriously when I approached them. Whereas if I were from San Francisco or, like, Ohio or something, maybe . . . who knows? Maybe not.

DD: Yeah, that's part of it. The Hollywood mystique. You're like, "I'm from Hollywood. I live in Hollywood now."

MD: I started making a living at art the day I moved here, pretty much. Even though none of my art really has anything to do with being from here. My publisher's in Ohio. My agent's in San Diego. My DVD distributor's in Pennsylvania. But I kind of think that those deals all might've come together a little more easily 'cause of my return address, you know?

DD: Yeah. I have the same thing. My publisher is in Washington State and Seattle and then I have this big Tokyo Japanese thing, you know, and that's all Tokyo.

MD: Do you tour Japan?

DD: Yeah. Yeah. I've been there three times. I'm going back probably this December. I always go back in December. For some reason they always want me back in December. I think it's the Christmas season.

MD: You should hook up with a toy company there.

DD: I'm in negotiations with a toy company now actually to make dolls.

MD: So let's get back to writing and your writing career and stuff. Did you first self-publish before you got a publisher?

DD: Definitely.

MD: What did you make?

DD: Well, I made comic books you know, and then like I started, you know, I've also taught.

MD: Like Xeroxed or did you go to a printer and make them look like books or what were they?

DD: The first one was Xerox and then the second—they were Xeroxed, but I was fortunate enough for the third one—I made three self-published and the third one was really, really slick looking because it was like—and I remember people commenting on this a lot—that the color looked extraordinary for a color Xerox because in 1990 color Xeroxes were not that great but my friend worked for this printing place and did all of it at night and gave me like three or four hundred of them for free with these awesome color Xeroxed covers that at the time were totally state of the art, and they looked like what they look like now, super great. People were just really impressed with that, and I think that had a lot to do with that, and I put a lot of glitter on the covers.

MD: You hand did each one, right?

DD: Yup, yup, yup, yup.

MD: And how many did you press of that?

DD: I think I did 400 or something of those, and what happened—I feel really fortunate for the fact I was going to the San Francisco Art Institute and I learned animation there and majored in film because I've always wanted to have an animated TV series based on *Meatcake*, and I've always wanted to make feature films. Even as a child I knew that.

So when I got into art school, even though I am an illustrator primarily and a musician as a hobby secondary, I want to be a filmmaker. But it's hard, it's a lot of work, it's a lot of money, a lot of connections that a teenager from Idaho doesn't have. So I started doing what I could, which was playing with my band and doing the comics, and playing in Caroliner Rainbow and having these bandmates that were older than me and really into self-producing and self-distributing their music. Grux would take all these album covers out of a dumpster and pour house paint on them and cover them in dirt and Xerox the cover and I would take them to the preschool where I used to be a teacher and have the little kids color them in and glue them in

Figure 19.5 *More writing and art by Dame Darcy (from* Meatcake*).*

the front and just like lay them all out on the warehouse floor and make them in masses . . .

MD: How many would he make of each one?

DD: Oh jeez, thousands. Two thousand maybe?

MD: Hand done? Two thousand of them?

DD: Ya, but he had all of us . . .

MD: An army of people.

DD: Ya. And it was very D.I.Y., and I saw that and my boyfriend at the time, Brandon Carney, was about eight years older than me, and so he made his own band and made his own albums, and he was interested in having his own label, and he showed that I could do this and how to do it and then helped me distribute it and helped me catalog who I distributed it to and call them back every month and get my money from them and send them more stuff, and I was hooked up with Revolver, Forced Exposure, Matador Records.

So I had these mentors and people helping me out, but at the same time I was very self motivated. I drew the whole thing myself, my friends were photocopying them for free, I sat in my house day in and day out stapling them like a maniac, collating them myself, taking them around to stores in San Francisco, keeping track of everything, picking it back up again. I was doing all of this when I was 18-19 years old.

MD: When I'm putting stuff together like that alone in my room, I feel some kind of interesting power. Do you feel that, too? Like you feel like you're touching the world's mouth from your room. Do you feel something like that? What do you feel when you're doing that folding and stapling all your art?

DD: Yeah, well, that's also weird . . . because like I've had more than one person come up to me at different times in my life and tell me they found out about me because they saw something that I'd drawn and photocopied and didn't want anymore left at the photocopy place.

MD: Wow. Like by accident?

DD: Yeah. That's how they found out about me.

MD: That's great.

DD: And I think that's awesome. Also, I would put flyers up all over Haight Street and stuff advertising my comic book and people would steal them all.

MD: I used to put flyers on trash, too. I'd be wheat pasting on poles and I'd wheat paste a few flyers on trash on the street. A couple people would come to shows because of that. They were like, "That's so cool that you put your poster on the trash."

DD: I know. That's really good. It's so punk rock.

MD: Has anyone ever told you that your art saved their life or talked about a suicide or anything like that or . . .

DD: Ya, I get suicidal people writing me all the time.

MD: You attract weirdoes. Why is that?

DD: Cause my book is fucking weird.

MD: How did you get a publishing deal?

DD: After I self-published my stuff, I sent it to all the independent publishing companies that I thought would be interested in it, and I became friends with Peter Bagge. I think Peter Bagge rooting for me helped me get into Fantagraphics. Peter Bagge is the most awesome feminist guy ever. He's so cool, I loved his book with Girly Girl in particular, and he's so into helping people out. He's the biggest philanthropist. He's really, truly what the spirit is of being an independent punk rock artist. He really is awesome, and I still love Peter Bagge.

MD: Seems like a lot of famous people are really into your stuff. Like, I know Margaret Cho is, Courtney Love. . . . Who else are some of your well-known fans?

DD: Well, I know that Christina Ricci and Winona Ryder have my dolls. I know that Thurston Moore—Thurston Moore has always been super nice to me, too. Will Oldham, I've done shows with him, Royal Trux, I toured with Michael Gira from The Swans. I got a Christmas card from Jarboe last Christmas, and it just made my life because, like, as a teenager she was my idol and to have her write me a Christmas card and see me as a contemporary is awesome. I was hanging out with Crispin Glover the other night, he's pretty funny. I'm going to try to hit him up to be in *Gasoline*.

MD: That's your . . .

DD: My current book that I just finished writing but I have to do the illustrations for and now I need to transcribe it into a screenplay.

I wrote a part in it for Margaret Cho. One of the girls in it is this pretty Asian girl that lives with another girl on an island, and they make their own honey and stuff like that, and I wrote that part for Margaret Cho 'cause I thought she'd like it because she's kind of old fashioned like that.

She's awesome, I love Margaret Cho. I watch her comedy routines, and you don't know whether to laugh or cry. They inspire that sort of feeling because she's so right on, like she's saying stuff that nobody says and needs to be said, it's important.

MD: How many have you sold of your biggest selling book?

DD: You know, I'm not really sure what the numbers are—I'm really bad that way, I don't keep track. Now that I get published, I just write the thing, give them the stuff, call them for my checks and catalogue and answer my own fan mail. But once I'm done with something, I put it out there, and then it's their baby. Just give me the cash . . . I don't care. I'll do stuff to promote it all, but meanwhile I'm just on to the next project. I don't even think about it anymore.

MD: Ya. That's kind of a good way to be. I think it keeps you from worrying too much about the results. Its very process oriented rather than goal oriented, which is the way I encourage people to be with art. Because it's a saner way to be.

DD: Right. I don't know if I'll ever have a child, and I kind of don't care. The reason is that you create your art and your image, you put it out in the world, it lives after you do and influences people beyond what you can do by just having a child.

MD: Do you ever get letters of people saying you've changed their life in an intense and positive way?

DD: All the time, all the time.

MD: That helps me get through struggling to pay the rent. I can go two weeks on one letter like that. You don't get that when you're working in an office.

DD: No, no. And it really means a lot to me. My problem is that because I'm struggling so much and because I have to move all the time, I lose all their letters. You just reminded me there are girls that write me. Girls in particular, hundreds and hundreds and hundreds of girls. Little girls, older women in their fifties, whoever, and they always write me the most encouraging letters like, "Oh, me and my sister read your book all the time, and we love fairies, and we like to play with dolls, too. And we live in this fantasy world and my sister is so cool and it makes me feel like that's the thing. . . ."

There really aren't a lot of female role models and mentors in today's society that are really right on. I'm not about flaunting my body and being this slutty babe, you know? It's not like I'm not about being pretty or being feminine, however. I'm not primarily about being a body at all, I'm all about my mind and my talent, and I always think about other girls. I never think about their bodies primarily.

You can get ahead, girls, without being slutty, you know? You can be smart and talented and still get ahead. Seriously. Or by being weird, or by being yourself, by being unique, by making your own clothing, by standing out. That's how you can get ahead. You don't have to play the fucking games. You can fucking make your own way. And that's my message to the girls, and I know that they pick up on it, and I get, you know, little girls, 14-year-old girls writing me and stuff, and I totally dig it. You know?

(Look on the CD-ROM in the goodies folder for a taste of this interview in audio format.)

Interview transcribed via Internet by Cassidy Coon and Carla Segurola.

Michael Bérubé

www.michaelberube.com

(Interview done via e-mail while Dean was on a train on book tour in Germany.)

MD: You were the first person I ever met who had a computer in his home. I thought it was pretty damn cool.

Michael Bérubé: No kidding—that would've been 1986, I guess, when I got a knockoff of a Leading Edge PC for about $900, and I don't know where the $900 came from. But I wrote my dissertation on the thing, with the 4-3/4" floppy disks and all. And now here we are talking to each other by way of this 1-google-byte Pentium-6, 1-billion MHz machines. Which is all well and good, but I still want to see those flying cars we were promised back in the 1965 World's Fair.

Figure 19.6 *Michael Bérubé.*

MD: Okay. Hey, Bérubé. By answering, you consent to have your answers used free in a new book by Michael W. Dean, tentatively entitled, *$30 Writing School*. Michael is not required to use the interview, but probably will. And he may edit for length and continuity. He will run his final draft by you for approval if you ask.

(Michael doesn't know you, but he loves you and promises to use your words for good, never for evil.)

I will also need a high-rez photo. E-mail or snail mail a photo, I can scan it and mail it back. And a bio.

Also, wanna tour Europe with me sometime? Play drums? We can get Todd back on guitar.

MB: I'm the Paterno Family Professor in Literature at Pennsylvania State University and the author of four books, including *Life As We Know It: A Father, A Family, and an Exceptional Child*, which was a *New York Times* Notable Book of the Year in 1996. I've written over 100 essays for a wide variety of academic journals such as *American Quarterly*, the *Yale Journal of Criticism*, *Social Text*, *Modern Fiction Studies*, and *The Minnesota Review*, as well as more popular venues such as *Harper's*, *The New Yorker*, *Dissent*, *The New York Times Magazine*, the *Washington Post*, the *Nation*, and the *Boston Globe*. I was born in New York City in 1961. Played drums in Baby Opaque in the early 80s, a band in Virginia that Michael Dean sang and played bass in.

MD: Did I tell you my daughter is in her second year at the University of Oregon? What a trip. . . . How old are your sons now?

MB: Nick is 17 and Jamie is 12—you got started before I did, of course. A kid in college—Jesus. Anyway, yeah, if you're planning on touring Germany and need a band, I can probably come along if it's in the summer. I'll tell Janet that I'm going out to get some groceries and I'll be back in a couple of weeks—2004 or 2005 will work for me. I have better drums now, too. And Nick is taking lessons.

MD: What books have you written?

MB: *The Aesthetics of Cultural Studies.* Edited collection. Forthcoming from Blackwell in 2004.

The Employment of English: Theory, Jobs, and the Future of Literary Studies. New York University Press, 1998.

Life as We Know It: A Father, A Family, and an Exceptional Child. Pantheon, 1996. Paperback edition published by Vintage, 1998.

Higher Education Under Fire: Politics, Economics, and the Crisis of the Humanities. Edited with Cary Nelson. Routledge, 1995.

Public Access: Literary Theory and American Cultural Politics. Verso, 1994.

Marginal Forces / Cultural Centers: Tolson, Pynchon, and the Politics of the Canon. Cornell University Press, 1992.

MD: How many copies has each sold?

MB: *Marginal Forces*, maybe 700 copies. *Public Access* (hah!), 2,500. *Higher Ed Under Fire*, no idea, maybe 3,000. *Life as We Know It*, 15,000. *Employment of English*, 2,000.

MD: Do you make a living writing?

MB: No.

MD: How do you make a living?

MB: Teaching at a college.

MD: Why do you write?

MB: To advance—and, occasionally, discover—my political beliefs; to contribute to public and scholarly debate; because I love working with ideas and working with prose.

MD: Did *Life as We Know It* have an outline? I loved it but felt it digressed a lot (which is probably why I liked it). How important are outlines? And how important is revision?

MB: It had a 10,000-word prospectus, much more detailed than an outline, and I followed it pretty closely. In order words, the digressions were built in from the start. Revision is absolutely crucial, though. I wrote most of the book in a 10-week span in fall 1995 but rewrote chapter two (the abortion debate) substantially in February to

March 1996. I went over everything with my diamond-cutter's magnifying glass and revised things meticulously before I sent them to my editor.

MD: Tell us about your writing and editing process.

MB: No formulas, really. I almost always write at home on this laptop or on the road on this laptop—almost never in my department office. I try to write in roughly 1,000-word bursts then take a break. I edit as I go, usually paragraph by paragraph, and then look it over when I'm done for the day, but don't trust myself to do any real editing until the prose has lain around for two to three days. Longer (a week or two) if the material is more dense and scholarly, shorter (overnight) if it's more journalistic. I like to write, these days, with Brian Eno's early-1980s ambient music on my *tres* cool, 1950s-idea-of-the-future personal sound system. I cannot write to vocal music—it throws me off.

When I'm a visiting speaker at a university or in NY on business, I *love* to hole up in a coffeehouse and work. I also get a lot of good writing done on Amtrak. I've written about ten to twenty of my published essays (first drafts) in bars, coffee shops, hotels, and on trains.

MD: How long did you write before you had a book published?

MB: Hard to say. In 1977 I wrote an Ambrose Bierce-influenced short story for the high school lit magazine, and in 1980–82 wrote a number of oddball "feature" pieces for the *Columbia Spectator* (newspaper) and the *Columbia Jester* (humor magazine). One of those *Jester* essays was picked up for a humor anthology under contract to Dell, but that book was never published. I kept writing for campus publications at Virginia—and Charlottesville's very own *Live Squid* magazine, if your memory serves! But my first "officially" published essay was a scholarly article on the black poet Melvin Tolson, published in the Afro-Caribbean journal *Callaloo* in 1989. Then I published another academic essay in 1990. In June 1991, I got my first nonacademic essay published in the *Village Voice*; my book had been finished and delivered to Cornell University Press in January 1991 and was published in April 1992. So when my book was accepted, I'd only published two scholarly essays; by the time it came out, I'd published four long things in the *Village Voice* and the *Village Voice Literary Supplement* and had finally begun my program of world conquest by 2020.

MD: What's different about breaking into print, with books versus periodicals?

MB: Well, just about everything, and the main difference is academic versus nonacademic. I assume that the academic side of things isn't going to be of much interest (or use!) to you or your readers, but it's a pretty reliable system. You send something to a journal, they get one or two "referees" to read the thing, they produce one-two page "reader's reports," and on the basis of these you get either (a) accepted,

(b) rejected, or (c) invited to revise and resubmit. Magazine publication in the nonacademic media is even more of a crap shoot. I sent my first essay in 1991 to *Harper's*, asking a friend if I could use his name in an innocuous way ("X suggested that I send this to you," in my cover letter), and they turned it down—I got a nice, personal, and (I think) wrongheaded response from a senior editor (he thought this whole PC thing would blow over). I then turned to a friend—a prominent lesbian historian, Lisa Duggan—and asked about submitting to the *Voice*, and she gave me a thumbs up. I sent it to the VLS, where she'd published in the past, and they decided to go with it and put it on the cover of the *Voice*. Go figure.

Anyway, Michael Dean, from that point on there was really no difference, for me, between being a struggling musician and being a freelance writer. Whatever gig you get, you want the booking agent to invite you back, even if it was the Gig from Hell in a place you never want to visit again. *You* want to be the one who says no, at the very least. For a writer, that means (among other things) you want to come in on time with a nice clean manuscript. An editor at *Transition* (a kind of quality-bookstore journal) once told me I was always welcome because I was a "quick edit," which is a little like having the sound man and the club owner say, "You guys can come back anytime." And magazines are just like clubs in this way, too: Word gets around. You play a good set at the *Village Voice*, you might get the Wednesday night slot at the *Nation*, and depending on who reads your review of X in *Dissent*, you might get a call or an e-mail from *Mother Jones*, and so forth. That's the way it's gone with me and magazines for the past 10 years—and then when an editor moves from *Lingua Franca* to the *Boston Globe* and gives you a call, you might find yourself given 1,800 words to talk about the war in Iraq in the *Boston Globe*. So much depends on who the booking agent is.

Books are much more ritualized. Agents, narrative proposals, and so forth. Again, you'll get some credibility based on your magazine work, but it's the difference between playing club gigs and getting a record contract, more or less.

MD: Does being a published writer affect your status as an educator and vice versa?

MB: Yes, partly because I'm a better reader of student writing thanks to all my experience dealing with professional editors at newspapers and magazines, and partly because I deal with a wider range of people and political debates than most of my colleagues.

MD: Ever get fan mail? Hate mail? Examples please.

MB: Yes and yes, but I'm sorry I haven't kept any examples. I get about 10–15 pieces of fan mail a year, all by e-mail, most of it having to do with *Life as We Know It*. I get hate mail usually right after I publish something somebody doesn't like— my criticisms of the fringe-left group ANSWER (Act Now to Stop War and End Racism) in 2002-03 drew rafts of crazy-ass responses from the last remaining Leninists in the U.S., who basically tried to show that my opposition to war in Iraq was somehow a form of support for war in Iraq, and my criticisms of Bush and company usually get me a small stream of illiterate rantings from far-right wingnuts.

MD: Do you have any hobbies? Do you still play music?

MB: I'm not in a band right now and haven't been since moving here. But I occasionally play with people when they have guitars with them, and I've sat in on a few bands in the past couple of years—when invited, of course. I play in a men's hockey league here in State College—I play on two different teams, one in the "A" division and one in the "B" (there's some grumbling about my being in the B league, because while I'm an average player in the A league, I'm one of the dominant players in B, and who knows, they may eventually kick me out). Each team plays a 40-game schedule from Labor Day to Easter, and I usually miss about 10 games a year because of my academic obligations, but still, I wind up playing about 60 games in all. So it's not really a hobby—it's closer to an obsession. There's a team photo of my A league team on my Web site under "hockey." I also play golf and softball whenever I can.

MD: How do you balance family life with creative life?

MB: I learned to type faster.

MD: How does an artist age gracefully?

MB: I wouldn't know, being so young and all.

MD: What do you do for kicks? How much time do you spend writing?

MB: For kicks, ice hockey and music. How much time I spend writing—hard to say, because I write tons of academic-dreck things (memos, letters of recommendation, reader's reports for journals and university presses) that don't fall under the heading of "my" work. But I'd say that I spend about 30–40 hours a week writing, and that in an ordinary week, "my" work consists of only a few hours in that total. When I'm in the middle of working on something, however, I can spend pretty much all my waking time on it if my schedule permits me to.

MD: Mac or PC?

MB: PC.

MD: Tell us about the book tour you did.

MB: It was weird and difficult. When I got back, Pantheon asked me how it went, and I said, "With the exception of Seattle, where for some reason I was scheduled to appear at the U of Washington Bookstore instead of the Elliot Bay Bookstore, and where UW had scheduled four other readings the same day and had publicized the wrong time for mine, and where, as a consequence, I read from my book to a former student, a friend's father, and a homeless guy, I tended to get about 30–40 people for my readings in Boston, Chicago, San Francisco, and St. Louis, I read for about 30 minutes or so, and then people asked questions for about an hour." They said, "That's amazing! That never happens!" And I said, "Huh?" And they said, "Usually an author reads for about 30 minutes to an audience of about five, and then someone asks, 'Where did you get the idea for that character?' and the author replies, and that's it—so if you're drawing crowds like that, full of people who are really interested in the subject, you really should think about getting yourself a lecture agent." To which I said, "Right, and that way I could be out of town all the time and never have to see my family again."

The tour lasted over two weeks, Monday to Friday, and I went home on the weekend—radio interviews and a 15-minute TV appearance in New York, a ludicrous cable-channel appearance and a bookstore reading in Boston, a radio interview and bookstore reading in Chicago, likewise in St. Louis plus a 5 minute TV appearance that aired at 3:30 a.m. Eastern time on CBS, a bookstore reading in San Francisco, a bookstore reading in Seattle. The people who showed up tended to be parents of or advocates for people with disabilities, and often they'd read something about my book in the local papers, because I was reviewed in the *Boston Globe*, the *Washington Post*, the *New York Times*, and so forth right around the same time, that is, mid-October 1996. It was emotionally draining, dealing with some of these people's questions, and at almost every radio interview, someone would come up to me afterwards—the sound technician, the receptionist, whoever—and tell me about their son/niece/uncle/cousin who has a significant disability. I still carry many of their stories around with me today.

Most people say book tours are completely unglamorous and a general waste of time unless you've got a real bestseller on your hands. Mine wasn't a waste of time, and they did put me up in some seriously luxurious hotels, the most outrageous of which was the Four Seasons in Chicago, so it was occasionally glamorous by my standards.

MD: What are you writing now?

MB: I'm trying to get a proposal accepted for a book about the recent history of the U.S. left, and I've got about a half-dozen essays in the pipeline on various subjects—contemporary literature (Don DeLillo and Colson Whitehead), disability issues, Great Books, cultural studies, and so on. Mainly academic things, plus one or two ideas for magazines.

MD: Any closing advice for up-and-coming writers?

MB: Read everything you can get your hands on.

Kimberly Valentini

Figure 19.7 *Kimberly Valentini.*

MD: How did you become a literary agent?

Kimberly Valentini: I started with the company as an administrative assistant and assistant to the president and eventually worked my way up to being an agent. Being the assistant to the president of this agency helped me learn a lot of valuable lessons about being an agent. It was really good hands-on experience. Definitely not something that could be taught in a classroom. So if you are looking to be an agent, I say the best thing to do is start early and get in somewhere as an intern. But don't be passive and just do the filing and answering the phones, actually read what you are filing, listen to the conversations, and if you are copied on an important e-mail with the request that you respond with someone's contact information, read the whole string of e-mails to understand how the deal was done.

MD: What do you look for in a writer?

KV: Basically, good writing skills and an interesting story to tell that hasn't been told before. Someone who is cooperative and a good worker is always helpful. I also like to know that they are going to meet their deadlines.

MD: What do you not like to deal with in a writer? Is there anything that would make you pass on a second project with someone who is selling books?

KV: One of the most important things is timeliness. I might consider not working again with an author if they prove to be someone who repeatedly can't make a deadline.

MD: How do you find most of your writers?

KV: Most of my authors come to me through referral from another author. But it isn't rare to pick up an author from a blind submission.

MD: Do you have to like a book to agent it?

KV: That depends. Some agents would say no, but personally I think it helps. If I have an interest in the book other than making money on it, I am much more dedicated in my search for a publishing house. I have tried to sell stuff that I was not interested in, with little success. Interest helps the passion and dedication.

MD: Is it harder to sell fiction than nonfiction?

KV: Fiction is definitely a harder sell because it is so subjective. It's also hard to get a publisher to back an unknown author. Sometimes it just clicks, though, and those times are good.

MD: What other types of writing are difficult to sell?

KV: If you have a strong proposal and a good platform, your book should be an easy sell.

MD: Can you please give us the rundown of a typical day for you?

KV: I take a lot of phone calls and read and write a lot of e-mails. Some of my day is spent reading submissions, helping authors strengthen their proposals, researching potential publishers, pitching proposals. The good days are when an offer comes in that I can negotiate, and when there is a contract to review.

MD: What other types of writing are easier to sell?

KV: Good writing is always easy to sell.

MD: Do you write? Do you have plans to get your writing published?

KV: I do love to write but joke that if I can't sell my own writing, I might as well help others sell theirs.

Jackie Cohen

Figure 19.8 *Jackie Cohen.*

Jackie Cohen: I'm a columnist for *Men's Edge*; freelance writer for titles including *Wired, Paper, ReadyMade,* and scores of other titles. I'm a former senior editor of *The Industry Standard*, which had the dubious distinction of being the fastest-rising and the fastest-falling magazine in the history of publishing. At its peak in 2000, it was selling more ads than any other weekly publication, including *People* and *Business Week*.

I have a master's in English Lit, which editors seem to think is interchangeable with a master's in journalism or an MFA in creative writing, but I think the difference is that I've read a heck of a lot more than my peers with writing degrees.

MD: A lot of people think they can write.

JC: No kidding! But so many people call themselves "writers," when they're really hobbyist writers. I mean, they'll describe themselves in a Craigslist personal ad first and foremost as a "writer," and then maybe in the twentieth sentence they divulge what their real career is. Writing is a pastime for many but a vocation for few.

MD: Not all who say they can write, can. How did you first know you were good?

JC: I have a love-hate relationship with writing, so while I guess you could say I've known since I was in high school or younger, I am hard pressed to say when I was able to admit to myself that I am good, as you put it.

Outsiders began commenting on my writing in high school. I was on the school newspaper for two years, and it was obvious that my copy was cleaner than most of the other kids'. The teacher-adviser to the paper, Mrs. Panos, could find nothing to criticize about my writing, and so she'd take to commenting on my appearance— I had a Mohawk in high school, so Mrs. Panos kept saying, "If you'd do something with your hair, you could get into Cornell." She kept saying Cornell as the school of choice, interestingly, not something like Columbia, which is like the Harvard Law School for journalists, carrying prestige for both its undergraduate and graduate programs, which have the unique distinction of being the only BS and MS you can get in journalism—that is a bachelor of science or a master's of science, when all other programs call it a bachelor of arts or master's of arts. Many people say this kind of nomenclature is pretentious, and that Columbia J School is more beneficial as a networking opportunity rather than an educational opportunity. I get to reap the benefits of the networking by having lots of former co-workers who went to Columbia, so from time to time I am regaled with the highlights of the chatter on the alumni mailing lists! My senior year, more than half of the school literary magazine was filled up with my writing, and people complimented me on it.

But at that age, growing up in suburbia, I didn't see writing as a career option. The message I'd gotten from the media was that it was too competitive, and I didn't want to be like that. That was half a lifetime ago, and looking back on that, I'd say I've found a happy medium. Getting overly competitive can make for some unhappy newsroom dynamics that I don't care to be a part of, so I guess I compete to the extent that I need to, not enough to make myself crazy about.

Anyway, I got similar feedback on my writing in college, but other than editing a campus feminist rag, I didn't really see myself as a "pro" until I broke into the newsstands, so to speak.

MD: Do you make your whole living as a writer? What exactly do you do for a living?

JC: Yes. I got my first publishing job right out of school but didn't get to writing full time until two years into things when I made it to the associate editor level. I had an easier time making my entire living as a writer when I was committed to one masthead full time. Now as a freelancer I am more vulnerable to economic vicissitudes. When you're an employee, you get a consistent paycheck and benefits like insurance, and that's a real safety net compared to independent contracting—which is like living from paycheck to paycheck and never knowing when the next one is coming. A magazine can bump your article a month ahead, and that means your income is bumped a month ahead, and when you're not sitting in their newsroom, you're the last one to find out about the scheduling change. It's very difficult to plan a budget as a freelancer, so it helps if you have backup funds—the best way to do it is to work really hard to accumulate enough funds to cover yourself during dry spells that aren't even your own fault. More than a decade ago, someone had commented to me that if she didn't have a trust fund as a backup, she wouldn't be able to support herself as a freelancer. I think that having the inheritance money can make you lazier about getting work, because you're not as financially needy. But some people are motivated by other things besides money.

MD: How does freelancing work?

JC: Freelancing is the writing industry's answer to temping, without the agency in the middle. You need to hustle for every single writing assignment you get, which makes it a lot more work than being a staff writer, where you only have to sell one editor on your ideas, and by virtue of repetition you have a much keener sense of what that editor wants. I DO NOT RECOMMEND THAT PEOPLE START OUT THEIR WRITING CAREERS AS FREELANCERS BECAUSE IT'S A MUCH, MUCH, MUCH STEEPER HILL TO CLIMB. I'm not saying this out of self-interest at all. It's just that my writing has continued to evolve over the years as I have worked in different places and with different people. Had I not been working in-house with various editors, I would have missed out on a lot of very valuable learning experiences and networking opportunities. The elitist aspects of this business also tilt the scales against people who start out their careers as freelancers and do nothing but. There's definitely a chicken-and-egg situation with respect to getting your first writing jobs, but the fact of the matter is that there really isn't any such a thing as an entry-level freelance gig. Also, editors are usually overwhelmed with pitches even from people they know, so if they don't know you, they're probably not going to be receptive. And if you're new to them, they're not going to take the time to explain what they want from you.

MD: How did you get started in writing magazine articles?

JC: I got an editorial assistant job out of graduate school simply by answering an ad in the *NY Times*, which is the only major metropolitan paper where there are journalism jobs listed in the classified section. New York is the place to be for people aspiring to get into the business, and I honestly think that the geographical difference between me and my writer friends outside of NYC explains why I got a jump on the market—although having the graduate degree probably helps, too.

MD: Do you write about stuff that interests you, stuff you think will sell, or both?

JC: Both. I mean, I find out about stuff that sells while working on something I'm interested in, and vice versa. However, it's taken me a good nine years of writing before I got to the point where I was able to make a living writing about what I enjoy. I spent the previous years writing about stuff I consider boring, but that's what you have to do—you have to start somewhere. What cracks me up, however, is all the presumptions made by people when you're still in the stage of your career where you aren't writing about what you want, but rather about what is paying your bills: People were puzzled by my employment within what is now *American Banker*, wondering why a radical chick like me was working for what they presumed to be just like an actual bank. Hello! A newsroom is a newsroom, and while the subject matter might taint the environment a little bit, the fact is that most of the people there would rather be writing about something else!

MD: How much will you change for an editor? Do you work with editors? How?

JC: Whatever the editor wants, I change it, no matter how painful it is—and when there's an excessive amount of rewriting to be done, I'll try to take a break from it so I don't feel overwhelmed. Now, book editors and magazine/newspaper editors are two different animals. Book editors seem to be much more hands off, asking the writer to make all of the changes and very often not subjecting the manuscript to copyediting at all. Since newspapers and magazines are usually catering to shorter attention spans, the rewrites are more thorough, and there's copyediting involved. The more prestigious the title, the more editing! Some of the reasons why book editors don't get too involved with copyediting is because of the scope of the project—it's one thing to copyedit something that's 1,000 words, and another matter to copyedit something that's 100,000 words. However, the sad result is that books always have typos in them, especially the first editions. The only time I don't see glitches is in a classic that was originally published long ago and thus has had the benefit of many printing runs to weed out mistakes. Anyway, when an editor asks for changes, I do whatever they ask. Why? They are paying for it, and as a freelancer you come to regard the editor as your client. Furthermore, when you write about something, you get really close to the subject matter and to the writing itself. Ultimately, that creates a blind spot for you because you are no longer approaching it afresh. So the editor's perspective is much closer to that of the average reader. So even when I'm thinking "duh!" about some kind of feedback, I have to tell myself that if the editor doesn't understand what the hell I wrote, then the reader isn't going to get it.

Apply this question to the setup you'd find at *Wired* or *The Industry Standard* and you have somewhat of a comedy routine. You see, the blend of editors is deliberately set up to be a mix of technology experts and general interest marquee-type editors.

NOTE

I asked her what this meant, and she replied:

"M'kay, an example of a marquee is the big board on top of a movie theater, advertising what's playing at the movie house. So a marquee-type name is someone they can boast about to the public on their promotional materials, you know, name-drop for advertising and marketing, and people know who you're talking about. In the example of *Wired*, their current EIC is Chris Anderson, formerly one of the bureau chiefs from the *Economist*. He's a marquee name.

"It also implies what I've alluded to previously: Publishing can be a real name-dropping business since it's a small world, and the more marquee names you drop, the better."

JC: Your technology types are going to do what are called the substantive edits, as in: "Are you sure that this fact is right?" or "Can you find out more about this?" The general interest marquee-types are going to be like, "I don't understand what this means. Clarify." So, I used to be one of the techie types at the *Standard*, so I would inevitably end up in some kind of debate with my executive editor, who was a general interest marquee type. He'd change something like "software running on a central server" to "application server," and I'd go up to him and explain that he inadvertently changed the meaning of the phrase because application server is specific techie jargon. My point here is that a good editor also *listens*, and if you explain yourself, there is a way to find a common ground or compromise. However, I do keep these kinds of things in mind when deciding whether to pitch a story to *Wired* or *B2.0* and who to bring it to, knowing that some people are better at preserving facts than others! Publishers don't tend to require that their editors take classes in management, and that can cause a whole set of other problems.

There are lots of editing styles, but the ones I think work the best are the ones that make life easier for the writer rather than harder or more disruptive—or when an editor makes you go back and requery a source about something you know is irrelevant or nonsensical, and you have to explain to them that you are asking because your editor wants you to, and you're doing everything in your power not to just blurt out that your editor is incompetent!

MD: Which comes first: The story or the deal?

JC: Only in a booming economy does the deal come before the story!

MD: Do you write the story and then try to sell it or do you sell them on the idea?

JC: I never write anything ahead of time, I always sell it first. Every word is paid for around here.

MD: What are some of the best resources you have found when it comes to finding what a magazine wants and how to contact it?

JC: Reading *Media Bistro* and networking. The more time you work in the business, the more contacts you amass and the more successful your former co-workers all become—it's like your network grows on its own. I think of my former employers as my alma mater.

MD: How do you get to the $1 a word level?

JC: Experience! But understand that there are a lot of factors that affect freelancer pay at different titles—most of the overhead costs in publishing are the actual paper and printing, so personnel take a back seat to that.

MD: What is the starting level?

JC: There are places that pay nothing, and that's where most people start out if they're starting their careers as freelancers, without any full-time masthead experience. But then you use your clips to sell your writing to the next place, where maybe you'll get a penny a word. The best thing to do is to try to get an internship at the best publishing outfit you can. It's much easier to score magazine internships than actual magazine jobs, but once you've got that on your resume, you can play it up and sell your experience to the next place. Piling on extra internships doesn't make your first paying job better. I know people who did years and years of internships out of Columbia, but it didn't get them further ahead than the people who did fewer apprenticeships.

Lots of really prestigious places don't even pay much. But the highest-paying magazine in the business is *Playboy*, at up to $5 per word. Apparently inflation hasn't kept up with the publishing business, and I read that in order for pay rates today to be comparable to what they were for the media in the 1920s, we'd need to be earning $9 per word! Nice, eh?

So after you get an internship, try for something community oriented or a trade publication. The former will get you started writing general interest pieces sooner. The latter will probably pay more and give you more of a shot at being promoted—getting editing or management experience only helps you get the next writing gig, hopefully somewhere with a higher readership and better pay. After interning, you're likely to have to be an editorial assistant somewhere and then leave after a year to go into writing. Sometimes people are able to go from college right into an entry level writing job, but that involves either relocating to hicksville (for hideously low pay) or joining a trade publication. The great thing about trades, however, is it's easier to get promoted, and that's what makes you marketable to other publishers. This is exactly how I have carved my path, although I didn't plan any of it. I literally fell into my first gig, and then everything took off from there as I learned the business.

NOTE

I asked her, "Can you give me some examples of trade pubs?"

She said, "Trade has a different meaning in journalism than it does in books, which define it as a paperback whose dimensions are larger than those of the titles that can fit in the racks at supermarkets and the like. To the journalist, trade refers to a publication devoted to participants in an industry. A trade publication can be a newspaper or magazine, and sometimes they do appear on newsstands even though they're trades, like in the case of *Adweek*, *Billboard*, and *Variety*, which are all trades.

"*The Hollywood Reporter* is considered a trade publication, while *Entertainment Weekly*, *Premiere*, and *Rolling Stone* are not. *Computerworld* is a trade publication, *Wired* is not. *The Journal of Commerce* is a trade publication, but *Business Week* isn't.

"Some of the top trade titles include: *American Banker, National Law Journal*, and *Women's Wear Daily*. Because these are the best ones in the biz, staffers very often 'graduate' from them to the major leagues. I have a former co-worker who went from the *New York Law Journal* (same company as *National Law Journal*) to *The New York Times*, taking a demotion from special reports editor to copyeditor at *NYT*, which is how the paper filters newcomers. Copyediting is considered to be less prestigious, even though some say it's instrumental.

"At trade publications your ultimate value to the company comes from the knowledge of the subject matter that comes with the territory. Become an expert and you get promoted. Being that expert can also make you a recruitment candidate for a bigger publication that needs someone with expertise. My career is a fabulous example of getting the right knowledge at the right time. I spent three years rising through the ranks of what is now *American Banker* (when I was there it was another subsidiary of Thomson, and they merged all of their banking titles under one roof). I developed an amazing reputation among my colleagues and sources, and that all contributed to my momentum. So there I was, an expert in online finance, and imagine my excitement when I read the following in *Wired News*: 'John Battelle has left *Wired* [magazine, where he was the founding managing editor] to start a new publication. We think it's a weekly. We think it's about e-commerce.' I thought, wow, that's my lucky break for the newsstand. And that's what it became."

MD: Can you really make a living, and what does it take to make a real living at freelance writing?

JC: Yes, if you are prepared to "mix it up." I mean, I have 12 years of experience, and technically half of that has been for newsstand publications. But as a freelancer you've got to be flexible and cast your net widely. If I just held out for book reviews (usually about $25 a pop, plus a free book), I'd be broke. Notice the diversity of the publications I've written for over the past three years (freelancing): *Genome Technology*, *The Storage Reporter*, *Paper*, *Men's Edge*, *Wired*, *Penthouse*, *Hustler*. I can usually turn around the stuff for the trades much faster than the newsstand stories, so in a way the trades can be better pay since they use my time more efficiently.

I know people who make up to six figures as freelancers, but these are highly productive people with lots of experience and a big network of contacts. To pull that off, you'll want to mix in some longer-term contractual writing or editing gigs—and be prepared to work seven days a week. I'd rather read fiction on the weekend.

Freelancing is much more effective if you've been a full-time editor or writer somewhere. The reason editors hire a freelancer is to get something taken care of efficiently. The non-newsstand magazines I write for usually don't change a thing in my copy because I'm at a higher level of experience than the people they have on staff. Newsstand magazines will simply not give you a second assignment if they don't like the work you did or if it was a hassle to get it rewritten.

MD: How did you get your foot in the door at the different magazines with which you have worked?

JC: For full-time gigs, you apply for the job. Send out clips (writing samples) with that resume and cover letter, and your writing is what opens the doors—that's what you're judged on. As a freelancer, you're doing almost the same thing, and still the writing samples sway the editors' decisions for or against you. I started out as an editorial assistant and worked my way up. Some people hit glass ceilings at various stages, but I haven't crashed into one yet—unless you factor in the fact that I'm stuck in San Francisco when I should be in New York. The higher up you go, the harder it gets to move from one job to another unless you're compromising something.

The best example of this comes from my conversations with one of my exquisite former bosses, Jonathan Weber, who was editor-in-chief of *The Industry Standard*. In talking about his prior experience as technology editor at the *Los Angeles Times*, he said that ownership of the paper changed in a way that a lot of employees disliked, so many planned to leave. But for these people to leave, it would take years and years. I mean, how do you meet or beat a gig at the *LA Times*? How often do you think jobs open up at that level, even when the economy is in great shape? What would be a next move for anyone coming from the *LA Times*? It would have to be the *NY Times*, *WSJ*, maybe the *London Times* or *FT*. Otherwise, an editor-in-chief spot would have to open up at another title, so the higher up you get, the slower the turnover. In a recession, the only reason why jobs open up at that level is when someone dies!

MD: Is there a structure or rules to writing magazine articles? How does it differ from other styles of writing—newspaper, nonfiction?

JC: The more prestigious magazines and newspapers tend to blur the lines between fiction and nonfiction, at least in terms of story organization and writing style. The inverted pyramid format tends to be the domain of trade publications and smaller circulation metro newspapers. Inverted pyramid is where you put the most important information in the lead paragraph and then place the rest of the facts in the story in descending order based on their significance. The point of this is to make it easier for editors to cut the length of the story when they're on a deadline. Savvier editors tend to plan better and can forecast the desired length of a story—or maybe it's just that they manage their time better so they're not as rushed when size issues come up. Nonetheless, lengths are often subject to change based on the other stories that are coming in, but sometimes advertising is a factor. Magazines usually have a desired ratio of editorial pages to ad pages, and if the sales reps don't meet their projections for the issue, then stories are likely to get cut to keep the story-to-ad ratio intact.

The Wall Street Journal is considered to be the best example of good feature writing, and what we really mean by that is news stories formatted as narratives, which makes them more compelling reads—instead of being something you *have* to read, it becomes something you *want* to read. *The New York Times* is another great example of this style. Notice the prevalence of anecdotal leads—that is, it starts out telling a story rather than hitting you in the face with facts—and then instead of a first-paragraph lead, you have what's called a "nut graph" coming in somewhere around paragraph three to six, where the thesis statement is presented.

Read a lot of publications, and you'll find that the ones with a million-plus circulation tend toward the feature-in-a-news-story format, while the ones with smaller readerships go for the more straightforward inverted pyramid—or otherwise they'll use a formulaic hybrid of the two. A good writer can adapt to both of these styles. Actually, if you want to succeed in this business, you've got to be flexible and prepared to adjust to different "house styles" of different publications.

That said, the other difference between journalism and other forms of writing is the emphasis on reporting—interviewing people on the phone or in person—and avoidance of editorializing, or expressing your own opinions. This will vary from one title to another, of course. And by geography: The Brits love to editorialize! If you're a columnist, for example, you're supposed to voice your opinion, and very often you don't quote anybody, as is the case with my column in *Men's Edge*. However, if you're doing straightforward news or features, you want to be inserting a quote every three graphs—maybe every other graph. Doing it excessively, however, will undermine your article and annoy the editor.

"Tracking people down" is what a good journalist does!

My current headache has been trying to track down Arnold Schwarzenegger for a *Men's Edge* piece about how the governor balances work and working out. I didn't get him, of course, but what I did was try to track down people who've dealt with him or even people who've spotted him. I wound up calling health clubs and Nautilus-type suppliers in the Sacramento area, plus the ghostwriters he worked with in authoring his encyclopedia of bodybuilding.

MD: What topics sell?

JC: If it's news, it sells! But if you take a macroeconomic look at the news, you can figure out where the paying assignments are at a given point in time. Watch the business news on television if you don't already. Where there's money in the economy, there's advertisers, and where there's advertisers there are editors with freelance assignment budgets. Today, you'd be rolling in the dough if you made yourself an expert in health care, technology, and the military. Entertainment stories sell in any economy.

MD: Any closing comments or advice?

JC: The grass is always greener on the other side: People who majored in journalism in college wish they'd studied history or English, and often the English majors wish they'd studied journalism in college. But I think eventually the two camps even out with experience.

From our e-mail exchanges:

JC: *$30 Writing School?* You know, my family paid a hell of a lot more money than $30 to educate *me*. So if it's only going on your Web site, the competitive bitch in me screams out. I'm sure you will get to interview many people with far better credentials than yours truly, and you will have to make the same decisions that I would if I were in your shoes. (I would pick Jerry Stahl over Jackie Cohen, hell yeah!) Nonetheless, how the hell could I refuse the opportunity to spout off a bit?

Hell yeah, you have to be competitive in this business or you will never sell a thing. Of course, I'm big on helping friends get ahead, and the karma always rebounds in a beautiful way. Writing may be a lot more democratic thanks to the Internet and whatnot, but at its heart it is still an elitist business. (The ultimate in competitiveness is U.K. publishing, and when the bloody Brits come over here for journalism jobs, they always get promoted over the goddamned Yankees. I love the Brits.) I guess it's easier to help established writers, but then again, it's not like I get approached by college students for help or anything. (Thank God the alumni association doesn't have my current details!)

Trying to get paid for something for the first time is a chicken-and-egg game: Everyone asks if you've been published somewhere else before, so where the hell do you get those first clips? Thank God for the Internet, school newspapers, and the growing number of community-focused publications for giving aspiring writers their first lucky breaks. Of course, you can advise people to look to 'zines for their first clips, but editors can tell the difference between a 'zine and a real magazine. Same goes for self-published versus professionally published—the average Joe might not be able to tell which is which, but the people in the business know.

Many writers say that writing books are bullshit—even the ones who have penned their own writing books say that. (Such is the attitude in Stephen King's *On Writing*.) As for the journalism world, Bill Blondell's *The Art and Craft of Feature Writing* is considered the bible—it's like *Cliff's Notes* on the *Wall Street Journal*'s stylebook. Anyway, I used to shun writing books because I prefer to read "primary sources," but in recent years I have checked out a few titles within this space. Be able to admit to the fact that a lot of the advice is crockery—hell, find passages worthy of poking fun at and go to town ribbing 'em, if your publisher allows it.

I much prefer reading fiction over nonfiction and can't help but read with a critical eye. No matter who the author is, I find myself fighting the urge to break out a red pencil. I read a lot of crap that somehow makes it onto the bestseller list, yet the writer lacks a basic understanding of style and usage—book publishers are allegedly short on copyediting. You have a Ph.D. in literature [*Jackie, what in heck's name makes you think that? I got kicked out of high school and flunked out of community college.*], so I don't need to clarify what I'm talking about here. It's simply that book publishers allegedly have different budgets and different priorities than news organizations, which specifically pander to people with short attention spans. (Think: commuters.)

Everyone I've talked to who's gone to journalism school (and I know a lot of Columbia alumni in particular) agrees that writing school itself is bullshit and that you learn more from sitting in a newsroom than sitting in a classroom. Regardless of whether your assignment comes from a teacher, an editor, or yourself, the more you write, the better you get. And even more importantly, you need to read a whole lot.

I know I seem like this radical chick, but I'm part of a dying breed because I've read the classics (and even studied Latin and ancient Greek). That makes me a more powerful writer than my many friends who've just got journalism degrees. The point is that the more I read, the more I realize how unoriginal everything is—I always predict the endings, which can make me an annoying movie-going companion, ha, ha, ha. Even in the news world, nothing's ever really news—Someone's always done it before, but the people who want you to write about them insist that they're the first. Hence my bit about maintaining a competitive edge. This business is the most competitive it gets.

As far as freelancing goes, it is much, much, much easier to do so after you have at least a few years of full-time masthead work to bank on. Not only am I better positioned to prove my credibility with editors, but I have a trove of contacts to utilize and a pile of favors to trade in on—everyone I assigned work to when I was an editor becomes someone I can now hit up for assignments. When the economy crumbles, the people who've done nothing but freelance find that their work opportunities disappear, as those of us who have been employed full-time gobble up all of the available assignments.

The sex writing is a much newer portion of my career, and to be perfectly honest I still make more money writing about other subjects—namely technology. And that brings up a whole other beef I have with the "how-to-write market," which is most annoying within the erotica genre. The "I want to copy Susie Bright" mentality is laughable. She made it big, and there's a whole entourage of bimbettes trying to copy her every move, and by using her as their only role model, they inadvertently shoot themselves in both feet. Most of them don't know there is indeed a glass ceiling for sex writers, because they're trapped under it.

Back when I was just 24, I was offered a job as an assistant editor at *Forum*, which is a spin-off of *Penthouse*. I was very excited about the offer, but my girlfriend at the time warned me not to take the job, or at least not to take something like that so early in my career. Her reasoning: Unless the offer is for something more prestigious like *Penthouse* or higher, taking a sex publishing job so soon in your work history will keep you from doing anything other than sex writing. I took her advice and still aver that she was dead-on. Ask any of the so-called sex writers out there what they have written for mainstream publications, and listen to the silence!

Cheers,

Jackie

(The following is Jackie for some reason answering the questions I intended for Hubert Selby, Jr. I like her answers, so I left it.)

MD: If an editor suggests a change, where do you draw the line?

JC: I do what the editor asks me to do because they're the one paying. I've also been an editor before and know that writers who balk might not be invited back. An editor is one step removed from the story, so if he/she/it can't understand what I'm trying to convey, then the average reader is going to be even more confused. As an editor, I look for places where people will lose interest in the narrative, whether because they don't get it or because they got bored.

MD: How come in *Requiem for a Dream*, the pupils dilate, not constrict, every time people shoot opiates?

JC: I know the question wasn't intended for me, but I noticed this, too. I think he wanted to depict a made-up drug, rather than a real one, because none of the characters ever said the name of the drug they were on.

MD: You write like people talk, specifically, like how some Americans talk. Was this a conscious attempt at style or did it just happen?

JC: Most writers suck at approximating how people talk. Authors park massive narratives and descriptions in quotes when most people aren't very articulate in speech, even educated people! I mentioned that I type fast enough that I can capture what a source is speaking as he/she/it says it, and you better believe that the transcript is loaded with ums, ers, ahs, sentence fragments, and other garbage.

MD: Do you write from an outline?

JC: It depends on the assignment, but certainly less when I'm on a deadline and more so for longer projects. An outline is a curse and a blessing.

MD: Do you write on a computer or a typewriter?

JC: I type 80 WPM, which is hard to beat in handwriting. But sometimes handwriting is better, which is why I'm considering a tablet PC.

MD: What's it like to be you?

JC: Michael, what's it like to be you?

Dan Gookin

Dan Gookin has sold over 15 million books and has been translated into 32 languages. He helped develop the *For Dummies* series, which changed the face of publishing.

Books that Dan has written include *PCs for Dummies*, *Word 2002 for Dummies*, *DOS for Dummies*, *Buying a Computer for Dummies*, *PCs for Dummies Quick Reference*, *Troubleshooting Your PC for Dummies*, and *Dan Gookin's Naked Windows XP*. He's written many, many more, all of which are now obsolete thanks to advancing technology.

Figure 19.9 *Dan Gookin.*

MD: What's your URL?

Dan Gookin: I suppose the closest thing would be my bellybutton, which is my only physical link to another human being, though it hasn't been used for over 40 years now.

On the Internet, my Web page is www.wambooli.com. That's only one of them. I have more. Somewhere. Please note that I have a free weekly newsletter that anyone can subscribe to. Thanks!

MD: Why did you start writing how-to and tech books? When? How?

DG: The voices in my head made me.

Back in 1982 I bought my first computer. By 1984 I had upgraded it enough and bought a printer, so that I finally had my word processing system. I sent articles to every possible publication. The first place that accepted a piece was a local computer magazine in San Diego, the *Byte Buyer*. I started writing more stuff for them—humorous pieces about computers.

Eventually I got noticed at a local computer book publishing house, thanks to my online friend Morgan Davis. I began work at CompuSoft Publishing in 1985 where I "researched" computer books. I can't say that I ghost wrote any of them because the owner won't let me, but I contributed heartily to *The BASIC Handbook, 3rd Edition* and the *IBM Basic Handbook* and other books during my 18-month tenure there.

As the publishing house began to seriously downsize, I was led to Bill Gladstone of Waterside Productions, a computer book literary agency. Bill took me on, and soon I had my first computer book with my own name on it published in 1987. By 1989 I had written over a dozen books on computers.

MD: Do you write articles or tour or do teaching or lecturing?

DG: I used to do the article thing. Thanks to attending the AppleFest in Boston in 1988, I met a lot of magazine editors. That was the key to getting published in a magazine; get face time with the editors. Once they connected my face with a real person, it was easy to get magazine assignments. At one time I was writing for over six different publications and had a regular monthly column.

Eventually the magazine stuff became too time consuming. I was kind of at the peak of my game writing for *INFOworld* and *PC Computing*, but I calculated that the time spent working on each article divided by the payment netted me about $2/hour, so I gave that up.

I give speeches, but have never connected with a speaking bureau. I wish I had; I'm a very good speaker.

MD: You've sold millions of books. Are you rich?

DG: I am rich because I am a father who has four boys who love him dearly. Wealth is measured by those who love you, not by how much you have squirreled away.

Money wise, yes, selling millions of books nets quite a few quatloos. It doesn't work out to "a dollar a book," sadly. But I made enough so that during my peak years I've paid over $6,000,000 in income taxes. I would have rather had that money myself, but the government has the nukes and, well, they'd rather waste my earnings in their own fashion.

MD: What sort of lifestyle do you live?

DG: I am a simple boy who loves to cook and sew.

I would say I have a lifestyle similar to a doctor, though without all that damn golf playing and, no, thank you, I do not think of myself as a god. I have no recreational vehicles, but I do have a grand piano, two pinball tables, and the Galaga arcade game. That's about as wacky as I get.

My main hobby is working in my woodshop, where I also do electronics and stained glass work. I've made a table and some cabinets and do some home repairs.

I mow my own lawn and clean my own house. Every Sunday night I clean out the cat's box. And I do my dishes by hand.

MD: What do you spend money on?

DG: Nothing really. I'm slowly spending it on furniture for my new place, specifically shelves. Houses don't come with bookshelves because people tend to watch idiot TV instead of read. So I have many books on the floor. Most of my money gets put into the bank or investments.

Once I year I spend lavishly to take my boys on vacation to some exotic place. Last year we went to Disneyland and California Adventure and to San Diego to see my folks. This year we're going to Cedar Point to ride all them roller coasters.

I also spend money on my house. The basement just flooded, and I lost the game cube and PlayStation plus lots of laser disks in the flood.

MD: How did you find an agent and a publisher?

DG: One of my co-workers at CompuSoft Publishing gave me Bill Gladstone's business card in 1986. Having an agent helps. But consider that the computer book publishing world works backwards: The publishers think of the ideas and then look for warm bodies to write the books. Honestly, I'm not treated like a "real" author in the computer book world. Over the past 10 years I've proposed dozens of ideas to publishers, and they've followed through with maybe three of them—to my credit.

MD: Have you authored a series? How does that work differently versus just writing single books?

DG: There are no more single books. They say there are, but there really aren't. The same is true in fiction more or less, where the publishers want series and trilogies.

I created *DOS for Dummies*. The entire *Dummies* series is a derivative of that work. The publisher tried to take credit, but because I'm alive and vocal, he never could entirely steal the credit away. Of course, I'm still here, and he's long gone.

MD: Have you written any fiction? Is it financially rewarding?

DG: Written tons. Never published. Eventually I plan on making the switch to fiction, which is my true love. I have to wait for my other house to sell before that can happen. Presently I'm juggling two hefty mortgages and until the old "palace" sells, I'll have to plug away at computer books.

MD: What is your work schedule like? What's a typical day for Dan?

DG: Jessica, my love slave, wakens me by massaging my feet with her naturally large breasts. But then I wake up and realize that it's 7:30 and I really don't have to get up. So I wake up at 8:30 and realize that I still don't have to get up. So I wake up at 9:30, do the bathroom ritual, get dressed, and walk the awful 20-foot trek into the home office.

I spend about two hours answering e-mail, sometimes more—and I still don't get it done. I make it a policy to put my e-mail address in every book and encourage people to write. Despite the fact that I tell them I DO NOT TROUBLESHOOT, all the questions are troubleshooting and I answer them anyway—unless I'm really backlogged, and then I just start playing a game.

Up until lunch I try to clean up some loose ends and get work done on various products, spiff up the Web page and other things.

From lunch on I work on whatever the priority is.

I try to hit the gym on Tuesdays and Thursdays.

And I generally work late afternoons and well into the evening.

If I'm on deadline, the only thing that changes is that I put off the e-mail until the pile gets so huge that I just nastily reply to everyone that I DO NOT DO TROUBLESHOOTING.

I take Friday nights and Saturdays off to play with the boys or work in the woodshop or do some other project.

MD: How much freedom do you get to put yourself into the books you write?

DG: That's not the question, the question is how much of my free spirit will the silly publisher tolerate and not edit out of the book.

It's not as bad as it used to be, but back in the old days, just mentioning "Jesus" or "God" in a book caused a major uproar. And sometimes you get those damn female editors straight out of university who feel they have to correct the masculine injustices done to the English language. I once had some feminist nutball strip out "rule of thumb" from a poem—which made the poem non-rhyming—because of some nonsense drilled into her back in college.

Eventually, though, over time you find good editors who know that EDITING IS NOT REWRITING. I value such editors and use them again and again.

MD: Do you consider what you do to be art?

DG: Only when I write about Microsoft beta software.

MD: Do you ever feel torn between being artistic and being commercial, or do you see them as interconnected? How?

DG: My work isn't art. It's temporary nonsense. I may write an excellent book, one with wit and a smart pace with spice and life and more energy than in most novels. But the book is only around as long as the product. So while I do put my all into every book, I recognize that I'm essentially writing in chalk on a sidewalk.

MD: Do you use a laptop? What kind?

DG: I have an Apple G4 PowerBook.

MD: Do you like writing at home or out of the house (like in a local coffeeshop), or out on the road?

DG: I don't do the "road" thing. When I travel it's for fun. Back when it used to be for work, I would take the laptop, but that was merely to check e-mail, which piles up obnoxiously because everyone wants me to TROUBLESHOOT THEIR COMPUTER.

I do occasionally take the laptop down to the local coffee shop to test my programming (as a break from writing) or to write short pieces that don't require a computer. Otherwise, I need about two or three computers to write on: One for testing, one for writing, and another because I'm greedy.

MD: Do you get fan letters? Has anyone ever said, "You changed my life"?

DG: All the time.

MD: Do you consider yourself to be a nerd?

DG: No. I'm a fiction writer trapped in a computer writer's career. I'm probably keeping some damn nerd somewhere from making it as a computer book author. In the meantime, I don't think John Grisham, Stephen King, Michael Crichton, or Tom Clancy are quaking in their boots.

MD: What were you like as a kid?

DG: Younger. Cuter.

MD: Do you have groupies?

DG: Yes. Typically middle-aged to older women as well as a few old codgers. I think the women groupies come around because I actually respond to e-mail.

MD: What operating system do you have on your computers?

DG: You name it, I got it.

MD: What program do you write in?

DG: Mostly Word 2000. I have a dedicated Windows 98 system with Word 2000 on it and nuthin' else. It's the most stable system in the office.

MD: How important is an outline to your writing?

DG: Vital. Books don't happen without outlines. Even fiction that I dabble in has outlines. It's not good writing unless you know where you're going and the stops along the way.

Most books are simply overstuffed outlines. In fact, the original *WordPerfect for Dummies* started as a 10-page outline, then a 20-page outline, then each "chapter" from the outline was copied and pasted into each chapter that eventually became the book. That's how I work.

I do reserve the right to change the outline. Sometimes some topic turns out to be more quickly covered or more elegantly presented than others.

MD: How do you work with your editor?

DG: Via e-mail.

MD: Have you ever had an editor change something you were very unhappy about? Please explain.

DG: Many times.

At one press they had three editors that the book passed through. Each had a different colored pencil. So they would print out my manuscript, then each editor would take a crack at it. There were at least four marks from each editor on every page of the book—none of which improved readability or did anything other than prove to the editor's boss that they were "doing their job."

The editing was nitpicky. They would reverse a clause, for example; for example, they would reverse a clause—which does nothing for the text, but yet it gets them their little colored pencil mark on a page. Ridiculous!

Then they would edit out humor. I hate that. At one point they edited one of my jokes because, they said, "Our German translator would have trouble with that one." I mean—FORGET THE MILLIONS OF AMERICANS WHO WOULD GET THE JOKE!

Funny, but the books I did with those publishers never did as well as the books with publishers who had editors who understood what editing was all about.

Most of the time they would change things back when I would request them. But there was one book I utterly gave up on. It was an "educational book," and the editing was so bad and so severe that it left my text utterly bereft of personality or life. The silly thing was, even after I told them I wanted my name off the book, that publisher wanted me to write more books for them. I gently turned them down.

MD: How do you feel about Kazaa?

DG: Not all pirates have wooden legs and parrots on their shoulders. Theft is theft. I will not support or help anyone who pirates things.

MD: What's it like being you?

DG: The same as everyone else, but hungrier. I have no switch inside my brain to tell me when to stop eating, so weight has always been a problem. I'm currently on a diet and trying to lose 100 lbs. I've lost 20 so far, but it's hard to tell because of my hideous girth.

Beyond that I'm actually kind of aloof. I could walk through a mine field and not know it because I'm usually thinking some other thought or going over something in my head.

I look forward to growing old and becoming a geezer. A thinner geezer, a geezer with fiction books under his belt, but that pretty much sums it up.

MD: Any closing comments?

DG: As the progenitor of the *Dummies* series, I do get asked often how to start oneself as a writer. The best answer I can give people is to be consistent. Sit down and write. Having ideas isn't enough; it's the art of planting one's butt in a chair and writing, creating words.

Writing isn't a social activity. You must be able to tolerate long hours with just yourself and the keyboard. If you're easily distracted, then you must learn to budget your time. Writing takes time.

They say that you need to write at least one million words before you get any good. So start writing those one million now. Use it as training. Keep writing and writing. And don't be afraid to show your stuff to people. If you are, then you'll never be a writer; writers need feedback.

There is no such thing as "writer's block." I've never had it. The solution to writer's block is to lower your standards. Trust me, it works. If you don't believe me, you'll never be a writer.

After you have something worthy, get an agent. Good agents will provide you with good feedback. Believe them. If they have suggestions or recommendations, follow them. In exchange for their commission, you get a person who is well connected with editors in specific fields, so the agent can properly place and sell your book.

Do not self-publish. Avoid the vanity presses. If your stuff isn't ready for a real publisher, then it's crap. Keep working at your craft until what you write is ready for real publication. Yes, there are exceptions, but not enough to be mathematically significant. Trust me.

Generally speaking, most beginners can throw away the first paragraph of whatever they're writing. Consider it the warm-up paragraph.

Writing is about getting to the point. Get to the point! If you're not getting to the point, then you're writing poetry and will die hungry and poor. And ugly.

Don't fret over spelling. Don't fuss over grammar. That's why God created editors.

Read Strunk & White's *Elements of Style*.

Read Bryson's *The Mother Tongue*.

A good editor is a guide. They help shape your thoughts and ensure that your text is clear and, where desired, non-ambiguous. Editors do not rewrite text. They may tell you to rewrite text, but they don't do it themselves. And remember that it is your text, and you have the power to overrule any edit. The key word is STET, which is Latin for "Restore my damn text!"

Meet your deadlines.

Don't be afraid to self-edit. Don't be afraid to write from the middle outward or the back frontward.

If you're using a word processor, SAVE! Save often. Save now.

If you show your stuff to 10 people, and nine love it but one guy really hates it, then he is wrong.

Best,

DAN

Appendix A

Recommended Reading

Magazines

Writer **magazine:** Some of the articles are great, though a lot of the ads are aimed at selling you stuff you don't need.

Written By **magazine:** Magazine of the Screenwriter's Guild. Again, some of the articles are great, though a lot of the ads are aimed at selling you stuff you don't need.

Whole Earth Catalog: A very out-of-print source book from the sixties. Do a search online to find various excerpts.

This phonebook-size periodical tome was published by Northern California hippies in the sixties to promote science, interconnectivity, and new ways of thought through technology. Sounds pretty dismissable until you consider the fact that these same hippies ran a pre-World Wide Web commercial Internet connectivity service (one of the very first), and there is a good chance that without them, you wouldn't know what the Internet is.

This catalog was one of my first D.I.Y. influences and blew my young mind when I found my older sister's copy at age eight.

These folks were also very into geodesic domes and their inventor, scientist/societal visionary Buckminster Fuller. I met Fuller when I was a kid, and it changed my life forever in deep ways.

Here's something he wrote that kinda sums up him and this whole movement:

"I see God in the instruments and the mechanisms that work reliably, more reliably than the limited sensory departments of the human mechanism. . . . All organized religions of the past were inherently developed as beliefs and credits in 'second hand' information. Therefore it will be an entirely new era when man finds himself confronted with direct experience with an obviously a priori intellectually anticipatory competence that has interordered all that he is discovering."

Books

$30 Film School

$30 Music School

The Artist's Way (Julia Cameron with Mark Bryan). Cool lady teaches us how to give up the artistic blocks we inherited as kids.

The Writer's Journey: Mythic Structure for Writers (Christopher Vogler). Read it slowly and savor it.

Ebert's "Bigger" Little Movie Glossary (Collected by Roger Ebert). Great observations about cliches in movies. "Any main character who wears glasses will, at least once, take the glasses off to express some deep emotion or give an impassioned speech." "Every explosion is shown at least three times, from three different angles, and the sound track has three 'booms' on it, even though it's only one explosion."

Eats, Shoots & Leaves: The Zero Tolerance Approach to Punctuation (Lynne Truss). Funny, cranky English book. A good (and hilarious) list of what to avoid if you're writing (or directing) a film.

Chicago Manual of Style

Strunk and White's *Elements of Style*

Writer's Market 2004

AP Guide to News Writing (Rene J. Cappon). Good even if you don't write news.

The Deluxe Transitive Vampire: The Ultimate Handbook of Grammar for the Innocent, the Eager, and the Doomed. If all English books were this much fun, all kids would be writers.

Mother Tongue: English & How It Got That Way

Jeff Herman's Guide to Literary Agents

Write the Perfect Book Proposal: 10 That Sold and Why

Get in the Van (Henry Rollins)

Ernest Hemingway on Writing

On Writing (Stephen King)

Fahrenheit 451 (Bradbury). Half-century-old sci-fi about book burning. Has a lot on the value of books and writing.

Future Shock. 1970 bestseller told us then everything that is happening now and how to not be destroyed by it.

The Ethical Slut. Best attempt I've ever seen at explaining how to make polyamory work. You'll need it after your book hits big. I did.

The Redneck Manifesto. Mike and I thought it was the best first book we'd ever read.

Should you read books on how to write? I would say there are only a few I would recommend: The ones I mentioned earlier, *The Writer's Journey* and Stephen King's *On Writing*. Other than that, I would just *write* and read anything *but* writing books. I would read the other King, Larry King. His book *How to Talk to Anyone, Anytime, Anywhere* will teach you more about life and thus make you a better writer than most books on writing. Read Ice T's autobiography, *The Ice Opinion*. Read Edmund J. Pankau's *Hide Your Assets and Disappear: A Step-by-Step Guide to Vanishing Without a Trace*. This book is incredibly useful, especially for anyone wanting to become what he calls a PT (permanent traveler). You don't have to be committing fraud to be a PT, but with today's mobility, a writer with a laptop can, and probably should, have no fixed address.

I'm sort of a PT, even thought I maintain a residence. The best PTs have a lover in every port. That makes it easier.

It's important that you read a lot to be a good writer. If you aren't a good reader, you probably will never be a good writer.

Appendix B

Recommended Surfing

$30 WRITING SCHOOL

Recommended Surfing

www.freelancesuccess.com

www.anotherealm.com/prededitors: Preditors & Editors.

Craigslist.org

www.RockForCats.com

www.mediabistro.com: Great resource for writers, especially magazine writers. It has classes on lots of cool stuff, as well as tutorials on how to pitch to specific magazines. Our loving nickname for them is "Media Beastie."

www.verbaladvantage.com: Verbal Advantage (or as we call 'em, "Gerbil Advantage"). An amazing CD set with lessons on improving word power and vocabulary. I heard some on Kazaa and liked it a lot. Worth buying.

www.m-w.com: Merriam-Webster online. Searchable dictionary and thesaurus. Don't forget to sign up for their free word-of-the-day service.

www.VisualThesaurus.com: http://www.visualthesaurus.com/online/index.html

www.jpkvideo.net: Good cheap Web hosting from my friend J.P.

Appendix C

What's on the CD-ROM?

The models on the CD interface are Cassidy Robb Coon, her rooster, Baby Roo, and a lovely AlphaSmart word processor.

Movies

Video of my Connie Martinson TV interview.

Interview with me on French TV.

Trailer for *DIY or DIE*.

Hubert Selby Jr. interview (audio only).

Release Forms

Software (all are working versions):

   Word processing:

      AbiWord for Windows.

      AbiWord for Red Hat Linux 9.

      FinalDraft for scriptwriting.

   Emailfwdthing: For stripping formatting from e-mails.

   WallMaster: Wallpaper displaying utility.

   MouseCount tailored for this book.

   Quark templates for book and cover.

Scans of My Rejection Letters

Book proposals.

Book reviews.

My press releases from various projects.

Photo or scans of various outlines with my work-in-progress notes.

Cool *$30 Writing School* wallpaper.

Tour diary from European backpack tour and photos to inspire your writing.

Rich Text Format document of the first quarter of one of my scripts (*Hollywood: The Last American City*).

Final draft document of the first quarter of one of my scripts (*Hollywood: The Last American City*).

Other assorted goodies for inspiration.

The CD-ROM stuff will run faster from your hard drive than from the CD. Copy the CD to the desktop. Then right-click on the folder, go to Properties, and remove the checkmark for Read-Only.

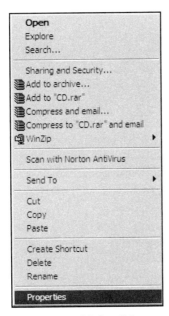

Figure C.1 *Right-click on the folder to access the Properties box.*

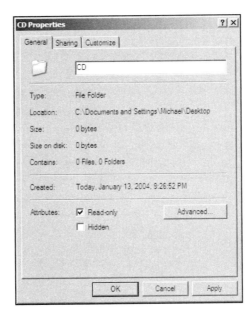

Figure C.2 *The Properties box.*

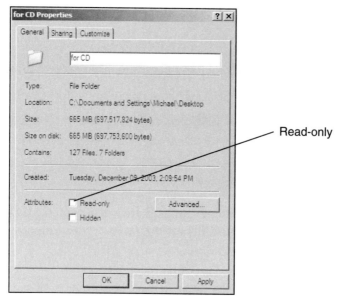

Read-only

Figure C.3 *The Properties box with Read–Only unchecked.*

Apply to all folders.

Feel free to give the CD on to someone else after you do this. Information wants to be free. Pass it on.

"Whoever has his art on the most people's hard drives when he dies, wins."

—me

Index

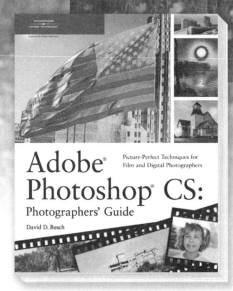
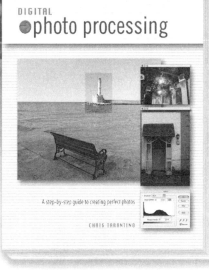

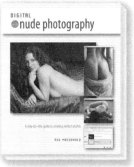

License Agreement/Notice of Limited Warranty